E 267 .S66 2008
Spring, Matthew H. 1973-
With zeal and with bayonets
only

D0782282

WITHDRAWN
UNIVERSITY LIBRARY
THE UNIVERSITY OF TEXAS RIO GRANDE VALLEY

LIBRARY
THE UNIVERSITY OF TEXAS
AT BROWNSVILLE
Brownsville, TX 78520-4991

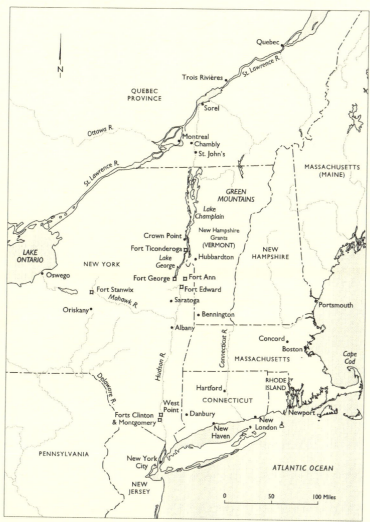

**Map 1. The Northern Theater**

A duplicate of map 3 (Southern Theater) was erroneously printed on page xix (albeit with the name Portsmouth correctly spelled). The above map of the Northern Theater is intended to appear on that page.

# WITH ZEAL AND WITH BAYONETS ONLY

## C&C

CAMPAIGNS & COMMANDERS

GREGORY J. W. URWIN, SERIES EDITOR

# CAMPAIGNS AND COMMANDERS

GENERAL EDITOR

Gregory J. W. Urwin, *Temple University, Philadelphia, Pennsylvania*

ADVISORY BOARD

Lawrence E. Babits, *East Carolina University, Greenville*
James C. Bradford, *Texas A&M University, College Station*
Robert M. Epstein, *U.S. Army School of Advanced Military Studies, Fort Leavenworth, Kansas*
David M. Glantz, *Carlisle, Pennsylvania*
Jerome A. Greene, *Denver, Colorado*
Victor Davis Hanson, *California State University, Fresno*
Herman Hattaway, *University of Missouri, Kansas City*
John A. Houlding, *Rückersdorf, Germany*
Eugenia C. Kiesling, *U.S. Military Academy, West Point, New York*
Timothy K. Nenninger, *National Archives, Washington, D.C.*
Bruce Vandervort, *Virginia Military Institute, Lexington*

# With Zeal and with Bayonets Only

## The British Army on Campaign in North America, 1775–1783

Matthew H. Spring

LIBRARY
THE UNIVERSITY OF TEXAS
AT BROWNSVILLE
Brownsville, TX 78520-4991

University of Oklahoma Press : Norman

Library of Congress Cataloging-in-Publication Data
Spring, Matthew H. (Matthew Hasler), 1973–
With zeal and with bayonets only : the British Army on campaign in
North America, 1775–1783 / Matthew H. Spring.
p. cm. — (Campaigns and commanders ; v. 19)
Rev. and expanded version of thesis (Ph. D.)—University of Leeds,
2001.
Includes bibliographical references and index.
ISBN 978-0-8061-4152-7 (paper) 1. United States—History—
Revolution, 1775–1783—British forces. 2. United States—History—
Revolution, 1775–1783—Campaigns. 3. Great Britain. Army—
History—Revolution, 1775–1783. I. Title.
E267.S66 2008
973.3—dc22                   2008013656

*With Zeal and with Bayonets Only: The British Army on Campaign
in North America, 1775–1783* is Volume 19 in the Campaigns and
Commanders series.

The paper in this book meets the guidelines for permanence and
durability of the Committee on Production Guidelines for Book
Longevity of the Council on Library Resources, Inc. ∞

Copyright © 2008 by the University of Oklahoma Press, Norman,
Publishing Division of the University. Manufactured in the U.S.A.
Paperback published 2010.

All rights reserved. No part of this publication may be reproduced,
stored in a retrieval system, or transmitted, in any form or by any
means, electronic, mechanical, photocopying, recording, or
otherwise—except as permitted under Section 107 or 108 of the
United States Copyright Act—without the prior permission of the
University of Oklahoma Press.

2   3   4   5   6   7   8   9   10

FOR MY PARENTS, ROGER AND ROSEMARY,

WITH MUCH LOVE AND GRATITUDE

# Contents

# Illustrations

*A gallery of seven illustrations of British soldiers by artist Don Troiani appears after page 161.*

# Tables

# Preface

The historiography of the American War of Independence (or Revolutionary War) is now so vast that anyone who seeks to augment it ought, perhaps, to begin by justifying his intention, particularly when the work in question focuses on the already well-studied British war effort.[1]

Over the past few decades, academic historians (especially Americans) of the American War and its contending armies have written a great deal on topics such as strategic planning, logistics, and social history. Yet if the ultimate purpose of all armies is to fight, and if therefore the most fundamental task facing the military historian is arguably to study combat, it is perhaps ironic that we should still have relatively little detailed analysis of the way in which the respective armies operated on campaign and in action. What we have instead is an ever-increasing number of colorful campaign and battle narratives, composed predominantly by nonacademic historians for a popular (predominantly American) audience. Much of this material suffers from serious deficiencies. First, it is uneven, being heavily concentrated on the dozen or so most famous engagements (and especially on the handful of British battlefield defeats). More important, many such works tend to be unreliable and unbalanced in that they exhibit a chauvinistic and self-congratulatory tone and contain factual inaccuracies and errors of interpretation that stem from too much cribbing from existing secondary accounts. In addition, such authors have generally tended—for obvious reasons, and with predictable results—to prefer rebel American eyewitness accounts to those penned by British, Provincial, and German participants, which have often been ignored or discounted. If these criticisms appear unduly harsh, it should be stressed that those American historians who have (especially in recent decades) incorporated a truly scholarly approach to their studies of campaigns and engagements have produced accounts that have radically altered our interpretation of those contests, even in terms of basic chronology.[2] I have drawn on these impressive studies extensively in the course of this work.

Despite this handful of revisionist studies, our understanding of the British Army's performance in the field has remained limited. Interestingly, more has been written about how the British soldier looked on campaign than how he fought, due largely to the efforts of dedicated amateur historians and living-history enthusiasts who have pieced together evidence for how British military clothing and equipment was adapted to local conditions.[3] As a consequence of the relative lack of interest in British tactical methods, however, many historians of the American War have persisted in describing what they sometimes (tellingly) call the British "military machine" in combat in terms that are far more reminiscent of the conventional European battlefield clashes of the Seven Years War. Their narratives of engagements from Bunker Hill to Guilford Courthouse are laced with the image of serried ranks of grim-faced, pipe-clayed, red-coated automata advancing relentlessly in perfect cadence to thudding drums and squealing fifes, with regimental colors snapping at their heads. Most dramatically conveyed before the age of cinema in Howard Pyle's epic canvas depicting the British advance in line at Bunker Hill, this image continues to thrive today through the warped efforts of the Hollywood mythmongers.[4] In reality, as I hope to show in the course of this work, the King's troops won the vast majority of their battlefield engagements in America because they tailored their conventional tactical methods intelligently to local conditions—very much as they had done in similar circumstances during the French and Indian War (1754–63).

The aim of this work is to gain a picture of how British forces in America performed at the operational and especially the tactical level. Although it has been necessary to look at contemporary drill manuals and other military treatises, by far the most useful evidence are the plentiful diaries, memoirs, official letters, and private correspondence that British and German officers and enlisted men composed during and soon after the war. Many of these will be familiar to students of the American War; it is my hope that, in reexamining these sources, I have brought something fresh to the table.

As the American War was overwhelmingly an infantryman's conflict, the particular focus of this work is on the infantry. This means that some important topics (including cavalry and artillery tactics) have been given a relatively light treatment, while others (including siegework and the roles of the engineers and the medical services) have not been addressed at all. Moreover, if a topic has received good coverage elsewhere (such as the themes of British officers' motivation or of the conduct of amphibious operations), I have declined to trespass upon it here.[5] With regards to combat, this work focuses on the kind of clashes in which each side comprised a minimum of about a thousand men and in which British, Provincial, or German regulars formed the majority of the Crown forces engaged. This study will not concern itself very much with the kind of small-scale skirmishes that occurred on an almost daily basis, when royal troops (whether in garrison or in the field) were engaged in security duties, intelligence gathering, or foraging—not least because these chaotic encounters are the most difficult to analyze.

I have followed a number of conventions in writing this work. First, for the benefit of the reader, when quoting primary sources (whether in manuscript or printed form), I have modernized quixotic eighteenth-century spelling, punctuation, and capitalization and have reproduced abbreviated words in full. I have, however, used square brackets to indicate where I have added words to render the original meaning more clear. I hope that the relative ease with which many of the sources can be accessed in published form will make this decision less unpalatable to those readers who prefer the original style. Second, wherever possible, I have cited the published versions of primary sources rather than the original manuscript sources. Third, I have thought it proper, for the sake of continuity with the (predominantly British) sources employed here, to use the political terminology that British soldiers, statesmen, and observers favored. Thus I have referred to those colonists in arms against Britain neither as "Americans" (an inappropriate usage anyway in the context of a civil war) nor as "Patriots" but as "rebels." Likewise, those colonists who supported the King I have termed "loyalists" (or "Provincials," for those colonists serving in British-raised military units) rather than the pejorative "Tories." Furthermore, I have employed the term "regulars" to distinguish uniformed, full-time soldiers of whichever side from militia. Therefore, I may refer to the New Jersey Volunteers as "Provincial regulars" or the 1st Maryland Continental Regiment as "rebel regulars." Fourth, I have always tried to indicate whether a witness's evidence was penned contemporaneously with events or much later; and if the former, I have referred to the author by the rank that he held at that moment if possible. Lastly, bearing in mind the heavy plagiarism that occurred when participants went to print after the war, I have always attempted, where a number of sources contain very similar passages, to employ the original.[6]

For reference purposes, I have drawn extensively on a number of secondary works. As a guide to the numbers of troops present at engagements, I have used Greg Novak, *"We Have Always Governed Ourselves": The War of Independence in the North* (Champaign, Ill.: N.p., n.d.), and *"Rise and Fight Again": The War of Independence in the South* (Champaign, Ill.: Rue Sans Joie, 1988). For the numbers of casualties incurred at engagements, I have utilized Howard Peckham, *The Toll of Independence: Engagements and Battle Casualties of the American Revolution* (Chicago: University of Chicago Press, 1974). Indispensable for all purposes has been Mark M. Boatner, *Encyclopedia of the American Revolution*, 3rd ed. (Mechanicsburg, Pa.: Stackpole Books, 1994).

# Acknowledgments

This book is a revised and expanded version of the doctoral thesis that I wrote at the University of Leeds between 1998 and 2001.[1] I should, therefore, first express my gratitude to that institution for the generous funding that it provided to enable me to undertake my research. Sincere thanks are also due to Professor John Childs, who kindly acted as my research supervisor and to whom I am I indebted for his encouragement, expert guidance and patience. I should add that the friendly and expert staff of the university's School of History and the excellent Brotherton Library (particularly the ladies of the interlibrary loan section) proved an immensely helpful resource.

Nor would I have been able to write my doctoral thesis, or to re-shape the thesis into a book, without the invaluable assistance that I received from various other quarters. Dr. John Houlding very kindly read innumerable drafts, gave me the benefits of his vast expertise on the eighteenth-century British Army, suggested new lines of enquiry, and provided crucial biographical information on the British officers who served in America. In the United States, before I started my research, Pauline and Mark Blair kindly provided me with a base for a thoroughly enjoyable driving tour of the numerous well-preserved and well-presented historical sites pertaining to the southern campaigns. Thereafter, a number of extraordinarily kind Americans shared the fruits of their own research on the British Army's performance, pointed me to (and in many cases provided me with copies of) sources that I would not otherwise have employed, or offered the kind of fascinating insights into minor tactics that, at a distance of over two centuries from the war, one can only gain by participating in living-history events like those run by the Brigade of the American Revolution. Principal among these open-handed individuals were Don Hagist, Robert Selig, Linnea Bass, Stephen Gilbert, Todd Braisted, Radford Polinsky, Jay Callaham, Tom McGuire, and Eric Schnitzer. In Leeds I gained enormously from my many exchanges on eighteenth-century warfare with my fellow researchers Stephen Brumwell, Kevin Linch, and Craig Robinson, whose excellent company helped enliven my years of research; while Mark Lodge very kindly provided much valuable information on the services in America of the 33rd Regiment of Foot. Last but not least, my brother Jamie and my old schoolmate Gareth Lukes regularly sweated blood in helping me shift my rapidly swelling personal library from place to place.

In the years since I completed the thesis and entered the teaching profession, Dr. John Houlding and Prof. Gregory Urwin have continued to provide much needed encouragement and support. Indeed, without their tactful prodding, this book would probably never have seen the light of day. I am similarly grateful to my fiancée, Sarah Day, for her long-standing toleration of what must have seemed my eccentric fascination with what is, for Britons, a distant and little-remembered lost war. In particular, I am especially grateful for her having patiently endured my neglect of her during weekends and school holidays, when I closeted myself away to work on the manuscript. For this, I owe her a very special debt of thanks.

Finally, I should thank my grandmother, Agnes Hasler, for having gifted me the book, over two decades ago, that first aroused my continuing fascination for this period of history.

# MAPS

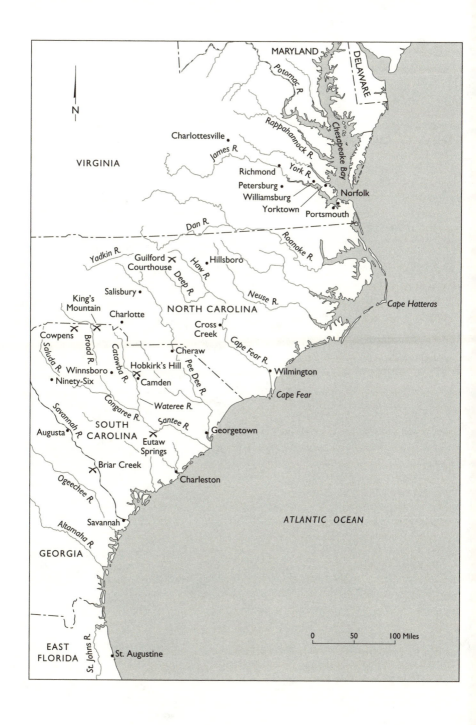

MARYLAND

DELAWARE

*Potomac R.*

*Rappahannock R.*

Chesapeake Bay

Charlottesville

VIRGINIA

*James R.*

Richmond

*York R.*

Petersburg

Williamsburg

Yorktown

Norfolk

Portsmouth

*Dan R.*

*Roanoke R.*

*Yadkin R.*

Guilford
Courthouse

*Haw R.*

Hillsboro

*Deep R.*

Salisbury

*Neuse R.*

King's
Mountain

NORTH CAROLINA

Charlotte

Cross
Creek

Cowpens

*Broad R.*

*Catawba R.*

Cheraw

*Cape Fear R.*

Cape Hatteras

*Saluda R.*

Winnsboro

Hobkirk's Hill

*Pee Dee R.*

Wilmington

Ninety-Six

Camden

Cape Fear

*Congaree R.*

Wateree R.

*Savannah R.*

SOUTH
CAROLINA

*Santee R.*

Augusta

Eutaw
Springs

Georgetown

Briar Creek

Charleston

*Ogeechee R.*

*Altamaha R.*

Savannah

ATLANTIC OCEAN

GEORGIA

*St. Johns R.*

EAST
FLORIDA

St. Augustine

0    50    100 Miles

N

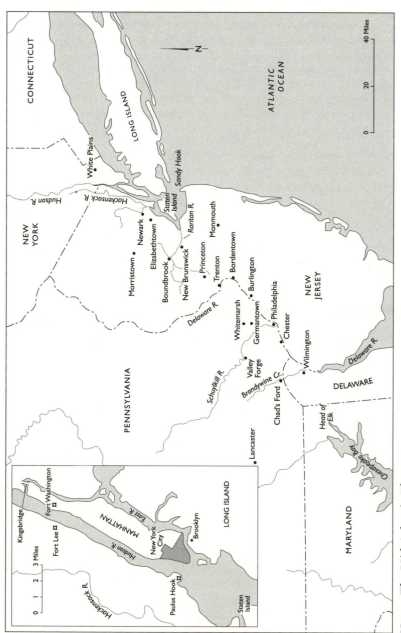

**Map 2. The Mid-Atlantic Theater**

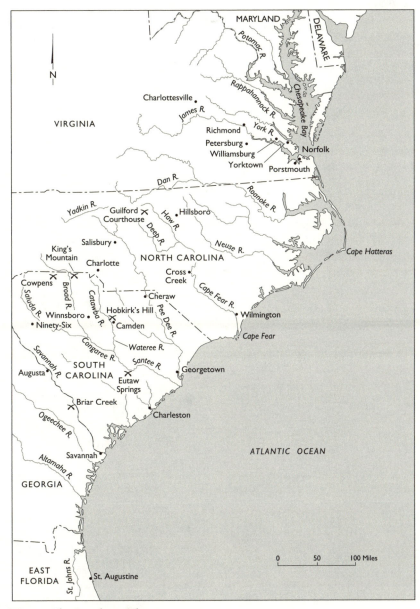

**Map 3. The Southern Theater**

# WITH ZEAL AND WITH
# BAYONETS ONLY

# 1

# THE ARMY'S TASK

It is not a war of posts but a contest for states dependent upon opinion.

Nathanael Greene to Brigadier General Thomas Sumter,
8 January 1781

In the short term, the attempt to restore royal authority in North America by force of arms depended on the ability of the British Army to achieve three related objectives. These were to defeat and disperse the rebels' conventional military forces; to encourage the populace to cease supporting Congress's war effort, and even to transfer that support to the Crown; and to induce the rebel leadership to give up the armed struggle in favor of a political settlement.

## THE REBEL LEADERSHIP

In the first three quarters of the eighteenth century, Great Britain successfully waged war against a variety of enemies that included the great powers France and Spain and the insurgent Jamaican Maroons and Jacobite rebels. Supported by the Royal Navy, British troops engaged in what would today be styled conventional, guerrilla, amphibious, and counterinsurgency warfare in theaters as diverse as the plains of Flanders, Germany, Iberia, and India; the Scottish Highlands; the North American wilderness; and the jungles of the Carib-

3

bean. Arguably then, Britain's armed forces should have been well prepared to deal with the conflict that erupted in the American colonies in 1775.

But in one vital respect, the American War presented Britain with an unprecedented military and political problem: she was neither contesting for limited political, territorial, or commercial advantage nor even attempting to defend and uphold royal government against usurpation by an insurgent movement. Instead her war aim was the dismantling of an established enemy regime. This regime effectively gained control over the thirteen colonies in the months before the outbreak of hostilities as the leaders of the colonial opposition worked through sympathetic provincial assemblies, committees, and militia officers to marginalize royal authority and to prepare for the clash with the mother country that few of them feared, many of them eagerly anticipated, and most of them assumed would be of brief duration.[1] Once the shooting started in April 1775, all vestiges of royal authority were speedily eliminated throughout the colonies save in those few enclaves occupied in force by Crown troops, the last of which (the port of Boston) the British evacuated in March 1776. Between then and July, when British forces began to concentrate on Staten Island for the great offensive that Lord North's ministry expected would break the revolt, the rebel leadership and its supporters effectively controlled every inhabited acre of the colonies.

The task of dismantling this hostile regime was rendered more difficult by the uncompromising stance of its leadership. Once these men had gained full control of local and national government, they were understandably reluctant (as Captain William Duff tartly put it in April 1778) "to relinquish it, and return to their original obscurity."[2] Although they dared not say so publicly, the radicals at the head of the colonial opposition were never genuinely interested in a political accommodation with the mother country over the issues that had fueled American resentment since the 1760s. In July 1776 they judged that the time was right to declare America's independence, not least because they knew that the ministry had empowered its military and naval commanders in the colonies (General William Howe and Vice Admiral Richard Lord Howe) as peace commissioners and feared that American popular opinion would galvanize behind a movement for reconciliation if it were allowed to gather momentum.

This assumption of full sovereignty not only facilitated the rebels' efforts to attract European allies but also enabled Congress to dismiss imperiously the limited peace overtures made by the Howe brothers in August 1776 and by the Carlisle Commission in 1778.[3]

The dismantling of the rebel regime was also complicated by the fact that it had no political center of gravity, the elimination of which would have brought about its immediate submission. The thirteen rebellious colonies were essentially a confederation of self-governing states, not a centralized state on the European model; although Congress assumed the functions of a national government, it was an extralegal body with little real power over the various state legislatures. Hence the temporary restoration of British control in New Jersey, Georgia, and South Carolina in 1776 and 1779–80 had little effect on rebel authority in neighboring states, while the fall of the rebel capital, Philadelphia, in 1777 merely temporarily displaced Congress.

Despite these problems, one should not assume that an advantageous political settlement was permanently beyond Britain's reach. Most eighteenth-century conflicts ended with a negotiated peace once the belligerents' governments calculated that the economic and political costs of continued military effort would outweigh the likely benefits. In the case of a war for independence like that in America, a precedent of sorts existed in the way the Austrians translated militarily ascendancy into a favorable negotiated end to the Rákóczi Uprising (1703–11). A similar outcome in America was less improbable than it might at first appear. Most of the key rebel leaders were men of means with a great deal to lose by maintaining their resistance to the bitter end. In addition, the colonies were, politically, culturally, and geographically, far from perfectly united. On one level the tensions between local and national interests undoubtedly hampered the rebels' attempts to coordinate their war effort, as evinced by the perceived tardiness with which the various state governments fulfilled their obligations to support the Continental Army and its operations.[4] Indeed, more skillful and sustained British diplomacy might have succeeded in exploiting the kinds of internal rivalries that led Ethan Allen to enter into negotiations over the future of Vermont between 1780 and 1783. Alternatively, the nominal independence of each state from its neighbors made possible the option of a compromise peace based on the principle of *uti possidetis* (the retention of territory by the possessors at the close of hostilities), especially from 1779, when the British overran and (at least temporarily) subjugated large tracts of the South.[5]

Particularly during the war's early campaigns, some soldiers and statesmen believed that British military success might bring the rebel leadership to the negotiating table. As Howe put it in January 1776, "From what I can learn of the designs of the leaders of the rebels . . . , it is my firm opinion they will not retract until they have tried their fortune in a battle and are defeated."[6] Crucially, the rebel leaders were able to rebuff British peace proposals in 1776 and 1778 because, in both years, the Crown was not negotiating from a position of strength. When the Howes made their modest overture in August 1776, they had neither smashed General George Washington's army nor even prized New York City from its control. Similarly, in 1778 news of French intervention and the imminent abandonment of Philadelphia fatally weakened the British diplomats' hand. Yet had British arms succeeded in puncturing the rebels' confidence in the inevitability of colonial victory, the leaders of the revolt might well have changed their tune.[7]

## THE CONTINENTAL ARMY

The Continental Army was the foremost obstacle to the restoration of British authority in the colonies. Divided between six commands (or departments), this regular-style, permanent military establishment was brought into being by Congress in June 1775 to make possible a coordinated and sustained challenge to British military coercion. With the support of local militia and state-controlled regular forces (which could not independently undertake major operations), the Continental Army's commanders were tasked with eliminating or inducing the withdrawal of Britain's military forces and thereby breaking her capacity and/or will to dispute American independence.

This task took far longer than most of the rebel leaders initially envisaged, principally because they grossly miscalculated their ability to force a favorable military decision. To resolve the war speedily, rebel armies needed to adopt the strategic offensive and overwhelm the Crown's forces and their fortified bases, especially the major coastal population centers (including Boston, New York City, Philadelphia, Savannah, and Charleston) on whose port facilities the British depended. Yet as the failure of the operations against Canada (1775), Newport (1778), Savannah (1779), and South Carolina (1780) demonstrated, the rebels were only rarely able to assemble and maintain in the field the superior military resources (particularly heavy artillery and warships, which only their later French allies could provide) that they needed to prosecute major offensives successfully. Combined with the mobility that naval superiority conferred on Crown forces, this factor ensured that the British generally maintained the strategic initiative in America. Consequently, for the greater part of the war, the Continental Army was constrained to act on the defensive.

For the rebels, the simplest method of contesting British offensive operations was what might be styled a strategy of "forward defense." Washington and his ablest subordinates never doubted that "we should on all occasions avoid a general action."[8] Yet influenced by political considerations and impressed by the carnage at Bunker Hill, they initially believed that their forces could cover exposed assets like the principal major population centers by taking up strong (preferably fortified) positions that the British would not be able to force without incurring unsupportable casualties. In this fashion, in 1776 and 1777 Washington tried to hold New York City and Philadelphia, respectively, by fortifying western Long Island, Manhattan, and the northern shore of New Jersey and by attempting successively to contest a British advance over the Brandywine Creek, the South Valley Hills (the "Battle of the Clouds"), and the Schuylkill River. Likewise, in 1777 Major General Horatio Gates entrenched his army at Stillwater to bar the British drive on Albany, while in 1778 and 1780 Major Generals Robert Howe and Benjamin Lincoln attempted to defend Savannah and Charleston by offering battle outside the former and by attempting to withstand a siege of the latter.

The problem with this bold defensive strategy was that British armies (especially when supported by the Royal Navy) proved very capable of turning, encircling, or bypassing exposed rebel positions. This produced a string of variously disastrous reverses, the worst of which included the near-destruction of much of the main rebel army on Long Island in August 1776, the loss of 3,000 men at Fort Washington that November, and the capture of the southern army at Charleston in 1780. Moreover, the apparent collapse of popular support for the rebellion in New Jersey in late 1776 clearly demonstrated how closely the Revolution's survival was linked to the fortunes of the Continental Army. For the rest of the war, the overriding need to preserve the latter from disintegration restrained Washington's naturally bold temperament. As he warned Major General the Marquis de Lafayette in 1780, "we must consult our means rather than our wishes; and not endeavor to better our affairs by attempting things, which for want of success may make them worse."[9]

Consequently, after Washington's withdrawal from Manhattan in 1776, and particularly after the fall of Philadelphia, the rebel conduct of the war tended to be characterized by a Fabian strategy. Prudent rebel commanders shunned major confrontations on any but the most advantageous terms by ensconcing their armies in inaccessible and/or virtually impregnable fortified camps in the interior (like Washington at Valley Forge in Pennsylvania or Morristown in New Jersey) or by exploiting space and topography to evade British pursuit (like Major Generals Nathanael Greene and Lafayette in the Carolinas and Virginia). By keeping their forces intact in this fashion, rebel commanders were nevertheless able to erode Britain's military ability and political will to continue the war. First, they were able to engage their forces against the King's troops under controlled conditions in what contemporaries called the *petite guerre*. In this nearcontinuous petty skirmishing, rebel commanders were able to drain British manpower and blood their regulars and militia in the type of fighting that best suited their lack of formal military discipline and enabled them to win the kind of minor successes that boosted morale and stimulated popular support for the rebellion. Second, the rebels preserved the option of taking the offensive when the opportunity arose to strike a heavy blow; as Greene put it, "I would always hazard an attack when the misfortune cannot be so great to us as it may be to the enemy."[10] Hence Washington pounced upon isolated Crown forces at Trenton and Princeton in the winter of 1776–77, Stony Point in 1779, and Yorktown in 1781 and attempted (less successfully) to crush Howe's depleted army at Germantown in 1777 and to cut off Sir Henry Clinton's rearguard at Monmouth Courthouse in 1778. Likewise, after the "Race to the Dan" in 1781, Greene doubled back into North Carolina and sold Lieutenant General Charles, Earl Cornwallis his ruinous victory at Guilford Courthouse. Third, the rebels' ability to destroy isolated forces made it very dangerous for the British to disperse troops in garrisons. By default, this left the countryside (where most of the population lived) in rebel control thanks to the efforts of the local militia.[11] As Greene put it in South Carolina in May 1781, "if [the British] divide their forces they will fall by detachments, and if they operate collectively, they cannot command the country."[12]

If the Continental Army stood squarely in the way of the restoration of royal authority, it was necessary for the British to neutralize it. As historians have been so fond of pointing out, the most direct way to achieve this would have been (as the turncoat Brigadier General Benedict Arnold pointed out in October 1780) "to collect the whole British army to a point and beat General Washington (which would decide the contest)."[13]

Here, however, we must pause to recognize that there were significant strategic, operational, and tactical constraints on the implementation of a battle-seeking strategy in conventional eighteenth-century European warfare before the French Revolutionary and Napoleonic wars (1792–1815).[14] Perhaps the principal cause of this phenomenon was the eighteenth-century state's limited ability to replace its expensively recruited, trained, and maintained long-service professional soldiers. In the field this limitation manifested itself in a concern not to lose troops unnecessarily to sickness and desertion by exposing them to hardships like short rations and inclement weather. In turn this curbed a field army's mobility by shackling it to magazines, bread ovens, and baggage trains.

This lack of mobility militated against the adoption of a battle-seeking strategy in two ways. First, it was extremely difficult to bring on an engagement that was decidedly disadvantageous to the enemy. If a commander on the defensive believed that the conditions were unfavorable, it was usually possible for him to refuse battle by withdrawing. Conversely, if he was confident of success and was therefore prepared to stand and fight, it was less likely to be in the interest of the commander on the offensive to oblige him. Furthermore, unless one or the other commander made serious mistakes, an action that occurred by mutual consent was liable to exhaust both armies and cost each one between a fifth and a third of its numbers. A commander who won this kind of hard-fought battle was unlikely to be in a position to throw sizeable reserves of fresh troops into a pursuit of the scattered and demoralized enemy forces.[15] When the fruits of battlefield victories therefore frequently extended little further than possession of the field, the prospective "butcher's bill" made most commanders very cautious about the circumstances under which they were prepared to engage.

Second, it was not practical to undertake operations inside territory that was covered by enemy-controlled fortresses, for field armies (which did not commonly exceed 40,000 men) were usually too small to detach screening forces to protect their lines of communication against sorties by enemy garrisons. Indeed, before the 1790s, especially in the most commonly contested and thus most heavily fortified theaters (particularly the Low Countries, northern France, and northern Italy), the main objectives of offensive operations tended to be the siege and capture of key fortresses, either as springboards for further operations or as tangible strategic assets to be retained or bargained away at the peace negotiations that terminated most eighteenth-century conflicts. Even in less heavily fortified theaters, however, commanders often preferred to maneuver against the enemy field army's communications rather than to incur heavy casualties by attacking it directly, particularly if it was well posted. In the right circumstances it was possible, at limited cost, to induce an enemy force to abandon successive strong positions and make rapid withdrawals during which it was likely to suffer serious losses to sickness, straggling, and desertion, much as the Austrians succeeded in doing in 1744 when they drove Frederick the Great from Bohemia without a battle.[16]

Nevertheless, not all conflicts before the 1790s were wars of posts or maneuver. We should not forget that pre-revolutionary commanders shared the same basic incentive to seek battle as their successors: they could not effectively pursue their operational objectives while significant enemy forces remained in the field. With the right conditions, battlefield engagements offered commanders the prospect of dramatically altering the balance of forces in the campaign by inflicting disproportionate casualties on the enemy. For example, at the battles of Blenheim (1704) and Kunersdorf (1759), the vanquished forces incurred over 50 percent losses, while the battles of Poltava (1709) and Maxen (1759) led directly to the defeated armies' surrenders. By compelling the weakened enemy field force to withdraw to avoid further (and more disadvantageous) engagements, or indeed by knocking it out of the campaign altogether, a commander freed himself from enemy interference until winter terminated the campaign and gave the defeated a respite in which to recover. In 1781 the British commander in chief in India, Lieutenant General Sir Eyre Coote, insisted that forty years of service had taught him "a rule which a soldier ought never to lose sight of—if there is an enemy in the field, anywhere near, and in force, to a fortified town or garrison intended to be attacked, first to beat it, and so effectually as to be himself satisfied that it will not be able to rise again in strength sufficient to molest him whilst carrying on the operations of the siege."[17] Hence Frederick the Great drove off the Austrian army at Prague (1757) in order to place the city under siege, while The Duke of Marlborough smashed the French army at Ramillies (1706) so early in the campaign that he was able in the following months to snatch more than a dozen fortified towns in the Spanish Netherlands. Moreover, it was not only commanders on the strategic offensive who had an incentive to seek battle. Many engagements occurred because commanders sought to maintain control of objectives of strategic importance, whether by relieving a besieged fortress, as at Turin (1706) and Kolin (1757), or by protecting friendly territory from occupation, as with Ferdinand of Brunswick's victory at Minden (1759). Furthermore, those who had confidence in their troops' superior tactical effectiveness, like Marlborough and Frederick the Great, were understandably inclined to seek battle more consistently.

In the case of the American War, some of the strategic, operational, and tactical factors that made it difficult for commanders to bring about and exploit advantageous engagements in conventional European conflicts also rendered problematic the British task of neutralizing the Continental Army in battle. Indeed (as discussed in chapters 2 and 11), American conditions had the effect of exacerbating some of these constraints (including logistics, manpower shortages, and the problems of mounting an effective pursuit). In particular, if the relative dearth of extensive, large-scale, formal fortifications in North America prevented the conflict from becoming purely a war of posts (the sieges of Savannah, Charleston, and Yorktown were arguably the conflict's only serious operations of this kind), the rebels' proclivity for ensconcing their armies in strong defensive positions made it difficult for the British to attack them with advantage.

This was especially true of Howe's New York campaign of 1776. Although in January of that year Howe had expressed a hope to strike at the rebels in New York "before they could cover themselves by works of any signification," when he arrived at Staten Island in July, he found conditions disappointing.[18] Rather than obligingly dashing his troops against the rebels' successive defensive lines, between late August and early December, Howe employed a combination of maneuver and limited engagements to compel Washington to withdraw successively from Long Island, New York City, Harlem Heights, Westchester, White Plains, and eventually (with Cornwallis snapping at his heels) from New Jersey into Pennsylvania.

The British fully expected this series of reverses and retreats to bring about the gradual disintegration of the ragtag rebel army. Before the opening of the campaign, Captain Francis Lord Rawdon wrote that the consequences of a defeat would be "fatal to the rebels" because "[a]n army composed as theirs cannot bear the frown of adversity."[19] Another officer suggested that the capture of all the rebel troops on the Brooklyn Heights after the battle of Long Island would have triggered "probably the entire dispersion of their main body."[20] More explicitly, Captain Frederick Mackenzie observed days before the Kipp's Bay landing that "[t]he destruction or capture of a considerable part of the rebel army . . . would be attended with numerous advantages, as it would impress the remainder with a dread of being surrounded and cut off in every place where they took post, would increase their discontent, and [would] probably be the means of breaking up the whole of their army, and reducing the colonies to submission."[21] Howe calculated that, once the enlistments of the majority of Washington's remaining troops expired at the end of the year, the apparent hopelessness of the rebel situation would prevent the recruitment of a new army. In reporting how Washington's withdrawal from White Plains had forestalled a British attack, Captain the Honorable William Leslie observed that "most people seem to think that General Howe's intention was to endeavor to bring the rebels to a general engagement in order to disperse their army, which if once dispersed will be very different [*sic*, difficult?] to bring together, at least this season."[22]

Howe's intention to subject Washington's army to intolerable stresses proved partially successful, if not ultimately decisive: while the Virginian had around 28,000 men under his command at the start of the campaign, only about 5,000 accompanied him over the Delaware River in early December. Months later, during the Philadelphia campaign, Howe's Hessian aide de camp, Captain Friedrich von

Muenchhausen, was still working on the assumption that the rebel army would disintegrate under firm pressure, expressing the hope that "we can either force him to do battle on an advantageous terrain or to make a precipitous retreat. Either would mean the ruin of his army."[23]

If, especially early in the war, the rebels' preference for strong defensive positions gave British commanders every reason to seek alternatives to bloody frontal assaults, the relative tactical effectiveness of the contending forces gave them a powerful incentive to bring on open-field engagements. During Howe's inconclusive operations in New Jersey in June 1777, Captain Muenchhausen expressed the Crown forces' desire to put their superior discipline and military skill to the test: "Everyone in our army wishes that the rebels would do us the favor to take their chances in a regular battle. We would surely defeat them. I do not think that there exists a more select corps than that which General Howe has assembled here. I am too young, and have seen too few different corps, to ask others to take my word; but old Hessian and old English officers who have served a long time, say that they have never seen such a corps in respect to quality. The elite of the corps are the English grenadiers, light infantry, light dragoons, the Hessian grenadiers and *Jäger*. Every soldier serves with joy, and he would prefer to attack today rather than tomorrow."[24] An unsigned strategic memorandum penned in London in 1779 asserted that a Crown field army of 10,000–12,000 men "ever has been and will continue to be (considering the difference in the discipline of the British and American troops) sufficient to [defeat] any force the Americans have been [able to collect] since the first campaign, or will be able to collect."[25] Two years later, speaking of the victory of Lieutenant Colonel Francis Lord Rawdon's 900-strong force over Greene's army of 1,500 men, Major Frederick Mackenzie mused, "Having seen on every occasion what wonders are done by the British troops, against a very superior number of the rebels, it is to be lamented, that of late we have never had it in our power to attack them when there was any kind of equality."[26] To put it simply, British field forces in America were categorically defeated in battle only where they were greatly disadvantaged in terms of numbers and/or position, as at Princeton, Bemis Heights, and Cowpens.[27]

Only significant battlefield victories offered the British the prospect of neutralizing the Continental Army in a way that (as Lord

George Germain put it) "removed all apprehensions of further disturbance from the rebel troops."[28] As one example of this, when Clinton
congratulated Cornwallis on his victory over Lafayette at Green
Springs, he expressed a hope that it would "prevent his giving you
disturbance" during Cornwallis's pursuit of his current operational
objective—in this case the establishment of a naval station on the
Chesapeake.[29] Consequently throughout the war, British commanders were conscious that their primary objective was (as Germain put
it) "to bring Mr Washington to a general and decisive action."[30] Indeed, in 1777 and 1779 Howe claimed, "I do not now see a prospect of
terminating the war but by a general action," and that "my opinion
has always been, that the defeat of the rebel regular army is the surest
road to peace," while his successor, Sir Henry Clinton, asserted in
1779 that "to force Washington to an action upon terms tolerably
equal has been the object of every campaign during this war."[31]

## THE ARMED POPULATION

In eighteenth-century warfare, including most colonial campaigns,
military and political control over territory was generally concomitant
with the possession of its (usually fortified) major centers of admin-
istration and settlement. For instance, during the Seven Years War,
Britain wrested control of Canada, Cuba, and the Philippines by capturing Louisbourg (1758), Quebec (1759), Montreal (1760), Havana (1762),
and Manila (1762). In these conflicts civilians mostly remained passive
spectators (and victims) of the campaigns that unfolded around them.
When popular uprisings or insurgencies occurred, government forces
were usually able to defeat and disperse ill-armed rebel levies and (as
in the case of the British Army's punitive raids into the Highlands
after the last Jacobite uprising) terrorize recalcitrant populations into
submission.

      In the case of the American rebellion, the picture was very dif-
ferent. Perhaps the war's most unorthodox dimension, and the most
fundamental barrier to the restoration of British authority, was the
fact that the great majority of the adult white male population had
access to modern firearms and were (as one contemporary commen-
tator put it) "deep into principles."[32] From Massachusetts in 1774,
Brigadier General Lord Percy warned of the threat that the existence
of the colonial militia posed to British authority: "What makes an

insurrection here always more formidable than in other places, is that there is a law of this province, which obliges every inhabitant to be furnished with a firelock, bayonet, and pretty considerable quantity of ammunition. Besides which, every township is obliged by the same law to have a large magazine of all kinds of military stores. They are, moreover, trained four times in each year, so that they do not make a despicable *appearance* as soldiers, though they were never yet known to behave themselves even decently in the field."[33] Although the events of 1775 were to show just how determinedly the militia could fight when fully roused, Percy's low evaluation of its effectiveness was largely correct in the context of conventional military operations. Throughout the American War, militiamen's tendency to come and go as they pleased (often taking scarce equipment with them) caused senior rebel commanders much frustration, and their inability to stand up to British regulars in the open field contributed to a number of disastrous rebel defeats, most particularly the battle of Camden.[34]

Tactically, the militia proved far more effective when operating in broken terrain, employing what the British contemptuously styled a "skulking" method of fighting in actions where superior numbers, personal initiative, and enthusiasm were more potent factors than conventional military training and discipline. Indeed (as mentioned earlier), the militia's most important military contribution to the rebel cause was in the *petite guerre*. Crown troops often found their march through the country opposed by swarms of local irregulars in the manner experienced by Lieutenant General John Burgoyne in 1777: "Wherever the King's forces point, militia to the amount of three or four thousand assemble in twenty-four hours: they bring their own subsistence, and the alarm over they return to their farms."[35] These militia swarms were capable of mounting stiff resistance to small British forces (like the Concord and Danbury raiding columns) and on occasion inflicted sharp reverses on them (as at Bennington and King's Mountain). Similarly, British pickets, patrols, escorts, and flanking and foraging parties were at constant risk of hit-and-run attacks by prowling militia parties, especially in the South, where these "crackers" generally operated mounted.[36] These bitter little clashes were an unwelcome drain on British manpower, as Captain Banastre Tarleton acknowledged in July 1777 when he described the demise of two sergeants and one trooper in a rebel ambush on a British cavalry patrol in

New Jersey the previous month as "a great loss to the 16th Light Dragoons."[37] Four years later Cornwallis grimly made the same point: "I will not say much in praise of the militia of the southern colonies, but the list of British officers and soldiers killed and wounded by them since last June proves but too fatally that they are not wholly contemptible."[38]

But perhaps the most valuable overall role that the militia played in the rebel war effort was as an (as some historians have put it) "armed revolutionary constabulary": militia structures represented the nearest thing the local authorities had to a police force.[39] Before the war, the local rebel leaderships made certain of the militia's obedience by removing politically questionable officers. Consequently, throughout the conflict, wherever British troops were not immediately in force, the militia ensured popular compliance with the rebel government. It also forcibly suppressed loyalist activity, using terror where necessary. In short, the rebels' control of the militia ensured that (as Greene put it at Valley Forge) "[t]he limits of the British government in America are their out-sentinels."[40]

Given the potency of the militia, the control that the rebel leadership exerted over it, and the undoubted difficulties that a large-scale British military effort must inevitably have encountered in the face of widespread popular resistance, one might ask why the ministry rejected the alternative option for reestablishing British control over the colonies. That option, advocated by Lord Barrington (the secretary at war) and by Lieutenant General James Murray from Minorca, called for the occupation of the principal ports and the imposition of a close naval blockade that would have strangled the Americans' maritime trade and cut off the exports and imports upon which they depended. An accessory to this option was the employment of punitive action to stamp out defiance, such as the destruction of coastal towns that harbored rebel privateers or the encouragement of Indian raids on the frontiers.[41] Indeed, as the war dragged on and as the scale of disaffection became clearer, the option of employing what was euphemistically called "severity" against the rebellious colonists gained support from some frustrated British soldiers and statesmen.[42] Yet while both these options played to Britain's naval strength, it is not difficult to see why neither was fully implemented. To begin with, for reasons of economy the Royal Navy had been allowed to run down after the Seven Years War and was therefore not ready for full mobilization in 1775. Additionally, a predominantly naval strategy would inevitably have involved a prolonged and costly effort that would have increased the opportunities for the Bourbon monarchies to intervene and transform the colonial dispute into a doubtful side-show in a perilous global conflict. (The ministry was not to know, of course, that the military effort that it backed in the false expectation of a quick victory had the same outcome.) Lastly, an economic block-ade and especially the use of "severity" were liable to have provoked lasting popular bitterness in America, which would have been inimi-cal to the reintroduction of British authority.

If a military solution to the rebellion was the only viable strategy open to the ministry in 1775, it should be asked how the soldiers and statesmen who framed and executed Britain's war effort might have expected to restore and maintain royal government in America in the teeth of widespread popular resistance. Certainly this task would have required far more than the seizure and retention of the principal population centers. Crown commanders would also have needed to establish in the interior what Greene called "intermediate posts of communication for the purpose of awing the country and command-ing its supplies" and to have kept powerful mobile columns in the field to hunt down and disperse bands of intransigent partisans.[43] Unfortunately, the vastness of the theater and the meagerness of Brit-ish manpower resources put this quite out of the question. As Gen-eral Harvey, the adjutant general, bluntly asserted in June 1775, "at-tempting to conquer America internally by our land force, is as wild an idea, as ever controverted common sense."[44] In fact, as the British discovered in New Jersey in the winter of 1776–77 and in South Car-olina from 1780, even on a reduced scale Crown forces could not safely attempt to subdue via direct occupation a population that con-tained significant hostile elements while the Continental Army re-mained in being to threaten them with defeat in detail.

The simple answer to the question of how the British expected to conquer, and to keep subjugated, a hostile, armed colonial population is that they never intended to do any such thing. Instead they under-stood all too well that the restoration of royal authority in America was impossible without at least the acquiescence of the majority of the population. To British planners, this outcome was entirely realis-tic because, for the greater part of the war, their strategy remained firmly predicated on the assumption that the rebellion was the work

LIBRARY
THE UNIVERSITY OF TEXAS
AT BROWNSVILLE
Brownsville, TX  78520-4991

of an ambitious, artful, wicked minority that had deluded a gullible but essentially loyal population to submit to a republican "tyranny," that this authority was maintained by naked force, and that the majority of Americans desired the restoration of benevolent royal government.[45] This flawed interpretation of colonial public opinion, which prominent loyalists worked assiduously to bolster, upon which the ministry increasingly staked its political survival but which most senior military officers in America had rejected even before Yorktown underlined its bankruptcy, was probably at the root of Britain's failure to suppress the rebellion.

The contemporary British interpretation of colonial popular opinion flies full in the face of the traditional historiographical view of the American Revolution, which has tended to imply that the vast majority of the population was strongly committed to the cause of independence, or at least inveterately hostile to Britain.[46] But in recent decades historians like John Shy have proposed an alternative and altogether more convincing model of colonial attitudes. First, whatever their private sympathies, a large proportion of the colonists (possibly the majority) appear to have remained essentially uncommitted, taking the path of least resistance by submitting to whichever party happened to dominate locally. Second, the loyalties of those Americans who chose to play an active part in the conflict were frequently shaped less by ideology than by prewar ethnic, political, economic, religious, and personal rivalries and were liable to change according to circumstances.[47]

If Shy's model is accurate, then the British assessment of colonial public opinion, though flawed, was probably nearer the mark than historians have traditionally allowed. Specifically, British soldiers and statesmen were probably correct in believing that colonial public opinion was malleable: it was possible, as Clinton put it in February 1776, for Britain "to gain the hearts and subdue the minds of America."[48] Throughout the war, British commanders expected to bring about a collapse in popular support for the rebellion by means of successful military action, which they believed would discredit the revolutionary authorities by demonstrating the futility of continued resistance. Some of the methods by which they sought to achieve this aim were quite subtle. For example, Howe later claimed that he had raised no redoubts to protect his camp and outposts at Germantown prior to Washington's unexpected attack, "because works of that kind are apt to induce an opinion of inferiority, and my wish was, to support by every means the acknowledged superiority of the King's troops over the enemy."[49]

Yet the main way by which British commanders sought to demonstrate to the general population the pointlessness of opposing the King's troops was to score operational successes against the rebels' military forces. For instance, in December 1780 Cornwallis reported how the appearance of the apparently invincible Lieutenant Colonel Banastre Tarleton driving the partisans before him had quieted the unruly population between the Santee and Pee Dee rivers: "Tarleton . . . pursued [Lieutenant Colonel Francis] Marion for several days, obliged his corps to take to the swamps, and, by convincing the inhabitants that there was a power superior to Marion who could likewise reward and punish, so far checked the insurrection that the greatest part of them have not dared openly to appear in arms against us since his expedition."[50]

Crucially, it was not just Crown commanders who realized that British military success had the potential to dampen popular support for the rebel cause. Rebel military commanders likewise demonstrated enormous sensitivity to the population's perception of the course of military operations. For example, a month after Cornwallis wrote his report, Brigadier General Daniel Morgan warned Greene that a rebel retreat would have "the most fatal consequences": it would not only destroy "[t]he spirit which now begins to pervade the people and call them into the field" but also cause the militia to desert and even to switch sides. When Morgan nevertheless shortly afterward moved his detachment toward the Broad River in order to keep out of striking range of Cornwallis's army, he was at pains to assure Greene that this movement had been necessary "at the risk of its wearing the face of a retreat."[51] Likewise, in early May 1781, in relating to Washington the reasons why he felt obliged to avoid battle with the superior British forces in Virginia, Lafayette expressed concern about "what the public will think of our conduct."[52] Weeks later he returned to the theme, informing the rebel commander in chief that he was "determined to skirmish, but not to engage too far" because "[w]ere I to decline fighting, the country would think itself given up."[53]

If British soldiers and statesmen identified operational success against the rebels' military forces as the main way to trigger a popular rejection of revolutionary authority, the battlefield provided the most conspicuous arena for what Germain styled "proving the superiority of the British troops over the army of the rebels."[54] For example, two months after the battle of Bunker Hill, Burgoyne wrote that not the least of the victory's fruits was that "it re-establishes the ascendancy of the King's troops in public opinion": "I believe in most states of the world, as well as our own, the respect and control and subordination of government at this day, in great measure depends upon the idea that trained troops are invincible against any number or any position of undisciplined rabble; and this idea was a little in suspense since the 19th of April."[55]

The concept that signal British battlefield victories over the Continental Army would influence the colonists to abandon the rebel cause formed a central plank of Howe's plans for the New York offensive, Britain's greatest military effort in America. In April Howe advised the ministry that there was not "the least prospect of conciliating this continent until its armies shall have been roughly dealt with," while in June he asserted that a battlefield victory, "once obtained, and prosecuted immediately upon the arrival of the reinforcements, would not fail to have the most intimidating effects upon the minds of those deluded people."[56] By the time his army arrived at Staten Island in July, Howe was "still of the opinion that peace will not be restored in America until the rebel army is defeated," and he reiterated that to make an "impression upon the enemy's principal force collected in this quarter" would remain "the first object of my attention."[57] That summer Captain Alexander McDonald expressed Howe's intention more concisely: "after a few beatings, the people will begin to return to their senses by degrees, until the whole, wearied with disorder and panting after the sweets of peace, shall by a general defection forsake and leave their leaders to condign punishment."[58]

Once again evidence exists that rebel officers shared the British view that rebel defeats had a deleterious effect on popular support for the rebellion. For example, in a letter written a fortnight after Washington's defeat at Brandywine, the rebel adjutant general, Timothy Pickering, expressed his disgust at the way the militia of Pennsylvania and Delaware had deserted in droves: "How amazing, that Howe should march from the Head of Elk to the Schuylkill, a space of sixty miles, without opposition from the people of the country, except a small band of militia just round Elk!"[59]

Crown commanders did not just expect military successes to trigger a popular rejection of rebel authority, however. They also hoped these successes would influence the people to throw in their lot with the King. From the beginning of the war, British statesmen and soldiers expected Americans to play a part in crushing the rebellion, whether by taking up arms against their disloyal countrymen or, more importantly, by providing Crown forces with logistical support and intelligence while using their own moderating political influence to further the cause of a negotiated political settlement. Hence the abortive "southern expedition" of 1776 was designed to support major loyalist uprisings that were expected to restore speedily British authority in Virginia, the Carolinas, and Georgia, while Howe's offensives of 1776 and 1777 (and even Burgoyne's drive on Albany in 1777) were planned on the assumption that the King's troops would receive some material support from the "friends to government."

Shrewd British observers were realistic enough to appreciate that the scale of this support depended largely on the progress of operations. For example, months before the New York campaign, Howe prophesied that "there are many inhabitants in every province well affected to government, from whom no doubt we shall have assistance, but not until his Majesty's arms have a clear superiority by a decisive victory."[60] Similarly, three days before the battle of Freeman's Farm, Lieutenant William Digby recorded his belief that, if Burgoyne's army obtained a conspicuous battlefield success, "many of the country people would join us, but not till then—they choosing to be on the strongest side."[61]

Historians have criticized British strategy, both for not having properly exploited local support during the first three years of the war (particularly by raising more Provincial corps and loyal militias) and then, once Bourbon intervention forced a reevaluation, for having relied on the military potential of militant loyalism too completely.[62] Here we should sketch the essentials of the "southern strategy" (as it is known to historians) that was implemented from 1778.[63] To compensate for the necessary reduction of Britain's military commitment in America, this plan called for loyal Americans to play a greater direct military role in the process of suppressing the rebellion. In short, British regulars were to be used (as Major General James Robertson testified in Parliament in 1779) "to assist the good Americans to subdue the bad ones."[64] Starting with Lieutenant Colonel Archibald Campbell's expedition to Savannah in late 1778, this "Americanization" of the war (a term not used by contemporaries) involved a shift in operational focus to the more sparsely populated South, where the British erroneously believed that militant loyalism was prevalent. The new plan prescribed that Crown regulars were to recover these colonies piecemeal, organizing the inhabitants of each newly recovered area into new, loyal militia units that would carry out similar constabulary and security functions to those that the original rebel militias had provided. This, they believed, would free the precious regulars for the work of exporting "counterrevolution" (again, not a contemporary term) to new areas. But by 1781 the failure of the southern strategy had confirmed many senior officers' suspicions that the loyalists were nowhere in America numerically strong or determined enough to maintain British control without continued, heavy support from Crown regulars.

For obvious reasons, this "Americanization" of the war heightened the British incentive to achieve military success against the rebels as a way of encouraging elements of the population to come out openly in support of Crown forces. For example, after Guilford Courthouse, Cornwallis reported that he had accepted the challenge to attack Greene's much larger and well-posted army because he was "convinced that it would be impossible to succeed in that great object of our arduous campaign, the calling forth the numerous loyalists of North Carolina, whilst a doubt remained on their minds of the superiority of our arms."[65] Again, it was not only Crown officers who believed that battlefield victories influenced Americans (even supposed rebel supporters) to avow openly the King's cause. For instance, Brigadier General Stevens of the Virginia militia reported to Governor Thomas Jefferson that, as parties of fugitives from the shattered rebel army made their way northward after Cornwallis's great victory at Camden, "the inhabitants rose in numbers, took and disarmed the chief of our men."[66] According to rebel colonel Otho Williams, these fugitives were betrayed by "many of their insidious friends, armed, and advancing to join the American army." When these latecomers learned of the catastrophic rebel defeat, "they acted decidedly in concert with the victors; and, capturing some, plundering others, and maltreating all the fugitives they met, returned, exultingly, home."[67]

The extraordinary (if temporary) collapse of popular support for the rebellion within British-occupied New York and New Jersey in November and December 1776 and in South Carolina in May and June 1780 appeared to demonstrate the political efficacy of a convincingly spun illusion of British military invincibility. In both cases, when the power of local rebel authorities was broken, most ordinary Americans did not immediately embark on a bitter partisan war against British occupation. Instead they either ignored rebel militia summonses or returned to their communities, where they commonly sought royal pardons and protections. Of course, in neither case did the British ascendancy last long, due to a resurgence in popular opposition that stemmed from various factors (including Washington's successes at Trenton and Princeton, the misbehavior of the King's troops, loyalist vengefulness, and Clinton's attempts to deny paroled southern rebels the option of neutrality) that have been too well documented to need reexamination here.

British commanders identified operational successes against the rebels' military forces—and particularly battlefield victories against the Continental Army—as the key to achieving victory in America. By inducing the disintegration of rebel forces or by compelling them to withdraw deep into the interior, British commanders expected to be able to restore royal authority by dispersing their own meager forces in fixed garrisons. Rebel reverses were also expected to pay a handsome political dividend: popular support for the revolt was expected to wither (thereby facilitating the reestablishment of royal government over a turbulent and armed population) and elements of the rebel leadership were expected to break ranks and seek terms. The astonishing (if temporary) collapse of the rebellion in New Jersey in late 1776 and in South Carolina in May–June 1780 gave British leaders some reason to feel confident in their assessment of the importance of clear military successes over the Continental Army.

# 2

# OPERATIONAL CONSTRAINTS

[W]ithout baggage, necessaries, or provisions of any sort for officer or soldier, in the most barren, inhospitable, unhealthy part of North America, opposed to the most savage, inveterate, perfidious, cruel enemy, with zeal and with bayonets only, it was resolved to follow Greene's army to the end of the world.

Brigadier General Charles O'Hara to the Duke of Grafton,
20 April 1781

O nly by neutralizing the rebels' military forces could the Crown have reestablished control over American territory, persuaded the rebel leadership to abandon the goal of independence in favor of a negotiated political settlement, and encouraged the colonial population at large to withdraw its armed support for the rebellion. Consequently, British commanders and statesmen identified military success against the Continental Army as the key to victory. Inconveniently, a number of factors conspired to render the British Army's operations in North America unusually problematic.

### "WE LIVE BY VICTORY"

If a convincing display of British military invincibility was required to undercut support for the rebellion, Crown commanders clearly needed to avoid military reverses. The course of Howe's operations in

1776 illustrates particularly well the degree of caution they exercised to this end. Traditionally, historians have censured Howe for having, they supposed, wasted the numerous opportunities to crush the rebels that Clinton, Howe's testy second in command, identified. Yet as William Willcox has demonstrated, the campaign around New York gave early signs that Clinton's propensity for precocious planning was not matched by a proclivity for bold action. For example, when the general unenthusiastically executed Howe's successful Kipp's Bay landing, he declined to deviate from his orders by attempting to interdict the rebel withdrawal from New York City into Harlem. Similarly, when he was sent to occupy Rhode Island at the end of the campaign, he made no attempt to trap the rebel defenders.[1] In forgoing opportunities to strike powerful blows against the rebels' military forces, Clinton demonstrated not only that he was no more desirous than his chief to fritter away his precious British and German regulars but also that he was acutely aware of the political damage that operational miscarriages wrought. As he himself put it: "My advice has ever been to avoid even the possibility of a check. We live by victory."[2] In this he was fully in accordance with Howe's own avowal that "a check at this time would be of infinite detriment to us."[3]

British military setbacks galvanized the rebel cause principally by prompting Americans to give active support to the revolution, whether by providing intelligence, enlisting in the Continental forces, or engaging in popular resistance to the King's troops. The best examples of the last were the escalations in local militia activity (whether spontaneously or in response to summonses) stimulated by the defeats at Trenton and Princeton in the winter of 1776–77, the disaster at Bennington in August 1777, and the series of partisan successes against isolated Crown detachments in the South Carolina backcountry from late June 1780. In January 1781, before Cornwallis's second invasion of North Carolina, Lieutenant Colonel James Stuart of the 2nd Battalion of Guards worried that "were any misfortune to happen to our army when advanced in this country they [i.e., the rebel militia] would increase to such numbers as would effectively cut off our communications with the sea. From what I have said you will easily perceive the difficulties that an army offering to penetrate this country must encounter. I sincerely wish that they may be well understood by our general, that no fatal consequences may ensue."[4] Presumably, Stuart was reflecting on how the New England militia and the southern "over-mountain-men" had respectively risen to crush the "Canadian army" at Saratoga and Major Patrick Ferguson's loyalists at King's Mountain.

Rebel successes also discouraged Americans from giving active support to the British. Howe provided an excellent example of this in his testimony before Parliament in 1779. Although one must remember that Howe was attempting to evade responsibility for the ultimate failure of Britain's military efforts in America in 1777, his version of events sheds light on British attitudes to the malleability of colonial public opinion. According to Howe, the inhabitants of Pennsylvania, lower Delaware, and lower New Jersey exhibited "equivocal neutrality" when the campaign opened. But British successes (particularly the capture of Philadelphia) "convinced the country of the superiority, and persuaded them of the established power of His Majesty's arms." This change in attitude produced an increase in the quality and quantity of "secret intelligence" that the general received from the population and what he interpreted as a new readiness "to assist offensively in compelling his Majesty's revolted subjects to their duty." According to Howe's version of events, the imminent collapse of the rebellion under the weight of apparently "insurmountable" difficulties was averted only by news of French intervention and the ministry's decision to evacuate Philadelphia, "by which measure the protection of his Majesty's forces was to be withdrawn from the province." Howe summarized the "sudden and melancholy change in our affairs" by concluding, "The rebels were inspired with fresh hopes; the friends of government were dismayed."[5]

Charles Stedman, a Philadelphia loyalist who served as a commissary under Cornwallis in the South, later highlighted a similar case that shows how even an apparent reverse curbed popular support for the British. In this case the supposed check was the incidental concurrency of Cornwallis's withdrawal over the Haw River after "Pyle's Massacre" (25 February 1781) with Greene's return into North Carolina: "The bulk of mankind being guided by external appearances, nothing could be more unfavorable to Lord Cornwallis's present views than this retrograde movement upon the approach of General Greene's army. If the loyalists were before cautious and slow, they now became timid to an excess, and dreaded taking any active measure whatsoever on behalf of the King's government more especially when they reflected on the disaster that had happened to Colo-

nel [John] Pyle, whose [loyalist militia] detachment was cut to pieces
within little more than a mile of Tarleton's encampment." Significantly, Stedman added, Cornwallis's intelligence broke down completely at this point, robbing him of a favorable opportunity to strike
at Greene before the latter was ready to fight.[6]

The obligation on British commanders to avoid even the appearance of a check often had a significant effect on operations. In defend-
ing his conduct of the Albany expedition, Burgoyne claimed that he
had made the fateful decision to take the overland route from Skenesboro to Fort Edward (rather than having fallen back to Ticonderoga
and then sailed down Lake George) partly because of "the general
impressions which a retrograde motion is apt to make upon the
minds both of enemies and friends."[7] Similarly, in reporting his battlefield triumph at Camden, Cornwallis explained why, despite long
odds, he had resolved to fight Gates's invading rebel army. On one
level was a narrowly military consideration: a retreat to Charleston
would have necessitated the abandonment of eight hundred sick and
a great quantity of stores. Uppermost in his lordship's thinking, however, was the obligation to preserve the impression of invincibility
that the fall of Charleston and other minor successes had established
in the people's minds. A retreat would have shattered this illusion
and stimulated an upsurge in popular resistance, which would have
brought about the collapse of British control throughout South Carolina and Georgia, "besides forfeiting all pretensions to future confidence from our friends in this part of America."[8] This sensitivity to
the population's response extended even to relatively minor details.
For example, after he had driven off Greene's superior army at Hobkirk's Hill, Lieutenant Colonel Francis Lord Rawdon reported his
concern to Cornwallis that Lieutenant Colonel Henry Lee's rebel dragoons had carried off several wounded men from the British rear,
"probably with intent to deceive the country people respecting the
event of the action."[9]

If Crown commanders believed that a successful end to the war
depended heavily upon the establishment in American minds of an
illusion of British military invincibility, it is understandable that they
were consistently reluctant to risk politically damaging operational
miscarriages that undid weeks or months of patient planning and
successful action. The frustration that the latter outcome elicited in
these officers is apparent in Brigadier General Charles O'Hara's de-

spairing judgment on the war in November 1780: "how impossible must it prove to conquer a country, where repeated successes cannot ensure permanent advantages, and the most trifling check to our arms acts like electrical fire, by rousing at the same moment every man upon this vast continent . . . in pursuit of their favorite independency."[10]

## MANPOWER

Estimates are that something like 250,000 different men actively served the rebel cause in a direct military capacity during the course of the American War. While we do not know how many of them were rendered incapable of further service by wounds or sickness, about one in ten died. Furthermore, perhaps a third of all regulars and half of all militiamen deserted. By contrast, Britain maintained an average of about 35,000 men in North America throughout the war, of whom an estimated 19,000 had been lost (through death, discharge, desertion, or capture) by 1779.[11] In all, perhaps 50,000 regular British soldiers (excluding the Provincial and German corps) served in North America (excluding the West Indies) during the course of the conflict.[12] Even a superficial comparison of these fragmentary statistics indicates that the total number of rebel casualties must have dwarfed the corresponding British figure.

The rebels' war effort managed to withstand such enormous losses because of the unconventional means that they employed to raise and maintain their military forces.[13] Three striking facts emerge. First, a very high proportion of the adult male population actively served as rebel regulars or militia—perhaps half the total eligible. Second, in the majority of cases, this service did not comprise one continuous period but several. Third, most of these separate periods can be measured, not in years, but in months or even weeks. For instance, while almost all adult males were liable for militia service and were obliged to turn out for immediate local defense, the quotas of men that were required for short periods of militia service away from home were commonly selected by ballot. Similarly, although a tough core of experienced veterans gradually developed within the Continental Army, its ranks were nevertheless in considerable flux. This was due not only to chronic wastage from sickness and especially desertion but also to the means by which new recruits were obtained. At the start of the war, the Continental Army generally offered short-term enlistments, which nearly led to its disintegration at the end of 1775 and 1776. But because the longer enlistment terms (three years or the duration of the war) introduced in 1777 to rectify this problem were so unattractive, rebel authorities had to resort to drafting men (typically for no longer than nine months, from spring to winter) from the militia to keep the Continental Army in being. This was the situation that led Captain Johann Ewald of the Hessian *Feldjägerkorps* to observe in 1781 that "in no monarchy in the world is levying done more forcibly than in this country, where it is said without distinction of position, 'serve or provide your man [i.e., a paid substitute], else you lose your goods and chattels.'"[14]

The rebel authorities' ability to keep the Continental Army in being by means of relays of short-term recruits and drafts, and to summon large numbers of militia into the field for short periods, was in stark contrast to the Crown's situation.[15] From 1775, British and Provincial regulars were enlisted on an almost entirely voluntary basis for three years or the duration of the war (at the King's option). Throughout the conflict, the army experienced severe problems in finding enough men, despite extemporizations that included increasingly generous bounties and other incentives, the authorized recruitment of Roman Catholics and some pardoned criminals, the raising of new regiments "for rank," and the very limited military presses instituted in 1778 and 1779 to stimulate voluntary enlistments. One problem the British faced was the popular fear of transoceanic voyages and pestilential climes, which made many potential recruits (as one pamphleteer observed in 1775) "mighty shy of enlisting" in any corps serving in or destined for America.[16] Once the conflict there escalated into a global struggle, the army began to scrape the bottom of the manpower barrel to obtain (as the secretary at war put it) "any man that could be made of the smallest use."[17] For example, when the 80th Regiment was raised in 1778, it sought recruits between eighteen and thirty years of age who were at least 5 feet, 4 inches tall. The next year the 94th Regiment was permitted to enlist men between the ages of fifteen and forty and as short as 5 feet, 3 inches tall.[18] Predictably, this had an effect on the quality of the rank and file in America, one French commissary at Yorktown having noted how "small" most of the surrendered redcoats were.[19] This shortness was not merely a cosmetic flaw, for infantrymen shorter than 5 feet, 6 inches had difficulty carrying their packs on the march.[20]

Contemporary observations on the standard of the Royal Artillery's enlisted men in America further illustrate this crucial point. Only well-built men could manhandle heavy artillery pieces effectively, and in peacetime the corps recruited selectively. Hence in October 1776 Captain Georg Pausch of the Hesse-Hanau artillery described the Royal Artillery as containing "the tallest, strongest, and best-looking troops which can be seen in the entire world." This claim Pausch substantiated less than a year later when he noted that all of the corps' thirty-odd enlisted men killed and wounded at the battle of Freeman's Farm measured between 5 feet, 10 inches and 6 feet.[21] According to the letters of the senior Royal Artillery officer in America, within two years these high standards were a distant memory. By March 1779 Major General James Pattison's 4th Battalion of the Royal Artillery was over 250 men short of its establishment. Six months later Pattison lamented the numerical and qualitative inadequacy of a recently arrived batch of drafts and recruits: "hard times indeed and great must be the scarcity of men when the Royal Artillery is obliged to take such reptiles." He particularly wished the Irish newcomers "again in the bogs from whence they sprang" and despaired that only five of a recently arrived batch of 178 drafts and recruits had spared him the pain of looking at them by deserting or dying en route. Disdaining that "such warriors of 5' 5 1/2" I never saw raised before for the service of Artillery," Pattison questioned the generosity of his fellow commanding officers in Britain in having parted with these "whippers-in" and "postilions." Indeed, so physically unimpressive were the arrivals that, when the Board of Ordnance refused to send carbines for them, the exasperated Pattison observed caustically, "I will try how far the strength of these diminutive warriors is equal to carry muskets *cut down.*"[22]

Because the British could not match the enemy's ability to replace casualties, the principle of "conservation of force" exerted a crucial influence over the conduct of operations. In particular, commanders had to exercise caution selecting the circumstances in which they were prepared to engage their forces in combat. As Lieutenant General James Murray observed from Minorca, the rebels would have been well advised to lose a battle every week: "it may be discovered that our troops are not invincible, they are certainly not immortal."[23]

In 1779 Howe's testimony to the parliamentary enquiry into his handling of the command repeatedly stressed this point: that "the most essential duty I had to observe was, not wantonly to commit his Majesty's troops, where the object was inadequate"; that "any considerable loss sustained by the army could not speedily, nor easily, be repaired"; that "one great point towards gaining the confidence of an army . . . is never to expose the troops, where . . . the object is inadequate"; that, while on the one hand, "the defeat of the rebel regular army is the surest road to peace," on the other hand, "a material check to his Majesty's arms might have been productive of fatal consequences to the interests of this country in America"; and that, despite this, "I never delayed to seize an opportunity of attacking the enemy, consistently with my duty of weighing the risk of ruining the cause I was engaged in by a considerable loss of troops."[24] Significantly, Howe's officers appear to have approved of his care not to fritter away his men's lives. As one put it in September 1776, "the difficulty of getting troops, and such troops, is so great, that we ought not to hazard our men without the evident prospect of accomplishing our purpose."[25]

In fact, British commanders could not afford to inflict casualties on, and sustain them at the hands of, the rebels at anything like an equal rate of exchange. Howe explicitly made this point when he later asserted that, had he permitted his victorious troops to storm Brooklyn Heights toward the end of the battle of Long Island, "[t]he loss of 1,000, or perhaps 1,500 British troops, in carrying those lines, would have been but ill-repaid by double that number of the enemy, could it have been supposed they would have suffered in that proportion."[26] Similarly, after Cornwallis took possession of Fort Lee (19 November 1776), he ordered Captain Ewald to let the retiring rebel garrison escape without molestation, explaining that "[w]e do not want to lose any men. One *Jäger* is worth more than ten rebels."[27] In April 1781 the French officer Baron Ludwig von Closen made a similar point when he observed (with pardonable exaggeration) that "[t]he Americans lose 600 men in a day, and 8 days later 1,200 others rejoin the army; whereas, to replace 10 men in the English army is quite an undertaking."[28]

The need to conserve the Crown's military forces in America also exerted a restraining influence on the general course of operations. In particular, commanders could not afford to lose men to sickness or desertion in the same proportion as the enemy, whose leaders routinely exposed their predominantly short-service troops to highly unconventional levels of deprivation. Traditionally, historians have made much of the differing extents to which British and rebel armies depended on baggage trains in America. Yet necessity rather than altruism required Crown generals to provide their troops with the commodities that (as discussed in the next section) were necessary to maintain their health and morale. Ewald put this point very simply in commenting on the willingness of rebel troops to undergo unconventional levels of privation: "Deny the best-disciplined soldiers of Europe what is due to them and they will run away in droves, and the general will soon be alone."[29] British commanders seem to have been successful in avoiding this outcome, for their desertion rates were inconsiderable despite the potential inducements and opportunities that existed in the New World.[30]

## LOGISTICS

Britain's military effort to subjugate the rebellious colonies posed unprecedented logistical challenges. While historians have shown how supplies were acquired in the British Isles, transported across the Atlantic, and then administered in America, it is arguable that insufficient attention has been given to the ways in which logistical considerations affected British operations.[31]

The difficulties of feeding campaigning armies exercised a dominating influence on contemporary European warfare.[32] Especially problematic were the needs of draught, cavalry, and riding horses, each of which daily needed about fifty pounds of green forage or half that amount dry (to say nothing of occasional issues of hard feed) to remain in condition in the field.[33] Too bulky for transport, forage had to be obtained and consumed more or less *in situ*. It was possible in winter to take troops into the field for brief periods by divorcing them from almost all their horses, which Howe did when he prevented the force with which he probed Washington's position at Whitemarsh in December 1777 from taking along its wagons (including his own vehicle).[34] Yet the absolute impossibility of conducting major operations without transport and artillery ensured that serious campaigning was limited to the growing season.[35] On the positive side, field armies in America (especially in the sparsely settled northern wilderness and southern backwoods) not only were small by European standards but also contained proportionately fewer horses. Hence, while in conventional European campaigns one in every four or five days had to be given over to a "grand forage" involving almost all the troops as mowers or escorts, in America such affairs were generally necessary only if an army exhausted the local forage by remaining static for too long. Such was the case when Burgoyne's advance stalled along the Hudson in September and October 1777.[36]

The men's nutritional needs were less straightforward. The common soldier's nominal daily ration was up to one pound of bread and one pound of meat, plus varying quantities of "small species" (butter, cheese, oatmeal, rice, peas, vinegar, sauerkraut, etc.). But in the field the soldier generally received instead up to one and a half pounds each of meat and bread.[37] Moreover, to circumvent the use of cumbersome field ovens, this "bread" normally took the form of pre-baked, compact, long-lasting hard "biscuit" (though sometimes the troops were issued with the flour to make their own "cakes").[38] Despite the disciplinary problems caused by drunkenness, the troops also required alcohol. This included occasional issues of porter and especially spruce beer to combat scurvy, but the soldiery expected a daily gill of rum to alleviate the arduousness of service in America.[39] As loyalist Lieutenant Anthony Allaire put it after the backwoods operations that culminated in the disaster at King's Mountain, "rum is a very essential article, for in marching ten miles we would often be obliged to ford two or three rivers, which wet the men up to their waists."[40]

That America was, in operational terms, a hostile country made the provisioning of a British field army particularly problematic. In conventional European campaigns, civilian contractors commonly arranged for the bulk purchase and delivery of comestibles. In this way provisions had been obtained for the King's troops in North America during the French and Indian War, and Congress was able to employ a similar system to supply its own military forces during the American War. By contrast, the closure of colonial markets to Crown agents in 1775 thereafter compelled British commanders in America to feed their troops predominantly on provisions shipped across the Atlantic. Contrary to expectations, royal forces never relinquished this precarious and expensive transatlantic logistical lifeline because they proved unable to break the rebels' control over any substantial tracts of territory for more than a short period, as in New Jersey in late 1776 and in South Carolina in mid-1780.

The leading authority on the British logistical effort in America has pointed to the failure to maintain sizeable food reserves at Crown bases like New York or Charleston as one of the principal contributing factors in Britain's defeat, specifically because of the way this inhibited strategic planning.[41] Arguably more significant were the problems involved in forwarding the supplies from the warehouses through hostile country to the troops in the field. In conventional European campaigns, armies were more or less dependent on their logistical "tails," supplies having been shuttled to them by road or preferably by water from temporary depots or magazines in the rear. Once again, however, what was commonplace in other theaters, and what the rebels could themselves usually do, was next to impossible for the British in America.[42] Vice Admiral Samuel Graves encapsulated the problem when he observed that the movement of a British field army in America resembled "the passage of a ship through the sea whose track is soon lost."[43] Of course, during the wilderness campaigns of the French and Indian War, British commanders had employed chains of fortified depots to relay supplies through country that was similarly hostile.[44] Yet they were able to do this because of their great numerical superiority. By contrast, the British forces that combated the American rebellion were (as Lieutenant General Thomas Gage protested in August 1775) "too small to divide or allow of large detachments to open the country for supplies or keep up posts of communication."[45] To traverse even limited distances, supply convoys needed massive escorts to guard against prowling rebel bands. During the Pennsylvania campaign, for example, Howe was twice compelled to employ three whole battalions to escort provisions convoys coming up from Chester and Philadelphia to his field force at Germantown and Chestnut Hill, respectively.[46] Illustrative of the stranglehold that this problem exerted on British operations in America is Howe's abortive feint through New Jersey toward the Delaware River in June 1777. Although this thrust was intended to dupe Washington into leaving his inaccessible camp in the Watchung Mountains to defend Philadelphia, the Virginian declined to take the bait because he knew that Howe simply could not break contact with his bridgehead at New Brunswick.[47] Indeed, over two months earlier, the

British commander in chief had already committed himself to a sea-borne invasion of Pennsylvania for the very same reason.[48]

As this latter point suggests, it was possible for commanders to circumvent the impracticability of the depot system by relying upon water carriage, particularly in conjunction with the Royal Navy. Vessels ranging from small riverine craft to large seagoing transports were able to relay supplies up to the army from the rear or to accompany it in the fashion of a "floating magazine." This option was particularly attractive when the army was operating along the coast, as during the successive operations against New York, Rhode Island, Savannah, and Charlestown between 1776 and 1780. For operations farther inland, however, a means of interior navigation compatible with the army's axis of advance was necessary. Viable routes included the corridor formed by the St. Lawrence River, Richelieu River, Lake Champlain, and Lake George, which the "Canadian army" utilized in 1776 and 1777, or the Hudson and Delaware rivers and Chesapeake Bay, which Howe, Clinton, and Cornwallis variously employed between 1776 and 1781.[49] Nevertheless, even where such interior navigation was available, the insecurity of overland communications restricted an army's maximum operational range to about fifteen to twenty miles from navigable water.[50] Furthermore, like overland communications, water carriage was vulnerable to interdiction. This the Howe brothers discovered after the seizure of Philadelphia in 1777, when they found themselves embroiled in a bitter struggle to prize open the Delaware River before the occupying army starved. Cornwallis's experience in the Carolinas in 1780–81 was similar. Rebel irregulars jeopardized the main supply route up the Santee River from Charleston to Camden and then, after Guilford Courthouse, prevented the garrison of the coastal base at Wilmington from dispatching supplies up the Cape Fear River to Cornwallis's battered army at Cross Creek.[51]

If it was impracticable to supply Crown forces in the field by road or water, it might be argued that more use could have been made of local resources. A strategic memorandum penned in London in 1779 asserted that America was "a country full of provisions."[52] Indeed, that same year Cornwallis testified before a House of Commons Committee that one of the attractions of a campaign in Pennsylvania in 1777 had been that Howe had expected to draw upon ample local supplies of livestock and flour.[53] Moreover, during Clinton's overland withdrawal from Philadelphia to New York in 1778, Commissary Daniel Wier succeeded in acquiring something like ten days' provisions from the apparently "devoured" and "inimical" New Jersey countryside by drawing on the army's perennially short supply of specie.[54]

In reality, however, Crown troops could never have subsisted in the field entirely on local foodstuffs. Wier's success was the exception that proved the rule. The country folk did not generally brave rebel patrols to sell their animals and produce to the King's troops because they could not easily redeem the paper commissary receipts with which they were customarily paid. In addition, transport shortages, the speed of the army's movements, and the hostile nature of the countryside all conspired to restrict the distance that commissaries could roam to seek out, requisition, and cart back comestibles. In short, the only local foodstuffs that the army could depend upon were those it encountered in its immediate path. Such local pickings included the deer and pigeons that Carleton's soldiers shot in the woods around Lake Champlain in October 1776, the unripe potatoes that Burgoyne's men pulled up at Fort Edward in July 1777, and the livestock that Howe's troops gathered as they advanced through Pennsylvania in August and September 1777.[55] Moreover, even these pickings were slim in the more sparsely settled regions or when the British were traversing areas through which rebel forces had already passed, as was commonly the case. Nor should one assume that all locally available comestibles were always of value. For example, Cornwallis's men had little leisure to bake the barreled flour that they found as they chased Washington's disintegrating army through New Jersey in November 1776.[56]

Cornwallis's field army attempted to live off the land when it invaded North Carolina in September–October 1780 and January–April 1781. The southern backwoods was one of the least promising regions in the colonies for this experiment because (as Lieutenant Colonel James Stuart of the Guards observed in January 1781) it was "quite covered with wood and very thinly inhabited and therefore by no means calculated to maintain even a small army."[57] The later recollections of participants like Roger Lamb (a sergeant in the 23rd Regiment in 1780) bear ample testimony to the difficulties that the army experienced in wringing adequate provisions from the country it traversed: "Sometimes we had turnips served out for food when we came to a turnip field; or, arriving at a field of corn, we converted our canteens into rasps and ground our Indian corn for bread. When we could get no Indian corn, we were compelled to eat liver, as a substitute for bread, with our lean beef."[58] Even this hand-to-mouth existence was threatened when the army was pressed, as when it made its grueling fortnight-long withdrawal from Charlotte in October 1780 without tents and rum, along roads churned into mud by incessant rain. John Robert Shaw was a private in the 33rd Regiment in 1780, and his later account of the retreat emphasized the troops' gnawing hunger: "We made our retreat like lost sheep, not knowing where to go, no forage, no provisions for our men, though marching day and night. At this time I saw an English guinea offered for a bit of cornbread not larger than my two fingers. Hard times with us indeed—16 days without a morsel of bread. In this starving condition we made our way to Winnsboro."[59] The account of the same bitter withdrawal penned later by the loyalist Charles Stedman, who served as a commissary with Cornwallis, also focused on food shortages: "Sometimes the army had beef, and no bread; at other times bread and no beef. For five days it was supported upon Indian corn, which was collected as it stood in the field, five ears of which were the allowance for two soldiers for twenty-four hours. . . . The water that the army drank was frequently as thick as puddle. Few armies ever encountered greater difficulties and hardships."[60]

During Cornwallis's longer and deeper second invasion of North Carolina, the army's deprivations were even worse. In part, this was because the earl destroyed almost all the baggage (including all the vehicles save the ammunition, salt, and hospital wagons) to streamline his army for the "Race to the Dan."[61] But once again the main reason why Cornwallis's veterans suffered so much was that the sparsely settled province could not provide the army with adequate provisions. When the last elements of Greene's army crossed the Dan River into Virginia (15 February 1781), Cornwallis had to withdraw, first to Hillsboro, thence to Alamance Creek, because the rebels had consumed all the local resources and the British could not subsist even by slaughtering the draught oxen and requisitioning food from local houses.[62] John Robert Shaw later recalled the short rations that the troops received during the month-long interval between the end of the "Race" and the battle of Guilford Courthouse: "At this time the scarcity of provisions was so great that we had but one pound of flour for six men per day, with very little beef and no salt the half of the time. With this allowance, my messmates and I made two meals a day, which we managed by first boiling the beef, and then taking it out. And having mixed our pound of flour with some water, we put it into the kettle in which the beef had been boiled; and when sufficiently heated, we took it off the fire and let it stand until it cooled. This served us for breakfast, and the beef we kept for dinner; and as for supper, we were obliged to do without it."[63] According to Lamb, when the elusive Greene finally gave battle, "[t]he British army had marched several miles on the morning of the day on which they came to action. They had no provisions of any kind whatever on that day, nor until between three and four in the afternoon of the succeeding day; and then but a scanty allowance, not exceeding one quarter of a pound of flour and the same quantity of very lean beef."[64]

With no secure way of bringing up supplies from the rear, and with little likelihood that the troops could live off the land, British field armies almost inevitably had to carry with them at least a proportion of the victuals needed to sustain their operations. While the soldier was able to could carry up to four days' rations on his person, wheeled vehicles or pack animals conveyed provisions to sustain the army beyond this short period, in the manner of a "rolling magazine."[65] For example, according to Cornwallis, Howe's army in Pennsylvania in 1777 carried with it about "22 days' rum, 6 days' pork, [and] 12 or 14 days' bread."[66] Here we should be clear about the numbers of vehicles that were needed to assemble such a provisions train. If we suppose that a four-horse wagon could carry 2,000 pounds of rations (excluding the containers), then Howe's 12,500-strong army at Brandywine would have required more than 131 wagons and 524 horses merely to carry two weeks' supply of biscuit.[67] When smaller vehicles were employed, the numbers required were even greater. The table that Nathaniel Day (Burgoyne's commissary general) drew up in preparation for the Albany expedition (more commonly referred to today as the Saratoga campaign) shows that he envisaged employing two-horse Canadian carts that could carry a load of eight hundred pounds. Taking into account the containers and reckoning the ration at three pounds, Day's calculations showed that 1,000 men needed thirty-nine such carts to carry their provisions (excluding alcohol) for ten days' campaigning (see table 1).[68]

Table 1. Land transport necessary (in number of carts) for the
provisions train of Burgoyne's invasion force from Canada, 1777.

| | Number of days | | | | | | | | |
|---|---|---|---|---|---|---|---|---|---|
| | 1 | 2 | 3 | 4 | 5 | 10 | 20 | 60 | 90 |
| 10,000 Men | 38 | 75 | 113 | 150 | 188 | 375 | 750 | 1,250 | 3,375 |
| 5,000 Men | 19 | 38 | 57 | 75 | 94 | 188 | 375 | 1,125 | 1,688 |
| 4,000 Men | 15 | 30 | 45 | 60 | 75 | 150 | 300 | 900 | 1,350 |
| 3,000 Men | 12 | 23 | 34 | 45 | 57 | 113 | 225 | 676 | 1,014 |
| 2,000 Men | 8 | 15 | 23 | 30 | 38 | 75 | 150 | 450 | 675 |
| 1,000 Men | 4 | 8 | 12 | 15 | 19 | 39 | 75 | 226 | 339 |
| 500 Men | 2 | 4 | 6 | 8 | 10 | 20 | 38 | 113 | 171 |

Note: Calculations are those of Commissary General Nathaniel Day.

Beyond provisioning, campaigning troops also required access to what is known collectively as baggage. First, British field armies could not usually establish static hospitals unless they intended to abandon their inmates to the enemy. Instead, the army had to carry its sick and wounded along with it unless the injured could be evacuated by water, as Howe did after Brandywine when he delayed his pursuit of Washington in order to secure a post at Wilmington, Delaware.[69] Hence when Cornwallis destroyed his train before invading North Carolina in January 1781, he nevertheless retained four wagons for the sick and wounded and a number of others to carry hospital stores, salt, and ammunition.[70] Second, an army needed a varying amount of specialist equipment, like engineers' tools, traveling forges, and the horse-drawn pontoons (employed by the main and "Canadian" armies in 1777–78).[71] Third, it needed enough ammunition to see it through several engagements. Common field practice was for the Royal Artillery to administer central stocks while each battalion maintained its own supply of one hundred rounds per man—sixty on the soldier's person (thirty-six in his cartridge pouch and twenty-four in his knapsack or haversack), with the rest in the regimental baggage.[72]

Fourth, the troops needed camp equipage. The soldiery's five-man tents could not be moved save on pack animals or wagons, so from the New York campaign onward, British troops in the field increasingly slept instead either under the stars or inside ad hoc "wigwams" or "huts" constructed from brushwood, fence rails, and cornstalks.[73] Nevertheless, tools (listed by one contemporary authority as ten shovels and five mattocks per company and one hatchet per tent group) still had to be carried in the regimental baggage.[74] The rest of the camp equipage was part of the men's full marching order: a knapsack containing "necessaries" and blanket, a haversack for rations, a water canteen, and a tin camp kettle (one per five-man tent group)—a load that, in addition to accoutrements, firelock, bayonet, ammunition, and regimentals, weighed over sixty pounds.[75] One should note that for short periods the men were able to do without knapsacks and camp kettles by utilizing blanket rolls and filling their haversacks with several days' precooked rations. (Presumably this is what Anspach musketeer Private Johann Döhla meant when he recorded in 1778, "The common British soldier is swift, marches easily; and in general, the English nation is very swift and light on their feet, and the soldiers have very light and airy clothing and do not carry heavy loads when they are in the field.")[76]

Finally, a campaigning force needed a varying amount of personal baggage for its officers. Traditionally, historians have scorned these men as self-indulgent dilettantes who took absurd amounts of personal paraphernalia into the field. Some evidence can be marshaled to support this unflattering picture. For example, one Quaker lad later recalled that the short, portly, well-dressed, and genteel British officers whom he encountered before the battle of Brandywine "did not look as if they had ever been exposed to any hardship; their skins being as white and delicate as is customary for females who were brought up in large cities or towns."[77] More damning was Captain Johann Ewald's criticism of British and German officers' preference for campaign portmanteaux crammed with fripperies like hair powder, pomade, playing cards, and light reading, which he claimed contrasted poorly with their rebel counterparts' apparent satisfaction with knapsacks containing only spare linen and well-thumbed military treatises.[78]

The quantity of officers' baggage taken into the field did cause on occasion serious problems, as on the Albany expedition.[79] Burgoyne's trouble originated in the latitude that he gave his officers to make their own arrangements for transporting their gear once the army quit the bateaux on the lakes.[80] Although he warned them to bring along only the most essential field equipage, most (presumably unconvinced that the rest of their baggage would reach them from Canada when the campaign closed) apparently declined to do so.[81] Consequently, the regulation number of animals allowed to each battalion (thirty-eight for the officers and staff in addition to the sixteen for the enlisted men's tents) appears to have been ignored.[82] Instead, most officers brought horses from Canada or obtained them locally in the weeks following the fall of Fort Ticonderoga (6 July).[83] After the army's disembarkation at Skenesboro (10 July), Burgoyne recommended those officers still without a means of moving their baggage to return all nonessential gear to Ticonderoga and to make do with whatever they could stuff into a knapsack.[84] Yet once the army left for Fort Edward (24 July), interference with the provisions and ammunition wagons provoked a series of increasingly censorious official injunctions that culminated in a threat of cashiering.[85] In short, the excessive amount of baggage brought on the expedition appears to have exacerbated the transport difficulties that ultimately helped derail Burgoyne's early progress.

Taken as a whole, however, the evidence regarding officers' baggage is less damning. In particular, tighter control was exercised in the main army. During Howe's campaigns, subalterns were excluded from taking riding or pack horses into the field, and each battalion had transport allocated to it.[86] For example, in September 1776 Howe allowed each British and German battalion four and six two-horse wagons respectively, and in advance of the Pennsylvania campaign (before the sea voyage from New York ravaged the army's draft horses), he made allowances for four per line battalion.[87] The system seems to have worked satisfactorily, despite occasional orders against the overloading or other misuse of these wagons.[88] For example, the equipage that John Peebles (a lieutenant, then captain, in the 42nd Regiment) took into the field between 1776 and 1778 comprised some spare clothing, a canteen, bedding, and a small personal marquee. This was hardly extravagant by contemporary European standards or even by those of Continental Army officers, if we can trust the list of clothing that Captain William Alexander of the 7th Pennsylvania Regiment claimed to have lost at Brandywine.[89] Furthermore, when transport was short, British regimental officers also dispensed with marquees (they usually used common soldiers' tents instead, typically two officers to a tent) and frequently made do without their portmanteaux.[90] Days after the battle of Long Island, Captain the Honorable William Leslie enthused: "It is now a fortnight [that] we have lain on the ground wrapped in our blankets; and, thank God (who supports us when we stand most in need), I never enjoyed better health in my life. My whole stock consists of two shirts, 2 pair of shoes, [and] 2 handkerchiefs, half of which I use, [and] the other half I carry in my blanket like a peddler's pack."[91] Likewise, in 1777, when the long sea voyage to Head of Elk decimated the army's draught horses, Lieutenant Loftus Cliffe wrote, "Our field equipage . . . was reduced to two shirts and a blanket and a canteen for each officer."[92] The letters of Lieutenant William Hale show that these were not isolated incidents. Throughout the New York and Pennsylvania campaigns, he and his brother grenadier officers generally had access only to some spare linen, their canteens, and shared tents. Indeed, by the time Hale went into winter quarters in 1776 and 1777, his appearance was extremely ragged, and in early 1778, when his baggage failed to catch up with him at Philadelphia, the impecunious junior officer was reduced to borrowing to purchase an entire new suit of clothing.[93]

Clearly, British field armies required sizeable provisions and baggage trains. Throughout the war the main army maintained an average of more than seven hundred wagons and carts and about four thousand horses (half of them draught animals), and these figures increased by hire or purchase when it went into the field.[94] For instance, when Howe and Clinton respectively evacuated New Brunswick in June 1777 and Philadelphia in June 1778, their armies were reportedly encumbered by nine- and twelve-mile baggage trains comprising one thousand and fifteen hundred vehicles, respectively, of all kinds (roughly one per ten men).[95] At the other end of the scale, the force that Tarleton led to defeat at Cowpens in January 1781 was accompanied by about thirty-five wagons (or one vehicle per thirty-odd men).[96] It was no simple matter to obtain this amount of transport locally, as Howe and Clinton discovered in 1777 and 1780 when extended sea voyages from New York ravaged the health of their armies' horses. Most disastrously, in 1777 Burgoyne's failure to assemble the huge train that his army needed once it left the lakes stalled his advance at Forts Edward and Miller. For six fatal weeks his commissaries struggled to bring up provisions both to feed the army and to accumulate the month's reserve it needed before crossing the Hudson and resuming operations.[97]

Even when successfully assembled, a provisions and baggage train that comprised hundreds of sluggish vehicles drastically curbed a field force's mobility, particularly when heavy rain muddied up the roads (as during Howe's Pennsylvania campaign).[98] According to the aforementioned strategic memoranda of 1779, "the immense baggage, etc. has been the bane of the British operations, and are . . . a great obstruction to sudden and quick movements and pursuits, without which nothing can ever be done with an enemy as lightly accoutered as possible and who perhaps never means to come to a decisive action if they can avoid it."[99] Although it was possible for a commander to march his troops ahead of the train, the danger of doing so in a hostile country was demonstrated when, in fleeing the Cowpens battlefield, Tarleton's party of dragoons ran into a band of rebel irregulars who had already begun to loot his baggage.[100] Moreover, the larger the train, the more care the commander needed to take on the march to cover it against enemy blows.[101]

Here, an obvious tension existed between two conflicting interests: maximizing the army's mobility and minimizing the stresses and strains that hardship and deprivation exerted on it. The practice of doing without bulky tents to save transport illustrates this tension well, for the drawback (as Guards officer Lieutenant Colonel James Stuart warned from South Carolina in January 1781) was that "to live in the woods" during inclement conditions produced "the worst consequences" for the men's health.[102] For example, with few local houses and barns in which to shelter, Howe's troops suffered terribly during the three-day equinoctial storm that terminated the "Battle of the Clouds" (16 September 1777). According to engineer Captain John Montresor, "the prevailing distemper of the fever and ague" brought on by the cold and wet incapacitated almost half his engineers, artificers, laborers, and wagoners and compelled Howe to provide all corps in the army with empty wagons to carry their swollen numbers of sick.[103]

When British commanders could not provide their troops with regular rations, this damaged the men's morale.[104] In particular, the inability to provide rum provoked, as Lieutenant Loftus Cliffe put it, "the horrors of the soldiery."[105] In the field protracted shortages caused soldiers to plunder, desert, sicken, and die. After Cornwallis's "very shattered, exhausted, ragged troops" arrived at Wilmington (7 April 1781), Brigadier General O'Hara admitted that the arduousness of the second invasion of North Carolina "has completely destroyed this army." The general's pessimistic letter to the Duke of Grafton provides details of the decline: "[W]hat remains are so completely worn out, by the excessive fatigues of the campaign in a march of above a thousand miles, most of them barefoot, naked and for days together living upon carrion, which they had often not time to dress, and three or four ounces of unground Indian corn. . . . *Entre nous,* the spirit of our little army has evaporated a good deal. No zeal or courage is equal to the constant exertions we are making."[106] Field returns serve to illustrate the damage that Cornwallis's army had sustained: the 3,224 rank and file present and fit for duty on 15 January 1781 had fallen to 2,440 by 1 February; to 2,213 by 1 March; and to 1,723 by 1 April.[107] This represents a fall of almost 50 percent in a little over six weeks. Allowing for serious combat losses (especially at Cowpens and Guilford Courthouse), it is clear that several hundred men must have died, deserted, or been taken prisoner while straggling. One of the latter was Private John Robert Shaw of the 33rd Regiment. Days before Guilford Courthouse, when a party of rebel dragoons captured him and an equally famished accomplice after the two had strayed from camp on an illicit private foraging expedition, Shaw's companion burst into tears. Shaw himself later candidly expressed that "for my part, I thought it very good fortune."[108]

### Intelligence

Lack of reliable intelligence also seriously hampered British operations in America. The problem was twofold. First, British commanders often had a very inadequate knowledge of the country around them. Henry Lee, one of the rebels' most successful commanders of light troops, later recalled: "There was throughout our war, a lamentable ignorance of the topography of the country in which we fought, imposing upon our generals serious disadvantages. They had to ascertain the nature of the ground by reconnoitring, or by inquiry among the inhabitants. The first was not always practicable; and the result of the last was generally defective."[109] Lee's lament is striking when one considers that the rebels were fighting on home ground, that they had the sympathy if not the active support of probably the bulk of the population almost wherever they went, and that they acted generally on the defensive. How much more difficult must the situation have been, then, for the British? When Clinton ordered Lieutenant Colonel Archibald Campbell to lead the expedition against Savannah in late

December 1778, the Scotsman confided in his diary: "It was a matter of great concern, that there was not a chart of Georgia in the possession of any officer in this army nor any information of the roads, swamps or creeks, which could be depended upon, for directing our operations into the interior parts of the province. . . . The only resource therefore left me, was such information as I could procure from the people of the country for 20 miles in front, before the troops were ordered to march; from which information I was enabled to make a rough sketch of the road . . . [that] was corrected from my own observations the day thereafter."[110]

This problem was not confined to the sparsely populated South. Howe later testified in Parliament that the difficulty of gaining accurate information on the lie of the land had adversely affected his operations in the middle colonies:

> With regard to the knowledge of the country, so necessary to be obtained previous to . . . movement . . . I beg leave to mention the difficulties we labored under in that respect throughout the war. The country is so covered with wood, swamps, and creeks, that it is not open in the least degree to be known, but from post to post, or from accounts to be collected from the inhabitants entirely ignorant of military description. These circumstances were therefore the cause of some unavoidable delay in our movements. . . . I assert it with firmness, that almost every movement of the war in North America was an act of enterprise, clogged with innumerable difficulties. A knowledge of the country, intersected, as it everywhere is, by woods, mountains, waters, or morasses, cannot be obtained with any degree of precision necessary to foresee, and guard against, the obstructions that may occur.[111]

Here one specific example will suffice. According to the journalist of the Hessian *Feldjägerkorps*, three days after Howe's army landed at Head of Elk in August 1777, it marched to Elktown, which was found to be deserted: "We had no reports about the enemy, and no maps of the interior of this land, and no-one in the army was familiar with this area. After we had passed the city, no-one knew which way to go. Therefore, men were sent out in all directions until finally a Negro was found, and the army had to march according to his directions."[112] Interestingly, when the army evacuated Philadelphia in June 1778 and commenced the march through New Jersey back to New York, it was necessary for Clinton to ask for a number of local Provincials from the Queen's Rangers to act as guides.[113]

In 1775 Burgoyne neatly summarized the second main intelligence deficiency under which the British labored in America: "We are ignorant, not only of what passes in [rebel] congresses, but want spies for the hill half a mile off."[114] What the general meant by this was that Crown commanders often lacked accurate information about the enemy's numbers and movements because the local people were reluctant or unable to provide it.[115] At Winnsboro in November 1780, an irritated Cornwallis made the same complaint to Lieutenant Colonel Francis Lord Rawdon: "All my accounts about [Major General] Smallwood agree with yours, but mine are: 'I went as far as Fishing Creek, and there Billy McDaniel's wife told me that she saw Dicky Thomson, who said he saw young Tommy Rigdom that just came from camp, etc. etc.' "[116]

The operational implications of this inability to get accurate information were very serious. As Lieutenant Colonel the Honorable William Harcourt put it, "from the want of intelligence we frequently, nay generally, lose the favorable opportunity for striking a decisive stroke."[117] Moreover, inadequate intelligence left the army vulnerable to enemy designs. The day after Greene surprised and nearly defeated Lieutenant Colonel Alexander Stewart at Eutaw Springs, the British commander pointedly reported his powerlessness "to gain intelligence of the enemy's situation." He ascribed this to his inability to engage local spies, combined with the rebels' habits of "waylaying the by-paths and passes through the different swamps" and detaining flags of truce.[118] As Stewart's case suggests, the fact that British commanders often operated under a blanket of ignorance was particularly serious because the enemy did not generally suffer the same constraint. In late November 1777, after Howe's Pennsylvania campaign, Major General Grey lamented that the general population was universally disaffected: "Consequently, [we receive] no intelligence to be relied on, [while] at the same time every movement made by the [King's] troops [is made] known [to the enemy] as quick as possible. This will make the affair, in my opinion, tedious, if not doubtful."[119]

## TOPOGRAPHY

The topography of the American colonies seriously obstructed the British goal of neutralizing the rebels' military forces. As one moved farther from the coast into the more thinly settled interior, the country became progressively more rugged, peaking in the chain of Appalachian mountain ranges than run from the White and Green mountains in the North to the Blue Ridge in the South. The operations of the "Canadian army" in 1776 and 1777 and the "backwoods" campaigns in the South unfolded in the hinterland, a wilderness of dense forest and swampland scarred by extensive ravines and laboriously winding watercourses, interspersed here and there with farm clearings and small settlements.[120] While there were significant topographical variations between the various colonies' more developed and accessible seaboard regions, where most British operations took place between 1776 and 1778, in general the face of this country emerges from the writings of eyewitnesses as an undulating (especially in the North) patchwork of fenced (and in New England, walled) fields, woodland, and dense thickets crisscrossed with numerous creeks and rivers, cut here and there by ravines and serviced by an undeveloped network of roads and tracks.[121]

While the topography of North America might not have been ideally suited to major operations, one should be wary of the pervasive assumption that it was somehow unique. Strikingly, British and German officers in America occasionally noted resemblances between the countryside around them and their own homelands.[122] Certainly the wild backwoods and even the settled seaboard differed markedly from the open plains of Northwest and Central Europe. But eighteenth-century European armies commonly campaigned in theaters like the Iberian Peninsula and Eastern Europe, which varied significantly from this stereotype. Furthermore, one should remember that one of the reasons why close-order tactical methods were modified during the French Revolutionary and Napoleonic wars was the dramatic change that the process of enclosure had wrought in the decades after the Seven Years War. This process left British officers particularly worried by the threat of French invasion because of the army's relative lack of effective light troops.[123]

The topography of North America nevertheless did strongly favor the rebels' customary Fabian-style operations. First, it provided them

with vast space in which to maneuver. For example, during the "Race
to the Dan," Greene was able to retreat for 250 miles through the
Carolinas—a distance not much short of Marlborough's celebrated
march to the Danube—before Cornwallis was forced to give up the
pointless and enervating chase.[124] Second, it helped battle-shy rebel
commanders evade unwanted engagements; skillfully conducted rebel rearguards were able to dampen British pursuit by breaking down
bridges, contesting every village and wood, setting ambuscades, and
shielding the main army's march route from prying enemy eyes,
much as Colonel Otho Williams retarded and misled Cornwallis's
advance during the "Race."[125] Third, the country provided ideal positions for commanders on the defensive, as Major General Charles
Grey stressed before Parliament in 1779 in his testimony on Howe's
operations in the middle colonies: "That part of America, where I
have been, is the strongest country I ever was in; it is everywhere
hilly, and covered with wood—intersected by ravines, creeks, and
marshy grounds, and in every quarter of a mile is a post fitted for
ambuscades. Little or no knowledge could be obtained by reconnoitring. . . . America is, of all countries, the best calculated for the
defensive. Every one hundred yards might be disputed; at least that
part of it which I have seen."[126] Last, but certainly not least, America's broken and restrictive country provided the ideal arena for the
petite guerre: the near-continuous state of petty skirmishing that
best enabled the rebels to grind down the British war effort, both
militarily and politically.

Five main factors made it extraordinarily difficult for British commanders in America to secure the kind of battlefield engagements in
which they sought to neutralize the rebels' military forces. First, they
had to exercise caution in avoiding even minor operational reverses
that would galvanize the rebel cause and stimulate popular resistance. Second, their limited manpower resources constrained them
to avoid exposing their troops unnecessarily to hardship and to exercise restraint over the conditions in which they were prepared to
engage the enemy. Third, logistical considerations (particularly the
dependence upon trains and/or water transport) grievously limited
their field armies' mobility. Fourth, the problems of obtaining intelligence on the face of the country and the enemy's numbers and
movements made it difficult to operate successfully. Fifth, the local

topography strongly favored defensive operations, enabling prudent rebel commanders to shun unwanted major engagements.

Of these five factors, the British perhaps made greatest strides in overcoming the second. Throughout the war, Crown commanders, officers, and men displayed an unconventional willingness to cut logistical corners to enhance mobility—a phenomenon that led John Graves Simcoe (the former commanding officer of the Queen's Rangers) to boast later that "[t]hey despised all those conveniences without which it would be thought impracticable for European armies to move."[127] Cornwallis's army took this process furthest by attempting to subsist off the land for over two months during the invasion of North Carolina in 1781. Yet despite the troops' sacrifices, the earl not only failed to catch and smash Greene's army but, in "converting his army into light troops" (as Henry Lee put it), he also irrevocably damaged it in a way the British, unlike their rebel opponents, could not afford to do.[128]

# 3

# GRAND TACTICS

They had imagined (which to say the truth our former method of
beginning always at the wrong end had given them some reason to
suppose) that we should land directly in front of their works, march
up and attack them without further precaution in their strongest
points. They had accordingly fortified those points with their
utmost strength, and totally neglected the left flank, which was
certainly incapable of defense. It was by our marching round to this
quarter that we had so totally surprised them on the 27th [August],
so that the possibility of our taking that route seems never to have
entered into their imaginations.

> Captain Sir James Murray to his sister, 31 August 1776

As previously explained, despite the operational constraints under which British armies labored in the field, Crown commanders identified the defeat and dispersal of the rebels' conventional military forces as the prerequisite for the restoration of British authority.
Once again, battlefield engagements offered the most direct means of
neutralizing Congress's armies.

### BRINGING THE REBELS TO ACTION

Unfortunately, the goal of bringing rebel armies to action was easier
said than done when their commanders were (in Howe's words) "stu-
dious to avoid it, unless under most favorable circumstances."[1] In

conventional European campaigns, the simplest way to force the enemy to fight was to threaten or attack an object of strategic importance, such as a vital fortress. In America there were few such objects that the rebels would not (reluctantly) have sacrificed to avoid committing themselves to action under adverse conditions. These included the cities of New York, Philadelphia, and Charleston, which in 1776, 1777, and 1780 the rebels vainly attempted to defend for political as much as for military reasons.[2] Nor could the rebels have abandoned the forts in the Hudson Highlands, because, with New York City in British hands, they bestrode the vital communications between the middle colonies and New England.[3] Significantly, both before and after he came to the command, Clinton composed numerous abortive plans for offensives up the Hudson, most of which aimed to compel Washington to risk a major action in defense of the forts.[4]

If it was not easy for the British to induce the rebels to fight to protect a particular strategic object, it was nevertheless possible (as Clinton advised Lord Germain in London in May 1777) to draw them into battle by "chicanery."[5] British commanders in America resorted to several techniques to achieve this end. The first was to deceive the rebels by a *ruse de guerre* into committing themselves to an unfavorable action, as Cornwallis did at Green Springs when he duped Brigadier General Anthony Wayne into attacking what he believed was an isolated rearguard on the rebel side of the James River. The second technique was to engineer a situation whereby the rebels' retreat was physically obstructed, as when Howe attempted to trap Lafayette's exposed division on Barren Hill against the Schuylkill River (19–20 May 1778) and as Cornwallis tried unsuccessfully to do during the "Race to the Dan," hoping to pin the rebels against the swollen Catawba, Yadkin, or Dan rivers. The third technique was to threaten to cut off part of the rebel army with the aim of presenting its commander with the unenviable choice of fighting to sustain it or leaving it to its destruction. This was Clinton's intention during the initial stage of the battle of Monmouth, where he hoped to drive back Major General Charles Lee's advanced guard against one of the three ravines that cut across at right angles to his line of march, the British commander in chief "judging that Mr. Washington's situation must become critical should he venture to commit himself among those defiles in support of his advanced corps."[6]

Howe's fruitless fortnight-long campaign in New Jersey in June 1777 provides examples of all three techniques in practice. Howe first endeavored to bring Washington down from the Watchung Mountains by thrusting inland from New Brunswick (on 14 June), threatening either to cut off Major General John Sullivan's exposed division at Princeton or to cross the Delaware River by pontoon and seize Philadelphia. One week later, when it became clear that Washington had not taken the bait, Howe retired to New Brunswick. From there (on 22 June) he retreated in a purposefully disorderly fashion to Perth Amboy, hoping that Washington would try to catch the British in the act of evacuating to Staten Island. When Howe received intelligence that Washington had indeed tentatively come down from the mountains, he tried again to catch the Virginian (on 26 June) by thrusting directly at him with one column while Cornwallis with the other attempted to hook around the rebel left in the hopes of blocking a retreat back into the mountains. This attempt also failed, however, largely because Washington was alerted to the threat when Cornwallis ran straight into Major General Lord Stirling's division.[7]

## ENVELOPMENT

Given that the British needed to neutralize the rebels' military forces in order to crush the rebellion in America, historians have commonly criticized Crown commanders for not having sought more energetically the total destruction of enemy field forces. The most effective means by which this might have been achieved was by envelopment, whether at the strategic level (by surrounding the enemy army and compelling it to surrender en masse, as Gates did to Burgoyne at Saratoga) or at the tactical level (as when the ferocious "overmountain-men" encircled and crushed Ferguson's loyalists at King's Mountain).

Of the senior British officers who served in America, Clinton proved the most consistent advocate of strategic and tactical envelopment. Soon after his arrival at Boston, the general recommended landing troops on Dorchester Neck in order to cut off the rebel forces on the Dorchester Heights. When the rebel occupation of Breed's Hill on the Charlestown peninsula effectively shelved this operation, Clinton responded by formulating a similar plan: to trap the redoubt's defenders by landing one force near the Neck and another at Charlestown itself.[8] Although his solution was rejected by Gage's council of war before the battle of Bunker Hill, it was apparent enough to have occurred in essence to a more junior officer in Boston: "Had we intended to have taken the whole rebel army prisoners, we needed only have landed in their rear and occupied the high ground above Bunker's hill [i.e., Bunker Hill itself, which overlooked the rebel redoubt on Breed's Hill]. By this movement we [would have] shut them up in the peninsula as in a bag, their rear exposed to the fire of our cannon and, if we pleased, our musketry. In short, they must have surrendered instantly or been blown to pieces."[9]

Probably Clinton's most interesting scheme for grand-tactical envelopment was the proposal that Howe used as the basis for his turning movement at Long Island—a factor that has led some historians to award the laurels for the battle to him rather than to Howe.[10] Clinton's original proposal (which was not executed in its entirety) had three elements. First, the British right would have penetrated Jamaica Pass by night before wheeling into the rebel rear the next morning. Second, the center would have made holding attacks to pin down the rebels there. Third, the British left would have stormed the Heights of Guan at their westernmost extremity, then rolled up the rebel positions on the crest from west to east. Had the plan been successfully applied, it would have sealed off almost all the rebel defenders from escape into the lines on the Brooklyn Heights. Nevertheless, Clinton's ambitious planning did not stop there. Both before and after the battle of Long Island, he unsuccessfully lobbied Howe to envelop (rather than simply displace) the rebels by landing a force around Kingsbridge that would have blocked the main exit route from Manhattan.[11] And toward the end of the year, in the hopes of more quickly terminating the war, he offered three ambitious plans as alternatives to the Rhode Island expedition, each of which involved a pincer-like offensive either against Washington's army or Philadelphia.[12] Not until 1780, however, when he masterfully shut up the rebel's southern army in Charleston and won the single greatest British victory of the war by capturing both it and the city by siege, was Clinton able to execute in its entirety one of his envelopment plans.[13]

British commanders in America rarely attempted strategic or tactical envelopments, for success depended on several extraordinary conditions. These included numerical superiority; a misplaced resolve on the enemy's part not to withdraw until it became too late to do so; the existence of impermeable natural barriers on the enemy's flanks and/or in his rear, which funneled his avenue of retreat; and/or the ability to place a detachment in the enemy's rear. Crown commanders rarely found these conditions in their favor. For example, after the New York and Pennsylvania campaigns, campaigning British armies did not often enjoy numerical superiority over the rebel field forces opposed to them. And after the fall of Fort Washington, prudent rebel commanders declined to adopt positions from which they could not easily withdraw. But even where the rebels' retreat from the battlefield was restricted in some way—as at Monmouth and Green Springs—it was usually impractical to place a detachment in their rear.[14] In those extraordinary circumstances where this might have been achieved, as at Bunker Hill, it was not attempted for fear that the detachment would have been "caught between two fires" (that is, between the forces that the British wished to cut off and the main enemy body).

### General Actions and Partial Engagements

In conventional eighteenth-century warfare, a "general action" signified an essentially linear battlefield engagement in which the fighting extended along most of the frontage of two rival armies.[15] Typically, the opposing armies drew up opposite to and parallel with each other in one or more lines of battle, with the cavalry massed on the wings. Thereafter, the elements of one army advanced and attacked until the fighting became general. When units in each first line were worsted, units from the supporting lines marched forward to replace them. Ultimately, the contest was decided when the pressure exerted on one line caused entire formations, and subsequently the entire army, to give way in disarray.

While some eighteenth-century general actions did indeed unfold in this fashion, the vast majority were much less clean cut. Styles of deployment varied considerably, especially with multinational field armies. Some generals placed cavalry within the line of battle to facilitate combined-arms tactics. Others strengthened their positions by incorporating natural and manmade features, such as elevations, woods, villages, rivers, and fieldworks, which produced markedly convex or concave lines. Likewise, topography and command limitations often compelled commanders to divide their lines into manageable portions and to assign a particular grand-tactical objective to each. Indeed, this was crucial if the general wished to achieve a decisive local superiority, or "mass," at one particular sector rather than seeking simply to overthrow the enemy army by assailing it from flank to flank. As the influential British military writer Colonel David Dundas put it in 1788, "it is never the intention of an able commander to have all his men at the same time in action; he means by skill and maneuver to attack a partial part, and to bring the many to act against the few."[16]

In comparison with these European battlefield clashes, which frequently pitted 50,000 to 100,000 men against each other over a frontage of several miles, the engagements of the American War were puny affairs. During the New York campaign, Howe had well over 20,000 troops at his disposal, and at Brandywine, Germantown, and Monmouth, the main British field army comprised between 9,000 and 14,000 men. Yet Burgoyne took only 7,000 troops on his doomed Albany expedition, and Cornwallis's field army in the Carolinas did not typically exceed 2,500. In fact, many engagements—such as Princeton, Hobkirk's Hill, Briar Creek, and Cowpens—involved a British field force of around 1,000 men. The marked tendency for such minor actions and even the most piddling combats to be termed "battles" in the historical record of the American War appears laughable in this light.[17] Nevertheless, as the editor of the *Annual Register* for 1781 pointed out toward the end of the war, the use of this terminology does have some merit: "Most of these actions would in other wars be considered as skirmishes of little account, and scarcely worthy of detailed narrative. But these small actions are as capable as any in displaying military conduct. The operations of war being spread over a vast continent, by the new plan that was adopted, it is by such skirmishes that the fate of America must necessarily be decided. They are therefore as important as battles in which a hundred thousand men are drawn up on each side."[18] In short, the miniature engagements of the American War often had an influence on the conflict that was profoundly out of proportion to their size.

Some of the Revolution's best-known engagements could certainly be described as general actions—particularly in the South, where the forces involved were smallest. Most, however, are less easy to categorize, largely because of the very broken and restrictive nature of the terrain on which they occurred. Contemporary and modern narratives and maps commonly confer a highly misleading degree of unity and order on fighting that was, in reality, extraordinarily confusing. For example, having viewed the field of battle at Brandywine, Major General the Chevalier de Chastellux noted discrepancies in the various accounts of the attack over Chad's Ford. He also noted: "It is equally difficult to trace out on the plan, all the ground on which Cornwallis fought. The relations on both sides throw hardly any light upon it. I was obliged therefore to draw my own conclusions from the different narratives, and to follow none of them implicitly." On visiting Freeman's Farm and Bemis Heights, the Frenchman was even more perplexed: "I avoid the word *field of battle;* for these two engagements were in the woods, and on ground so intersected and covered, that it is impossible either to conceive or discover the smallest resemblance between it and the plan given to the public by General Burgoyne."[19] Chastellux's trouble stemmed from the fact that the closeness of the country in which many engagements took place often prevented formations from deploying contiguously, in unbroken lines of battle. Instead the terrain partitioned the fighting into multiple, almost unrelated, combats. In some actions, seemingly at no point did more than a handful of battalions in either army draw up in line and operate in what Charles Stedman described as "a regular combined disposition for the attack."[20] This was particularly true where the fighting was especially fluid, such as the ragged, confused, seesaw battles of Germantown and Monmouth.

According to military convention, a partial engagement (or combat, or affair) was one where only a part of each army actively engaged. Technically speaking, some of the biggest and best-known battles of the American War were partial engagements in that a majority of the forces present on the field never properly engaged, as Lieutenant William Hale noted with interest after the battle of Monmouth: "I know not whether from want of inclination or abilities, but none of our generals have yet engaged more than three thousand of this army at one time, and in the last action scarce half that number was opposed to the whole rebel army. The brigades [of line infantry] have been looked upon as nurseries only for the flank corps."[21] Hale was not alone in making this observation. After Brandywine, Howe's Hessian aide de camp noted that "we had 62 cannon . . . of which we used not even 20, nor were more than half of our troops under fire," while one anonymous grenadier officer pointed out after Monmouth that "[t]he

[Third and Fourth] Brigades and other troops that were with us never came into action, for what reason I cannot say."[22] Likewise, in August 1778 Captain Patrick Ferguson wondered that "it never yet has been found practicable to bring 5000 men into actions."[23] This phenomenon requires some explanation.

## THE FLANK BATTALIONS

Hale's observation that the line battalions were "nurseries" for the flank corps points to the reason why the majority of British forces present were not properly engaged at any of the main army's battlefield actions in the middle colonies. Military historians have generally condemned the common eighteenth-century practice whereby the flank companies were detached from their parent regiments and combined in composite battalions of grenadiers and light infantry, not only because the battalion thereby lost its organic skirmishers but also because it proved an inadequate alternative to the establishment of genuine light infantry units.[24] In March 1789 John Graves Simcoe (former commanding officer of the Queen's Rangers, one of the most successful of the "partisan" corps formed during the American War) wrote to the King to protest the continued deficiency of true light troops in the army: "As a substitute for such a corps the chosen men of the British Army are thrown together to form light infantry; which in the American War was so numerous, that the loss of it would have been almost the loss of the army, and this was well known, and frequently said by the general officers. . . . [E]mployed as the light infantry were, merely as a first line, there is not an officer in the Army, but knows that it was a most ruinous drain upon their respective regiments."[25] Simcoe's observation was almost certainly colored by the catastrophic loss of most of Cornwallis's light troops at the Cowpens, which hamstrung his lordship's operations in North Carolina in 1781 because (as the loyalist Charles Stedman pointed out) light infantry were indispensable in operations in a wooded and thinly settled country.[26] But like Hale, when Simcoe mentioned that the light infantry served as the British "first line" in America, he clearly had the campaigns in the middle colonies in mind.

With the proviso that the commanders frequently altered their campaigning forces' command structure according to the changing operational situation, we can make some general points about field organization. In the southern campaigns British field armies were not generally large enough to warrant the employment of more than one march column, even if the poor road network had not made this impractical; they therefore usually deployed and fought as a united entity. Moreover, in these operations light infantry and especially grenadiers made up a small proportion of most British forces in the field; the flank battalions had returned to New York with Clinton after the fall of Charleston.[27] Because they commonly acted as vanguards, the small numbers of light troops that campaigned in Georgia and the Carolinas did sometimes spearhead attacks that were delivered over a narrow frontage. For example, the light infantry of the Guards Brigade led Cornwallis's column in its opposed crossing of Cowan's Ford (1 February 1781), while the flank companies of the Volunteers of Ireland fronted Lieutenant Colonel Francis Lord Rawdon's attack at Hobkirk's Hill. Yet because most of the principal southern engagements were general actions, flank companies typically fought in the line of battle, usually in the "post of honor" on the extreme right flank (as at Camden, Cowpens, Green Springs, and Eutaw Springs).

The picture in the northern campaigns was different. In the field British armies were commonly organized into two (or infrequently three) divisions or columns, which generally marched within supporting distance of each other (in parallel, if roads permitted, or one behind the other, if not). Commonly, these divisions were unequally "weighted": whichever was expected to see the heaviest action was made numerically stronger and assembled predominantly from the field army's choice units, including the flank battalions. Because it maneuvered nearest to the enemy on the march and was first into action, this stronger division was known as the "Advanced Corps." Hence in October 1777 Captain the Honorable Colin Lindsay declined to continue as an aide de camp and instead "desired to go into the light infantry, which is at present the most active service."[28] Likewise, in December 1778 Lieutenant Francis Laye of the Royal Artillery successfully petitioned for his guns to be attached to the British grenadiers, for he was anxious to make his name by serving alongside the troops that were always "first into action."[29] Indeed, a month after Monmouth, Captain Patrick Ferguson was able to observe to the commander in chief that on the battlefield "the Advanced Corps hitherto carried every thing before them with the assistance of a brigade or two [of line troops] occasionally."[30]

When the main army went into the field in the middle colonies between 1776 and 1778, the status of the Guards Brigade as household troops guaranteed their inclusion within the Advanced Corps—a situation that was presumably justified by a superior level of esprit de corps and skill at arms to that in most line regiments.[31] Yet in the main army, as in Burgoyne's "Canadian army" in 1777, the backbone of the elite Advanced Corps comprised the flank battalions, which were unanimously considered "the flower of our army."[32] Flank company officers —and especially light company officers—were among the youngest, toughest, most dynamic, and ambitious young gentlemen in the army, seeking preferment by embracing the most active, dangerous, and demanding line of duty.[33] These officers endured privations in the field that were uncommonly severe by European standards. Moreover, Lieutenant Hale's letters make it clear that his brother grenadier officers took encouragement from the fact that their men never complained of their more acute hardships.[34] Martin Hunter, who served in America as a light company officer, echoed Hale's sentiments. Speaking particularly of the Pennsylvania campaign, he later asserted that, despite the hard conditions that the "light bobs" experienced, "desertion from us was scarcely known": "The light infantry were always in front of the army, and not allowed tents. We generally quartered our men in farmhouses and barns, or made huts when houses were not conveniently situated, and we were always so near to the enemy that the men never pulled off their accoutrements, and were always ready to turn out at a minute's warning."[35]

Along with the *Jäger* and light dragoons, the British light battalions performed the lion's share of the army's march security, outpost watch, and reconnaissance, duties that had to be performed even after the rest of the army had gone into winter quarters. As an example, after the two light battalions returned from a foraging expedition beyond the Schuylkill on the last day of 1777, they occupied the brick barracks at the northern limits of Philadelphia. This enabled them to succor the nearby chain of works that covered the city's landward approaches, to patrol aggressively the neutral ground outside the city, and to spearhead any expedition made from within. As Sergeant Thomas Sullivan of the 2nd Battalion of Light Infantry put it, the light infantry's post was "in the front going out, and the rear coming home."[36] Captain Sir James Murray expressed it similarly: "We have

always something to do and something to expect; if *atra cura* is anywhere to be avoided, it is in a light infantry company in America."[37]

Like their officers, the enlisted men of the flank battalions were
exceptional individuals, carefully chosen from among the regiments'
battalion companies. But at least in many corps, this selection process was seemingly undertaken with different criteria, depending
upon whether the corps was on active service or not. Writing in Britain in 1781, former officer John Williamson asserted that, while grenadiers and light infantrymen were supposed to be appointed according to their "strength, size and courage" and their "spirit and alacrity"
respectively, these qualifications were "seldom particularly attended
to." Instead, he complained, many regiments simply filled those
companies with the tallest men (grenadiers) and with the shortest
and youngest men (light infantry).[38] Data from the annual reviews
appear to confirm Williamson's point. As just one example, when
the 4th Regiment was reviewed in April 1774 shortly before embarking for America, the average heights of the grenadiers, hatmen, and
light infantrymen were almost 5 feet, 11 inches; almost 5 feet, 8
inches; and almost 5 feet, 7 inches. The tallest grenadier, hatman, and
light infantryman measured 6 feet, 2 inches; 6 feet; and 5 feet, 8 1/2
inches.[39]

Military theorists deplored this state of affairs. In 1768 military
writer Captain Bennett Cuthbertson asserted that a grenadier company composed of men selected on the basis of "a full face, broad
shoulders and well-proportioned legs," as well as height, was "much
superior in point of marching, and every sort of fatigue, to one, which
only boasts of size." As for the light company, Cuthbertson judged
that it should "be composed of chosen men, whose activity and particular talents for that duty should be the only recommendation
to their appointment."[40] Another military writer, Captain Thomas
Simes, agreed. In 1777 he argued that the soldiers of the flank companies "should be men whose health, strength, and activity can most
be depended upon; that are good marksmen; and in point of marching,
etc. are superior to those who pique themselves of size: it is a mistaken opinion that size alone is a qualification for either. These men
should be accustomed to move at the rate of four miles [in] the hour
without being the least fatigued, and twenty-four miles a day when
necessity demands it, without distress."[41]

During the American War, the practice of those corps on active service in the colonies seems, quite sensibly, to have reflected the theorists' views. When it was necessary to transfer hatmen from the parent corps to the flank battalions, regimental commanding officers were directed to send only suitable men "fit for that service."[42] In the case of the grenadiers, an imposing physique undoubtedly remained a prerequisite.[43] But other criteria undoubtedly influenced the selection process, especially in the case of the light infantry. Untried recruits were not usually thought appropriate material, whatever their build or agility.[44] For instance, to assist Captain Wolfe in completing the 40th Regiment's light company in June 1777, Lieutenant Colonel Thomas Musgrave ordered the battalion companies' commanding officers to create a pool of potential recruits by selecting "two of the properest [sic] men they have, of a twelvemonth's standing as soldiers in the regiment."[45] Moreover, surviving muster lists show that many men were returned from the flank companies to the battalion, as if they could not (or could no longer) meet the demands made of them.[46] Of course, troublemakers or men liable to desert were not wanted. For instance, in May 1779 Clinton ordered the transfer of a number of NCOs and privates from the 57th Regiment's light company to the battalion on the grounds that they had been guilty of behavior that "renders them unworthy of the distinction of serving in a flank corps."[47]

On active service in America, proven physical stamina was certainly the most important criterion for transfer to the flank battalions, especially to the light infantry. This much is clear from the fact that these soldiers became renowned for their physical endurance. In bids to get into action at Harlem Heights, Germantown, and Monmouth, the grenadier battalions respectively "trotted about three miles without a halt to draw breath," covered most of the five miles from Philadelphia "in a kind of half-running march," and "ran for three miles without stopping."[48] As for the light infantry, in mid-June 1776, as the rebel invaders of Canada fled up the Richelieu corridor, three light companies jogged three miles to St. Johns in pursuit of the enemy rearguard.[49] Similarly, at the action outside Savannah, rebel colonel George Walton observed Captain Sir James Baird's light infantry as they completed their wide outflanking march through the swamp on the rebel right, "hopping over the little difficulties with great agility."[50] In his account of the failed expedition to destroy Lafayette's division at Barren Hill, Martin Hunter claimed that the flank battalions had marched an astonishing sixty miles in twenty-four hours without losing a single man. His explanation for this was that "[t]hey were in good wind, as we generally marched out of Philadelphia every day ten or twelve miles to cover the market people coming in."[51]

The flank battalions—and particularly the light infantry—were composed of tough veterans, hardened by constant, severe, and successful active service. And, at least in the northern campaigns, British commanders employed them to maximum effect on the battlefield.

### TURNING MOVEMENTS

When British commanders encountered rebel forces posted in defensive positions (which, particularly in the early campaigns, commonly incorporated fortifications like redoubts, breastworks, and shallow trenches that neutralized British musketry and artillery fire), they had two main options: either dislodge the enemy by means of an attack or displace them by skilful maneuvering. Because commanders did not covet the ground beneath the rebels' feet, they usually proved reluctant to dash their forces obligingly against the enemy position when it appeared too strong to carry without heavy losses. Hence Lieutenant Loftus Cliffe commented approvingly after the Kipp's Bay landing, "as General Howe is determined . . . not [to] run our heads against their works (which is what they have all along hoped for), they will find themselves confoundedly disappointed both in their numbers and their strongholds."[52] Howe later made this point explicitly with reference to his operations in 1776: "I do not hesitate to confess, that if I could by any maneuver remove an enemy from a very advantageous position, without hazarding the consequences of an attack, where the point to be carried was not adequate to the loss of men to be expected from the enterprise, I should certainly adopt that cautionary conduct, in the hopes of meeting my adversary upon more equal terms."[53] As discussed in chapter 1, during the New York campaign, Howe successfully employed skilful maneuvering and limited engagements to force Washington to abandon one position after another in a series of near catastrophic retreats.

When British commanders judged that it was practical to attack the rebel forces, however, they generally declined to make costly frontal assaults along the length of the enemy's line, preferring instead to defeat it by turning a flank. This is what Howe did at Long Island and

Brandywine and what Lieutenant Colonel Archibald Campbell did outside Savannah.[54] Such a turning movement echoed the grand-tactical design that Frederick the Great employed during the Seven Years War, known (not entirely accurately) as the "oblique order." In short, like the Prussian king before them, British commanders sought to engage only a fraction of their forces seriously, with the aim of effecting mass on one of the rebels' flanks—the weakest sectors of their line. This was feasible, at least during the northern campaigns, because the British were able (again, like Frederick) to capitalize on the superior mobility of the elite formations concentrated within the Advanced Corps, which (as we have seen) comprised picked men who were able to bear up better to the physical strain of the inevitably long flanking marches.[55]

For British commanders, the chief attraction of the flank attack was its major psychological effect on unsteady enemy troops, which was vastly out of proportion to the physical force involved. As one of their opponents, Major General William Heath, shrewdly observed: "A few shots on the flank and rear of an enemy serves to disconcert them more than a heavy fire in their front. The point of decision here lies not in the force, but in the mind. A company of 50 men cannot fire more shots in the same given time on the flank, or in the rear, than they could in the front; but these few shots will have more effect on the minds of the enemy than the fire of a whole regiment in their front."[56]

More potent even than the moral effect of an enfilading fire, however, was the frightening prospect of having the line of retreat cut off. This fear cast inexperienced troops into irretrievable panic. Days after the battle of Long Island, Admiral Lord Howe's secretary noted of Washington's army: "Nothing terrifies these people more than the apprehension of being surrounded. They will not fight at any rate, unless they are sure of a retreat."[57] For example, at Germantown the rebel battalions that had penetrated farthest assumed the worst when they heard the sounds of the assaults against the British-held Chew House in their rear. One Continental officer lamented that the heavy smoke and dense fog "increased the fear of some to fancy themselves flanked and surrounded, which like an electrical shock seized some thousands, who fled in confusion, without the appearance of an enemy."[58] Similarly, a Virginian militia officer posted on the right wing of the second rebel line at Guilford Courthouse later recalled what happened when the militiamen apprehended that British troops had penetrated the line farther along and were pushing into their rear: "This threw the militia into such confusion that, without attending in the least to their officers (who endeavored to halt them, and make them face about and engage the enemy), [Colonel John] Holcombe's regiment and ours instantly broke off without firing a single gun, and dispersed like a flock of sheep frightened by dogs."[59] Again, the British party involved in this incident need not have been more than a company or platoon in strength. Captain Johann Ewald encouraged his *Jäger* when in action to disperse and get onto the enemy's flanks and rear, "whence often an officer or non-commissioned officer with a few men can completely chase away the enemy." This, he claimed, occurred during the action at Spencer's Ordinary, "where a non-commissioned officer by the name of Sippel got into the rear of the enemy with 6 to 8 men. The result was that 300 men, Englishmen, Anspach, and Hessian *Jäger*, who were almost in the hands of the enemy already, beat back an American corps of 1,000 men, the elite of their army."[60]

Even where an outflanking attack did not produce this kind of instantaneous collapse or where rebel commanders succeeded in deploying a new front to face the threat (as Major Generals Sullivan, Stirling, and Adam Stephen did with their divisions at Brandywine), these hurried alterations were liable to dent inexperienced troops' confidence. Henry Lee later opined that any retrograde movement generally produced disorder in the ranks.[61] And even before the Guards Brigade had arrived in the colonies, Brigadier General Edward Mathew saw fit to make the following announcement: "The Brigadier flatters himself that the corps will never have occasion to go to the right-about in the presence of the enemy. But as it may happen to be necessary to change the disposition and take ground to the rear, he wishes it may be clearly understood by every soldier as not meaning a retreat; and that, therefore, this maneuver may be executed with as much steadiness and good order as any to the front."[62] One may glean the motive behind Mathew's reassurance from comments made after the war by Ewald, who stressed that "you have to take into consideration that people who retreat are always discontented. The common soldier, who rarely can guess and understand the secret plans of the general, believes, as soon as he has to take a few steps backward, that everything is lost. Added to this has to be the panic, which is rarely missing in a retreat, which is really inexplicable but shows that the courage of a man is periodic."[63] The best example of the confusion that a forced redeployment could create occurred toward the end of battle of Cowpens, when Captain Andrew Wallace's company of Virginia Continentals was ordered to wheel backward on the left in order to re-fuse the right flank of the rebel main line against the turning attack undertaken by the 1st Battalion of the 71st Regiment. Instead the company simply turned about and began marching toward the rear, prompting an unintentional staggered withdrawal by the whole rebel line. Although in the event this outcome was probably fortuitous in that it triggered the premature and chaotic British pursuit that left Tarleton's line vulnerable to the shattering rebel counterattack that broke it, in different circumstances this undeniable blunder might well have resulted in disaster.[64]

A flank attack had two other major attractions. One of these was that it permitted a commander to achieve overwhelming local superiority, or mass, even when his total forces were outnumbered. For instance, although the opposing armies at White Plains each numbered something like 14,000 men, Howe's storming of Chatterton's Hill pitted around 4,000 Crown troops against the 1,600 defenders. Similarly, the British and rebel armies at Brandywine comprised around 12,500 and 11,000 men respectively, yet when Cornwallis opened his attack around Birmingham Meetinghouse, his 7,500 troops initially faced less than half that many rebels. Moreover, as explained earlier, the troops that performed the flank attack were usually the cream of the royal army: the light infantry, British and Hessian grenadiers, Guards Brigade, and Jäger.[65] A third major attraction of the flank attack was that it addressed the concern that dominated British strategy and tactics in America, what we might call "conservation of force." In theory the troops used to pin the enemy's attention (by demonstrating in their front) often sustained inconsiderable casualties because they only pushed their attacks in earnest once the enemy army was already starting to crumble under the pressure of the flanking attack. Indeed, as Rodney Atwood has pointed out, after the battle of Long Island, the letters of Hessian officers at all ranks gave no hint that the writers were aware of how little they had been required to do at the Flatbush Pass.[66]

Successful flanking movements were possible only when clear intelligence on the lie of the battlefield and/or the rebel dispositions was available. This was demonstrated most dramatically at Bunker Hill, where lamentable ignorance of the terrain (neither the Charlestown peninsula nor the surrounding waters had been properly surveyed and sounded) handicapped British planning and helped derail the initial plan.[67] Campaigning British generals in America could not often obtain reliable intelligence because the bulk of the local population was rarely prepared or able to assist them in this manner (as noted in the last chapter). One important exception to this was the Pennsylvania campaign, during which a number of loyalist guides rendered the army invaluable services. Captain Ewald recorded of the march to the battle of Brandywine that "Lord Cornwallis had sent me a guide who was a real geographical chart and almost a general by nature. During the entire march I often spoke with him regarding the area which was beyond the horizon. He constantly judged so correctly that I always found the enemy there where he presumed him to be. His description was so good that I was often amazed at the knowledge this man possessed of the country."[68] Likewise, prior to the battle of Savannah, Lieutenant Colonel Archibald Campbell personally climbed a tree to trace the extent of the rebel line of battle and questioned a slave from Governor Wright's plantation. The latter was able to inform him of a little-known route through the swamps that led into the rebel right and rear. Armed with this information, Campbell planned and executed one of the most brilliantly successful (if generally unknown) turning attacks of the war.[69]

The type of wide turning movement that British commanders favored in America had three principal drawbacks. The first was time: to pass unperceived into the enemy's flank, it was necessary for the corps that undertook the turning attack to make a significant detour. The delay in opening the battle that this occasioned sometimes left the British with insufficient time to pursue the beaten rebels before nightfall (as will be seen in chapter 11). The second drawback (and one related to the first) was that it gave an alert and enterprising enemy the opportunity to beat the widely separated elements of the British army in detail. At Long Island the rebels had no idea of Howe and Clinton's progress until it was too late to do anything about it. At Brandywine, by contrast, Washington had intelligence of the wide British outflanking march early enough (between eleven o'clock and noon) to order an assault of his own over the creek, with the intention of crushing Lieutenant General Wilhelm von

Knyphausen's dangerously isolated division. Rebel forces had already driven back advanced British elements at Chad's Ford when false intelligence reached Washington (at around half past one) that the flanking column had disappeared. Believing wrongly that Howe wished to lure him from his strong position over Brandywine Creek and into a trap, Washington cancelled the attack.[70]

The third drawback to the turning movement was that, unless the defeated troops' escape route was somehow obstructed and/or powerful cavalry forces were available to pursue the enemy effectively, a turning movement tended to have the effect of dislodging the enemy forces rather than killing, wounding, and capturing them. An engineer officer, Captain John Montresor, later pointed this out when he bemoaned the fact that Howe had always allowed the defeated rebels the proverbial "golden bridge" from the field.[71] The battle of Long Island provides a good example of this. As already discussed, Clinton initially proposed to envelop the rebel forces on the Heights of Guan. In the event, however, Howe ordered Major General Grant (commanding the left) to demonstrate in the front of Stirling's division and to launch a frontal attack only when Howe's column (on the right) had got into the rebel rear. Because of this, and because of the heroic holding action fought by Stirling's Maryland and Delaware Continentals, about half of the rebel defenders escaped.[72]

### Frontal Attacks

On the battlefield in America, British commanders generally preferred to achieve mass by means of turning movements. In almost all the engagements where they succeeded in doing this, the British drove the rebels from the field, inflicting more casualties than they sustained. This leaves us with a number of important engagements (including Bunker Hill, Princeton, Freeman's Farm, Germantown, Bemis Heights, Monmouth Courthouse, Camden, Cowpens, Guilford Courthouse, Hobkirk's Hill, and Eutaw Springs) in which Crown commanders did not successfully execute, or even attempt, a flanking attack. Some of these were general actions; others, only partial engagements. In most, however, the King's troops fought under significant disadvantages in terms of numbers and/or position and suffered heavy casualties accordingly. Indeed, almost all these actions were either Pyrrhic tactical successes or outright defeats.

If we concentrate our attention on those engagements in which the British were clearly on the tactical offensive, Bunker Hill appears to stand out as the best example of the tactical bankruptcy of frontal attacks against a more numerous and strongly posted enemy.[73] We have already seen that, at the council of war before the battle, Clinton's colleagues rejected his envelopment plan as unsafe. The prickly Clinton interpreted this as professional jealousy and insecurity: "Mr. Gage thought himself so well informed that he would not take any opinion of others, particularly of a man bred up in the German school, which that of America affects to despise." His inference was that the hallmark of the "American school" was a distinct lack of tactical imagination: "These people seem to have no idea of any other than a direct at[tack]." Significantly, he later recorded that, when Brigadier General Sir William Erskine carried to headquarters Clinton's elegant proposal for a double envelopment of the rebel lines on the Heights of Guan on Long Island, the commander in chief and Major Generals James Grant and James Robertson criticized his proposal as "savoring too much of the German school" and "German jargon." Indeed, Clinton alleged that Erskine had heard Howe advance the astonishing theory that "as the rebels knew nothing of turning a flank, such a movement would have *no* effect."[74]

Whatever the merit in Clinton's criticism of the "American school," the British did not intend to launch a frontal attack at Bunker Hill. Instead the plan on which Gage, Howe, Clinton, and Burgoyne agreed before the battle involved a turning movement. It called for a British force to land on Moulton's Point at the eastern tip of the Charlestown peninsula, to advance along its northern shoreline toward Bunker Hill, and then to swing south toward the rear of Breed's Hill, thereby compelling the rebels to evacuate the redoubt.[75] This plan makes sense when one remembers that the British generals initially believed the redoubt was a redan (that is, open at the rear, or northern side).[76] In the event, the rebels reacted to the landing by throwing militia behind a rail fence that lay in the path of a British advance toward Bunker Hill and by constructing several flèches to cover the gap between the fence and the breastwork abutting the redoubt.[77] Nevertheless, Howe's improvised second plan was based on the first. In the initial, unsuccessful attack, Brigadier General Robert Pigot's left wing demonstrated in front of the redoubt and breastwork, engaging the defenders in a long-range firefight. Meanwhile, Howe led the right wing against the militia ensconced behind the rail fence and sent the light infantry in column along the beach to penetrate the narrow gap between the fence and the Mystic River.[78] Had not Colonel John Stark's militiamen barricaded this strip of beach in time to repulse the column, Howe's turning movement would have compelled the rebels successively to abandon the fence, the flèches, the breastwork, and ultimately the redoubt. Instead, while the precise sequence of events is confused, it is clear that the momentum of the British advance quickly broke down, and the troops became embroiled from flank to flank in sustained firefights in which the rebels had the advantage in terms of numbers and position, inflicting predictably heavy casualties on the redcoats.[79] Eventually, Howe succeeded in carrying the redoubt by means of an alternative turning movement. While the light infantry demonstrated in front of the rail fence and Pigot's wing moved frontally against the redoubt, the rest of Howe's wing accessed the redoubt's rear by penetrating the breastwork.[80]

The situations at the battles of Freeman's Farm, Bemis Heights, and Hobkirk's Hill were comparable to that at Bunker Hill. In each case the rebels foiled British attempts to turn their positions and instead embroiled the King's troops in sustained and costly close combats in which numbers and/or position told heavily against them. When in September 1777 Burgoyne's army felt its way forward through the wilderness groping for Gates's fortified position against the Hudson at Stillwater, the British commander's intention would appear to have been to repeat his coup at Fort Ticonderoga. That post had fallen with unexpected ease on 6 July after the British had seized a nearby eminence from which to bombard the fortress. Indeed, Burgoyne had derided the defenders by writing, "They seem to have expended great treasure and the unwearied labor of more than a year to fortify, upon the supposition that we should only attack them upon the point where they were best prepared to resist."[81] Although Burgoyne's intelligence on Gates's position must have been limited, at the battle of Freeman's Farm he almost certainly intended his left and center columns to engage the enemy's attention while the right (and strongest) column gained the higher ground beyond the extreme left of the rebel position and cannonaded the lines in enfilade. Eighteen days later, when Burgoyne led out a reconnaissance in force and was defeated at the battle of Bemis Heights, he was again intending to probe the rebel left in preparation for a concentrated assault the next morning.[82] In both actions the rebels thwarted Burgoyne's designs by sallying out of their lines in strength: they having concentrated their efforts against Brigadier General James Hamilton's center column at Freeman's Farm, and against both flanks of Burgoyne's single line at Bemis Heights. A similar pattern seems to have occurred at Hobkirk's Hill, where Lieutenant Colonel Francis Lord Rawdon's surprise attack failed to turn the rebel position. The result was a sustained action that cost each side an equal number of casualties before the unexpected collapse of the 1st Maryland Regiment compelled Greene to order a withdrawal.

The heavy British casualties at Princeton and Monmouth Courthouse can be explained by the fact that both actions were, loosely speaking, meeting engagements in which successful initial British attacks lost their momentum as more and more rebel troops poured onto the field and embroiled the redcoats in unequal close combats. At Princeton Lieutenant Colonel Charles Mawhood's 17th Regiment speedily routed in turn Brigadier General Hugh Mercer's and Colonel John Cadwalader's brigades. It was only when the gross of Washington's army arrived on the field and threatened to envelop Mawhood's vastly outnumbered command that the British fled.[83] At Monmouth Clinton desisted in his design to trap Major General Lee's advanced corps once it recoiled in disarray onto Washington's main body behind the West Ravine.[84] Probably the majority of the British casualties to musketry and artillery were sustained, quite uselessly, during this phase of the action. Here, when the forward elements of Clinton's strike force contacted Washington's much superior forces, they had to endure an extended cannonade from Comb's Hill while the light infantry and Queen's Rangers (who had, rather inconveniently as it turned out, advanced farthest) extracted themselves.[85]

What of the British frontal attacks at Camden, Cowpens, and Guilford Courthouse? Typically historians have concurred with Brigadier General Morgan's opinion of Tarleton's military abilities: "I knew my adversary, and was perfectly sure I should have nothing but downright fighting."[86] But other factors than ineptitude constrained both Cornwallis and Tarleton to attack the enemy frontally at these three actions. By the time of the southern campaigns, the more prudent rebel commanders had learned to fight only in defensive positions that could not be turned easily. As should now be clear, to turn the enemy's position the British needed to be able to perceive it and to be able to push a turning force onto the enemy's flank, preferably undetected. While Tarleton had local loyalists with him at Cowpens who were able to provide an accurate outline of the face of the country thereabouts, the lie of the terrain hid the rebels' dispositions. Indeed, Tarleton was only able to get an idea of the extent of the rebel skirmish line by ordering his cavalry to gallop along its length and draw the riflemen's fire.[87] Likewise, Cornwallis reported that, when his army marched to attack Greene at Guilford Courthouse, "[t]he prisoners taken [that morning] by Lieutenant Colonel Tarleton, having been several days with the advanced corps, could give me no account of the enemy's order or position, and the country people were extremely inaccurate in their description of the ground." A personal reconnaissance permitted the earl to see only the disposition of the first militia line.[88] Moreover, at Camden and Cowpens the rebels anchored their flanks on boggy ground that precluded any turning movement until Cornwallis had broken the rebel left, and Tarleton had contacted the third rebel line.[89] Hence at all three actions, it is difficult to see what alternative option there was to a frontal attack.

Unfortunately, by this late stage in the war, the more prudent rebel commanders had learned to draw the sting from British attacks by creating a "defense in depth," in which successive lines of rifle- and musket-armed militia blunted the British advance before it reached the last line of defense, which comprised rebel regulars. (Indeed, at Eutaw Springs Greene even employed this tactic offensively by using his militia as a first wave with which to de-range the British line before his Continentals advanced against it.) Hence at Cowpens and Guilford Courthouse (and indeed at Eutaw Springs), the British were condemned once again to commit their outnumbered forces to sustained and costly close combats in which the rebels were able to exploit their advantages of numbers and/or position to best effect.

THE GENERAL OFFICER IN ACTION

Having sketched the range of British grand tactics in America, it is useful here briefly to touch upon the influence that British commanders wielded on the battlefield once the action commenced. As in conventional European warfare, once the plan of attack was agreed and the troops had deployed and begun to advance, a British field force's commander and his staff typically observed the combat unfold from a vantage point. For instance, at Brandywine local boys studied Howe in fascination as he and his aides de camp (perched on Osborne's Hill in the rear) watched Cornwallis's division make its attack.[90] As appropriate, British generals shifted their positions to better observe and/or influence the action. Thus on the day before the battle of Freeman's Farm, Burgoyne directed, "In case of an action the Lieutenant General will be found near the center of the British line, or, he will leave word there where he may be followed."[91]

Whether a commander remained stationary or moved, however, he could exert only limited control over the ebb and flow of battle, particularly when distance, terrain, smoke, or fog obscured his view or when the action was too far away for him to intervene promptly.[92] In close terrain like thick woodland, it was possible for the commander to influence events only within his immediate environs. During the confused attack against the second rebel line at Guilford Courthouse, a straggling Sergeant Roger Lamb probably saved Cornwallis from capture or worse. As the earl trotted unwittingly straight toward the enemy, the Irishman pulled up his horse and led the general to the relative safety of the 23rd Regiment—an incident that hints strongly at Cornwallis's impotence from the moment the British line entered the woods.[93] This phenomenon was not uncommon; the consequence was that regimental officers in America were compelled to adopt a highly unconventional degree of tactical autonomy in action (as discussed in chapter 7).

The presence of a commander to whom the troops felt genuine attachment undoubtedly improved their morale. On campaign such popular generals were able to squeeze greater efforts out of their men. Early in 1776 Captain Francis Lord Rawdon wrote of Howe: "He is much beloved by the whole army. They feel a confidence in him which cannot fail of producing the best effects whenever the troops take the field."[94] Similarly Commissary Robert Biddulph wrote from Charleston of Cornwallis after the battle of Camden, "The great confidence the army place in him, will enable him to carry the world before him." In January 1781 Biddulph added: "His army is a family, he is the father of it. There are no parties, no competitions. What may not be expected from a force so united, a leader so popular and patriotic?"[95] Part of Cornwallis's powerful appeal to his embattled little army was his evident willingness to share its hardships. Former redcoat Roger Lamb boasted that on campaign in the South, his lordship had "fared like a common soldier," eating the same wretched food and not even allowing himself the distinction of a tent—"in all things [he] partook of our sufferings, and seemed much more to feel for us than for himself."[96] When in February 1781, during Cornwallis's second invasion of North Carolina, it became necessary to destroy most of the train in order to lighten the army for the "Race to the Dan," the officers—led by Cornwallis—publicly burned their own baggage. According to Stedman, such was the power of this dramatic gesture, and so zealous were the officers and men to undergo any hardship in the promotion of the King's service, that the destruction of most of the army's wagons was "acquiesced in without a murmur," despite the fact that the soldiers thereby lost all prospect of rum or regular provisions.[97]

This kind of adulation translated well to the battlefield. While neither British generals nor regimental officers appear to have indulged in theatrical bravado or showy speeches to boost their troops' morale, they do appear to have sought the same effect via a display of calmness and confidence.[98] According to Corporal Thomas Sullivan, during the preparatory artillery bombardment of Chatterton's Hill, "General Howe stood in the rear of the cannon, and his undaunted courage and resolution animated the troops, seeing themselves commanded by so bold and prudent a commander."[99] One anonymous British officer recorded Howe's similarly inspiring behavior at Brandywine, during the respite on Osborne's Hill before Cornwallis's hard-marching division advancing to the attack: "Sir William Howe with a most cheerful countenance conversed with his officers and invited several to a slight refreshment provided on the grass. The pleasing behavior of that great man on this occasion had a great effect on the minds of all who beheld him. Everyone that remembers the anxious moments before an engagement may conceive how animating [is] the sight of the commander-in-chief, in whose looks nothing but serenity and confidence in his troops is painted. In short, the army resumed their march in full assurance of success and victory."[100] Although it seems unlikely that British generals wore full dress in the field, their appearance was nevertheless imposing. One Quaker lad later recalled how impressed he was by the sight of Lord Cornwallis as his division made its wide outflanking march at Brandywine: "He was

on horseback, appeared tall and sat very erect. His rich scarlet clothing, loaded with gold lace, epaulets, etc., occasioned him to make a
brilliant and martial appearance."[101]

Once the troops engaged, the general was able to inspire them
further by exposing himself to enemy fire, though officers' opinions
differed as to the propriety of this conduct. For Lieutenant William
Digby, the bravery that Burgoyne and Brigadier General Simon Fraser
displayed at Freeman's Farm did the pair nothing but honor.[102] But
Major Stephen Kemble criticized Clinton for his actions at Monmouth, where the commander in chief "showed himself the soldier,
but not the wise general, on this occasion, exposing himself and
charging at the head of a few dragoons."[103] During that action, to the
"inexpressible surprise" of Lieutenant William Hale, Clinton led the
2nd Battalion of Grenadiers in a tumultuous pursuit of the retreating
rebel van, an exploit that Hale alleged did not improve Clinton's
standing in the army: "The General by his rashness in the last action
has totally lost the confidence both of the officers and soldiers, who
were astonished at seeing the commander of an army galloping like a
Newmarket jockey at the head of a wing of grenadiers and expressly
forbidding all form of order."[104]

For a senior officer to expose his person in this manner was dangerous, for the consequences of his incapacitation were severe. Hence
Howe's recklessness at Brandywine made his aides de camp worry—
not only for his personal safety but also for the conduct of the campaign in the event of his death.[105] Similarly, Brigadier General Fraser's
conspicuous efforts in rallying the faltering British line at Bemis
Heights resulted in a mortal wound that Lieutenant William Digby
thought "helped to turn the fate of the day. . . . When General Burgoyne saw him fall, he seemed then to feel in the highest degree our
disagreeable situation."[106]

British commanders in America were not quite as unimaginative in
their battlefield tactics as historians have represented them. They did
actively seek engagements, and wherever an attack was practicable,
they preferred to use their best troops to achieve mass on the enemy's
flank, to turn the rebels' dispositions, and so dislodge them speedily.
When this tactic was successful, it produced battlefield victories in
which the rebels suffered disproportionate (if not necessarily heavy)
casualties. Yet wherever topography, poor intelligence, and/or the

rebel commander's skill precluded successful turning movements, the King's troops found themselves having to engage at much less favorable odds. On occasion the potency of furious British bayonet rushes managed to overcome this disadvantage (as at Camden, where most of the rebel militia gave way at the first charge). But at those engagements in which Crown forces were drawn into general actions against superior numbers of rebel troops on unfavorable ground, where consequently the action degenerated into a series of sustained and costly close combats, then the British generally suffered disproportionately. This kind of grand-tactical derangement was especially serious when one remembers that eighteenth-century commanders generally exerted limited control over engagements once the fighting began.

# 4

# MARCH AND DEPLOYMENT

The moment the head of the British column passed the rivulet, the
different corps, in quick step, deployed to the right and left, and
soon were ranged in line of battle.

Henry Lee, *Revolutionary War Memoirs*

Thus far we have established that the British Army's principal
objective in America was the dispersal of Congress's conventional military forces. We have also surveyed the various operational
factors that obstructed this goal and the grand tactics that Crown
commanders employed to facilitate it. It is now necessary to examine
how British troops reached the battlefield and deployed for action.

### THE BATTALION'S TACTICAL ORGANIZATION

Most of the British regular infantry regiments that served in America
comprised a single battalion of ten companies, with a further two
"additional companies" in the British Isles whose task was to obtain
recruits.[1] On active service the two flank companies were almost
invariably detached from their parent unit to form composite grenadier and light infantry battalions, leaving the eight remaining center
("hatman," or "battalion") companies to form "the battalion" proper.
During the course of the war, these regular battalions rarely met

their paper strengths, which were augmented in 1775 and again in 1779. As an example, in mid-July 1779 the 33rd Regiment's eight battalion companies at New York together comprised 375 rank and file (corporals and privates), which meant that it was 73 rank and file short of its establishment (the return did not specify whether the regiment had its full complement of sixty-four officers, sergeants, and drummers).[2] But these figures included individuals who were sick, wounded, on duty, or in captivity; or who (in the officers' cases) were on detachment as staff or engineer officers, had not yet joined the battalion, or were absent with leave.[3] Hence the number "present and fit" at any one time would have been significantly lower, particularly when the battalion was in the field. As an example, on the eve of the battle of Camden, the 33rd Regiment's eight battalion companies with Cornwallis mustered only 238 officers and enlisted men.[4]

The infantry's main fighting formation was the battalion line. The British Army's *1764 Regulations* prescribed that the battalion should draw up in three ranks with intervals of six inches between each file.[5] (Theorists generally allowed eighteen to twenty-four inches per file.)[6] According to military writer Captain Bennett Cuthbertson, these file intervals were necessary to prevent the soldiers "struggling for a proper place" and thereby producing "disorder and confusion."[7] Yet for reasons that will be explained in chapter 6, for most of the American War the infantry's default line formation was two deep, with the files at eighteen-inch intervals.

Because the company was an administrative subunit, before action the adjutant was supposed to "tell off" the battalion into equalized tactical subunits to facilitate the various maneuvers and firings: two wings, four grand divisions, eight subdivisions, and sixteen platoons.[8] According to the arrangement laid down in the *1764 Regulations*, in combat the field officers (along with the adjutant) oversaw the battalion, while the "eldest" (or "first") captain took charge of the "color reserve" in the center-rear.[9] Consequently, the companies were supposed to draw up in line in such a fashion (see figure 1) that the second- and third-eldest captains were able to take command of the battalion's two wings, while the second-, third-, fourth-, and fifth-eldest captains could command the four grand divisions. If the battalion was called upon to fire or to maneuver by platoons, then a number of the supernumerary subalterns ordinarily posted in the rear of

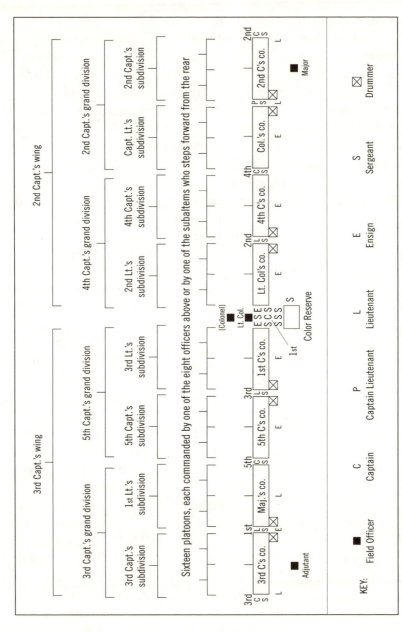

**Figure 1. Officers' posts and command responsibilities, according to the _1764 Regulations_.**

the battalion (nearest their own companies) were available to march forward and take command.[10]

If this neat arrangement was appropriate for a peacetime review, in the field the absence of key officers (for reasons mentioned above) would have made it unworkable. Particularly during prolonged campaigning, these officer shortages became very pronounced. For instance, at the battle of Camden, the 23rd and 33rd Regiments and the two battalions of the 71st Regiment mustered only ten, thirteen, and fifteen officers (the 23rd and 71st did not have a single field officer).[11] Six months later, shortly before Cornwallis plunged into North Carolina, only five officers remained with the 2nd Battalion of Guards.[12] Provincial corps like the Queen's Rangers were usually less prone to this problem because their perennial shortage of enlisted men created an artificially high officer-to-men ratio.[13]

In the event of the absence of key officers like the senior captains, it was necessary for battalion commanding officers to improvise an alternative to the specific command arrangement laid down in the *1764 Regulations.* The simplest alternative was to reorder the sequence of the companies within the battalion line to reflect the seniority of the officers who were present. This is probably why Corporal Thomas Sullivan's account of the storming of Chatterton's Hill at White Plains specified that Captain James Grant's company of the 49th Regiment, and not the colonel's, was the "2nd right-hand company of our battalion."[14] Indeed, we have good evidence for this phenomenon as it relates to the 47th Regiment during the Albany expedition. When, ten days before the battle of Freeman's Farm, two of the battalion companies were detached to garrison Diamond Island on Lake George, Lieutenant Colonel Nicholas Sutherland issued the following order:

> The [remaining six] companies will fall in upon the parade and encamp as follows till further orders [in the following sequence]:
>
> Captain [John Dormer] Alcock's, the right.
> [Lieutenant] General [Carleton]'s, the left.
> Lieutenant Colonel's, left of Captain Alcock.
> Captain [Richard] L'Estrange's, right of the General's.
> Captain [William] Sherriffe's, right of the center.
> Major [Paulus Aemilius Irving]'s, left of the center.

Assuming that the practice of retaining a color reserve under the command of the senior captain was dispensed with (as seems to have been the case in America), and bearing in mind that Alcock was now the only remaining captain with the battalion (excluding the field officers), this sequence ensured that the two or three senior officers commanding companies were in the right positions in the battalion line to be able to take charge of its two wings or three grand divisions—Captain Alcock and Captain Lieutenant Henry Marr (who commanded Carleton's company in his absence) for the two wings, and Alcock, Marr, and the senior lieutenant, Thomas Story (who commanded Sherriffe's company in his absence) for the three grand divisions.[15]

If a battalion's shortage of officers was so severe that the reordering of the companies within the battalion line was insufficient to ensure efficient command and control, how might the battalion commanding officer have proceeded? After the war George Hanger ridiculed Roderick Mackenzie's unlikely claim that Major Timothy Newmarsh was still "posting the officers" of the 7th Regiment when the British line moved forward at Cowpens: "The idea of posting officers I am at a loss to comprehend; such an expression was never before used in any military production, nor was such a practice ever adopted in the field. Every officer, when a regiment is ordered to *form*, of course knows his proper station without being *posted*."[16] As Hanger's rebuke implies, command arrangements were established well before the battalion came to action. When Major General Eyre Massey took a small force from the Halifax garrison into the field in September 1777, he instructed that each battalion's four grand divisions and eight subdivisions were to be styled "1st" to "4th" and numbers "1" to "8". More importantly, he ordered that commissioned officers were to command the former but that the oldest and most experienced noncommissioned officers were to take charge of the latter. Massey explained that, whether a whole battalion, a wing, a grand division, or a subdivision was sent "on services of fatigue or enterprise," this system would ensure that "the same men will inseparably act with the same officers."[17]

Massey's orders clearly demonstrate that, contrary to the impression given in the *1764 Regulations*, it often would have fallen to subalterns and even sergeants to shoulder direct command responsibility in the field. Ensign Frederick Robinson, an American, was sixteen when on 26 February 1779 he was obliged (by the fact that his captain was—as he put it—absent flirting in New York) to lead his company of the 17th Regiment against rebel militia during Major General William Tryon's amphibious raid on West Greenwich (or Horseneck), Connecticut.[18] In hindsight Robinson did not consider himself to have been equal to this task: "That I was not a very able warrior as to personal efforts may be judged from the following anecdote. In endeavoring to get up to the enemy, to whose fire we were exposed, but did not return a shot, we were checked in our career by a stone wall, which baffled my efforts to get over. A stout young corporal of the company, seeing my difficulty, seized me by the waistband and threw me over with as much ease as he would have thrown a pebble, saying at the same time, 'Now, young gentleman, take care of yourself.' " Robinson was again exercising authority beyond his capabilities at the rebel storming of Stony Point, where he once again found himself indebted to an experienced noncommissioned officer: "On this occasion I commanded one of the advanced companies, which must have been accidental, as I was much too young for so important a situation. Upon so severe a trial, I acted, as many older officers no doubt had done before, and since—I obeyed the directions of an experienced sergeant, who also saved my life by shooting a man who had leveled his firelock at me within ten yards."[19] Additionally, the young "gentlemen volunteers" like Thomas Anburey, who attached themselves to British regiments in America in the hopes of earning a free commission, must also have assisted in directing the battalion in action.[20]

In theory every regular British corps was able to perform an impressive repertoire of "core" maneuvers and firings (those prescribed in the *1764 Regulations* and that the regiment had to demonstrate at the regimental review) as well as "customary" (or nonregulation) ones. In reality most of these differed only in detail. For instance, a battalion was able to deploy from line into column and back again in numerous ways; likewise it was able to fire volleys by wings, grand divisions, subdivisions, or platoons. In the field, however, battalions executed only a small number of these, and the most common maneuver and fire unit employed in America appears to have been the subdivision (which corresponded more or less with the company).

Indeed, one officer who served with the 1st Battalion of Light Infantry in America later questioned the need for different tactical and administrative nomenclature for the company/subdivision. Instead he argued that "[a] company is a company; weak or strong a company" and advocated that it "be divided in plain, familiar language—in half, quarters, and if this is not sufficient, into eighths."[21]

Because battalions in America seem most commonly to have maneuvered and fired by subdivisions, the order in which the companies were ranged in line during combat lost much of its significance. Indeed, in May 1777, before the opening of Burgoyne's expedition, Major General William Phillips informed the infantry of the "Canadian army" that "[t]he changing the order of companies at times, in drawing up the battalion, will make the soldiers ready in forming on general principles, without regarding local stations of companies."[22] And when the journalist of the Hessian *Feldjägerkorps* recorded the landing of the First Division of Howe's army at Head of Elk (25 August 1777), he noted that "the men were immediately formed by companies, without regard to seniority, in order to be prepared to resist the certainly nearby enemy."[23] The later testimony of the aforementioned former officer of the 1st Battalion of Light Infantry in America confirms the point: "The precedence of companies being well understood to be established as the parade order—but in formation of line from column, convenience or rapidity of movement [is] to supersede seniority."[24]

Another command practice that was probably disregarded in the field in America was "sizing." In order to facilitate the maneuvers and firings, convention dictated that the tallest, shortest, and medium-sized men of each subdivision should compose the front, center, and rear ranks respectively, with each rank's biggest men on its flanks and the smallest at its center (or vice-versa).[25] Even before the war military writer Captain Cuthbertson had recommended amending this practice by posting "the most expert and attentive" soldiers on the flanks of each platoon and company where they could regulate the firings and wheelings. Accordingly, in the Queen's Rangers the "two files in the center, and two on each flank [of each company], were directed to be composed of trained soldiers, without regard to their size or appearance."[26] A more substantial barrier to sizing, however, was the 1st Battalion of Light Infantry's custom of permitting front-

and rear-rank men to pair up at will: "Upon service, the front-rank man [is] to be permitted to choose his comrade and to do all duties with him, and always to cover him. This will prevent the exact sizing of the men, which certainly adds to the appearance of the company. The front rank may be sized."[27] It is difficult to say how widespread this practice was; certainly in January 1780 Major Patrick Ferguson's new Provincial corps, the American Volunteers, adopted it.[28]

## THE MARCH COLUMN

In opening this section, we must remind ourselves that for most of the American War, the King's troops abjured the linear formation employed by "heavy infantry" in conventional European warfare (three ranks with closed file intervals) in favor of two ranks and open files. (This theme is explored fully in chapter 6.) This shift had implications for the types of columnar formations that the redcoats employed in America, both on the march and in maneuvering.

Of all the army's core and customary maneuvers, the majority dealt with the business of deploying from line into column and back again. Indeed, in 1782 military writer Lieutenant Colonel William Dalrymple lamented the lack of uniformity with which different British regiments formed columns.[29] Most relevant for our purposes are the march and maneuver formations that appear to have been employed most regularly in the field in America: the "column by companies" (or "subdivisions" or simply "divisions"), the "column by half companies" (or "platoons" or "half divisions"), the "column by quarter companies," and the "column by double files."

When the commanding officer wanted the battalion to deploy from line into a column of companies, half companies, or quarter companies, the simplest method was for the relevant units to make a quarter wheel simultaneously (see figure 2a). This turning was usually performed clockwise, it having been most common to march "by the right." For instance, on 20 June 1778, during Clinton's withdrawal from Philadelphia to New York, Knyphausen's Second Division "marched this morning from their right in half divisions wherever the road would admit of it, the country which the army marched through becoming more open."[30] Alternatively, the battalion was able to deploy from line into column to the front. In August 1780 Lieuten-

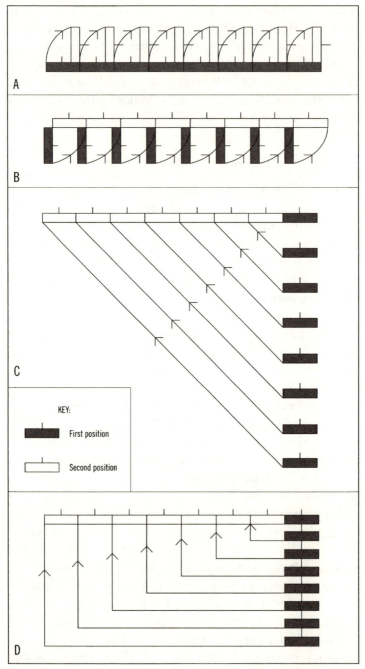

KEY:

First position

Second position

**Figure 2.** Common methods by which a battalion of eight companies (subdivisions) deployed from line into column and back again.

ant Colonel Henry Hope outlined the preferred method of doing this in his tactical instructions to the 1st Battalion of Grenadiers:

> When the battalion is ordered to advance in column from any particular company or division, the officer commanding it will give the word to march; [the officer commanding] every other company alternately doing the same when the preceding one has got to a proper distance, and carrying his division into the line of march (remembering always to caution his men to which flank they are to oblique and dress). If the company first put in motion is of the right wing, it is to be followed by the next upon its left; if it belong to the left wing of the battalion, [then it is to be followed] by the [company] next upon the right, and so on, alternately. But if the column moves in a smaller front than [that] of a company, [then] the divisions of one company are never to intervene between those of another.[31]

Assuming for a moment that a given battalion in two ranks comprised eight companies, each of thirty-two rank and file, then the column by companies, half companies, or quarter companies would have proceeded on a frontage of sixteen, eight, or four files, howsoever it was formed.

Battalions were able to move in either an "open column" (where the distance between the front rank of one maneuver division and the front rank of the next corresponded with its frontage in the line) or a "closed column" (meaning that the intervals between the successive maneuver divisions were reduced to a minimum).[32] While the closed column took up less road space and was often used for night marches, its main drawback was that deployment into line could only be achieved to the front by files.[33] Conversely (as discussed in the next section), it was possible for an open column to deploy into line in any direction.

When the battalion was passing a defile or crossing a bridge, it was possible for the commanding officer to compress the column's frontage temporarily by closing the file intervals of each maneuver division. But on narrow trails the battalion employed an alternative march formation, the "column of double files." According to a disapproving Clinton, marching by files was common during the French and Indian War, and Howe revived the practice for the 1776 campaign.[34] Confirmation of this is contained in the first official report that Major Carl Baurmeister, Hessian adjutant general in America, made after the landing on Long Island: "These woods . . . are thickly grown with large trees and are full of gullies and ravines, which make it impossible for even three men to walk abreast, not to mention a platoon. Hence we were compelled to follow the example of the English, that is, to form in columns, two men abreast and rather far apart, as if lined up for someone to run the gauntlet."[35]

A two-deep battalion line might have deployed into a column of double files in two ways. The simplest method was for the rank and file of each maneuver division to face to the right (or the left), which transformed the battalion's two ranks instantly into two files.[36] The 49th Regiment seemingly employed this elementary maneuver when it escorted the army's baggage to Bedford during the battle of Long Island, Corporal Thomas Sullivan having recorded that "the front rank [marched in one file] on one side of the road, and the rear rank [in another file] on the other."[37] An alternative way to deploy into a column of double files was from the battalion's center. According to this method, the two files (that is, the four men) at the very center of the battalion stood fast while the rest of the rank and file turned ninety degrees right or left to face them, the rear-rank men stepping behind their front-rank partners. When the two center files marched forward, the battalion's left and right wings (now the left and right files of the column) then simply filed out to cover them. In 1778 Lieutenant Colonel Archibald Campbell required the battalions of his expeditionary force not to deploy from line into a column of double files by any other method.[38]

As in conventional European warfare, a British field force on campaign in America would have proceeded in one or more columns of march, depending on the availability of parallel roads. Commonly the order of the units within the march column was spelled out each day in general orders. As an example, on 10 February 1781, during the "Race to the Dan," Cornwallis gave out that the army was to be ready to march (that is, with the packhorses loaded and the men under arms) at 6:30 A.M. the next morning in the following order: (1) The *Jäger*, (2) British Legion cavalry, (3) half of the army's pioneers, (4) two 3-pounders, (5) Lieutenant Colonel James Webster's Brigade (23rd Regiment, 33rd Regiment, 2nd Battalion of the 71st Regiment), (6) two 6-pounders, (7) Regiment von Bose, (8) North Carolina Volunteers, (9) two

6-pounders, (10) Brigadier General O'Hara's Guards Brigade (1st Battalion, 2nd Battalion, Grenadier Company, Light Company), (11) the army's packhorses, accompanied by each corps' quartermaster sergeant, (12) half of the army's pioneers, (13) the army's wagons, and (14) one officer and twelve dragoons.[39] Alternatively, because field forces generally encamped in a fashion approximating the line(s) of battle, it was possible for the army simply to move off its ground "from the right" (or alternatively "from the left").[40] This would have ensured that the order of the battalions in the line(s) from right to left (or from left to right) became the order of march within the march column(s). Lastly, one should also note that it was possible for a number of battalions drawn up in line together to form a march column from the center; the battalions having alternately fallen out of the line into their appointed places in the march column.[41]

Here it should be pointed out that, contrary to popular imagination, it would have been pointless for the men to have maintained their exact dressings and step when not in the enemy's presence. Instead British troops on the march in America would have resembled the picture that Dundas painted in 1788: "In common route marching, the same regularity of step cannot be required as is necessary in the operations of maneuver. The battalion or column may be carried on at a natural pace of two miles an hour; the attention of the men may be relaxed, and the ranks and files loosened, so as to move with the greater conveniency [sic]."[42]

Light troops with the column usually performed screening duties. For example, Captain Johann Ewald led the advanced guard of Cornwallis's division during its outflanking march at Brandywine; his force consisted of sixty foot and fifteen mounted *Jäger*, with the light companies of the 17th and 42nd Regiments following behind in support.[43] Strong flanking parties, usually drawn from the battalions themselves, were also thrown out at varying distances on either side of the column, with orders (as Bland put it in 1727) "to examine all the hedges, ditches, and copses which lie near the road."[44] For example, before Howe's column commenced its flanking march on the eve of the battle of Long Island, the commander in chief ordered that "each regiment will have a flanking party of a non-commissioned officer and 4 men per company under the command of a commissioned officer of the regiment."[45] Likewise, during the army's withdrawal toward Perth Amboy toward the close of his abortive operations in

New Jersey in June 1777, Howe ordered the two parallel columns to maintain flanking parties of one captain and forty men per corps.[46] This was exacting work in broken country, particularly when under fire, because the flankers had to slog their way over or through walls, fences, hills, streams, woods, and underbrush to stay abreast of the column. Indeed, during the return march of Lieutenant Colonel Francis Smith's column from Concord to Boston on the first day of the war, fatigue and casualties quickly conspired to overwhelm the flankers' efforts to fend off the growing swarms of militia. In fact, the bloodied column was only saved from disintegration when it reached the relative safety of Lexington Heights, where the fresh battalion companies of Brigadier General Lord Percy's relief force threw out strong flanking parties to protect Smith's exhausted men. Many of the rebel casualties were incurred when these flankers trapped and killed militiamen whose attention was fixed on the column, as at Menotomy.[47]

Usually the army's baggage followed in the rear of the column if the army was advancing and at the front if it was withdrawing in the face of the enemy. Whole battalions covered the vehicles during the march. Thus at the battle of Long Island, the two ranks of the 49th Regiment marched on either side of the baggage, while the three battalions of the 71st Regiment covered the wagons' left, right, and rear during the march of Knyphausen's division to Chad's Ford at Brandywine.[48]

British march discipline in America does not appear to have been particularly good—a phenomenon that, in the face of a more competent enemy, would have exposed Crown armies to disaster. One common failing was the frequency with which alarming gaps opened up between the battalions within a march column.[49] Much of the danger must have stemmed, however, from the two-deep line formation that the King's troops employed in America, for as Lieutenant Colonel William Dalrymple observed in 1782, "whenever the depth of the battalion is reduced, the extent must be increased; and, the column of march being lengthened considerably, the movement of great bodies becomes more difficult."[50] This phenomenon was particularly marked when the army marched in a column of double files, which as Captain Cuthbertson pointed out in 1768, "often subjects a battalion to enlarge itself from front to rear, more than is ever, if possible, to be wished."[51] Indeed, Howe's Hessian aide de camp later blamed the custom of marching by files for Lieutenant General Phillip Leopold von Heister's failure to bring up his division as quickly as Howe wanted at White Plains.[52]

## PARALLEL AND PROCESSIONAL DEPLOYMENT

When a march column contacted the enemy, it deployed into line of battle to fight. With the "parallel" method of deployment, the column was brought onto its ground along a line of march that was parallel with the alignment of the enemy forces. This parallel march climaxed when the head of the column reached an assigned point; whereupon the different battalions within the column simultaneously deployed into line to the left or right, facing the enemy, and were ready to do battle.[53] This would appear to have been what one rebel officer observed at Guilford Courthouse when he saw the British "forming their line of battle, by filing off to the right and left."[54] Major General Heath also appears to have witnessed parallel deployment at White Plains prior to the storming of Chatterton's Hill: "A part of the left column [under Lieutenant General von Heister], composed of British and Hessians, forded the river [Bronx], and marched along under the cover of the hill, until they had gained sufficient ground to the left of the Americans; when, by facing to the left, their column became a line, parallel with the Americans."[55] With the parallel method, it was perfectly straightforward for a battalion in a column of double files to deploy back into line: all the men had to do was simultaneously to face to the left or right.[56] Similarly, if the battalion was in an open column of companies, half companies, or quarter companies, the maneuver divisions simultaneously executed a quarter wheel to the left or right (see figure 2b). As Lieutenant Colonel Charles Mawhood reminded the Fourth Brigade in May 1777, "If one regiment or the whole brigade has marched from the right, and is ordered to form to the left, [then] the whole wheels together and dress[es] to the right."[57] As should be clear from Heath's testimony, the advantage of the parallel manner of deployment was that, in theory, all the units in the march column were able to deploy into line almost instantaneously.

A small problem arose if the battalion had marched by the right and needed to form line to the right (rather than to the left). If the commanding officer did not wish to reverse the order of the battalion's maneuver divisions within the line, then a circuitous maneuver was required. In Mawhood's words, "the leading division wheels to the right, [and] every other division passes that which is in front of it, and then wheels and dresses to the right."[58] The drawback to this movement was that it could not be executed instantaneously: the tail-end maneuver-division (as in Mawhood's example), or the very last two men in the column (in the case of a column by files), had to cover almost twice the length of the column itself to reach its proper station in the line. A year and a half later, Lieutenant Colonel Campbell offered a timesaving alternative in the tactical instructions he issued to the expeditionary force he led against Savannah: "Should the army, battalion or detachment be upon its march from the right by half- or quarter-companies, and it is ordered to form for the reception of an enemy moving towards the right of the line of march, the first order will be, *to the rear change your front!* On which, the men of the front rank in each half- or quarter-company will go to the right about, and . . . change places with those in the rear rank. By wheeling the half- or quarter-companies to the left, the army, battalion or detachment is instantly formed to the left for action. (The same to be observed should the army have marched from the left, and be under the necessity of forming to the left.)" Here Campbell calculated that it was acceptable to reverse the order of the maneuver divisions within the battalion line if one also reversed the order of the files within each. Although he acknowledged that this maneuver "will occasion the right of the army, battalion or detachment to become the left," he argued that "the ceremonials of parade" should "give way to the essentials of service," adding that "[a]n army, battalion or detachment ought to be ready to meet or fight an enemy at all times and in every direction." In short, because the rebels were expected to exploit their knowledge of the swampy, wooded terrain to launch surprise attacks on the march column's flank or rear, it was necessary to employ methods of deployment that could be "executed in the shortest space of time, and with the least fatigue to the troops."[59]

An alternative to a parallel deployment was the "processional" method (or *Deployiren*) evolved by Frederick the Great before the Seven Years War. According to this tactic, the march column approached the enemy line perpendicularly. When the lead unit reached its ground, it deployed into line to its front; meanwhile each successive battalion moved out of the column obliquely to its appointed place in the line. To speed up deployment, it was possible for the two or more parallel columns to deploy in this fashion simultaneously. For example, after his disastrous defeat at the action at Briar Creek, Brigadier General John Ashe testified that the attacking Crown forces "came down about three in the afternoon in three columns six-abreast."[60] Likewise, during the last phase of Howe's flanking march at the battle of Brandywine, Cornwallis's division forked into three columns as it traversed Osborne's Hill. Howe's Hessian aide de camp (who watched the deployment with his chief from the hill) described the moment that these three columns almost instantaneously deployed into line of battle for the attack at Birmingham Meetinghouse: "At four in the afternoon our two battalions of light infantry and the Hessian *Jäger* marched down the hill. They marched first in a column, but later, when they approached the enemy, in line formation, deploying to the left. Soon after this the English grenadiers did the same in the center, almost at the same time; just a little later, the English Guards formed the right wing. Behind the English grenadiers were the Hessian grenadiers; behind the light infantry and the *Jäger* was the 4th English Brigade. The 3rd English Brigade was in reserve on top of the hill. The two squadrons of dragoons, who were close to us, halted behind the left wing of the Hessian grenadiers."[61]

When a battalion in column (whether by companies, half companies, or quarter companies) deployed to its front, the lead maneuver division stood fast while the others marched to their appointed stations in the line. They did this in one of two ways, either obliquely along the most direct path (see figure 2c) or (less commonly, in the case of a closed column) by files (see figure 2d). A variation upon this theme was outlined in instructions to the 1st Battalion of Grenadiers in 1780: "When [the companies are] ordered to form the battalion upon any given company or division, [then] the officer of that company or division orders it to halt and immediately see[s] that his line is dressed in such direction as may be pointed out by the commanding officer. The other divisions either advance obliquely, or go about and retire obliquely, in the nearest line to their proper front in battalion."[62] Conversely, if the battalion had originally deployed from line into a column of double files from the center, then a different maneuver was required to redeploy back into line to the front. Here the two center files (meaning the four men leading the column) simply stood fast while the rest of the men ran up obliquely left or right to their stations in the line.

## The Line of Battle

In European warfare the ideal deployment of an army for battle followed a conventional formula: "The method and order of arranging
the troops in order or line of battle . . . generally consists of three lines,
viz. the front line, the rear line, and the reserve. The second line
should be about 300 paces behind the first, and the reserve at about 5
or 600 paces behind the second. The artillery is likewise divided along
the front of the first line. The first line should be stronger than the
rear line, that its shock may be more violent, and that, by having a
greater front, it may more easily close on the enemy's flanks."[63] Additionally, both the brigades and their component regiments were supposed to take their place in the line of battle, as also in camp and
cantonments, in a pattern that accorded with their seniority within
the army.[64] Furthermore, it was necessary to leave intervals between
the battalions that were large enough to prevent the flanks of adjacent
corps from brushing, though not so large as to enable enemy forces—
particularly cavalry—to penetrate and roll up the line.

British commanders in America were perfectly aware of the advantages of this conventional manner of deployment. Indeed, on occasion they drew up orders of battle for their armies that closely mirrored it, as Howe did at Halifax in May 1776 (see figure 3) and as
Lieutenant Colonel Campbell did at Savannah in December 1778 (see
figure 4).[65] Major General Phillips's order of battle, composed at West-
over, Virginia, in April 1781, deserves to be quoted in full:

When the troops form it is to be done in the following manner:
the infantry and hussars of the Queen's Rangers, with a detachment of *Jäger* and [Captain John] Althause's rifle company,
form the advanced guard, under Lieutenant Colonel Simcoe.
The first line to be composed of the light infantry; the second to
be composed of the 80th and 76th Regiments, who will form
three deep, and in compact order. The grenadiers and light infantry of the 80th, with the American Legion, to form the reserve under Major [James] Gordon. The cavalry of the Queen's
Rangers, to form with the reserve, till such time as they may be
called upon the wing of the first or second line.[66]

Unfortunately, these notional orders of battle tell us little about how
the King's troops really operated on the battlefield in America: at no

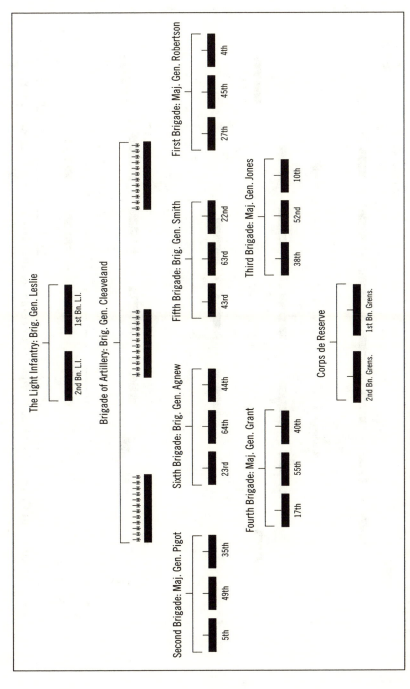

**Figure 3. Howe's (notional) order of battle, Halifax, 16 May 1776.**

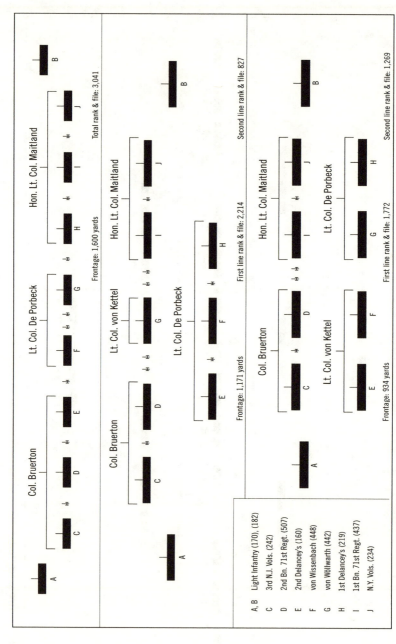

Key:
- A, B — Light Infantry (170), (182)
- C — 3rd N.J. Vols. (242)
- D — 2nd Bn. 71st Regt. (507)
- E — 2nd Delancey's (160)
- F — von Wissenbach (448)
- G — von Wollwarth (442)
- H — 1st Delancey's (219)
- I — 1st Bn. 71st Regt. (437)
- J — N.Y. Vols. (234)

Col. Bruerton   Lt. Col. De Porbeck   Hon. Lt. Col. Maitland

Total rank & file: 3,041

Frontage: 1,600 yards

Col. Bruerton   Lt. Col. von Kettel   Hon. Lt. Col. Maitland

Lt. Col. De Porbeck

Frontage: 1,171 yards

First line rank & file: 2,214

Second line rank & file: 827

Col. Bruerton   Lt. Col. von Kettel   Hon. Lt. Col. Maitland   Lt. Col. De Porbeck

Frontage: 934 yards

First line rank & file: 1,772

Second line rank & file: 1,269

**Figure 4. Lieutenant Colonel Archibald Campbell's three (notional) orders of battle, December 1778.**

time during Howe's 1776 campaign, or in the handful of actions and skirmishes that Campbell and Phillips fought in Georgia and Virginia, did their forces deploy and fight according to these plans.[67]

One significant discrepancy between the conventional European style of deployment and that practiced by British commanders in America was that these officers did not always observe the of deploying brigades and corps according to seniority. After the disaster at Trenton in December 1776, Howe cited this principle in defense of his decision to entrust the most exposed posts in New Jersey to the German mercenaries: "The left . . . was the post of the Hessians in the line, and had I changed it upon this occasion it must have been considered as a disgrace, since the same situation held in the cantonments as in the camp."[68] Similarly, at the battle of Brandywine, Howe observed the practice by allocating the First and Second Brigades to Knyphausen's division (the army's right wing). Moreover, within those two brigades the 4th and 5th Regiments (the "eldest" British line regiments in Howe's army) each appear to have deployed on the right, which means that they spearheaded Major General Grant's attack over Chad's Ford.[69] Yet at those actions where we know with certainty the arrangement of the corps within the line(s) of battle, the only noticeable nod to convention was that a choice unit or brigade normally filled the post of honor on the right (see figure 5). Indeed, so predictable was this tendency that, at the action at Stono Ferry, Major General Lincoln entrusted to his rebel regulars the rebel left, where they were pitted against the 1st Battalion of the 71st Regiment, and placed his militia on the right, opposite Lieutenant Colonel the Honorable John Maitland's Provincials and Hessians. Henry Lee later criticized Gates for not having done the same at Camden, where the deployment of the militia on the rebel left condemned them to face the flower of Cornwallis's army, Lieutenant Colonel James Webster's brigade.[70]

A second significant discrepancy was the size of the intervals between the battalions. For instance, in the three orders of battle that Lieutenant Colonel Campbell drew up for his expeditionary force off Savannah in late 1778 (see figure 4), he allowed intervals of eight or sixteen yards between each battalion and its neighbor. Even more generously, Lieutenant Colonel Thomas Musgrave's tactical instructions to the Fourth Brigade in May 1777 prescribed fifty-pace intervals between each battalion.[71] This was partly because the rebels

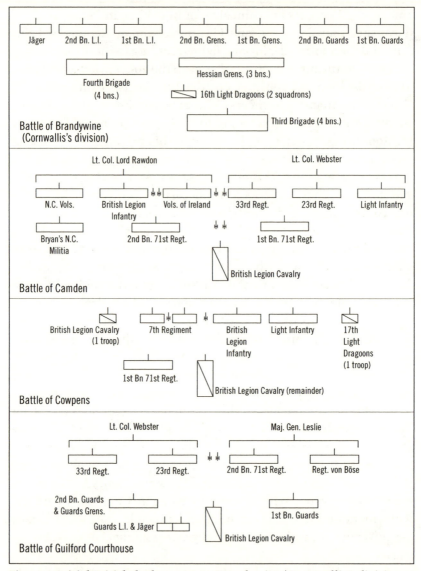

**Figure 5. Initial British deployments at Brandywine (Cornwallis's division at
Birmingham Meetinghouse), Camden, Cowpens, and Guilford Courthouse.**

possessed only limited numbers of cavalry, none of it the heavy type
that posed the greatest threat to infantry. But probably the main reason for these large intervals was the need to tease out the line of battle
to match the frontage covered by the enemy.

The same consideration motivated the most significant discrep-

ancy between the conventional European deployment and that which
Crown commanders generally practiced in America: the number of
lines employed. After the war Tarleton claimed that the King's troops
had escaped a catastrophic reverse at the rebels' hands until the battle
of Cowpens because "the multiplicity of lines with which they generally fought, rescued them from such imminent danger."[72] In a similar
vein Simcoe later recorded that, in actions in America, the Hessians
"usually formed the firm and solid second line to the British."[73] In fact
neither of these statements was quite correct. On occasion British
commanders did deploy a second line of battle to succor the first. One
such example was Cornwallis's division at the battle of Brandywine,
where part of the Fourth Brigade marched forward from the second
line to fill a yawning gap that had opened up between the light infantry and grenadier battalions during the fighting around Birmingham
Meetinghouse.[74] Another instance was the action at Green Springs,
where Cornwallis was powerful enough to deploy a second line in his
surprise attack on Lafayette's weak "corps of observation."[75] In a similar fashion the close-order Hessian battalions occasionally supported
the more loosely formed British corps' assaults. For example, during
the storming of Forts Clinton and Montgomery, Clinton posted the
Hessian Regiment von Trümbach in reserve "to cover our retreat in
case of misfortune."[76] The general repeated this exercise at the battle
of Monmouth, where he ordered the Germans to hold some rising
ground in his rear so that, were his brisk counterattack against the
rebel van rebuffed in disorder, "I should always have it in my power to
retrograde on the Hessian Grenadiers."[77] Yet in each case Clinton here
used the compactly deployed Hessians in a passive rather than an
active supporting role—in other words, as a rallying point in case of
defeat. Probably this stemmed from the fact that in action the Germans were incapable of keeping up with their swift-heeled British
allies (as we shall see in chapter 6).

The infrequency with which British commanders deployed multiple lines of battle was especially marked in the southern campaigns—a point that Tarleton's bitterest critic, Roderick Mackenzie, a
former lieutenant in the 71st Regiment, put most vehemently after
the war:

I would ask Lieutenant Colonel Tarleton in what action, during the [southern] campaigns of which he treats, did the mul-

tiplicity of his lines rescue the British troops from imminent danger? And on what occasion did their front line, or any part thereof, give way? I believe it will be found that it fell to Lieutenant Colonel Tarleton alone to lead the troops of Britain into a situation from which they could be driven by an equal, or even by double or treble their number. When Earl Cornwallis fought the memorable battle near Camden, his force, considerably under two thousand men, was opposed by upwards of six thousand. At Guilford, his Lordship, with not one third the number of his enemy, obtained a glorious victory over General Greene, the best commander in the American service. And Lord Rawdon upon Hobkirk's Hill routed the same general, who had now experience to his other talents; and this, though his numbers compared with his enemy, did not bear the last mentioned proportion. Many other proofs could be brought of the fallacy of our author's reasoning, but these which have been adduced will I trust sufficiently show the impossibility of forming a multiplicity of lines with so manifest an inferiority of numbers.[78]

Mackenzie's point (if not his figures) was accurate. In almost all their general actions in the South, the British were so outnumbered that, while the rebels were able to deploy multiple lines and/or reserves, Crown commanders were compelled to commit nearly all their units to a single line of battle, as Stedman put it, "in order to show a front equal to the enemy."[79] The alternative was to risk envelopment, as at Hobkirk's Hill. There Lieutenant Colonel Francis Lord Rawdon initially advanced with what Henry Lee later described as a "very narrow front" of two battalions: the King's American Regiment on the left and the 63rd Regiment on the right. When Greene ordered a counterattack, with the intention of enveloping the British force, Rawdon (in Lee's words) "no sooner cast his eyes on our disposition than he perceived the danger to which his unequal front exposed him; and, bringing up the Volunteers of Ireland into line, he remedied the defect seized by Greene in time to avert the expected consequence."[80] The story was similar at Guilford Courthouse, where "the great extent of the enemy's line" obliged Cornwallis and his subordinates to commit almost all of their forces in the battle's early stages.[81] This inability to keep units in support and reserve was risky. If the units in the line of battle were repulsed, they had nothing upon which to fall back—the fatal consequences of which were well illustrated at Cowpens. We should emphasize here that American topography often prevented British commanders from deploying even a single, unbroken line of battle. One example of this was at the battle of Long Island, where Major General Grant's left-hand column pinned Major General Lord Stirling's forces in place. As Stirling himself reported,

> The troops opposed to me were two brigades [the Fourth and Sixth] of four regiments each, under the command of General Grant; who advanced their light troops to within one hundred and fifty yards of our right front, and took possession of an orchard there and some hedges which extended towards our left. . . . On the part of General Grant there were two field-pieces: one howitzer advanced to within three hundred yards of the front of our right, and a like detachment of artillery to the front of our left on a rising ground. At about six hundred yards' distance, one of their brigades formed in two lines opposite to our right, and the other extended in one line to the top of the hills, in the front of our left.[82]

As Stirling's account shows, the undulating and cluttered terrain dictated the deployment of Grant's light troops, artillery, and infantry.

Another excellent example of how close country and/or limited space sometimes obstructed British deployment was the storming of Chatterton's Hill on the extreme right of Washington's position at White Plains. There Brigadier General Alexander Leslie's Second Brigade made a frontal attack while several Hessian corps tackled the right flank of the rebel position, which was held by Brigadier General Alexander McDougall's brigade. Corporal Thomas Sullivan of the 49th Regiment, who participated in Leslie's assault, subsequently penned a colorful account that deserves to be quoted at some length:

> [T]he General . . . ordered the 28th Battalion (that was [on] the left of the brigade) and the next [i.e., the 35th Regiment] to support [the Hessian attack]. They marched down the hill by companies, and crossed the river [Bronx] in a place more practicable [than the Hessians]. . . . The 35th and 49th Battalions marched down the hill by companies, formed, and advanced [up] the opposite hill (though under the enemy's fire) with the

greatest steadiness. Lieutenant Colonel [Robert] Carr, who commanded the 35th Regiment, behaved with great courage, being obliged to force the left of his battalion through the right wing of the 28th (they being [for] some minutes attacked by the main part of the rebels' line, and not in strength to advance). The 49th Battalion formed as well as the ground would admit, [and] every company engaged as they came up.... The hill was so narrow that the right-hand company of our battalion [i.e., the 49th Regiment] had scarcely room to form, until we beat the enemy some distance back.

At this point, Captain Lieutenant William Gore, who commanded the 49th Regiment's right wing, interrupted his men's firing when he mistook the blue-coated rebels opposite (who were shooting from behind a wall that ran across the crest of the hill) for Hessians:

During that [two-minute] interval, when Brigadier General Leslie saw our firing abate, and the enemy pouring in [fire] upon us, he imagined that we were retreating. [He] therefore ordered the 5th Battalion to come up immediately to our assistance. But before the 5th had any ground to form and join us, we observed our mistake, gave three cheers and three smart volleys, and ran close up to the enemy; who were beginning to retreat, as we were in close quarters.... This material post being gained, and the enemy routed, our brigade formed upon the hill; for during the engagement we were sometimes twelve deep, occasioned by the narrowness of the hill, and the large rocks and trees that were dispersed upon it.[83]

Sullivan's account discloses several interesting points about the dynamics of deployment. First, the 28th, 35th, 49th, and 5th Regiments forded the Bronx in column and engaged in that order (the battalions' losses tend to confirm this: sixty-seven, fifty-nine, twenty-eight, and three casualties respectively).[84] Second, the 35th Regiment deployed into line behind and to the right of the 28th Regiment so that, when it advanced, its left wing passed through the stalled 28th Regiment's right wing. Third, the 49th Regiment deployed and engaged, piecemeal, on the right of the 35th Regiment. Presumably, the 49th Regiment's companies (which had marched by the left before crossing the Bronx) successively wheeled into line to the left, thereby gradually filling up the limited space available (and maintaining their correct order within the battalion line). By the time the tail-end company in the column had come up, there was not enough room for it to deploy comfortably. Lastly, the same problem prevented the 5th Regiment from deploying at all.

Tarleton's detailed account of his initial dispositions at Cowpens provides another good example of how topography served to complicate deployment in America. On the morning of the battle, Tarleton's column proceeded thus: "Three companies of light infantry, supported by the Legion infantry, formed the advance; the 7th Regiment, the guns, and the 1st Battalion of the 71st, composed the center; and the cavalry and mounted infantry brought up the rear." Having arrived on the field, and having traced the positions of the riflemen who made up the rebel first line (which extended perpendicular to the British axis of advance along the Green River Road), Tarleton initiated his deployment. The order in which the infantry units arrived on the field dictated their position in the line of battle, from right to left:

The light infantry were ordered to file to the right till they became equal to the [left] flank of the American front line. The Legion infantry were added to their left; and, under the covering fire of a three-pounder, this part of the British troops was instructed to advance within three hundred yards of the enemy. This situation being acquired, the 7th Regiment was commanded to form upon the left of the Legion infantry, and the other three-pounder was given to the right division of the 7th. A captain, with fifty dragoons, was placed on each flank of the corps who formed the British front line, to protect their own [flanks], and [to] threaten the flanks of the enemy. The 1st Battalion of the 71st was desired to extend a little to the left of the 7th Regiment, and to remain one hundred and fifty yards in the rear. This body of infantry, and near two hundred cavalry, composed the reserve.[85]

It was not Tarleton's original intention to keep the Highlanders in reserve. According to George Hanger (a major in the British Legion but absent at Cowpens), this corps (less than 250 rank and file) was initially supposed to deploy on the left of the line. But "when moving up to form in line with the rest of the troops, whether from their not taking ground enough, or from some other circumstance, their right flank *brushed* the left flank of the 7th Regiment, and intermixed one with the other. Major [Archibald] M'Arthur, who commanded them, will not deny this fact."[86] Again, the problem was lack of space. The three infantry corps that composed the line may have totaled less than 500 rank and file. On the left was the 7th Regiment (less than 170); in the center, the British Legion infantry (around 200); and on the right, the composite light battalion (120–160).[87] Making allowance for intervals between the three corps, Tarleton's line would have extended over something approaching three hundred yards when the infantry formed two deep with open files.[88]

A blinkered reading of contemporary British drill books and military theory would tend to suggest that the tactical deployment of companies, battalions, and brigades invariably followed a formula that was governed by the principle of seniority. During the American War, however, more immediate and pressing circumstances like local topography and the enemy's own deployments tended to dictate British dispositions. Consequently, at many engagements—and particularly at Long Island, Germantown, and Monmouth—British battalions did not deploy, advance, and engage in strictly linear fashion but instead fought fluid and ragged combats that defy detailed sequencing and make nonsense of contemporary and modern battle maps. Even in those battles where the fighting was more recognizably linear in character, numerical inferiority usually prevented Crown commanders from deploying conventional multiple lines of battle. Against unsteady and imperfectly disciplined rebel forces, this did not much matter. But as the war progressed and the quality of the opposition steadily improved, it became increasingly hazardous for British troops to fight without adequate support.

# 5

# MOTIVATION

> History cannot produce examples of more ardent zeal in the service
> of their country, than that which characterized the British officers
> and soldiers in America.
>
> J. G. Simcoe, *Simcoe's Military Journal*

Historians have tended to agree that eighteenth-century states recruited their common soldiers predominantly from the unproductive human rubbish of society; that these paupers, runaways, criminals, and halfwits were indifferent to their sovereigns' interests; and that only the generous application of the lash, alcohol, and the dread of their own officers kept them in line and motivated them to brave enemy fire. In this traditional view these men were in every way inferior to the patriotic, volunteer citizen-soldiers who emerged in America and France in the last quarter of that century.[1]

This assessment is, however, questionable. One historian of the French Revolutionary Wars has disputed that the "professional" soldiers of the "old regime" armies performed less heroically in combat than their "revolutionary" counterparts. The implication of this, he argues, is either that ideological commitment had little to do with fighting effectiveness or that "old regime" values were able to motivate men as powerfully as "revolutionary" ideals.[2] One might make a similar case for the Crown troops who strove to crush the rebellion in America. Despite the paucity of documentary material from the ranks, testimonies to the enlisted men's patience and loyalty in adversity and to their bravery and spirit in action practically leap off the pages of the private as well as the public writings of the British and German officers who led them. Indeed, as Sylvia Frey concludes candidly in her social history of the British soldier in America, the King's troops appear to have battled the rebellious colonists with what might paradoxically be described as "revolutionary ardor."[3]

If we focus our attention initially on the factors that motivated the redcoats to brave enemy fire in America, then there is little evidence that their officers drove them forward into combat at the points of their swords. Similarly, while the men received generous alcohol rations to alleviate the arduousness of field service (when this was practical), British commanders did not commonly buoy up their spirits before action by issuing additional rations. In October 1776 Lieutenant Loftus Cliffe quipped that the affair at Harlem Heights had presented, "an opportunity of showing the difference of British and American *spirit*. Every one of the enemy's killed and wounded stunk infamously of rum. Their canteens still contained the remains of sheer spirits, [and] even their officers were in this manner urged on; when ours . . . had not, I dare say, drank their allowance of grog, which is four waters to a good deal less than half a pint of rum."[4] In fact throughout the war, British and German combatants frequently encountered intoxicated rebel troops in combat.[5]

## Esprit de Corps

To explain what kept the redcoats in the ranks and steeled them in combat, Frey points to what she calls their "corporate identity." In short, the paternalistic relationships between company officers and their men, and the ties of friendship and kinship that bound the rank and file, made a regiment a tight-knit, closed community. Over years of service the soldier developed a powerful sense of belonging to this community, which was further fostered, and expressed most visibly, by the regiment's colors and by the distinctions in dress that set it aside from other units.[6]

It is possible to raise some queries to Frey's thesis. First, eighteenth-century Britain's itinerant line cavalry and infantry corps did not possess the long-standing traditions and distinctions that are such a key ingredient of the regimental identities of their modern successors. In 1775 few of the seventy line infantry regiments had existed for more than a century, and none of the "youngest" twenty-one corps was more than twenty years old.[7] Hence regimental identity in most cases did not extend much beyond a number in the line (marked on the colors and on the uniform buttons), one of a handful of different-facing colors, and a unique pattern on the men's coat lace. Moreover, even the visible manifestations of regimental identity can be overdrawn. Even if historians have not exaggerated the reverence with which the regimental colors were viewed, only a minority of corps emblazoned theirs with distinctive devices, and "battle honors" did not exist.[8] Similarly, regimental distinctions in clothing and equipment (Highland kilts and broadswords; grenadier caps and hangers) did not always survive the service modifications that appear to have been common even before the troops took to the field in America.[9]

A more serious objection to Frey's thesis is that, as John Houlding has shown, for much of the time regiments simply did not exist as stable communities. First, line regiments in Britain and Ireland spent a majority of their time dispersed, supporting the civil power and the revenue service.[10] Second, one must not underestimate the high turnover in personnel, particularly in wartime. In the case of the officers, this was due to death, retirement, and especially promotion;[11] in the case of the enlisted men, the causes were principally death, discharge, desertion, and drafting (the transfer of rank and file from one corps to another, especially before a battalion left for or returned from foreign service).[12]

Table 2 contains a breakdown of the enlisted men of ten sample regiments at their last reviews in 1774–75 before they departed for service in America.[13] Although four-fifths of these men had spent at least three years with their regiments, and one quarter had been with them for ten years or more, over a fifth were young and inexperienced soldiers with less than the three years' peacetime service that eighteenth-century observers believed was necessary to produce a competent infantryman.[14] Moreover, the fact that these units absorbed numbers of recruits and drafts before their departure and during their service in America means that the proportion of younger soldiers in the ranks would have been higher than these reports indicate. For example, while the 33rd Regiment mustered 380 and 385 enlisted men when reviewed in 1774 and 1775, when it arrived in America in

Table 2. Number of enlisted men by years of service in ten sample regiments at their last reviews before embarkation for America.

| Regiment (date of review) | 1 or less | 2 | 3 | 4 | 5–9 | 10–14 | 15–19 | 20+ | Total enlisted men |
|---|---|---|---|---|---|---|---|---|---|
| 4th (7 April 1774) | 66 (15.6) | 32 (7.6) | 36 (8.5) | 30 (7.1) | 129 (30.6) | 75 (17.8) | 36 (8.5) | 18 (4.3) | 422 |
| 63rd (14 May 1774) | 40 (10.5) | 20 (5.3) | 56 (14.7) | 47 (12.4) | 107 (28.2) | 13 (3.4) | 81 (21.3) | 16 (4.2) | 380 |
| 49th (25 July 1774) | 57 (14.0) | 19 (4.7) | 17 (4.2) | 81 (20.0) | 102 (25.1) | 24 (5.9) | 53 (13.1) | 53 (13.1) | 406 |
| 55th (May 1775) | 31 (7.8) | 25 (6.3) | 28 (7.0) | 12 (3.0) | 183 (45.8) | 51 (12.8) | 22 (5.5) | 48 (12.0) | 400 |
| 46th (15 May 1775) | 39 (9.9) | 45 (11.5) | 27 (6.9) | 26 (6.6) | 208 (52.9) | 8 (2.0) | 17 (4.3) | 23 (5.9) | 393 |
| 42nd (30 May 1775) | 23 (6.1) | 44 (11.6) | 19 (5.0) | 33 (8.7) | 160 (42.3) | 39 (10.3) | 41 (10.8) | 19 (5.0) | 378 |
| 27th (7 June 1775) | 51 (13.6) | 24 (6.4) | 37 (9.9) | 35 (9.4) | 160 (42.8) | 11 (2.9) | 8 (2.1) | 48 (12.8) | 374 |
| 17th (9 June 1775) | 54 (13.5) | 24 (6.0) | 26 (6.5) | 40 (10.0) | 210 (52.5) | 7 (1.8) | 14 (3.5) | 25 (6.3) | 400 |
| 9th (17 July 1775) | 70 (18.0) | 59 (15.2) | 36 (9.3) | 77 (19.8) | 81 (20.8) | 7 (1.8) | 23 (5.9) | 36 (9.3) | 389 |
| 33rd (17 July 1775) | 44 (11.6) | 23 (6.1) | 50 (13.2) | 26 (6.8) | 147 (38.7) | 17 (4.5) | 65 (17.1) | 8 (2.1) | 380 |

Note: Numbers in parentheses indicate percentages of the regiment's total enlisted men.

1776, its numbers had increased by almost 100. Most spectacular was the growth of the 42nd Regiment, which swelled from less than 400 enlisted men in May 1775 to more than 1,000 the next year.[15] In short, the thirty-year-old veteran of ten years' service that Frey paints as the "typical" British common soldier of this period was not necessarily representative of the redcoats who fought in America.[16]

Despite these qualifications, Frey's judgment that regimental esprit was most firmly rooted in the human relationships within a corps is essentially sound. At one level was the relationship between regimental officers and their men. Some historians have characterized the former as remote and chilly figures.[17] Yet it is likely that the nature of this relationship differed from company to company and that the conditions of active service significantly altered its dynamics.

One factor that lends some weight to the idea that a paternalistic relationship existed between at least some officers and their men was that the proclivity of eighteenth-century common soldiers for amazingly irrational and irresponsible acts necessitated constant supervision.[18] There are numerous examples of British soldiers in America having indulged in this kind of behavior. The rebel Dr. Benjamin Rush reported in October 1777 of his visit to Howe's army: "One of their officers, a subaltern, observed to me that his soldiers were infants that required constant attendance, and said as a proof of it that although they had blankets tied to their backs, yet such was their laziness that they would sleep in the dew and cold without them rather than have the trouble of untying and opening them. He said his business every night before he slept was to see that no soldier in his company laid down without a blanket."[19] In another striking case, days after the British capture of Charleston in May 1780, idle soldiers stupidly cast armfuls of loaded muskets into a magazine, causing a massive explosion that razed part of the city.[20] Similarly, days before the battle of Guilford Courthouse, when rebel dragoons captured Private John Robert Shaw of the 33rd Regiment and another equally famished man of the 23rd Regiment who had strayed from camp in search of food, Shaw's companion simply burst into tears.[21]

This naivety was probably an important factor in the "filial" loyalty that some redcoats displayed toward their officers. This was especially the case when the latter found themselves in difficulty. At Lake Champlain in September 1777, when rebel raiders seized a party under the command of Ensign Thomas Hughes, his men offered to carry his few items of baggage on their rigorous trek through the wilderness into captivity. Hughes recorded his pride: "I am happy to say they were all so honest, that I collected them all after two weeks march through the country."[22] This kind of devotion was most powerfully expressed, however, when popular officers were killed. According to one Boston loyalist, at the battle of Bunker Hill, when the wounded Marine lieutenant Thomas Pitcairn heard that his father, Major John Pitcairn, had fallen, "he cried out, 'I have lost my father'; immediately the corps returned, 'We have lost our father.' "[23] Likewise, if an inaccurate report that the Queen's Rangers' beloved commandant had been killed during a raid into New Jersey in October 1779 provoked grief throughout the corps, the subsequent news of Simcoe's safety in captivity provoked equally profound joy.[24] In the heat of action, it was possible for this kind of grief quickly to transform into rage. To this, in part, Tarleton later attributed the heaviness of the rebel casualties at the affair at the Waxhaws, where the overturning of his horse by the rebel volley produced "a report amongst the [British Legion] cavalry, that they had lost their commanding officer, which stimulated the soldiers to a vindictive asperity not easily restrained."[25]

As in the cases above, common soldiers appear to have become particularly attached to officers who took obvious pains over their welfare. An example of this was the way in which the remaining enlisted men of the Convention Army reacted to their separation from their officers at Lancaster, Pennsylvania, after nearly four years of shared captivity. One of those officers was Ensign Thomas Anburey, and his later description of the event is such a powerful reflection of the bonds that could develop between officers and men that it deserves to be reproduced at length:

> The sight was too deeply affecting, and we hastened from the spot. Could you have seen the faces of duty, respect, love and despair, you would carry the remembrance to the grave. It was the parting of child and parent, the separation of soul and body. It effected that which the united force of inclement seasons, hunger and thirst, incessant barbarity, adverse fortune, and American insults heaped together, could never have effected—it drew tears from the eyes of veterans, who

would rather have shed their blood. As far as sounds could convey, we heard a reiteration of "God bless your Honors." It was such a scene as must leave an everlasting impression on the mind. To behold so many men, who had bravely fought by our side, who in all their sufferings looked up to us for protection, forced from us into a prison; where, experiencing every severity, perhaps famishing for want of food, and ready to perish with cold, they had no one to look up to for redress, and little to expect from the humanity of Americans.[26]

While the conditions that the captive Convention Army encountered were admittedly atypical, the parental concern that Anburey and his fellow officers seem to have demonstrated for their men's wellbeing was not. As Stephen Conway has pointed out, one phenomenon that badly damaged British fortunes in the struggle for American "hearts and minds" was the manner in which many company officers seem to have turned a blind eye to their men's transgressions against the populace in order to protect the offenders from the army's brutal sanctions.[27]

The diary of Highland officer John Peebles also sheds light on the paternalistic relationship that existed between at least some officers and their men. In May 1780, during the siege of Charleston, Peebles recorded his remorse at having knocked down a soldier in his company on parade. Although he felt the man had deserved the blow for his insistent denials of his obvious drunkenness, Peebles admitted, "I am sorry for it, for we should never punish a soldier in a passion."[28] In February 1782, having sold his captaincy, Peebles made a parting address to his grenadier company before leaving New York for Britain:

Royal Highland Grenadiers, I am sorry that I am going soon to leave you; in doing which I very much regret my leaving so respectable a regiment and corps as that to which I belong, and the company I have the honor to command, with whom I have served so long with satisfaction and pleasure to myself. If any of you has any claims or demands on me as your captain, I shall remain here for some days yet, and will readily listen to them and satisfy them with justice. And as I intend to take the first opportunity of going home to Scotland, if you have any letters to send, or anything that I can do for you there, I will do it with pleasure. And Gentlemen, I earnestly hope that you will always preserve that good name you are so justly possessed of, whether in quarters or the field. And in all your future services I sincerely wish you all that honor, success and happiness which your merit and good behavior so well deserves.

Peebles's moving address clearly conveys his fatherly pride in, and concern for the welfare of, his grenadiers. His further comments demonstrate that his sentiments were genuine and, indeed, reciprocated: "I could hardly make an end of this little speech, my voice faltered, and my knees shook under me. I was glad to get into my room where my heart swelled at the thoughts of it. I saw the poor fellows were affected too—I ordered them five gallons of rum to make a drink of grog in the evening."[29]

Whether or not the relationship between officers and their men was commonly marked by paternalism, bonds of comradeship undoubtedly developed between the enlisted men, particularly within the mess or tent group, the nearest thing to what, in modern military parlance, is known as the vital "primary group."[30] Eighteenth-century commentators were well aware that men from small, close-knit village communities often experienced shock and depression when they were first thrust into the unfamiliar world of their new regiments.[31] To obviate this feeling of dislocation, military writer Captain Bennett Cuthbertson advised commanding officers to keep associates together when they enlisted rather than to allocate recruits between the various companies by lot, "as nothing binds them more strongly to the service, than having their friends and relations about them, employed in the same pursuits."[32] How commonly this happened is difficult to say. Interestingly, when Private Thomas Sullivan and his fellow recruits joined the various companies of the 49th Regiment at Cork in 1775, he noted in his journal that he was separated from his friend.[33]

If commanding officers did not invariably heed Cuthbertson's advice, the importance of comradeship in the ranks was well understood. Its benefits are powerfully conveyed in an instruction that Major Patrick Ferguson issued to his Provincial corps, the American Volunteers, with which he arrived at Savannah in January 1780:

It is recommended to the officers to promote among the soldiers of the several detachments a free choice of comrades, who ought never to be separated when it can be avoided; but [who instead should] always ... compose one file, to assist and defend each other, in action; ... to share in hardships as well as in danger for their mutual advantage and relief; to sleep and mess together; to take care of each other in sickness, and of one another's arms and necessaries during absence. Three of these files, if afterwards so [fused] into one mess, would at all times easily rally together and stand by each other, so as to add much to their own safety and increase the strength of the detachment. This fellowship will naturally be agreeable to men of good disposition and much increase their confidence in action. The man who at any time behaves unfaithfully by his comrade must be despised, and he who abandon[s] his friend in danger [must] become infamous.[34]

As his last sentence indicates, the Scotsman was particularly keen to harness what modern military psychologists have identified as perhaps the most powerful influence on soldiers' behavior (and indeed, sometimes the cause of their misbehavior) both in and out of combat: the fact that the members of the primary group were anxious not to appear to each other in a contemptible light. In 1777 another officer and military writer, Captain Thomas Simes, elaborated on this theme. Simes pointed out that, in the event of an amphibious landing, the battalion companies of a corps might be called upon to support its flank companies while the latter pushed forward to pursue the retreating enemy: "Those [grenadiers and light infantrymen] being chosen men are attentive to their behavior, and the praises and reproaches which each man has to expect from witnesses from [sic, with] whom he is to pass his life, are powerful inducements to those [men] of the battalion [companies] to follow their example. They dread having reason to blush at their conduct before a comrade, and in some measure it is this salutary dread that constitutes what we term the spirit of corps, which preserves and cherishes the courage of a soldier."[35] Such moral forces must inevitably have been proportionally stronger in those corps where men served together for years at a time. As discussed below, at least during the early years of the American War, this gave the British an inherent advantage because of the short-service enlistment terms on which the rebels' military forces tended to rely.

One factor that fostered a sense of either belonging or alienation within a corps was regional identity. While it was common for the

English, Scottish, Irish, or Welsh officers and men to congregate with their peers in other corps to celebrate their own saints' days, such bonds were particularly useful if they united the entire regiment.[36] Such was the case with the Volunteers of Ireland, who observed St. Patrick's Day in 1780 with a belligerent new regimental song that celebrated the men's Irishness.[37] But the case for recruiting along regional lines went further than the stimulation of ethnic chauvinism. Military commentators like Captain Cuthbertson believed that recruiting along county lines made it easier to entice men into the ranks: "Regiments, which confine themselves to particular counties, have generally the best success; young men being most desirous of enlisting into a corps, where they are certain of meeting many countrymen, and perhaps relations. Besides, it is a spur towards rallying their ambition, to see some of their friends, who probably enlisted only a few years before, return among them in the character of non-commission-officers, or sometimes in a higher station."[38] Similarly, one anonymous pamphleteer asserted in 1775 that, while the Irish and Highlanders alike were eager to serve "provided they go in bands of their countrymen . . . the report of every recruiting sergeant will show how few of either country can be prevailed on to enlist in old regiments, where they are strangers to all, and all are strangers to them."[39]

One product of regional recruitment was the rivalry that developed between the various regiments. For example, one officer later recalled the "feeling of jealousy" between the 76th Regiment ("MacDonnell's Highlanders") and 80th Regiment ("Royal Edinburgh Volunteers") in America, which only began to subside in 1780 once "[t]he Highlanders had made great progress in acquiring the English language."[40] Yet this rivalry potentially had beneficial effects. The aforementioned pamphleteer argued that, should the army adopt the policy of regional recruitment, "regiment would then vie with regiment in action to preserve its distinction."[41] In fact, in November 1777 one French officer in rebel service opined that one of the great strengths of Howe's army was that it was "composed of English, Scotch, Irish, and German corps" and therefore "full of a spirit of emulation."[42]

During annual regimental reviews, data was compiled on the ethnic makeup of the officers and enlisted men, expressed as English (including Welsh), Scottish, Irish, or foreign. This information shows that certain regiments tended deliberately to target their recruitment in particular areas, including all Highland and some Lowland regiments and some of the "New Corps" that appeared from 1777.[43] In America the Volunteers of Ireland was another example, raised in 1778 specifically to leech Irishmen from the Continental Army.[44] Moreover, some regiments were clearly using particular areas as core recruiting grounds long before they received official county designations.[45] One example was the 33rd Regiment, for which in the summer of 1782 Cornwallis obtained the title of the "West Riding Regiment" because "the 33rd Regiment of Infantry has always recruited in the West Riding of Yorkshire, and has a very good interest and the general good will of the people in that part of the country."[46] John Robert Shaw, a Bradford lad who enlisted in Leeds in 1777, experienced this goodwill firsthand when he marched to London. There he encountered "a Yorkshireman . . . who made it a constant rule to treat all the Yorkshire recruits enlisted for the 33rd Regiment, having himself been an old soldier, and served the King in that regiment formerly in Flanders."[47]

But in most cases neither the territorial titles that a few corps retained as a relic of their original foundation nor the country designations that they received in 1782 signified the composition of the personnel. For example, when the 27th Regiment ("Enniskillings") was reviewed in 1775, twenty-five of the thirty officers, but only 175 of the 374 enlisted men, were listed as Irish.[48] Similarly, when the 12th Regiment ( "East Suffolk") was ordered in 1787 to provide drafts for corps destined for India, Colonel Thomas Trigge protested on the grounds that this would alienate opinion in the regiment's well-established recruiting grounds—Yorkshire and Lancashire.[49] Furthermore, anyone who enlisted in Britain with the additional company of a unit that was on foreign service had no guarantee he would join that regiment, for recruits who arrived in America were frequently "sold" to other corps if it was not convenient to forward them.[50]

While there were obstacles in the way of the development of what Frey called a regiment's corporate identity, it is undeniable that some officers incited some soldiers to greater efforts in combat in America by appealing directly to their esprit de corps. One of the best examples of this occurred at the battle of Camden, according to the testimony of one of the officers of the Volunteers of Ireland: "The enemy . . . threw in horrid showers of grape. . . . I commanded a company, and lost more than half the number I took into the field, and the company next [to] me lost two-thirds. For half an hour the event was doubtful. . . . Our regiment was amazingly incited by Lord Cornwallis, who came up to them with great coolness, in the midst of a heavier fire than the oldest soldier remembers, and called out, 'Volunteers of Ireland, you are fine fellows! Charge the rascals—By heaven, you behave nobly!' At that time we wanted something to encourage us."[51] Another well-known instance occurred at Guilford Courthouse, where Lieutenant Colonel James Webster (of the 33rd Regiment) reanimated the 23rd Regiment's faltering advance by riding out to its front and calling out "with more than even his usual commanding voice (which was well known to his brigade) '*Come on, my brave Fusiliers.*' "[52]

In some cases where officers made battlefield appeals to battalions' esprit, they were clearly invoking the units' real or perceived superior military effectiveness relative to other corps. After the sterling performance of the sharp-eyed German *Jäger* during the siege of Charleston, Captain Johann Hinrichs reported with pride that "[l]aughing eyes now beam upon us, and an incessant cheer is our reward whenever a Briton sees the greencoats."[53] Likewise, when Cornwallis's shrunken, hard-bitten army arrived at Petersburg in May 1781 from the grueling campaigns in the Carolinas, one officer with Brigadier General Arnold's force recorded, "Words can ill describe the admiration in which this band of heroes was held by the two Scotch regiments, and even by the battalions of light infantry—the elite of the army, who had fought and generally led in every action during the war."[54]

If successful service was the most striking manifestation of a battalion's military effectiveness, its regular conduct and smartness was another. When Corporal Roger Lamb of the 9th Regiment encountered the 33rd Regiment in Dublin in early 1775, the Irishman was deeply impressed by its "discipline and military appearance": "The men mounted guard in a superior style. Each sentinel, during the two hours he remained on his post, continued always in motion, and could not walk less than seven miles in that time. The soldier was ever alert and alive in attention; when on duty—all eye—all ear. Even in the sentry box, which the sentinel never entered unless when it rained, he was not allowed to keep the palm of his hand carelessly on the muzzle of his firelock, which, if the piece were loaded, was considered dangerous and always an awkward attitude for the soldier. This soldierly character they always maintained while they served in North America." Lamb added that in America the 33rd and 23rd Regiments (the latter of which—significantly—he chose to join in 1778) "furnished an example for cleanliness, martial spirit, and good behavior," a circumstance he ascribed to "the care and attention of their colonels, who were unremitting in trying to make their men excel in discipline, duty, and general propriety of conduct."[55]

Like the commanding officers of the 23rd and 33rd Regiments, Brigadier General Pattison strove to maintain the "regularity of discipline and military appearance" of the Royal Artillery in America. On 1 January 1778 he reminded the regiment's men at Philadelphia of the need "to render their behavior as much superior as possible as their pay to that of other corps," a state of affairs that, he added, "has for many years distinguished in a peculiar manner the Royal Regiment of Artillery." Pattison warned the men that to achieve this goal, he was resolved "to punish all neglects of duty, irregularity and slovenly, unsoldierlike [sic] behavior and appearance, which the good of the service requires."[56] In August 1780, before (the by then) Major General Pattison returned to Britain, he wrote to the remaining senior officer of his own 4th Battalion in America: "I trust that the *esprit de corps* now so happily prevailing will not suffer any relaxation of that discipline . . . necessary to support the honor and credit of it . . . and that I shall have the pleasure on rejoining the corps to find it in a state not less respectable than when I quit."[57]

Pattison's desire to uphold the Royal Artillery's creditable reputation emphasizes the fact that esprit de corps has historically been most potent within supposed elite units. As discussed in chapter 3, the composite flank battalions were considered the "flower" of the British Army in America; the evidence concerning their powerful esprit de corps is therefore particularly strong. After the war Martin Hunter (a light company officer in America) touched on the relationship between these elite units in some rather extraordinary comments on his men's superior plundering skills: "The 52nd Light Infantry were famous *providers*. They were good hands at a grab. Grab was a favorite expression among the light infantry, and meant any plunder taken by force; a lob, when you got it without any opposition. And I am very certain there never was a more expert set than the light infantry at either grab, lob, or gutting a house. The grenadiers used to call us their *children*, and when we got more plunder than we wanted we always supplied our *fathers*."[58] Captain George Harris used precisely the same familial metaphor in describing the emergency concentration of the flank battalions in New Jersey after the Trenton disaster. Harris was clearly moved by the light infantry's reaction when they found themselves joined by his grenadiers: "You would have felt too much to be able to express your feelings, on seeing with what a warmth of friendship our *children* (as we call the light infantry) welcomed us: one and all crying, 'Let them [i.e., the rebels] come!' 'Lead us to them, we are sure of being supported!' It gave me a pleasure too fine to attempt expressing; and if you see a stain on the paper, pray place the drops to the right motive, for the tears flowed even at the thought, so that I could not stop them."[59]

While the flank battalions did not possess regimental colors, their esprit de corps was stimulated by certain other distinctions. This was particularly true of the grenadiers, who sported expensive fur caps (worn occasionally in action as well as on ceremonial occasions[60]) and whose two fifers and two drummers per company had at their disposal two of the most celebrated marches in musical history, "The Grenadiers' March" and "The British Grenadiers."[61] As an impressed Lieutenant Martin Hunter witnessed, these symbols proved a powerful spur to the grenadiers' motivation when Cornwallis's division deployed for the attack at Brandywine: "It was here, before we attacked General Washington, that [Lieutenant] Colonel [William] Medows made the famous speech to the 1st Battalion of Grenadiers, which he commanded: 'Grenadiers, put on your caps; for damned fighting and drinking I'll match you against the world.' We marched to the attack in two columns, the grenadiers at the head of one, playing 'The Grenadiers' March,' and the light infantry at the head of the other."[62] Lieutenant William Hale, with the 2nd Battalion of Grenadiers, was electrified by the scene: "Nothing could be more dreadfully pleasing than the line moving on to the attack . . . believe me I would not exchange those three minutes of rapture to avoid ten thousand times the danger."[63]

Not surprisingly, the best-illustrated examples of senior officers having appealed in combat to their troops' esprit de corps concern the flank battalions. At Germantown, when the 2nd Battalion of Light Infantry (on outpost duty at the northern end of the town) was forced to withdraw in the face of Washington's surprise attack, Lieutenant Hunter witnessed how Howe attempted to stem the disorderly withdrawal of the light infantrymen ("always his favorites," as Hunter proudly added). As Howe rode up, "seeing the battalion all broke, he got into a great passion, and exclaimed, 'For shame, Light Infantry! I never saw you retreat before. Form! Form! It is only a scouting party.'" The general's reproof evidently stung Hunter and his brother officers, who took some satisfaction when three rebel columns promptly emerged from the fog and disabused Howe of his error by loosing a shower of grape in his direction: "I think I never saw people enjoy a discharge of grape before, but really all the officers of the 2nd Battalion appeared pleased to see the enemy make such an appearance and to hear the grape rattle about the commander-in-chief's ears, after he had accused us of having run away from a scouting party."[64]

While Lieutenant Loftus Cliffe was also surprised to see the light infantrymen retiring precipitately at Germantown despite their officers' calls to "stop, stop," such appeals to the flank battalions' esprit de corps generally appear to have been successful.[65] Captain John Money later testified that, when some men from Major John Acland's grenadier battalion broke ranks in panic during the hard-pressed withdrawal from Bemis Heights, they recovered themselves when some passing aides de camp called out to them "for shame."[66] A similar incident occurred on 11 October 1777, during operations against the rebel Delaware River forts. When exaggerated reports of a rebel sally against neighboring Carpenters Island panicked Major John Vattas of the 10th Regiment into ordering the evacuation of Province Island, his more resolute German subordinate, Lieutenant Friedrich von Berdot, failed to convince Vattas's frantically rowing hatmen to return to their posts by threatening to order his Hessian grenadiers to fire into the boats. Strikingly, however, Berdot succeeded in convincing two boatloads of British grenadiers (who were already halfway across the river) to return by pleading with them "to think of the insult they were inflicting on a corps which had won so much glory in the last campaign and whose name alone was formidable to the enemy."[67]

### Experience

Contrary to American mythology, the British battalions that attempted to subjugate the rebellion were not legions of perfectly drilled automata. As evidenced in the last section, a large proportion of men within each corps were recruits with limited service. Nor should one assume that the core of long-serving men were expert soldiers. As John Houlding has shown, infantry recruits of this era underwent an initial (or "material") period of training, during which they were taught military posture, elementary evolutions, marching, and weapons handling. In theory, once they were deemed "fit for the ranks," they joined their respective companies for ongoing (or "mechanical") drill. This comprised four main elements: the "manual exercise" and "platoon exercise" (basic training), and the "firings" and the "maneuvers" (advanced training).[68] In reality, because the army's peacetime civil commitments in Britain and Ireland commonly necessitated the wide dispersal of a regiment, training was largely constrained to those elements that could be practiced in smaller concentrations—in other words, a stultifying repetition of basic training. Save for a few weeks every year during the review season, it was only in wartime that advanced training—which could not be carried out profitably without the concentration of the regiment—was conducted really effectively and intensively in encampments at home and (more commonly) in the field abroad.[69] In America, while before the outbreak of the rebellion the battalions of the Boston garrison were able to exercise on the Common as often as their commanding officers thought proper, during the course of the war, Crown troops remained under similar training constraints to those that existed in peacetime in Britain and Ireland.[70] Every year in April and May, in preparation for the coming campaigning season, battalions commonly went out up to four times a week for two or three hours in the morning to maneuver or to fire. But weather, garrison duties, and operations in the field almost entirely precluded advanced training outside of these two months.[71]

The numbers of young and inexperienced soldiers in the ranks exacerbated training deficiencies, particularly during the war's early campaigns. In November 1775 Howe lamented, "this army, though complete in the spring, must have between 6 and 7000 recruits and of the worst kind, if chiefly composed of Irish Roman Catholics, [who are] certain to desert if put to hard work, and [who are] from their ignorance of arms not entitled to the smallest confidence as soldiers."[72] Recruits like Irishman Private Thomas Sullivan had to be given a crash course in initial and basic training in the weeks before their regiments departed for America.[73] Those who, like Private John Robert Shaw, joined their regiments in the colonies often had to be further "disciplined" by drill sergeants before they were allowed into the ranks.[74] For example, on Manhattan in October 1776, Lieutenant

Colonel Thomas Musgrave ordered that the 40th Regiment's recently arrived recruits exercise daily, weather permitting, until they were perfect in the rudiments of drill. Three weeks later he instructed: "As the duty of the battalion has become very easy, the awkward men and undisciplined recruits are to do no more duty with arms till they are more perfect in the essential part of the exercise and marching, etc.; to effect which, they are to be out three times a day if the weather permits under the inspection of [the] adjutant and drilled by Sergeants Benson and Parrot, who are to be struck off other duties till further orders. When the battalion parades, the recruits are to form on left of the whole, and the drill sergeants are to attend to their behavior in every respect."[75] Likewise, when 300 recruits joined their regiments in the "Canadian army" early in September 1777, Burgoyne ordered that they should undergo intensive drill and target practice for four hours per day to prepare them for the impending clash with Gates's command.[76]

Despite these efforts, there must always have been significant numbers of inadequately trained men in the ranks. As one example of this, Corporal Thomas Sullivan noted approvingly after the battle of Long Island, "The 23rd Regiment signalized themselves in this action, and showed such a good example, that undisciplined recruits among them that had not even received their regimentals fought with great courage."[77] These raw fusiliers were not the only half-trained redcoats who found themselves thrown into combat. When the men of the newly raised 71st Regiment ("Fraser's Highlanders") embarked at Greenock in April 1776, Lieutenant John Peebles of the 42nd ("Royal Highland") Regiment described them as "stout, raw and irregular."[78] Although (as one early historian of the army's Highland corps later pointed out) these men went to America in 1776 "without any training, except what they got on board the transport from non-commissioned officers, nearly as ignorant as themselves," the young Highlanders almost immediately went into action at Long Island. Thereafter, "[s]uch, indeed, were the constant and active duties, and incessant marching, actions, and changes of quarters of the 71st, that little time could be spared; and, therefore, little attempt was made to give them the polish of parade discipline till the third year of the war. Field discipline, and forcing their enemy to fly wherever they met him . . . they understood perfectly."[79] Those corps, like the Queen's Rangers, that shouldered a disproportionate share of the army's operational workload certainly rubbed along without "the polish of parade discipline." As Simcoe later explained: "A light corps, augmented as that of the Queen's Rangers was, and employed on the duties of an outpost, had no opportunity of being instructed in the general discipline of the army, nor indeed was it very necessary. The most important duties, those of vigilance, activity, and patience of fatigue, were best learnt in the field. A few motions of the manual exercise were thought sufficient. They were carefully instructed in those of firing, but above all, attention was paid to inculcate the use of the bayonet, and a total reliance on that weapon." Indeed, Simcoe added that it was not until August 1779 that "the officers commanding grand-divisions were ordered to make their men perfect in the whole of the manual exercise."[80]

Experience of peacetime soldiering was one thing, but (as Sir William Erskine put it before going to America in 1776), "nothing will make a soldier but service, and a damned deal of it too."[81] In particular, there was no substitute for combat experience. Because light troops performed the bulk of the scouting and security duties that generated most of the low-intensity contact with the enemy, it was possible for the infantry of the line to go through an entire campaign without coming directly under fire. This insulation against immediate physical danger was rudely shattered when armies or detachments engaged in earnest. Conventional linear-style combat was a profoundly stressful experience. Decades afterward, Roger Lamb could still vividly recall the horrifying sights (and probably also the ear-piercing sounds and gut-wrenching smells) of his second action as a young corporal with the 9th Regiment at Fort Anne in July 1777: "I had not been there five minutes when Lieutenant [Richard] Westrop, who was by my side, was shot through the heart. A few minutes after, a man a short distance upon my left received a ball in his forehead, which took off the roof of his scull! He reeled round, turned up his eyes, muttered some words, and fell dead at my feet!"[82]

If observers commonly expressed surprise when unseasoned troops responded well to the awful test of combat,[83] they were more than willing to ascribe reverses to the inexperience of untested recruits.[84] It is important to realize that the vast majority of the redcoats in America at the outbreak of the rebellion, or who arrived for the offensives of 1776, had never heard a shot fired in anger. Along with shortcomings in their training, this factor almost certainly explains the lack of discipline that the redcoats sometimes exhibited in combat early in the war, which caused one surprised rebel eyewitness to record of skirmishing that followed the Pell's Point landing, "I saw [in the British troops] as great irregularity, almost, as in a militia; they would come out from their body and fire single guns."[85]

Predictably, the best evidence for this phenomenon concerns the opening clashes of the conflict. Lieutenant John Barker recorded that, after Major John Pitcairn's light infantry excitedly swept the militiamen from Lexington Green, the officers experienced difficulty in reforming them because "the men were so wild they could hear no orders." Of the return march from Concord, he judged that "our soldiers . . . , although they showed no want of courage, yet were so wild and irregular, that there was no keeping them in any order; [and] by their eagerness and inattention they killed many of our own people."[86] Three days afterward Gage publicly rebuked the soldiers for their disorderliness: "As . . . the men in the late affair, though they behaved with much courage and spirit, showed great inattention and neglect to the commands of their officers (which, if they had observed, fewer of them would have been hurt), the General expects on any further occasion that they will behave with more discipline and in a more soldierlike manner."[87] In criticizing the redcoats' poor fire discipline and marksmanship during the return march, one flank company officer pointed out that the men lacked the "coolness and steadiness which distinguishes troops who have been inured to service" because "[m]ost of them were young soldiers who had never been in action." He added, "A good deal of this unsteady conduct may be attributed to the sudden and unexpected commencement of hostilities, and the too great eagerness of the soldiers in the first action of a war."[88] The same complaint was made by Lieutenant Richard Williams of the 23rd Regiment, who lamented that a friendly fire incident on 25 June 1775 during the siege of Boston had been caused by "the hurry and inattention natural to young troops; most of our regiment here being composed of recruits and drafts who, never having seen service, foolishly imagine that when danger is feared they secure themselves by discharging their muskets, with or without aim. . . . Theory is nothing but practice, and it requires one campaign, at least, to make a good soldier."[89]

But not everyone believed that recruits were such a liability in combat. Indeed, as Christopher Duffy has shown, eighteenth-century soldiers proved incapable of bearing the strain of battle if they were exposed to it too frequently—a phenomenon that contemporaries knew as "cannon fever."[90] Hence some commentators (like the afore-mentioned pamphleteer who argued in 1775 for the raising of "New Corps") asserted that "the fire of youth, the fire of emulation, the visions of preferment, even the spirits arising from novelty, [and] the inexperience of danger, all impel raw soldiers to exertions which vet-eran soldiers will shun if they can."[91] Johann Ewald later wrote of his experiences as a captain with the Hessian *Feldjägerkorps*, "The young people of sixteen to eighteen years of age . . . , since they did not yet know the dangers of war, were the ones who attacked best, and upon whom one could rely in critical circumstances."[92] He added of the corps' baptism of fire in America in October 1776, "My old sol-diers were the first who perceived our situation, and I was forsaken by many of them, but the young lads stood by me in the innocence of their hearts, and to them I owed the preservation of myself and my party."[93]

Nevertheless, like former redcoat Roger Lamb, most commenta-tors accepted that only "habit and the usage of fighting" was able to supply "coolness and self-possession in action" and thereby remedy what Lamb called the "confusion and lack of presence of mind [that] must attach to every young soldier":

> Men who are familiarized to danger, approach it without thinking, whereas troops unused to service apprehend danger where no danger exists. No doubt, before the commencement of a battle, a man, however he may class as a veteran, can-not fail to feel that his life hangs upon awful accident, and of course that natural instinct, if nothing else, which beats within us in anxiety for self-preservation, will cause a quick pulsation and agitate the breast. But the battle once begun, this anxious apprehension, which originates from the love of existence when we reflect in silence, is confounded and lost in the ardor and conflict of the engagement, wherein reflec-tion and thought suffer a temporary suspense, as much for the moment as if we were constituted without them.[94]

During the American War's early campaigns, the presence in the ranks of a small number of veterans of the Seven Years War facilitated the seasoning of the battalion's recruits.[95] For instance, when the 9th

Regiment came under fire at the battle of Trois-Rivières (8 June 1776), the old hands soothed the anxiety of those inexperienced men like Corporal Lamb: "This being the first skirmish I ever was engaged in, it really appeared to me to be a very serious matter, especially when the bullets came whistling by our ears. In order to encourage the young soldiers amongst us, some of the veterans who had been well used to this kind of work, said, 'there is no danger if you hear the sound of the bullet which is fired against you, you are safe, and after the first charge all your fears will be done away.' These remarks I found to be perfectly true many a time afterwards."[96] The proportion of seasoned soldiers in the ranks in America must have risen during the course of the war. Within the British armies in the South in 1780 and 1781, there was undoubtedly a hard core of veteran redcoats like Lamb—by then a sergeant in the 23rd Regiment—who were well accustomed to campaigning and combat and whose accumulated experience in turn facilitated the acclimatization of recruits to the demands of active service.

The existence of this hard core of veterans was particularly important because the development of a comparable group within the Continental Army was constrained by the short-service draft system that provided a significant proportion of its manpower.[97] Indeed, in a memorandum that he penned for Clinton in August 1778, Captain Patrick Ferguson judged that the redcoats' experience of several difficult campaigns offset the fact that Clinton's total forces were numerically weaker than those Howe had commanded. Although the army had lost some soldiers to sickness, Ferguson argued dispassionately that "it is only weeded of the weak men and will turn out as many to fight without having thousands of useless mouths to feed and a cumbersome hospital train to impede its movement." Furthermore, Clinton's 27,000 "seasoned" soldiers were "formed to service, accustomed to constant success, and confirmed by a long experience in the opinion that they have an enemy before them that will ever disappear at the gleam of their bayonets." Such physically tough and confident soldiers, Ferguson argued, could beat the same number of enemy troops as an unseasoned army of 40,000 men: "[E]very officer will allow it to be the strongest of the two, as its vigor and discipline would enable it to make more extensive and rapid movements, and to collect superior numbers at every point of attack. And from its numbers and healthfulness, it must subsist upon less and be in every respect much less encumbered." He concluded his argument with two striking points. First, field armies in America could not practically exceed 15,000 or 20,000 men. Second, considering that to date it had proven difficult to commit more than 5,000 men to action against the rebels at any one time, "all depends on the quality of the troops."[98]

Ferguson's assertion that the redcoats had become accustomed to victory leads to the last factor concerning combat experience: while the morale of inexperienced troops quickly collapsed in the event of military failure, they gained immeasurably from a successful taste of action.[99] This the redcoats enjoyed in abundance throughout the war. When Simcoe joined the Queen's Rangers as major-commandant, he found that the corps had grown enormously in confidence from its participation at Brandywine, despite the casualties it incurred there: "[I]f the loss of a great number of gallant officers and soldiers had been severely felt, the impression which that action had left upon their minds was of the highest advantage to the regiment: officers and soldiers became known to each other; they had been engaged in a more serious manner, and with greater disadvantages than they were likely again to meet with in the common chance of war; and having extricated themselves most gallantly from such a situation, they felt themselves invincible."[100]

### Antipathy for the Rebels

Eighteenth-century Englishmen were infamous for their xenophobia, which in America provoked Hessian captain Johann Hinrichs to execrate "the confounded pride and arrogant bearing of the English, who treat everyone that was not born on their ragamuffin island with contempt."[101] As Hinrichs's outburst suggests, the hearty English dislike of foreigners went hand in hand with a marked sense of self-assurance.[102] This conceit was not limited to the officer corps. Dr. Johnson believed that the ferocious courage in combat for which the redcoats were renowned proceeded from the Englishman's "want of subordination" and sense of individual worth: "they who complain, in peace, of the insolence of the populace, must remember, that their insolence in peace is bravery in war."[103] Edward Drewe, the disgraced ex-major of the 35th Regiment, made a similar observation after the American War, pointing to "the high-born spirit of the British soldiery," whom he described as "independent, [and] accustomed to the freedom of reasoning on the conduct of others, and of judging for themselves." He also claimed that they were motivated by "the love of fame, and their country."[104]

Self-assurance and xenophobia were seemingly key ingredients of the uncomplicated, chauvinistic patriotism that motivated some British officers and enlisted men. Although it is difficult to gauge the extent and depth of this patriotism (particularly within the ranks), it should be remembered that soldiers were regularly subject to rituals that were designed to reinforce their emotional attachment to King and country, as when the garrison at New York annually celebrated the sovereign's birthday by parading in their new clothing issues, loosing spectacular *feu de joie* and cheering.[105] There is evidence that these rituals were not without success. In 1781 Baroness Riedesel was struck by the stoicism and sense of duty displayed by the patients of a Crown hospital on Long Island: "When one would lament their fate, these good people would answer, 'We have fought for our King and are satisfied, and once we get back to Chelsea we shall be sufficiently rewarded!' "[106] In a similar fashion some British officers sought to motivate their men in combat by appealing directly to their national pride, as on two occasions when officers led forward their men at Brandywine and Monmouth Courthouse with the exhortations, "Come on, my Britons, the day is our own!" and "Come on my brave boys, for the honor of Great Britain!"[107] To judge from the journal of the siege of Penobscot (July–August 1779) by Sergeant William Lawrence of the Royal Artillery, such appeals would not have fallen on deaf ears. Lawrence recorded that the garrison returned the rebels' artillery fire "with the spirit of Britons," discharging their round-shot "with as good sulphur as Britons could give, and we hope they did proper execution." Elsewhere he wrote, "our picket behaved with the usual spirit of Britons"; the enemy's "vile intentions" to breach and storm the works were in vain, "as we was [sic] well lined with brave Britons"; and the garrison swiftly ejected the rebels from a foothold in the perimeter of the defenses "with the usual alertness of Britons."[108]

Another possible indicator of the uncomplicated patriotism motivating British soldiers in America was the number of them who ran the risk of close confinement or death by escaping rebel captivity and traversing sometimes hundreds of miles of hostile country to rejoin

Crown forces. Irishman Roger Lamb (who performed this feat twice, after he was captured at Saratoga and later at Yorktown) is the best known of these men. But Richard Sampson has positively identified more than 300 separate British escapees from the Convention Army who succeeded in rejoining Crown forces and has estimated that probably the majority of the 2,500 men who disappeared during captivity returned to the King's service at one time or another.[109] Indeed, so many escapees used enlistment in the rebels' military forces as a stepping stone to freedom that the resulting wastage of bounties, arms, and clothing prompted Washington in February 1778 to obtain a congressional resolution forbidding the further recruitment of British (but significantly, not German) deserters because of their (from his perspective) "treacherous disposition."[110]

What made so many British prisoners abscond? Clearly hardship, frustration, and mistreatment played an important role, as did the encouragement both of officers on the spot and of the high command at New York. According to Frey, regimental corporate identity provided an additional factor.[111] Yet this seems unlikely; the majority of the soldiers who made what, significantly, were styled "honorable desertions" from captivity to regain British lines were not rejoining their regiments and comrades but leaving them behind. Lamb himself is a good example: having escaped from the captive remnants of the 9th Regiment in New England, when he reached New York in November 1778 he enlisted in the 23rd Regiment and was promoted to sergeant. In short, a different kind of loyalty helped spur men like Lamb to risk their lives to rejoin British lines. From his perspective Lamb felt that to have accepted rebel inducements to desert "would amount to a dereliction of duty and his relationship with the old world, where he fondly hoped to cultivate the society of his early acquaintance."[112]

Concomitant with their patriotism was the hostile attitude of many British officers and men to the rebellion. Some historians have hunted for signs that Crown officers sympathized with the revolutionaries' "glorious cause."[113] In reality, as Stephen Conway has demonstrated, while there were a few conspicuous political malcontents, the majority of officers seem to have viewed the rebellion as an "unnatural" rejection of benevolent and lawful British authority.[114] Probably typical was the reaction of one who, when told by some local Quaker lads before the battle of Brandywine that Washington "was considered to be a good man," retorted "that he might be a good man, but he was most damnably misled to take up arms against his sovereign."[115] Nor should one imagine that many common soldiers viewed the revolutionary movement with much sympathy. Admittedly, after Irishman Thomas Sullivan successfully deserted from what he called the "English service" in June 1778, he recorded in his diary that since his arrival in America, he had yearned "to share the same freedom that America strove for" and that many of his comrades were "no less sensible of the oppression of many a family in the mother country than I was."[116] But Sullivan's ethnicity, his religious faith, his educated status, his grievance at his "ill-usage" in the army, and his marriage to an American woman in Philadelphia make it dangerous to generalize from his case.[117] In a similar fashion, whilst Burgoyne confided to the Secretary of the Southern Department some concern at the hesitation of some of the troops at Bunker Hill, he nevertheless was careful not "to convey any suspicion of backwardness in the cause of government among the soldiery, which ignorant people in England are apt to imagine."[118] Indeed, in Parliament in February 1776 Burgoyne firmly rejected an Opposition charge that the troops had misbehaved at that action because they disapproved of serving against the Americans.[119]

In fact British officers and enlisted men commonly expressed real hostility to the rebellion. While Sullivan may have had his own reservations, he nevertheless recorded soon after the battle of Bunker Hill that the British soldiery were "inveterate against the rebels, on account of their ambitious designs."[120] Indeed, both officers and men often lectured rebel captives on the badness of their cause and the impropriety of fighting against their King.[121] According to one anonymous correspondent, news of recent political developments in America (including the Declaration of Independence) outraged the men of the Brigade of Guards when it arrived at Staten Island in August 1776: "The Guards, on their arrival, were ordered to land and refresh themselves after a tedious voyage, but they desired to be led on directly to action, in resentment of the atrocious insults to their King and country. Their impatience was beyond expressing, when they were told of some indignities lately offered to the statue of their royal sovereign in New York."[122] Likewise, with Parliament's "Conciliatory Resolution" of 1778 in mind, Howe's Hessian aide de camp noted, "The common English soldiers are so angry about the Act of Parliament on non-taxation, etc., which is posted here that they tear down these proclamations during the night."[123]

The redcoats' antipathy for the rebels was rooted more strongly in other factors than political conservatism. Here again emerges the overweening national pride that consistently seduced eighteenth-century British soldiers and statesmen into underestimating the colonists. This scorn derived partly from the recollection of the unimpressive Provincial levies that served alongside British regulars during the French and Indian War, who Major General James Wolfe had blasted in one of his delightfully thunderous diatribes as "the dirtiest, most contemptible, cowardly dogs that you can conceive. There is no depending upon them in action. They fall down dead in their own dirt and desert by battalions, officers and all."[124] This kind of disdain for colonial military abilities was very much in evidence during the American War. Typical was Captain Francis Lord Rawdon's supercilious dismissal of the ragtag rebel army encamped around Boston in January 1776: "Indeed, I hope that we shall soon have done with these scoundrels, for one only dirties one's fingers by meddling with them."[125] Such attitudes died hard. Even as Washington's army was marching southward to trap Cornwallis at Yorktown, a British contractor at New York warned that "the contempt every soldier has for an American is not the smallest. They cannot possibly believe that any good quality can exist among them."[126]

Again, such opinions were by no means confined to British officers. As the rebel prisoners from Fort Washington were being marched to New York, one British sergeant confidently assured captive John Adlum that the war was near an end because nobody would henceforth join Washington's beaten army. When the militiaman retorted that British forces would finally be overwhelmed whenever they pressed inland and were separated from the fleet, "[t]he officer who was in front of the sergeant looked at me and smiled without saying anything, but I thought from the manner of his looking at me that he did not believe me. The sergeant said I was very much mistaken, and [that] he was sorry to see so young a lad as I appeared to be have such an opinion of the irresistible power of the British King, and that our fate was inevitable, for the next spring we would be a conquered people."[127]

Throughout the war, British commanders bolstered the troops' conviction of their martial supremacy over the despised rebels by lacing their general orders with colored reports of British successes. For example, after the repelling of Major General Sullivan's raid on Staten Island in August 1777, Clinton publicly thanked Brigadier General Campbell and the other officers and men of the 52nd Regiment, "who have so remarkably added to the numerous examples this war has produced, that no superiority of numbers can withstand Britons when they attack in earnest with the bayonet."[128] Of course, as the conflict dragged on, the gap in tactical proficiency between the contending forces narrowed significantly. Nevertheless, to the war's end what one British officer called "the flow of spirits and conscious superiority of our men" undoubtedly remained a potent asset in action.[129] As Simcoe put it, "The British soldier who thought himself superior, actually became so; and the ascendancy which he claimed was in many instances importantly admitted by his antagonists."[130]

One phenomenon that reveals the degree to which British soldiers of all ranks were convinced of their martial superiority over the rebels was the reluctance with which they accepted defeat. For example, as Captain Mathew Johnson disengaged the 46th Regiment's light company at the affair at Harlem Heights, "he had seven wounded, not one of whom would suffer themselves to be taken precipitately off, and some continued their fire after being severely wounded."[131] A similar scene occurred early in the battle of Germantown, when the signal was given for the embattled 2nd Battalion of Light Infantry to withdraw in the face of vastly superior attacking rebel forces. Martin Hunter, one of the battalion's lieutenants, later reflected, "This was the first time we had ever retreated from the Americans, and it was with great difficulty that we could prevail on the men to obey our orders."[132] Off the battlefield this phenomenon was just as conspicuous. According to Howe's Hessian aide de camp, when the army withdrew from New Brunswick to Perth Amboy on 22 June 1777, having failed to bring Washington to battle, "the passing troops . . . looked quite sullen because of the march back."[133] Out of Howe's sight, the redcoats vented their disappointment by firing houses along the way with a vindictiveness that their officers could not restrain.[134] One observer noted that the withdrawal "made our brave fellows almost gnaw their own flesh out of rage," and as the troops were ferried to Staten Island, they were filled with "mortification and resentment."[135]

Most striking of all, however, was the vexation that British troops exhibited when they were compelled to surrender. One rebel sergeant observed that the redcoats captured at Princeton "were a haughty, crabbed set of men, as they fully exhibited while prisoners, on their march to the country."[136] Significantly, in his account of the surrender of Burgoyne's army, Lieutenant Lord Francis Napier wrote that the rebel troops who lined the route that the "melancholy" redcoats followed on their way to lay down their arms "behaved with the greatest decency and propriety, not even a smile appearing in any of their countenances, which circumstance I really believe would not have happened had the case been reversed."[137] The best evidence for this phenomenon, however, concerns the surrender of Cornwallis's army at Yorktown. Unsurprisingly, the humiliation of defeat particularly affected the officers, who (as one New Jersey Continental officer gloated), "in general behaved like boys who had been whipped at school; some bit their lips, some pouted, others cried. Their round, broad-brimmed hats were well adapted to the occasion, hiding those faces they were ashamed to show. The foreign regiments made a much more military appearance, and the conduct of their officers was far more becoming men of fortitude."[138] Nevertheless, the common British soldiery also appeared conspicuously disgruntled. Allied onlookers reported that, as the resentful redcoats marched out of their shattered defenses, they appeared to have been drinking heavily; that they exhibited "disorderly and unsoldierly conduct, their step was irregular, and their ranks frequently broken"; that the rolling drums that accompanied them "beat as if they did not care how"; and that they "eyed the French with considerable malice depicted in their countenances."[139] According to the rebel Dr. James Thacher, "it was in the [surrender] field when they came to the last act of the drama, that the spirit and pride of the British soldier was put to the severest test, [and] here their mortification could not be concealed. Some of the platoon officers appeared to be exceedingly chagrined when giving the word 'ground arms,' and I am a witness that they performed this duty in a very unofficerlike manner, and that many of the soldiers manifested a sullen temper, throwing their arms on the pile with violence, as if determined to render them useless."[140] One of those British officers, Captain Lieutenant Samuel Graham, later wrote of the scene, "A corporal next to me shed tears, and, embracing his firelock, threw it down, saying, 'May you never get so good a master.' "[141] A French observer, Commissary Blanchard, similarly reported that "[t]he English displayed much arrogance and ill-humor during this melancholy ceremony; they particularly affected great contempt for the Americans." Although the Germans maintained discipline, "there was little order among the English, who were proud and arrogant" despite the fact that they had been "beaten and disarmed by peasants who were almost naked, whom they affected to despise and who, nevertheless, were their conquerors."[142]

It is significant that Cornwallis evaded the humiliation of surrendering personally to Washington at Yorktown by sending Brigadier General O'Hara in his stead and that the latter vainly attempted to deliver up his sword to the commander of the French forces, Lieutenant General Comte de Rochambeau.[143] Despite long-standing Franco-British rivalry, the animosity that British officers and men bore toward the American rebels was not mirrored by their feelings toward their French counterparts, whom Brigadier General William Medows pointedly described in orders to the reserve of Major General Grant's British expeditionary force on St. Lucia (all veterans of the American campaigns) in December 1778 as "our gallant and generous enemy."[144] Indeed, the civilized contact between these contending European forces contrasts strongly with the bitter and frequently atrocious nature of the struggle between the British and the American rebels. Captain the Honorable Colin Lindsay participated in the operations on St. Lucia, and he later recalled how the officers had had to exert themselves to prevent the British pickets and work parties from fraternizing with their Gallic counterparts. Lindsay wrote of the French: "their behavior was remarkably polite. Their chief surgeon was sent in to offer General Medows his assistance. The General's horse strayed out; they sent him back. Captain West, in giving his assistance to a wounded man, had dropped a silver-hilted sword; their working party carried it away; it was brought back by the next flag, and no money was suffered to be given to the soldier in return. Their sentries often, when they saw our soldiers passing near, would point to their arms, shake their heads, and laugh, but never fired." All in all, Lindsay mused, this was "a very different style of war from that which we had been used to in America."[145] In a similar manner, when the French expeditionary force joined Washington's army outside New York in summer 1781, the British responded by sending out flags with European gazettes for the French officers to read. Commissary Blanchard recorded, "The parleys between us and the English were displeasing to the Americans, and even to General Washington; they were unaccustomed to this way of making war." The Frenchman added that, after the capture of Cornwallis's army at Yorktown, the rebel officers "seemed displeased at the civility shown to the English prisoners, who, for their part, were very attentive to us."[146]

As earlier discussed, most Crown officers and men viewed the rebellion as "unnatural" and illegitimate. Another reason why the British were disinclined to treat the rebel military forces with the respect that they extended to French regulars was that, in important aspects, the rebels deviated conspicuously from European preconceptions of what soldiers were supposed to be. For example, the humble social origins of many rebel (particularly militia) officers left their European counterparts singularly unimpressed.[147] It is unlikely that this feeling was limited to British officers. For example, after the fall of Fort Washington, one British soldier explained to captive militiaman John Adlum that, unlike British officers, rebel ones were no good "[b]ecause there is but very few of them that appear gentlemen, [and] consequently [they] cannot have a proper sense of honour."[148]

The appearance of most rebel troops also left their adversaries less than impressed. Military commentators like Cuthbertson were adamant that "[an] exact neatness in the appearance of a battalion not only does honor to the attention of its officers . . . but gives great reason . . . to suppose that proper regulations are established in every other particular for the support of discipline."[149] When troops' persons, clothing, and arms did not meet such high standards, observers were inclined to doubt their military effectiveness.[150] Hence at Cape Fear in 1776, Clinton privately fussed over the amendments that regimental commanding officers had made to their men's impractical regulation uniforms: "a slouch hat begets a slouch look, that a slouch walk and slackness in every part of discipline."[151] Consequently, while the ragged, half-starved Continentals have become a treasured icon in American mythology, the sight of these gaunt tatterdemalions had quite a different effect on their enemies. For example, when the English adventurer Nicholas Cresswell set eyes upon Washington's "ragged, dirty, sickly, and ill-disciplined" troops in September 1776, he spat contemptuously, "If my countrymen are beaten by these ragamuffins I shall be much surprised."[152] Likewise, Captain Frederick Mackenzie noted of the shabby and unwashed rebel prisoners (many of whom were boys or old men) taken at Fort Washington that "few of them had the appearance of soldiers" and that "[t]heir odd figures frequently excited the laughter of our soldiers."[153] Such comments pepper the writings of British and German observers.[154]

It was, however, the nature of the rebels' armed resistance that provoked most hostility and contempt. In America, British and German regular soldiers regularly found themselves pitted against bands of un-uniformed, undisciplined irregulars, most commonly in the form of the militia. As in other such struggles, these irregulars' tendency to alternate between combatant and civilian status as it suited them infuriated their regular opponents. British officers regularly complained about the rebels' tendency to swear oaths of allegiance to the King in order to receive protections before going out in arms against British troops.[155] Indeed, in December 1776 Howe went so far as to order that armed men who fired on the troops or the inhabitants, and who lacked uniforms or officers, were to be summarily hanged as assassins.[156]

Particularly obnoxious to many British and German regulars were the irregular tactics that rebel parties commonly employed in the *petite guerre*. After the war, reflecting on his experiences in America as a captain with the Hessian *Feldjägerkorps*, Johann Ewald expressed his professional admiration for the half-trained rebel militia's skirmishing ability in wooded country: "What can you not achieve with such small bands who have learned to fight dispersed, who know how to use every molehill for their defense, and who retreat as quickly when attacked as they advance again, and who will always find space to hide. Never have I seen these maneuvers performed better than by the American militia, and especially that of the Province of [New] Jersey. If you were forced to retreat against these people you could certainly count on constantly having them around you."[157] Light company officer Lieutenant John Barker also illustrated these tactics when he recounted the harassment that the King's troops experienced at the hands of the Massachusetts militia during the return march from Concord: "before the whole [column] had quitted the town we were fired on from all sides, but mostly from the rear, where people had hid themselves in houses till we had passed and then fired. The country was an amazing strong one, full of hills, woods, stone walls, etc., which the rebels did not fail to take advantage of; for they were all lined with people who kept an incessant fire upon us, as we did too upon them but not with the same advantage, for they were so concealed there was hardly any seeing them." Barker added perceptively that the militia's attacks petered out once the redcoats approached the Charlestown peninsula, for "the rebels did not choose to follow us to the hill [i.e., Bunker Hill] as they must have fought us on open ground and that they did not like."[158] Reflective soldiers like Brigadier General Lord Percy conceded that the rebels could rarely "dare to form into any regular body" to oppose the King's troops because "they knew too well what was proper, to do so" and because "this country, being much covered with wood, and hilly, is very advantageous for their method of fighting."[159] Nevertheless, this (as Nicholas Cresswell put it) "skulking, cowardly manner of fighting" was repugnant to most European soldiers, and the enemy who chose to operate in this fashion was regarded as a "crafty, skulking, assassinating (though never a brave or generous) enemy."[160] While it might sound naive to modern ears, many British soldiers clearly resented the fact that the rebels were determined to destroy them without sportingly offering themselves up as a mark, one common redcoat having written scornfully that "[t]hey did not fight us like a regular army, only like savages."[161]

While undisciplined irregulars and urban or peasant uprisings were not unknown in Europe, British officers and men were taken aback by the ferocity and determination of the popular resistance that they often encountered in America. Indeed, years later veteran Roger Lamb deplored that the rebels had been motivated by "a sort of implacable ardor and revenge, which happily are a good deal unknown in the prosecution of war in general."[162] By seeking to ambush and destroy foraging parties, patrols, couriers, and even lone sentries, rebel irregulars in particular showed an infuriating disregard for the conventions of acceptable military conduct as understood by most European soldiers. One such breach of convention was the rebels' occasional trick of feigning surrender by "clubbing" their weapons, approaching the unsuspecting enemy, and then firing on them before making a quick getaway.[163] Another cause of resentment to European regulars was the rebels' employment of hunting rifles, with which (as Anburey later put it) "the life of an individual is sought with as much avidity as the obtaining a victory over an army of thousands."[164] During the siege of Boston, Lieutenant William Carter expressed typical disgust at the rebel practice of sniping: "Never had the British army so ungenerous an enemy to oppose. They send their riflemen (five or six at a time) who conceal themselves behind tress, etc., till an opportunity presents itself of taking a shot at our advanced sentries, which done they immediately retreat. What an infamous method of carrying on a war!"[165] Throughout the summer of 1776, while Howe's army on Staten Island prepared for the opening of the New York campaign, Admiral Lord Howe's secretary indignantly recorded a number of attacks by rebel sharpshooters, including the alleged killing of a British officer's child at play on Staten Island ("A Turk would detest so dirty an action").[166] For the British rank and file, the rebel rifleman represented a particular *bête noir.* Surgeon Thompson Forster, with Clinton's expeditionary force outside Charleston in June 1776, wrote that "the common men are highly exasperated against the provincials. They say it is not fair fighting, their aiming from their rifle-barrel guns." When two hundred of these sharpshooters subsequently surrendered at the battle of Long Island, Forster noted that the redcoats expressed their resentment against the prisoners' hated rifles, "most of which were broken to pieces by the soldiers on the spot."[167]

One of the striking indicators of this low esteem for the rebels was the intensity with which the British harangued them, both in and out of combat. Here one must be careful, for profanity was clearly something that came easy to the British lower orders. During the transatlantic voyage to America, Private Johann Döhla of the Bayreuth Regiment was horrified by the manner of the "thieving, happy, whoring, drunken" British tars, who "can hardly say three words without their curses, 'God damn my soul, God damn me.'" Once in America, the innocent young German judged of the common British soldiery that they "have only the vices of cussing, swearing, drinking, whoring, and stealing, and these more so than almost all other people."[168] The German was not alone in this estimation. Having experienced firsthand the inconvenience of British military occupation in the winter of 1776–77, with all the "swearing, lying, stealing, and blackguarding" that this entailed, one scandalized New Jersey resident complained of the British soldiery, "The last thing they do when they go to bed, and the first in the morning, is to remind God to damn their eyes, tongue, liver, pluck, heart and soul, and this they do more than a thousand times a day."[169]

Nevertheless, from what contemporaries steeled themselves to record, it is clear that the redcoats in America gave the enemy the full benefit of their particular genius for profanity. For example, witnesses noted that, during the two-week hiatus in Howe's operations after the battle of Long Island, impatient British soldiers and sailors loosed volleys of verbal abuse at Washington's troops on the far side of the East River.[170] As Captain Francis Lord Rawdon reported mischievously, when operations resumed and the redcoats were being rowed ashore during the Kipp's Bay landing, they continued to hurl violent expletives at the enemy: "The Hessians (who were not used to this water business, and who conceived that it must be exceedingly uncomfortable to be shot at whilst they were quite defenseless and jammed together so close) began to sing hymns immediately. Our men expressed their feelings as strongly, though in a different manner, by damning themselves and the enemy indiscriminately with wonderful fervency."[171] Likewise, one Connecticut rebel later recorded that, during skirmishing between the lines at New York in 1781, a party of British horsemen caught sight of him and "halooed to me, calling me 'a white-livered son of a bitch.' "[172]

A more explicit indicator of the redcoats' antipathy for the rebels was the verbal and physical abuse that they often meted out to prisoners. The experiences of rebel captain Alexander Graydon at the storming of Fort Washington are particularly revealing. First, a party of Highlanders initially responded to Graydon's attempt to surrender with an ineffective volley of musketry. He then had to dissuade an excitable mounted officer from having him and a fellow rebel officer killed out of hand. Almost immediately an exasperated Highlander savagely stripped the Pennsylvanian of a captured cartridge box upon which the royal cipher was conspicuously displayed. After Graydon had been marched off to join forty or fifty other rebel captives, mostly officers, the whole were subjected to an hour-long barrage of threats and insults. Finally, as the prisoners were transferred to New York, the column "was beset by a parcel of soldiers' trulls and others" who "assailed us with volleys of Billingsgate" and had to be held off by the guards.[173] Graydon's experiences were not atypical.[174]

The animosity that so many British soldiers felt for the rebels did not bode well for the latter if they found themselves within reach of British bayonets in combat. Indeed, in America the redcoats earned a grim reputation for ruthlessness (a theme explored in chapter 9).

Three main factors combined to produce the "zeal" that British officers and soldiers displayed against the rebels in America. The first of these was esprit de corps, which sprang from the bonds that developed between the men over years of service and from their well-developed sense of martial superiority over the enemy. The second was experience. Although there were few veterans of the Seven Years War in the ranks of British regiments by 1775, the Continental Army's much higher manpower wastage and its reliance on short-service drafts must have ensured that Crown corps more quickly became seasoned to campaigning and combat. The third factor was British antipathy toward the rebellion. That the King's troops harangued the rebels at every opportunity and often behaved harshly toward prisoners indicates that many of them viewed the rebels (and particularly rebel irregulars) with real hostility, not least because of the nature of the opposition they experienced in the *petite guerre*. Considering these factors, it is difficult to believe that the common British redcoat in America was much less strongly motivated to endure privation and to brave enemy fire than was his rebel counterpart.

# 6

# THE ADVANCE

The very small proportion of cavalry employed in the American wars, has much tended to introduce the present loose and irregular system of our infantry. Had they seen and been accustomed to the rapid movements of a good cavalry, they would have felt the necessity of more substantial order, of moving with concert and circumspection, and of being at every instant in a situation to form and repel a vigorous attack.

David Dundas, *Principles of Military Movements*

By the end of the Seven Years War, the "heavy" infantry of most states was trained to deploy in three ranks, with the files closed up almost elbow to elbow. This formation conferred several advantages in conventional linear warfare on Europe's plains. First, the formation's density enabled thousands of infantry to draw up together in continuous lines along frontages that, in terms of command and control, were manageable for company officers and sergeants, battalion commanders, and general officers. Second, provided the line of battle moved with circumspection, the proximity of the files within each battalion provided the men with a reassuring sense of security and helped them preserve their dressings. Third, such a line was powerful enough to achieve a tactical decision, for the formation (theoretically) concentrated the battalion's total firepower over the narrowest possible frontage. Indeed, even if one objected that the speedy breakdown of volleying in combat made it impractical for the third rank to fire, these men were still able to load for the front ranks or simply to reserve their fire for an emergency. Fourth, the men of the third rank were able to replace casualties in the first two, meaning that battalions were able to absorb heavy punishment without losing the solid, unbroken face or volume of firepower necessary to repel a vigorous enemy attack, particularly by heavy cavalry.[1] For all these reasons, the deployment of infantry in only two ranks was uncommon in conventional European warfare and usually signified serious manpower shortages.[2]

### "THE COMMON OPEN ORDER OF TWO DEEP"

If the British troops that participated in the conventional campaigns in Europe during the Seven Years War formed and fought three deep and in close order, the same was not true of their compatriots engaged in North America. There the operational and tactical context was very different. The prominent role played by Canadian and Indian irregulars, the total absence of cavalry, the broken and wooded terrain, and the need in action to spread available forces more thinly to cover more ground all militated against deep, compact formations. Instead, almost from the beginning of the French and Indian War, the redcoats in America deployed and fought two deep and with generous intervals between files.[3] Moreover, when the first authorized British light infantry companies emerged in 1771–72, the two-deep firing line was adopted as the basis of the woodland skirmishing disciplines drafted for them by Lieutenant General George Townshend (composed in 1772 for light companies on the Irish Establishment) and Major General William Howe (an experimental drill for a composite light battalion, tested in 1774). While Townshend prescribed an "open order" that incorporated file intervals of two feet, to be expanded or contracted as necessary, Howe specified three different interval "orders": "order" (two feet), "open order" (four feet), and "extended order" (ten feet).[4]

Surprisingly perhaps, the outbreak of rebellion in America in April 1775 revealed that the redcoats in Boston were unprepared to form, maneuver, and fight in any other than conventional European fashion. In August 1774 Gage had insisted that "[t]he troops are always to form three deep unless ordered to the contrary."[5] Predictably, the first day of hostilities underlined the unsuitability of close-order formations on enclosed and wooded ground. According to Lieutenant Frederick Mackenzie, when Brigadier General Lord Percy's relief column reached the heights overlooking Lexington, "we were ordered to form the line, which was immediately done by extending on each side of the road, but by reason of the stone walls and other obstructions, it was not formed in so regular manner as it should have been."[6] Weeks later, on 3 June 1775, Gage ordered the redcoats at Boston into two ranks, presumably because the rebels' lack of cavalry made it pointless and indeed counterproductive to invest manpower in a third rank: "The troops will draw up two deep on their regimental parades as well as on the general parade."[7] Hence Captain the Honorable Charles Stuart reported of Howe's initial deployment at Bunker Hill— the first set-piece engagement of the war—that "[t]he men were drawn up two deep on the beach in one line," while Clinton wrote disapprovingly that "our disposition on the 17th [June] was one long straggling line two deep."[8] Yet at this point Gage's redcoats retained their close order. This undoubtedly contributed to the major difficulties that the troops experienced during the battle (which Dundas would later encapsulate as the "deficiency of movement and want of flexibility in our solid battalions").[9] In short, those units that made the initial attack in line were described as having advanced "with rather a slow step," "in a slow and regular pace," at "a deliberate march," and at "a very slow march."[10] Although Howe reported that the infantry had advanced methodically and halted frequently "to give time for the artillery to fire," he blamed the difficulty and cost of the victory on the fact that "[t]he intermediate space between the two armies was cut by fences, formed of strong posts and close railing, very high, and which could not be broken readily."[11] These fences were clearly significant obstacles, Captain Thomas Stanley of the 17th Light Dragoons having reported that "the men were obliged to ground their arms to get over them."[12]

But one should understand that it was not only British infantry who experienced difficulties when traversing broken terrain in close order. Throughout the war, when rebel troops went onto the tactical offensive and attempted to maneuver in line in their customary compact formations, they appear to have experienced similar problems. One field officer recorded how, at Germantown, the attempt made by Major General Greene's left wing to advance down the Limekiln

Road "in line of battle" was frustrated because "the great number of post and rail fences, thickets and in short everything that could obstruct our march, threw us frequently into the greatest disorder."[13] Likewise, another rebel officer later blamed the "stiff German tactics" (presumably a disparaging reference to the drill manual drawn up for the Continental Army by Prussian Major General Friedrich von Steuben) that the British had abandoned, "from experience in our woody country," for the breakdown of the Pennsylvania Continentals' audacious counterattack at the action at Green Springs. In his estimation, "General [Anthony] Wayne's Brigade were drawn up in such close order as to render it utterly impracticable to advance in line and preserve their order—the line was necessarily broke by the trees as they passed [through] the wood."[14]

Despite the difficulties that the British grenadier and line battalions experienced during the initial attack at Bunker Hill, they retained their two-deep close-order formation for most of the siege of Boston. But on 29 February 1776, presumably in preparation for the abortive attack on Dorchester Heights (scheduled for the night of 5–6 March), Howe ordered all of his infantry to open up the files: "Regiments when formed by companies in battalion, or when on the general parade, are always to have their files 18 inches distant from each other, which they will take care to practice for the future, being the order in which they are to engage the enemy."[15] But then on 26 May, nearly two months after the army shifted from Boston to Halifax (where it arrived on 2 April) and two days before the start of a second round of field days on Citadel Hill in which the infantry exercised at brigade strength, Howe temporarily put the redcoats (excluding the light infantry) back into three ranks: "The grenadiers and battalions of the line are to form in future in three ranks with the files as formerly ordered at 18-inches intervals."[16] Possibly Howe did this either because Halifax lacked the space for several battalions to maneuver together in line when they were drawn up two deep or because the grenadiers and line infantry needed to practice moving in open order in three ranks before they attempted the more difficult feat of doing so in two.[17] Whatever the case, on 22 July, weeks after the army had quitted Halifax (10 June) and taken possession of Staten Island (2 July) and the day that the 42nd and 71st Regiments arrived from Britain, Howe changed his mind: "The 6 brigades and other corps upon the island are to form into two ranks until further orders."[18] Just over a week later, on 1 August (when the bulk of the outstanding reinforcements under Clinton and Cornwallis arrived), Howe made this formation definitive: "The infantry of the army without exception is ordered upon all occasions to form two deep with the file[s] at 18-inches interval until further orders."[19] The redcoats fought in this formation when they next went into action, at the battle of Long Island, Surgeon Thompson Forster noting that the Fourth Brigade "formed an extended line two deep ... on a considerable eminence."[20] Indeed, in the main army this remained the standard infantry formation throughout Howe's campaigns in the middle colonies.

It was not only Howe's redcoats who adopted the two-deep line at open files. On 29 June 1776, while Carleton's army constructed the flotilla with which they would wrest control of Lake Champlain in October, the infantry also adopted the formation: "The order of forming is to be at two deep, and the files 18 inches asunder."[21] Carleton may well have taken his cue from Howe, his own corps, the 47th Regiment, having joined his army from Howe's in May.[22] At any rate, the formation remained in force: a year later, on 20 June 1777, shortly after the opening of the Albany expedition, Burgoyne reminded the infantry of the "Canadian army" of "the present established rule of open files, and two deep."[23] Presumably this was the same formation that one rebel officer saw being employed when, before the battle of Bemis Heights, he witnessed a British battalion advance into open ground, where they "displayed, formed the line, and sat down in double ranks with their arms between their legs."[24]

Although what Clinton styled "the open, flimsy order of two deep in line" offended his "German school" military background (having served as aide de camp to Ferdinand of Brunswick during the Seven Years War), he declined to abolish it when he succeeded Howe in command in 1778. His reasoning was pragmatic: "We have succeeded always [with] it; the enemy have adopted it; [and] they have no cavalry to employ against it. Till a new enemy, therefore, comes, I shall content myself with supporting it always with something solid."[25] Thus, when the focus of the war shifted southward at the end of that year, two ranks with eighteen-inch file intervals remained the redcoats' standard battlefield formation. This is evident from the elementary maneuvers and three orders of battle that Lieutenant Colonel Archibald Campbell devised for the expeditionary force he led against Savannah in December 1778 (see figure 4).[26] Hence when

Campbell recorded his failed attempt to trap a rebel force at Mac-
bean's Creek (30 January 1779), he mentioned that the 1st Battalion of
the 71st Regiment "formed in line . . . in open order."[27]

In fact, Howe's formation remained the standard fighting formation for British infantry in America for the duration of the war. Indeed, both Clinton and Tarleton later blamed the catastrophic British
collapse at Cowpens largely on the instability of "that loose, flimsy
order which had ever been too much the practice in America" and on
"the loose manner of forming which had always been practiced by the
King's troops in America."[28] Likewise, in the tactical instructions
that he issued to his force in Chesapeake Bay in April 1781, Major
General Phillips alluded simply to "the common open order of two
deep."[29] Finally, on 12 October 1781, when Clinton's troops passed
Prince William in review on their way to board the transports that
would take them to relieve Yorktown, they did so "by sub-divisions,
two deep, in open order, and slow time."[30]

Although the German mercenary regiments that served in America are not the main focus of this work, it should be noted that they
too adapted their formations to local conditions. Rodney Atwood has
shown that the Hessian infantry regiments that joined Howe's army
in 1776 quickly abandoned the third rank but retained their close
order throughout the war.[31] In Canada at least some of the Brunswick
infantry corps were still exercising in three ranks in July 1776.[32] But
that same month Major General Baron Riedesel complained to the
Duke of Brunswick that the British wanted him to train his infantry
in what he styled the French system of open order in thin lines. He
added that he would teach them to secure the protection of the trees
as they advanced so they could meet the rebels on equal terms.[33]
Hence on 6 August Riedesel exercised his own corps, the Regiment
von Riedesel, in moving through woodland with skirmishers to the
front. On 3 September, after Lieutenant Colonel Friedrich Breymann's grenadier battalion had drilled in close order, three hundred
men of Riedesel's own regiment repeated their woodland exercise
in front of Carleton, Phillips, and Burgoyne.[34] Six months later, in
March 1777, Lieutenant Friedrich Julius von Papet of the Brunswick
Regiment von Rhetz recorded that, when Carleton and Riedesel reviewed the corps at Deschambault, "Each company had to conduct
special exercises . . . in three ranks. Next the entire regiment was
aligned two men deep and on orders from General Carleton eighteen-

inch intervals were taken between the men on either side."[35] According to Eelking, after the start of the Albany expedition, Riedesel ordered his officers to train their men to operate in open order, reserving
close order for the bayonet charge.[36] Nevertheless, Riedesel himself
later positively stated that the Brunswick infantry who saved the
British center from collapse toward the end of the battle of Freeman's
Farm with a last-minute flank attack advanced "with closed ranks."[37]
That the British never quite succeeded in weaning the Germans from
their close order was significant (as we shall shortly see).

### Speed versus Disorder

The redcoats in America adopted the two-deep line at open files in
1776, retaining it as their standard formation throughout the war
because it enabled them to advance more easily over broken ground.
One German officer with Burgoyne's Albany expedition made this
point explicitly when he wrote: "Here we have a special way of wag-
ing war which departs utterly from our system. Our infantry can only
operate two deep and a man must have eighteen inches space on
either side to be able to march in line through woods and brush."[38]
Johann Ewald later echoed this point: "The infantry . . . has to be
taught to march in line in the best order through thickets; between
two files there has to be an opening of a good pace."[39]

If the redcoats adopted Howe's open-order formation to facilitate
traversing broken ground during the advance, this begs the question,
how quickly did they move in action? Even on the European plains, a
close-order battalion could not advance any distance without the
ranks and files bulging and bunching unless it progressed at a deliberate pace and halted frequently to dress.[40] Hence in 1727 Lieutenant
Colonel Humphrey Bland had directed that "[i]n marching up to attack an enemy, the line should move very slow, [so] that the battalions may be in order, and the men not out of breath when they
come to engage."[41] By the 1740s the British Army had adopted the
practice of marching in step (the benefits of which the Hessians and
Prussians rediscovered after the War of the Spanish Succession),[42] and
long before the American War, three distinct paces had come into
general use. These were "ordinary" time (75 paces per minute) for
parades and reviews and for traversing rough ground in line, "quick"

time (120–150 paces per minute) for maneuvering or gaining ground, and the very rapid step (basically a run) for the bayonet charge.[43]

Although we have already noted the slowness with which the redcoats appear to have advanced at Bunker Hill, many contemporary military writers were convinced that it was perfectly possible to maneuver infantry in close order at a pace faster than the ordinary step. In 1768 Captain Bennett Cuthbertson recommended the latter only for when troops practiced new and unfamiliar maneuvers, "after which, it will be wrong to perform them in any other manner, than by the most rapid movement; as that most certainly must be the method, were it necessary to make use of any before an enemy."[44] Likewise, in 1782 Lieutenant Colonel William Dalrymple urged that British infantry need only march as slow as 80 paces per minute when manuevering in combat encumbered with full kit. As a standard step he instead recommended 100–120 paces per minute, which he described as "nothing more than an easy walk." Yet even this was not quick enough for his taste, and he additionally suggested that "[i]t might be accelerated occasionally to a kind of trot, and increased to one hundred a fifty in a minute. I am a great advocate for celerity."[45] In America, where the threat from cavalry was almost nonexistent, the case for celerity was even more convincing. In 1775 Colonel Timothy Pickering of the Massachusetts militia went so far as to recommend that, once a battalion had mastered maneuvering at the ordinary march, the troops should gradually quicken the pace "until by constant practice they are able to perform manoeuvres upon the full run."[46] From all this it seems difficult to believe that, once the redcoats in America adopted Howe's open-order formation in 1776, they would have needed to move in combat at anything less than the quick step. Indeed, Simcoe actually went so far as to forbid his Queen's Rangers ever to march in slow time.[47]

If Crown troops commonly began their assaults at around 120 paces per minute, then they would have covered around one hundred yards every minute (reckoning a pace as 2.5 feet). Common sense suggests that it would have been counterproductive to quicken the rate much above this until after the line came within maximum small-arms range of the enemy (about two hundred yards for smoothbores, three hundred for rifles). This was partly because a premature acceleration would have generated an unnecessary amount of disorder during this early stage of the advance, but mostly because it would only have fatigued the troops uselessly, especially if they had already marched many miles to the engagement. Tarleton's description of the British advance against the North Carolina militia at Guilford Courthouse seems to support this supposition: "The troops were no sooner formed than they marched forwards with steadiness and composure. The order and coolness of that part of Webster's brigade which advanced across the open ground, exposed to the enemy's fire, cannot be sufficiently extolled."[48] As contemporary and modern battle maps indicate that Cornwallis's army deployed into line of battle about five hundred yards from the Carolinians,[49] the attackers would not have entered the maximum "killing zone" of those men armed with rifles until the British line had covered about two hundred yards.

Once the line came within range of the enemy's small arms, it would have been sensible for the troops to quicken their pace to reduce the time they spent under fire. This consideration was clearly reflected in the training regimen laid down for the Queen's Rangers in 1779, which dictated that "the charge was never to be less than *three hundred yards*, gradually increasing in celerity from its first outset . . . [and] the pace adapted to the shortest men."[50] In fact the sources generally indicate that after 1775 the redcoats commonly accelerated to a kind of trot or jog long before they broke into a run for the bayonet charge. Thus in the northern campaigns, the King's troops "briskly marched up to" the enemy at Long Island, "briskly ascended" Chatterton's Hill, "advanced fearlessly and very quickly" at Brandywine, came on at Bemis Heights at a "quick step," stormed Fort Clinton "with as much velocity as the ground would admit," and "after a very quick march moved up briskly" against the enemy at Monmouth.[51] Likewise, in the South the redcoats "marched forwards briskly, or rather rushed with great shouts" at Savannah; were observed "advancing rapidly" at Briar Creek; and "rushed on with the greatest rapidity" (or "as fast as the ploughed fields they had to cross would admit") at Spencer's Ordinary.[52] Most expressively of all, one rebel militiaman at the battle of Cowpens later recalled that "the British line advanced at a sort of trot with a loud halloo. It was the most beautiful line I ever saw," while another reported that the King's troops "advanced rapidly as if certain of victory."[53]

Another indication of how quickly the redcoats advanced to the attack is that Howe's close-order Hessian battalions could not keep up with them in action. In 1777 Captain John Bowater of the marines censured the Hessians for not having amended their tactical methods to the same degree as the British, who had adopted the "discipline . . . of light infantry, which is the only method of proceeding in this country." Of the Germans he wrote, "They are exceeding slow, their mode of discipline is not in the least calculated for this country, and they are strictly enjoined by the Landgrave not to alter it."[54] The comparative laggardness of the Hessians (whom Lieutenant John Peebles evaluated as "slow but steady troops") was most clearly displayed at Brandywine.[55] Lieutenant William Hale participated in the attack at Birmingham Meetinghouse with Lieutenant Colonel the Honorable Henry Monckton's 2nd Battalion of Grenadiers and commented of the Germans:

> I believe them steady, but their slowness is of the greatest disadvantage in a country almost covered with woods, and against an enemy whose chief qualification is agility in running from fence to fence and thence keeping up an irregular, but galling fire on troops who advance with the same pace as at their exercise. . . . At Brandywine, when the line first formed, the Hessian Grenadiers were close in our rear, and began beating their march at the same time as us. From that minute we saw them no more till the action was over, and only one man of them was wounded, by a random shot which came over us. . . . They themselves make no scruple of owning our superiority over them, but palliate so mortifying a confession by saying "Englishmen be the Divel [sic] for going on, but Hesse men be soldier."[56]

Weeks later, when Monckton's grenadiers marched out of Philadelphia "at a half trot" toward the sound of the guns at Germantown, they passed the Hessian grenadiers, who (according to Jacob Mordecai, a young local eyewitness) were "smoking their pipes and marching at a steady pace." Once again the redcoats "were out of sight long before the Hessians were out of view."[57] In short, Howe's Hessian mercenary corps could not keep pace with the redcoats in America because they continued to employ their regulation ordinary and quick steps of 75 and 110 paces per minute (the latter for wheeling).[58] In April 1781, when Knyphausen finally (and vainly) asked the Landgrave for permission to put the Hessian infantry in America into open order, he explained, "I have found through experience that this method is of benefit here, for our troops, when they are fully closed up, are not able to march in line with the English, but lose thirty paces in every hundred."[59]

If Howe's close-order Hessian battalions were incapable of keeping up with the swift-heeled British infantry in action, Burgoyne expected the Brunswickers on the Albany expedition (who, as noted earlier, complied with the British request to adopt open order) to move fully as quickly as his redcoats. In May 1777 Burgoyne ordered, "The exercise of the troops under the Lieutenant General's orders is to be confined to firing with ball cartridges, bayonets fixed, and rapidity of movements in marching, evolutions and forming."[60] In June he further directed that in camp the picket was daily "to be exercised in marching and charging bayonets under the inspection of the brigadier of the day, in order that the British and German troops may acquire an uniformity of space and motion when acting together in line."[61] The diary of Captain Georg Pausch of the Hesse-Hanau artillery gives some idea of the sort of speed at which Burgoyne required his infantry to be able to maneuver. When daily drilling resumed in late January 1777, Pausch recorded approvingly that the Anglo-German garrison at Montreal underwent a bracing regimen of physical exercise that included running and marching. By May, however, the captain was not only troubled by the combined effects of heat and exertion on his "poor devils," but he had also come to realize with some concern that the British penchant for celerity of movement extended to the battlefield:

Every day on the parade ground I must execute their quick march with them, to my greatest displeasure. This would not be done by us, nor in Prussia, nor in the entire world, except when hunting with fleet horses and good hounds. During the winter this is an excellent exercise for the troops. In the summer and when it is warm, it is damaging to their health. To have the pleasure to watch it is ridiculous, and before the enemy completely unnecessary. Massed men can form no closed attack in this manner and if a retreat were to be made with this movement, not only would it be made with difficulty, but also all imaginable abusive language would be called forth from the journalists of Europe and America.

Elsewhere the horrified Pausch decried the British "quick march" as the "English gallop."[62]

Another indication of the rapidity with which British troops advanced is the fact that they typically went into battle as lightly accoutred as possible. Contrary to generations of scandalized historians, Howe did not send his infantry into battle at Bunker Hill in full marching order. Instead, the men paraded prior to embarkation only "with their arms, ammunition, blankets, and provisions ordered to be cooked this morning."[63] As discussed earlier (in chapter 2), from 1776 the redcoats commonly stripped to this light order in the field for days at a time. Even this reduced gear, however, was apparently too much to allow the troops to proceed in action with the requisite dash, Captain George Harris's grenadiers having gratefully appropriated the blankets left behind by the rebels after the Kipp's Bay landing "as several of our men had thrown off theirs on the 27th [August], when pursuing the enemy."[64] Indeed, it appears to have been entirely usual for British troops to "disencumber themselves of everything, except their arms and ammunition," prior to going into combat, as Tarleton required his infantry to do even before they deployed at Cowpens.[65] For example, one Quaker lad who watched Cornwallis's division make its attack at Brandywine later recorded that the fields in front of him had contained great heaps of blankets and gear, thrown together to relieve the King's troops for action.[66] Likewise, Captain Lieutenant John Peebles of the 42nd Regiment recorded that at Monmouth the battalions of the Third Brigade cast off their knapsacks before engaging.[67] And at Princeton, according to one local witness, "A party of them [i.e., redcoats from the Fourth Brigade] came into our field and laid down their packs there and formed at the corner of our garden about 60 yards from the door and then marched away immediately to the field of battle."[68] Possibly this was the same gear mentioned by one anonymous rebel sergeant who recalled that, after the first clash between the 17th Regiment and Washington's advanced guard, the redcoats "retreated eight rods to their packs, which were laid in a line."[69] According to the aforementioned local witness, when the troops of Cornwallis's main force arrived on the scene too late to succor the Fourth Brigade, they "began to plunder their fellow soldiers' packs, taking out what they pleased and leaving the rest in the dirt."[70]

A last clue as to how quickly the infantry advanced in action is the

way the men carried their firelocks. The customary method of supporting the weapon when at the halt or when marching and maneuvering was to shoulder it, like the men of the close-order battalions of
Cornwallis's second line whom one rebel officer spotted at the action
at Green Springs.[71] Common sense suggests, however, that a shouldered firelock would not have been very stable when the soldier
moved with rapidity, especially over difficult ground. There were alternatives, of course. The *1764 Regulations* prescribed that, when the
battalion attacked with the bayonet, "The front rank charges [fire-
locks] only, the other two [ranks] remain recovered."[72] According to
one American militia officer, to avoid becoming tired, British troops
were also able "to *slope*, to *support*, or to *advance* their firelocks, or to
*carry them in their right hands* [i.e., trail them]."[73] Interestingly, at
the storming of Fort Washington and at the battle of Bemis Heights,
rebel observers saw British troops "running across the island with
trailed arms" and coming on with a "quick step" with "trailed arms."[74]
Alternatively, in 1778 Simcoe ordered his Queen's Rangers to carry
their muskets into action "at the advance" because "he was fully
convinced of the truth of what an English military author had observed, that a number of firelocks were, in action, rendered useless, by
being carried on the shoulders, from casual musket balls."[75]

If the British adopted Howe's two-deep, open-order formation in
1776 to enable the troops to advance at speed over broken ground, this
benefit came at a cost, for it was very difficult for the men to maintain
their dressings on the move. Eyewitnesses rarely recorded that the
redcoats in America "advanced in a most excellent order" (as Lieutenant William Hale approvingly reported of the initial advances made by
the 17th Regiment at Princeton and the 2nd Battalion of Grenadiers at
Monmouth), presumably because these occasions were so rare.[76] To
get at the rebels, the British commonly had to scramble through
woods and brush, clamber over fences and walls, trudge through
ploughed fields, wade across watercourses, and scrabble up hills. The
assault on Chatterton's Hill provided a striking instance of how this
kind of terrain could derange the redcoats' ranks and files. There the
men of Corporal Thomas Sullivan's corps, the 49th Regiment, made
their ascent in a very ragged and uneven line: "during the engagement
we were sometimes twelve deep, occasioned by the narrowness of the
hill, and the large rocks and trees that were dispersed upon it."[77]

Yet it was not only on broken ground that open-order formations tended to become disordered. After being taken prisoner at York-town, Captain Johann Ewald witnessed the Rhode Island Regiment at exercise and "was greatly surprised that the men were not in close formation, arm to arm, but had consistently left a space for a man between every two men." Although Ewald thought this "a very good thing in penetrating a thick wood or underbrush with entire battalions," he added, "when such an open battalion comes through a wood into a plain, it looks just like the troops are advancing in the greatest confusion."[78] After the war, Dundas elaborated on this problem. He stressed that troops could only preserve their order when maneuvering if "each soldier is impressed with a religious observance of never relinquishing the touch of his neighbor." By contrast "[t]he perfect march of a battalion or line formed at open files, seems impossible; because its principal guidance, the touch of the files, is gone. Each man is necessarily employed to preserve a required distance from his neighbor; he is obliged to turn his head for that purpose, this distorts his body, a constant opening and closing takes place, [and] the whole must move loose and unconnected. If this must necessarily happen in the regulating battalion, its influence on a line may be easily imagined, and also the condition in which it will arrive near an enemy."[79] In short, when the troops were not locked into their place in the line by the men to their left and right, they could not maintain their proper dressings. Tarleton later made this point when he wrote of the initial British advance at Cowpens (where the battlefield was only lightly wooded) that "the troops moved on in as good a line as troops could move at open files."[80] As the war dragged on and the rebels' forces gradually improved in quality, the vulnerability of Howe's two-deep, open-order formation to determined resistance would become all to clear (as will be discussed later).

## OTHER LINEAR FORMATIONS

While two ranks with the files at eighteen-inch intervals remained the standard British infantry formation in America from 1776, this is not to say that the King's troops invariably formed and fought in this fashion. Although Tarleton and Clinton blamed the defeat at Cowpens on Howe's loose formation, Roderick Mackenzie (a former lieutenant in the 71st Regiment) asked bluntly, "If his files were too extensive, why did he not contract them?"[81] Mackenzie's objection reminds us that commanding officers, whether of armies or battalions, were perfectly capable of opening and closing the infantry's files and increasing and reducing the number of ranks to suit the immediate tactical situation. A good example of this was the small fight near Fort Ann (8 July 1777) in which Lieutenant Colonel John Hill of the 9th Regiment deployed his 190 redcoats in a single rank to prevent the more numerous rebels from turning his flanks.[82] Similarly, just over a fortnight before the battle of Brandywine, Hessian colonel Karl Emil von Donop expressed disquiet at the British infantry's tendency to fight "with its files four feet apart."[83]

Although we know little about what happened when corps went out to exercise outside of the campaigning season, it would appear that at least some regimental commanders trained their troops to employ different formations to meet different tactical scenarios. For instance, according to one of its former officers, the men of the 1st Battalion of Light Infantry were able to form in a minimum of one rank and a maximum of four, with two as the norm. They also practiced three alternative "orders" for the files (which were "by day always loose"): "usual order [at] 11 inches," "open order [at] arm's length," and "extended order from five yards to fifty."[84] Similarly, in January 1780 Major Patrick Ferguson laid down three distinct "orders" for his Provincial corps, the American Volunteers: "close (or charging) order, the files to be as near as may be without touching"; "common (or firing) order, three feet interval or at arm's length"; and "open (or skirmishing) order, four yards interval or twice the length of a man between the files."[85]

If some Crown corps in America employed different orders for different tactical scenarios, this begs the question, how would a battalion have shifted from one to another? Although one might have expected the unit to have opened or closed up on its center or flank, Simcoe's account of his minor victory at Spencer's Ordinary suggests a more likely method. When the Queen's Rangers formed for the attack, they initially spread themselves "with wide intervals [between the companies], and covering a great space of ground." During the attack, "each separate company kept itself compact" and maintained "intervals between the companies." From this we may infer that troops who advanced in what Ferguson called "firing order" would have, when commanded to adopt "charging order," simply closed up and dressed upon the center or flank of each company.[86]

Ferguson's "charging" formation is particularly interesting in that it signals that by 1780 an open-order bayonet rush was no longer seen as an appropriate tactic against the American rebels. (This theme is fully explored in chapter 9.) Suffice to say that the tactical instructions that Major General Phillips issued in Virginia in April 1781 lend further support to the notion that, late in the war, some British troops were readopting close order for the bayonet charge. As discussed earlier, when Clinton came to the command in 1778, he resolved always to employ compactly deployed corps in support of loosely formed attacking troops. Phillips's instructions, issued in April 1781 in the aftermath of Tarleton's disaster at Cowpens, strongly echo this concern. Because of their clarity, they deserve to be quoted in full:

It is the Major General's wish that the troops under his command may practice forming from two to three and to four deep, and that they should be accustomed to charge in all those orders. In the latter orders (of the three and four deep), the files will, in course, be closer, so as to render a charge of the greatest force. The Major General also recommends to regiments the practice of dividing the battalions, by wings or otherwise; so that one line may support the other when an attack is supposed; and, when a retreat is supposed, that the first line may retreat through the intervals of the second (the second doubling up its divisions for that purpose, and forming up again in order to check the enemy, who may be supposed to have pressed the first line). The Major General would approve also of one division of a battalion attacking in the common open order of two deep, to be supported by the other compact division as a second line (in a charging order three or four deep); [t]he gaining of the flanks also of a supposed enemy (by the quick movements of a division in common open order, while the compact division advances to a charge); and such other evolutions, as may lead the regiments to a custom of depending on and mutually supporting each other; so that should one part be pressed or broken, it may be accustomed to form again without confusion, under the protection of a second line, or any regular-formed division.

Simcoe, commanding the Queen's Rangers, especially approved of these instructions because they restored some solidity to Phillips's infantry, thus remedying the fact that the only Hessian corps on the expedition (the Regiment Erb Prinz) had remained with detachments from the British battalions to garrison Portsmouth and Norfolk.[87]

Days later, on 23 or 24 April, Phillips elaborated these innovative minor tactics into a single grand-tactical concept that incorporated his entire force. The rationale behind his (notional) order of battle (examined in chapter 4) was clearly that the loosely formed advanced light troops and the more compactly deployed supporting line battalions were to cooperate in the same fashion that he had previously prescribed for the two wings of a single battalion: "Should the particular difficulty of the country occasion the first line to take up new ground toward the rear, it may not be improper, perhaps, to do so by becoming a second line in the rear of the 76th and 80th [Regiments]; who will form openings, if necessary, for the purpose. It is to be observed, that the reserve is to be the point of assembly for the troops upon any difficult occasion. The impression made upon an attack by the advanced corps and light infantry will be supported in firm order by the second line."[88] Unfortunately, in none of the minor actions that he fought in Virginia did Phillips get the chance to implement his (notional) order of battle.

There is, however, some evidence to suggest that Cornwallis employed something like Phillips's grand-tactical concept in Virginia. Within a month of issuing his instructions, Phillips was dead, and his troops had been absorbed into Cornwallis's army at Petersburg.[89] In July the Hessian adjutant general in America reported from New York that Cornwallis had ordered his infantry henceforth to draw up in three ranks in close order, adding that at the action at Green Springs, the earl had advanced "some closed regiments."[90] At first glance this seems to contradict eyewitness testimony from two rebel participants in the action, who noted that "[t]he British advanced in open order at arm's length" and were "regularly formed, standing one yard distance from each other, their light infantry being in front of our battalion."[91] The confusion is cleared up by the evidence of another rebel officer, who noted that he "saw the British light infantry, distinctly, advancing at arm's length distance, and their second line in close order, with shouldered musket, just in front of their camp."[92] Thus it would appear that the infantry in Cornwallis's first line advanced in two ranks with open file intervals, while the second line deployed in close order—very much in keeping with what Phillips had recommended.[93]

## COLORS, MUSIC, AND CHEERING

British infantry regiments at this time possessed two flags: a King's color (the Great Union) and a regimental color (the field of which was the same color as the regiment's facings). In America these colors were mostly employed on ceremonial occasions, such as Howe's "Meschianza" (18 May 1778); when Clinton's troops marched triumphantly into Charleston in 1780; or sometimes at military punishments like the execution of deserters.[94]

It is likely that, on leading their corps out of quarters into the field, regimental commanders commonly left their colors in storage with the heavy baggage.[95] For example, in 1777 Lieutenant General von Heister reported of the Fourth Brigade's reverse at Princeton that "[t]he English regiments have no flags or cannon with them and so are saved the misfortune of losing them."[96] More explicitly, in January 1778 Major General Baron Friedrich Wilhelm von Lossberg wrote from Rhode Island: "They [i.e., the British] have their colors with them only when quartered, while we carry them with us wherever the regiments go. This is bad whenever a regiment is split up and put into works which are not closely together." On 6 December 1778 Lossberg restated his concern: "The country is bad for fighting. Nothing worries me more than the colors, for the regiments cannot stay together in an attack because of the many walls, swamps, and stone cliffs. The English cannot lose their colors, for they do not carry them with them."[97]

Despite this evidence, it is certain that some British regiments did take their colors into the field. Weeks after Burgoyne's capitulation at Saratoga, Gates informed Congress that the British general had assured him that his army had left its colors in Canada.[98] But the fact that Burgoyne had required the presence of the colors of "the eldest regiment" at his conference with the Indians at Skenesboro on 19 July shows that he was being somewhat economical with the truth.[99] In fact, Baroness Riedesel's diary reveals that her husband saved the colors of the Brunswick regiments from the rebels by burning the staffs and hiding the flags inside her mattress, which was later smuggled to Halifax.[100] While the baroness made no mention of the fate of the British colors, we know that Lieutenant Colonel John Hill likewise concealed those of the 9th Regiment in his baggage and presented them to the King on his return to England in 1781.[101] In the case of Cornwallis's surrender at Yorktown, the four German regiments appear to have handed over all their colors (eighteen in total), while three of the British corps seem to have surrendered theirs (six).[102] Although the unlucky 17th Regiment had already lost its colors when the rebels stormed Stony Point in 1779, there is no evidence for the fate of those of the other British units except for an unsubstantiated regimental tradition that the 23rd and 33rd Regiments concealed their colors before the surrender.[103]

Even if some British corps did take their colors into the field, for our purposes the most important question is whether they carried them into action, in conventional European fashion, to spur morale and act as a rallying point.[104] Perhaps the best evidence for this phenomenon concerns the expedition to St. Lucia. At a desperate moment during the battle of the Vigie (18 December 1778), with the ammunition nearly exhausted, Brigadier General Medows made a dramatic appeal to the 5th Regiment: "soldiers, as long as you have a bayonet to point against an enemy's breast, defend these colors."[105] Days later he instructed the redcoats of the reserve that, in the event of another French assault, the drums and fifes were to assemble around the colors of the 5th Regiment and play "The Grenadiers' March."[106]

The corps that composed Medows' reserve (the grenadiers, the light infantry, and the 5th Regiment) had previously served in the American colonies, and there are some references to the carrying of the colors in action there. For instance, one Pennsylvania militiaman saw a British regiment's colors during the storming of Fort Washington,[107] while at the battle of Camden, Sergeant Roger Lamb carried one of the 23rd Regiment's colors and Ensign Thomas Flyn carried the standard of the Volunteers of Ireland.[108] Similarly, we know that a few British flags were lost in combat. For instance, the 64th Regiment apparently forfeited its King's color at Eutaw Springs (it may have been presented to Greene by Congress in honor of his supposed victory)[109] while those of the 7th Regiment were taken at Cowpens.[110] Yet the fact that only one of Tarleton's three infantry corps (not counting the light infantry) lost its colors at this catastrophic defeat surely means that the others cannot have had any with them.[111]

In the final analysis, while practice almost certainly differed from corps to corps and from campaign to campaign, it seems likely that most regimental commanders would have been reluctant to take the colors into action because the slenderness of the redcoats' linear formations would have made it difficult to guarantee their safety. Significantly, British units in action in America do not appear to have deployed color reserves, as directed in the *1764 Regulations*.[112]

The evidence for the employment of martial music in combat is also somewhat mixed. At this time the army had at its disposal two types of military musician. One was the unofficial regimental bandsman. Not all regiments had a "band of music," but the typical band might have comprised half a dozen or more players with oboes, French horns, clarinets, and bassoons. Although these skilled musicians were officially mustered and paid as enlisted men, the captains and field officers bore the extra expense of retaining their services.[113] Additionally, although bandsmen accompanied their regiments into the field, they were not expected to fight save in an emergency—as at Hobkirk's Hill, after which desperate action Lieutenant Colonel Francis Lord Rawdon reported that he had been compelled to arm "our musicians, our drummers, and in short everything that could carry a firelock."[114] They were certainly a cut above the common soldiery; indeed, in the late 1760s the bandsmen of the 23rd Regiment attended the same Masonic Lodge at Holyrood House as their officers.[115] In addition, their skills were a marketable commodity, as the 62nd Regiment's bandsmen showed when they deserted to the rebels after the capitulation at Saratoga.[116] Again, as with the colors, the bandsmen's primary role was ceremonial.[117] Thus when Cornwallis took possession of Philadelphia and Clinton of Charleston, their troops were accompanied by "bands of music playing before them" and by oboists playing "God Save the King."[118]

More central to the army's everyday activities were the authorized regimental musicians. For most of the war, each company in a regiment of foot was authorized to have a pair of drummers, while each grenadier company was allowed an additional pair of fifers.[119] In practice some companies did not maintain their full complements of regimental musicians,[120] though in some corps captains and field officers sometimes paid private soldiers to serve unofficially as additional fifers.[121] Moreover, light company "drummers" and Highland grenadier company "fifers" actually employed horns and bagpipes.

In America, like the bandsmen, the authorized regimental musicians did sometimes play music on ceremonial occasions, as when the remnants of the 1st and 2nd Battalions of Grenadiers in turn presented arms and "beat a march" in honor of the other before their amalgamation in November 1778.[122] They also sometimes played music to lift the troops' spirits on the march, as when in Boston on 6 March 1775 the drums of the passing 43rd Regiment alarmed the Old South Meetinghouse occupants, who had collected to hear an inflammatory oration commemorating the anniversary, the day before, of the Boston Massacre.[123] Similarly, in March 1777, when Crown detachments twice sallied out of Perth Amboy to repel prowling rebel parties, they celebrated as they returned by beating a "triumphal entry" in order (as Lieutenant John Peebles sardonically put it) "to convince the general of his victory."[124] Occasionally the bandsmen accompanied the regimental musicians, creating an almost carnival-like atmosphere. According to one of Burgoyne's officers, as the British pursued the rebels up the Richelieu River toward Lake Champlain in June 1776, "The whole during the march showed the greatest cheerfulness, music playing and drums beating the whole way."[125] Conversely, the regimental musicians also sometimes played music to intimidate the enemy. As one example of this, Washington's adjutant general wrote of the early stages of the action at Harlem Heights that, as the British light infantry jubilantly pursued the retiring rebels, they "in the most insulting manner sounded their bugle horns as is usual after a fox chase. . . . It seemed to crown our disgrace."[126] Similarly, before dawn on the morning of the disastrous assault on British-held Savannah, the waiting men of the French assault columns heard the eerie skirl of bagpipes emanating from within the town—not from the 71st Regiment's usual campsite, however, but from the point of the British lines selected for the French attack. Vice Admiral Comte D'Estaing's wrote that the "*lugubre harmonie*" made a deep impression on his men; it was a sure sign that the British "wanted us to know their best troops were awaiting us."[127]

Contrary to popular opinion, the authorized regimental musicians did not necessarily provide a marching cadence as the troops maneuvered. Although in the late 1740s, British corps started to employ drums and fifes to set the pace, it gradually became clear that this practice was impractical, not least in action. By the 1770s, therefore, it was reserved for training recruits.[128] Instead the authorized regimental musicians' main purpose was—at least in theory—to relay orders, whether in billets or in camp, on the march or in action. Indeed, according to the *1764 Regulations*, two orderly drummers were to attend the commanding officer at the center of the battalion while the remainder posted themselves in the center-rear of the four grand divisions, from where presumably they relayed the signals beaten by the orderly drummers.[129] But by the American War, even this practice appears to have gone out of fashion. In 1768 Cuthbertson had recommended that troops should be trained to respond to vocal commands only, "because in action, the noise of the artillery and musketry generally renders it impossible to use any signals by drum, and therefore it can answer no purpose to have soldiers trained to what can never be attempted on real service."[130] This advice received official sanction a decade later,[131] and by the 1780s it had apparently become usual for the drummers (as Wolfe had instructed the 20th Regiment in 1755), and presumably also the fifers and regimental bandsmen, "to stay with their respective companies to assist the wounded men."[132]

For our purposes, the most important question is whether the authorized regimental musicians commonly beat or played signals or marches in action in America. Here the evidence appears inconclusive. As early as February 1776, Howe ordered the British regiments at Boston "not to use the drum or fife for marching or signals when in the field."[133] Hence, after the battle of Long Island, the Hessian adjutant general in America noted that the redcoats did not attack in the customary German manner, "namely, by sending their artillery ahead and continually beating their drums."[134] Conversely, Lieutenant Colonel Henry Hope's tactical instructions to the 1st Battalion of Grenadiers in 1780 did contain a number of "signals by drum":

*Preparative:* to begin firing by companies, which is to go on as fast as each is loaded till the first part of the *General,* when not a shot more is ever to be fired.
*Grenadiers' March:* to advance in line.
*Point of War:* to charge.
*To Arms:* to form the battalion (whether advancing or retreating in column) upon the leading division.
*Double Flam:* to halt upon the word "forward." In forming, the divisions [are] to run up in order.[135]

Interestingly, three years earlier at Brandywine, the drummers of the 1st Battalion of Grenadiers (accompanied perhaps by the fifers) beat "The Grenadiers' March" as Cornwallis's division opened its attack, one anonymous participant having recorded: "The line moving on exhibited the most grand and noble sight imaginable. The grenadiers beating their march as they advanced contributed greatly to the dignity of the approach."[136] How long the grenadiers' drummers continued to beat, however, is unclear. Even if they did not imitate the musicians of the Prussian Regiment von Bevern at Zorndorf (1758), who ceased playing and "removed themselves to safety" when the corps came under fire, once the British line came within effective musketry range of the rebels, the grenadiers would almost certainly have broken into a trot or a run.[137] This would necessarily have put an end to the drumming.

If British infantry in America did not commonly carry colors into action or march and maneuver to beating drums and squealing fifes, then they compensated for this by making a great deal of noise of their own. In conventional European warfare, advancing soldiers were ordinarily kept perfectly quiet to facilitate command and control, Bland having directed in 1727 that, "[i]n marching up to attack the enemy, and during the action, a profound silence should be kept, [so] that the commanding officers may be distinctly heard in delivering their orders."[138] In theory this silence was only to be broken in the event of a lively bayonet attack, as Wolfe had suggested in orders to his 20th Regiment in late 1755: "The battalion is not to halloo or cry out upon any account whatsoever, although the rest of the troops should do it, until they are ordered to charge with their bayonets; in that case, and when they are upon the point of rushing upon the enemy, the battalion may give a warlike shout and run in."[139]

During the American War, the redcoats often cried out both before, during and after the charge. While this noise was variously described as "cheers," "shouts," "huzzas," "hurrahs," and "halloos," what one German mercenary called the "usual English 'Hura!'" seems commonly to have comprised three cheers, made in rapid succession.[140] Presumably, the officers encouraged (and indeed probably orchestrated) this cheering because they calculated that the moral effect on raw and unsteady rebel troops outweighed any momentary impairment of command and control. Significantly perhaps, during the fighting on St. Lucia in 1778, Brigadier General Medows ordered the troops of the British reserve (all veterans of the American War) that, in the event of attack, they were to receive the French regulars "with three huzzas, and then to be perfectly silent and obedient to their officers."[141]

The best evidence for British cheering in action in America comes from rebel participants at Cowpens. After the action Brigadier General Morgan reported that "their whole line moved on with the greatest impetuosity, shouting as they advanced."[142] Other participants noted that "the moment the British formed their line they shouted and made a great noise to intimidate," that the King's troops "began the attack by the discharge of two pieces of cannon and three huzzas," that they pushed forward at the trot "with a loud halloo," and that Morgan intervened to counter the enervating effect of this cheering by ordering his troops to reciprocate, hollering to his men, "They give us the British halloo, boys. Give *them* the Indian halloo, by God!"[143]

The outbreak of hostilities in North America in 1775 found the British troops at Boston trained only to fight in conventional European linear fashion, and the first clashes highlighted the inappropriateness of the deep, close-order infantry formation on the broken and wooded local topography. In 1776 the redcoats readopted the kind of loose, shallow formation employed previously in the French and Indian War and more recently prescribed for British light infantry. This was done principally to enable the troops to traverse broken ground at speed, the enemy's lack of steady, regular troops (particular cavalry) having apparently negated the inherent instability of open order formations. Henceforth the British probably made their initial advances in action at about the quick step, accelerated to a trot or a jog when within small-arms range of the enemy, and then broke into a run for the bayonet charge. Although colors and martial music probably made only infrequent appearances in action, as the men came on they would have cheered repeatedly and threateningly to intimidate the unsteady rebels. For most of the American War, the King's troops made their attacks in this basic fashion. Only in the last year or two of active campaigning does there seem to have been a limited return to more conventional close-order tactics in response to the increasing combat proficiency of the Continental Army.

**Private, grenadier company, 38th Regiment, 1777**

Private, battalion company, 21st Regiment ("Royal North British Fusiliers"), 1777

Private, battalion company, 34th Regiment, 1777

**Private, light company, 63rd Regiment, 1778–1781**

**Private, battalion company, 33rd Regiment, 1780**

**Private, grenadier company, 42nd ("Royal Highland") Regiment, 1780**

**Private, battalion company, 71st Regiment ("Fraser's Highlanders"), 1780**

# 7

# COMMANDING THE
# BATTALION

The duty of my station when in engagements was to fill up the
intervals occasioned by killed and wounded, and to receive and
issue orders, etc. The duty of firing is left to the private men. The
business of an officer is to see that they do their duty properly, level
and fire well; and, if necessary, assist them with his exhortations to
inspire them with courage, and keep them from breaking and
confusion.

James Green, "Account of Green's Services"

Chapter 4 surveyed the various maneuver and fire divisions of the
battalion and the numbers and (nominal) posts of the officers
commanding them. This chapter explores what these officers did in
action.

## REGIMENTAL OFFICERS IN COMBAT

In eighteenth-century conventional linear warfare, the regimental
infantry officer took part in four main activities: he motivated his
men, directed them, kept them in good order, and engaged in personal
combat. At least on European battlefields, perhaps the first of these
four activities was the most important. Historians commonly assert
that eighteenth-century common soldiers braved enemy fire partly
because they were more afraid of their officers than of the enemy.

There is some truth in this. As Wolfe put it in his tactical instructions to the 20th Regiment in 1755, in action the cordon of supernumerary subalterns and sergeants in the battalion's rear were required "to keep the men in their duty." This meant they used compulsion—even lethal force—to prevent the men from taking off: "A soldier that quits his rank, or offers to fly, is to be instantly put to death by the officer who commands that platoon, or by the officer or sergeant in the rear of that platoon; a soldier does not deserve to live who won't fight for his king and country."[1] Roger Lamb, a veteran of the American War, later opined that this threat was effective: "A coward taught to believe that, if he breaks his rank and abandons his colors, he will be punished with death by his own party, will take his chance against the enemy."[2] British officers in America did occasionally resort to such threats in action, even if they do not appear to have carried them out. For example, Ensign John De Berniere wrote of the retreat from Concord that, as the militia's fire began to take its toll, "we began to run rather than retreat in order. The whole behaved with amazing bravery but little order. We attempted to stop the men and form them two deep, but to no purpose: the confusion increased rather than lessened. At last . . . the officers got to the front and presented their bayonets, and told the men if they advanced they should die. Upon this they began to form under a very heavy fire."[3] Less happily, Tarleton recalled that "neither promises nor threats" availed the frantic efforts to recover the troops from their panic after the collapse of his line at Cowpens.[4]

Although the threat of summary retribution must (if only subconsciously) have reinforced common soldiers' readiness to brave enemy fire, eighteenth-century officers principally led rather than drove their men into combat. As previously discussed, this sometimes took the form of stirring exhortations that appealed to national or regimental identity. Similarly, the officers probably orchestrated the loud cheering in which the redcoats commonly indulged during combat. But the main way that the officer motivated his men was by maintaining a resolute, steady demeanor, particularly before and during the advance. As Bland pointed out in 1727, "the private soldiers . . . form their notions of the danger from the outward appearance of their officers, and according to their looks apprehend the undertaking to be more or less difficult."[5] For this the officer needed presence of mind and, above all, physical courage—the essence of the eighteenth-century cult of honor and sine qua non of the gentleman-officer.[6] The need for these qualities intensified once the battalion engaged in close combat because the advanced position of the regimental officers who conducted the firings made them highly vulnerable not only to the enemy's fire but also to that of their own men (whether accidental or otherwise).[7] The officer's prominent position also ensured that any momentary lapse in resolution would have been highly conspicuous. Any who failed in this respect almost certainly would have been pressured into quitting the corps, as happened to two unfortunate officers of the Queen's Rangers after the battle of Brandywine.[8]

Like courage, stoicism was a key element of the officer's ability to lead by example. This manifested itself most often in reluctance on the part of injured officers to leave the battalion for medical treatment. A particularly impressive instance occurred at the battle of Freeman's Farm, as later related by Thomas Anburey:

> In the course of the last action, Lieutenant [Stephen] Harvey, of the 62nd, a youth of sixteen, and nephew to the Adjutant General of the same name, received several wounds, and was repeatedly ordered off the field by [Lieutenant] Colonel [John] Anstruther; but his heroic ardor would not allow him to quit the battle, while he could stand and see his brave lads fighting beside him. A ball striking one of his legs, his removal became absolutely necessary; and while they were conveying him away, another wounded him mortally. In this situation the surgeon recommended him to take a powerful dose of opium, to avoid a seven or eight hours' life of most exquisite torture. This he immediately consented to, and when the Colonel entered the tent with Major [Henry] Harnage, who were both wounded, they asked whether he had any affairs they could settle for him. His reply was, that being a minor, everything was already adjusted; but he had one request, which he had just life enough to utter: "Tell my uncle I died like a soldier!"[9]

Similarly at Bunker Hill (according to Captain the Honorable Charles Stuart), "not one officer who served in the light infantry or grenadiers escaped unhurt, and few had less than three or four wounds."[10]

In America courage was an even more essential commodity for

British officers because the hazards run in action there were seemingly higher than in conventional linear warfare. European officers generally considered it taboo to target individuals of consequence.[11] At Brandywine, for instance, Major Patrick Ferguson countermanded his order for three of his British riflemen to shoot down an unsuspecting mounted rebel officer and his aide de camp because "the idea disgusted me . . . ; it was not pleasant to fire at the back of an unoffending individual, who was acquitting himself very coolly of his duty."[12] By contrast, rebel troops appear to have been positively encouraged to kill British officers.[13] Indeed, at a dinner after the fall of Yorktown, captive Captain Lieutenant Samuel Graham noted that the unpolished Daniel Morgan "spoke with more volubility, perhaps, than good taste" on his riflemen's role in Burgoyne's downfall—and particularly of his having expressly ordered the shooting of Brigadier General Fraser during the battle of Bemis Heights.[14]

To combat the rebel tactic of picking them off in action, British officers commonly toned down their appearance. In the case of the Guards, this process started even before the troops departed for service. Hence one English journalist noted how "[t]he [Guards] officers who are ordered for America are to wear the same uniform as the common soldiers, and their hair to be dressed in the like manner, so that they may not be distinguished from them by the riflemen, who aim particularly at the officers."[15] In America Howe issued a similar instruction to the British and Hessian officers in his army days before he opened the New York campaign.[16] Although British regimental officers would have retained their scarlet (rather than brick-red) coats and their epaulettes and swords, they appear to have stripped the metallic lace from their button holes and hats, laid aside gorgets (and possibly also their crimson sashes), and (like the sergeants) taken up fusils.[17] These sensible measures probably enjoyed some success. After the battle of Long Island, Captain William Dansey reported with relief that the threat the rebel sharpshooters posed was "not so dreadful as I expected," though (as he added later) "such a bugbear were they at first [that] our good friends thought we were all to be killed with rifles."[18] Interestingly, when Simcoe was wounded and captured in October 1779 during the Queen's Rangers' raid into New Jersey, he heard one rebel regret that he had not shot him through the head, "which he would have done had he known him to be a colonel, but he thought 'all colonels wore lace.' "[19]

Nevertheless, whatever their appearance, British officers would have marked themselves out in action by issuing commands to and encouraging their men. Such was the case with the aforementioned mounted officer with the grenadiers at the battle of Monmouth, one rebel officer having recorded: "I ordered my men to level at him and the cluster of men near him. . . . He dropped [and] his men slackened their pace."[20] An even more striking instance occurred during the storming of Chatterton's Hill, as related by Corporal Thomas Sullivan of the 49th Regiment:

> Captain [Lieutenant William] Gore, who commanded the right wing of our battalion, seeing the rebels which we engaged on the right wing were dressed in blue, took them to be Colonel Rall's brigade of Hessians, and immediately ordered us to cease firing; for, says he, "you are firing at your own men." We ceased for about two minutes. The rebels, hearing him, made answer that they were no Hessians, and that we should soon know the difference. . . . The aforesaid captain was killed upon the spot: the enemy in his front took as good aim as possible at him, and directed the most of their fire towards the place [where] he stood, for they took him for the officer that commanded the regiment.[21]

Clearly the rebels singled out and peppered the unfortunate Gore precisely because he drew attention to himself in such spectacular fashion.

Officer casualties were probably disproportionately heavy in those engagements in America where British bayonet attacks failed to dislodge the enemy quickly because sustained fighting gave the rebels more opportunity to single out officers and shoot them down. Burgoyne later claimed that this had unfortunately very much been the case during the seesaw struggle in the center at the battle of Freeman's Farm: "The enemy had with their army great numbers of marksmen, armed with rifle-barrel pieces. These, during an engagement, hovered upon the flanks in small detachments, and were very expert in securing themselves, and in shifting their ground. In this action, many placed themselves in high trees in the rear of their own line, and there was seldom a minute's interval of smoke in any part of our line without officers being taken off by [a] single shot."[22] In a similar fashion, at Cowpens over two-thirds of Tarleton's infantry officers went down in the fighting that preceded the final, catastrophic British charge, according to Roderick Mackenzie, who was himself wounded.[23] Although officer casualties do not appear to have been grossly disproportionate in relation to those of the enlisted men, during the course of the war, some regiments and companies were clearly more unlucky than others. After the 52nd Regiment lost its fourth grenadier captain in three years at the battle of Monmouth, one of the corps' drummers observed with black humor, "Well, I wonder who they will get to accept of our grenadiers now. I'll be damned if I would take them!"[24]

Considering how (as we have seen) eighteenth-century officers often carried spontoons (or, less commonly in Europe, firelocks) in addition to their swords, one might have expected that they would have fought alongside their men in action. As Mark Odintz has convincingly demonstrated, however, in America this does not appear often to have been the case.[25] For example, when Brigadier General Alexander Leslie wrote to his brother about the death of Captain the Honorable William Leslie at Princeton, he reassured the earl, "I don't find he was too rash, as you seem to fear, or that he was out of the ranks."[26] More explicitly, after the battle of Monmouth, Lieutenant Hale regretted the fact that he and three brother-officers of the 2nd Battalion of Grenadiers had recklessly outpaced their companies during the initial breakneck British advance. Hale shamefacedly added, "I am told the general [i.e., Clinton] has expressed his approbation of the ridiculous behavior of the four subaltern officers . . . who had got foremost."[27]

That Hale took especial notice of the fact that one of his brother officers had dispatched a rebel with his sword during the pursuit ("as we all might have done") demonstrates that engaging in personal combat was an unusual exploit for an officer. Similarly, contrary to the recommendation of one officer and military writer who served in Britain, firelock-armed officers and sergeants in America were not encouraged to augment the battalion's fire in action.[28] At the opening of the Albany expedition, Burgoyne reminded his army that "[t]he attention of every officer in action is to be employed in his men; to make use of a fusil except in very extraordinary occasions of immediate personal defense, would betray an ignorance of his importance, and of his duty."[29] Likewise, in a memorandum composed around May 1776 at Cape Fear, Clinton complained that an officer could not properly command his men "while he is firing, loading, and playing bo peep behind trees." According to the general, when this happened the soldier, "when things become desperate talks of *every man for himself* and *sauve qui peut.*"[30] Months later, an incident at the storming of Chatterton's Hill appeared to vindicate Clinton's disapproval. He later described what happened when, having forded the Bronx River, two British battalions suddenly found themselves exposed to very heavy fire from the rebels atop the hill: "The officer who led them immediately formed in column for attack and advanced; the instant I saw the move I declared it decisive. But when the officer had marched forward about twenty paces he halted, fired his fusil, and began to reload (his column remaining during the time under the enemy's fire); upon which I pronounced it a *coup manqué,* foretelling at the same time that they would break. It happened as I said, and I could not help remarking to Sir William Howe that, if the battle should be lost, that officer was the occasion of it. I had scarcely done speaking when Lord Cornwallis came up with the same observation." Clinton's judgment on the affair was unequivocal: "General Burgoyne and I have often represented the absurdity of officers being armed with fusils, and the still greater impropriety . . . by which they neglected the opportunity of employing their divisions to advantage. These had no confidence in them, and they became in fact as the worst soldiers in their divisions."[31] In short, the officer could not properly carry out his duty to orchestrate violence and simultaneously be a direct agent of it.

The third activity that officers were expected to perform in action was to keep the men under order. This responsibility included supporting the sergeants in their main duties of filling vacancies and dressing the ranks and files—an important job when the men's natural instinct was to "bunch" under fire.[32] To facilitate this task, in conventional linear warfare officers and sergeants customarily carried spontoons and halberds; which were less useful as weapons than as tools with which to manhandle misaligned men into position. As mentioned earlier, the formation of two ranks at open file intervals customarily employed by the redcoats in America from 1776 precluded them from maintaining perfect dressings in combat. Despite this, however, the officers and sergeants needed to preserve a certain level of order, without which their control over the men would have broken down. This was especially critical when the battalion came under fire, met unexpectedly aggressive resistance, or routed one enemy force only to encounter a fresh one in its path. Any of these scenarios was likely, at best, to have dampened the men's ardor and to have temporarily diverted their attention from their officers. At worst, the battalion might have fallen into disarray, in which case it could neither have continued its advance, prevailed in the firefight, nor withstood a resolute enemy attack. Whatever the degree of confusion, it was the officers' immediate and overwhelming priority to restore full control over the bewildered or excitable soldiery.

As one instance of this, during the final assault at Bunker Hill, the adjutant of the 1st Battalion of Marines, Lieutenant John Waller, had to exert himself to restore order to the corps before it could resume its advance and storm the rebel position. Waller's account is so vivid that it deserves to be quoted at some length:

> when we came immediately under the work, we were checked by the severe fire of the enemy, but did not retreat an inch. We were now in confusion, after being broke several times in getting over the rails, etc. I did all I could to form the two companies on our right, which at last I effected, losing many of them. While it was performing, Major [John] Pitcairn was killed close by me, with a captain and a subaltern, also a sergeant, and many of the privates; and had we stopped there much longer, the enemy would have picked us all off. I saw this, and begged [Lieutenant] Colonel [William] Nesbitt, of the 47th [Regiment], to form on our left, in order that we might advance with our bayonets to the parapet. I ran from right to left, and stopped our men from firing while this was doing; and when we had got in tolerable order, we rushed on, leaped the ditch, and climbed the parapet, under a most sore and heavy fire.[33]

Similarly, during Lieutenant Colonel Charles Mawhood's first attack at Princeton, a "very heavy discharge" at forty yards brought down seven of the men in Lieutenant Hale's ad hoc grenadier platoon and forced the others to recoil some distance, where Hale "rallied them with some difficulty, and brought them on with [charged] bayonets."[34]

As Hale's experience indicates, sometimes the officers and sergeants could not restore their men's order while the enemy continued to present an immediate threat, in which case the whole had to retire some distance first. Thus at Concord, when the rebel militia's fire forced Captain Walter Laurie's three light companies at the North Bridge (in the words of one of the officers) "to give way, then run with the greatest precipitance," the four remaining officers did not succeed in halting the men until they reached the cover of the grenadier companies marching to reinforce them.[35] A similar phenomenon occurred at the battle of Eutaw Springs. There, when Lieutenant Colonel Alexander Stewart's line collapsed, it was necessary for the King's troops "to retire a little distance to an open field in order to form" under the cover of the fire from a detachment of the New York Volunteers, who posted themselves in an adjacent brick house.[36]

The last of the regimental officers' four main activities was to oversee the various maneuvers and firings of their troops. In theory, because the battalion was under the overall control of the field officers, this task did not demand a vast effort from the captains and subalterns. For example, if the commanding officer ordered the battalion to open fire at the halt by subdivisions, the eight officers in question simply had to step forward and give the signal in the predetermined sequence for their fire divisions to "make ready," "present," and "fire" (and then to "load"). Hypothetically, maneuvering the battalion generally demanded even less of the captains and subalterns, for most of the evolutions required no further verbal instructions than the initial command bellowed by one of the field officers. All the captains and subalterns had to do was to oversee their maneuver divisions as they executed the evolution—doubtless the sergeants would have shoved wayward men into place.[37] In short, in conventional linear warfare the directorial role of the captains and subalterns did not require them to display a great deal of tactical initiative. But as will become clear later in this chapter, it was a very different matter in America. There the British considerably loosened the ties that ordinarily bound the maneuver and fire divisions of the battalion so rigidly into a single tactical entity.

### Fragmentation of the Line during the Advance

In conventional linear warfare it was, as Bland had put it in 1727, "a fixed rule for every battalion to act, as near as possible, in concert with the whole, both in advancing, attacking, pursuing, or retiring together." This was because a battalion that did not regulate its movements "according to the motion of the line" risked being "surrounded by fresh troops, and cut to pieces, before the line can come up to their assistance." Here the principal threat was that the battalion might be "attacked on the flanks by the enemy's horse, who are frequently posted between the first and second lines for this purpose." In short, "the whole line must act like one battalion" or else risk destruction in detail: "While they [i.e., the battalions] keep in a body, they can mutually assist one another; but if they should separate in pursuing those they beat, the enemy may destroy them one after the other, with such an inconsiderable number of troops, that were they in a body, would fly at their appearance."[38] More succinctly, at the battle of Dettingen (1743), Lieutenant General Jasper Clayton directed one British regimental commander to "[k]eep your battalion in a line with the regiments on your right and left, [and] if you perceive any of them to give way, look sharp and guard your flanks."[39]

British commanders in America cannot have been unaware of the importance of what Bland recommended. Indeed, Howe made efforts to improve his battalions' ability to maneuver together in preparation for the New York campaign by holding a series of exercises on Citadel Hill at Halifax. During the first series of exercises in the second half of April 1776, Lieutenant General Lord Percy exercised the line battalions three at a time (that is, in brigade strength), while Major Thomas Musgrave exercised the light infantry and grenadiers eight or so companies at a time (that is, at battalion strength). During the second series of exercises in May and early June, Musgrave took out the newly organized flank battalions (four in number) and Percy the First to Sixth Brigades (each of three battalions).[40] Presumably, one of Percy's priorities was to practice the brigades in deploying and maneuvering together, Howe himself having later testified that at Halifax the army "received great benefit . . . from the opportunity of being exercised in line, a very material part of discipline, in which we were defective until that time."[41]

Yet despite Howe's exercises at Halifax, it does not seem that British battalions in America often regulated their movements in the manner recommended by Bland. This was largely because they did not need to do so. Since the rebels lacked the powerful cavalry forces maintained by European armies, and since only the cream of the rebel infantry was capable of maneuvering adroitly and aggressively, rebel field commanders often proved incapable of seizing the tactical initiative by, for instance, launching violent local counterattacks. Of course, the Continental Army did improve dramatically in quality over the course of the war. But even then the celerity with which the redcoats usually advanced, the extended frontage their battalions needed when drawn up two deep with open files, and the broken and/or wooded terrain that characterized most American battlefields all militated against the maintenance of a well-connected line of battle.[42] As the journalist of the Hessian *Feldjägerkorps* put it in recounting the attack of Cornwallis's division at Birmingham Meetinghouse at the battle of Brandywine, "We could not see the 2nd Battalion of Light Infantry [on our right] because of the terrain, and while we received only a few orders, each commander had to act according to his own best judgement."[43]

Throughout the war then, it was common for British lines of battle to bulge and even to fragment entirely as their constituent battalions diverged from a single axis and rate of advance to engage whatever enemy units presented themselves. In fact this phenomenon was so marked at some engagements (such as Monmouth Courthouse) as to make the precise sequence of events almost incomprehensible for the historian. Captain John André's account of the attack at Birmingham Meetinghouse illustrates vividly how the various corps conducted their maneuvers with only limited reference to those of their neighbors:

At about 4 o'clock the attack began near the [Birmingham] Meeting House. The Guards were formed upon the right, the British Grenadiers in the center, and the Light Infantry and Chasseurs [i.e., *Jäger*] on the left. The Hessian Grenadiers supported the Guards and British Grenadiers, and the 4th Brigade supported the Light Infantry and the left of the Grenadiers. The 3rd Brigade under [Major] General Grey was the Reserve. The Guards met with very little resistance and penetrated to the very height overlooking the 4-gun battery of the rebels at Chad's Ford, just as General Knyphausen had crossed. The Hessian Grenadiers were to their left and not so far advanced. The British Grenadiers divided after passing Birmingham Meeting House, the 1st Battalion inclining to the right and the 2nd pushing about a mile beyond the village of Dilworth. The Light Infantry and Chasseurs inclined to the left, and by this means left an interval which was filled up by part of the 4th Brigade. The Light Infantry met with the chief resistance at a hill on which the rebels had four pieces of cannon. At the end of the day the 2nd Battalion [of] Grenadiers received a very heavy fire; the 64th Regiment, which was near them was engaged at the same time. The rebels were driven back by the superior fire of the troops, but these were too much exhausted to be able to charge or pursue. The Reserve moved centrically in the rear of the whole and inclined successively to the parts most engaged.[44]

Howe's Hessian aide de camp understated the case when he wrote that, after the Fourth Brigade moved forward to fill the gap between the grenadiers and light infantry, "The new front was somewhat more sloping."[45] In reality, by the close of the battle, the battalions had become quite widely separated. For example, as the journalist of the Hessian *Feldjägerkorps* put it, "as the 2nd Battalion of Light Infantry had attacked so far to the right, we stood at a great distance from the army . . . until about seven o'clock in the evening."[46]

Where the fighting took place in thickly timbered country, it was plainly impossible to maintain a properly connected line during the advance. Thomas Anburey, who fought at Hubbardton as a "gentleman volunteer" with the grenadiers, later noted that "the woods were so thick, that little or no order could be observed in advancing upon the enemy, it being totally impossible to form a regular line."[47] Limited visibility was not the only factor that prevented the troops from maintaining a well-connected line of battle in woodland fighting, however. Some units inevitably encountered stiffer opposition than others, which consequently slowed their advance. As an anonymous Brunswick officer commented in the aftermath of the disaster at Bennington, "It is serious business fighting in wild woods and bushes, and one company may easily have better or worse luck than another."[48] A similar phenomenon was experienced at Guilford Courthouse, where, as Stedman later recalled: "The British line, being so much extended to the right and left in order to show a front equal to the enemy, was unavoidably broken into intervals in the pursuit of the first and second American lines; some parts of it being more advanced than others, in consequence of the different degrees of resistance that had been met with, or of other impediments arising from the thickness of the woods, and the inequality of the ground."[49]

Lieutenant Thomas Saumarez, with the 23rd Regiment on the British left, highlighted the role of these "impediments" when he related that, during the advance against the second rebel line, "[n]ot being able to attack in front, the Fusiliers were obliged to take the ground to their left to get clear of the brushwood."[50]

Tarleton's account of Guilford Courthouse conveys especially clearly how the British line became deranged as it fought its way through the woods. He recorded that, after Cornwallis's line had routed the North Carolina militia and plunged into the dense woodland that blanketed most of the battlefield, "[t]he broken ground and the extent of the enemy's front . . . occasioned the flanks to open from the center." What Tarleton meant by this was that, because the units posted on the extremities of the first rebel line maintained the contest after the militia had flown, the brigades of Lieutenant Colonel Webster and Major General Leslie drifted to the left and right respectively, leaving a yawning gap in the British center. This gap was filled by the 2nd Battalion and the grenadier company of the Guards, which were ordered up from the reserve. But the integrity of the British line was not restored for long. As the battalions engaged and forced back the various units of Virginia militia in the second rebel line, the fact that some units encountered "less opposition and embarrassment than others" conspired with "[t]he thickness of the woods where these conflicts happened" and thereby "impeded the British infantry moving forwards in a well-connected line." Consequently, some corps unknowingly outstripped the rest of the army and "arrived sooner in [the] presence of the Continentals." First to break out of the woods, on the left, was Webster with his own 33rd Regiment, with which (supported by the *Jäger* and the Guards' light company) he immediately attacked that part of the rebel third line that he could see across the open ground. Rebuffed in disarray, the mortally wounded Webster and his command remained in the woods "till he could hear of the progress of the King's troops upon his right"—which effectively meant until the end of the action, when he "soon after connected his corps with the main body." Next to emerge from the woods, in the center, was the 2nd Battalion of Guards, whose impulsive, unsupported attack the Continentals also bloodily repulsed. With the British left and center (if they could still be called such) now in confusion and the right stalled far behind in the woods, it was probably fortunate for Cornwallis that Greene now ordered a general withdrawal before the

2nd Battalion of the 71st Regiment and the 23rd Regiment came up. These had initially been part of Leslie's and Webster's brigades, but (in Tarleton's words) "had inclined from the divisions on the right and left."[51]

In combat in America then, the field officers were compelled to display an unconventional degree of tactical initiative in directing their respective corps, as Major General Phillips admitted in general orders prior to his thrust against Petersburg in April 1781: "As the present movements will be made in a difficult country, it becomes necessary that officers leading columns and commanding corps, should use and exert the intelligence of their own minds, joined to the knowledge of the service, in times of an attack, when they cannot immediately receive the orders of the Brigadier General [i.e., Benedict Arnold] or Major General."[52] It is worth stressing once again that this kind of order would have been unusual in most conventional European campaigns.

## The Company in Action

Unlike conventional European linear warfare, on American battlefields it was common for the companies within the battalion to operate as semiautonomous tactical entities, each one under the direction of its captain or senior subaltern. Indeed, individual companies were not infrequently detached from the battalion during combat to perform particular tasks. Although this phenomenon was most marked in the case of the light infantry, line battalion companies also sometimes acted almost independently in action, particularly in woody country. For example, Captain the Honorable William Leslie recorded of the battle of Long Island that, as Major General James Grant's and Brigadier General James Agnew's Fourth and Sixth Brigades deployed on the British left, "my company [of the 17th Regiment] was sent as a reinforcement to the advanced guard, who were much incommoded by riflemen."[53] Similarly, when Sergeant Roger Lamb found himself separated from the 23rd Regiment during the attack on the Virginia militia at Guilford Courthouse, he suddenly espied a single company of the Guards advancing to the attack. He later commented: "The reader may perhaps be surprised at the bravery of troops, thus with calm intrepidity attacking superior numbers, when formed into separate bodies, and all acting together; but I can assure him this instance was not peculiar: it frequently occurred in the British army during the American War."[54] The Irishman was well placed to comment on this theme, for he not only participated fully in Cornwallis's southern campaigns but also served in the northern wilderness with Carleton and Burgoyne in 1776 and 1777. He was therefore involved in some of the most confused and fiercely contested engagements of the eighteenth century.

Perhaps the earliest explicit expression of the unconventional degree of tactical independence that companies had to be able to exercise in action in America is contained in a series of tactical instructions that Major General Phillips issued to Burgoyne's army in May 1777, shortly before the opening of the Albany expedition. The thrust of Phillips's message to the captains was that Burgoyne required "that every company may form a respectable body singly, and though attached to its place in battalion, yet always ready to act separate from it, as the nature of the ground may require, or the nature of local service they may be sent on make necessary." Having recommended that officers drill their own companies (to ensure that they were "perfectly acquainted" with their men and the latter were "accustomed to the sound of their [officers'] voices"), Phillips observed, "It is well understood, that all regiments exercise by companies; but it is usually done with a view of joining in battalion." By contrast, he warned, the expected nature of the forthcoming campaign made it necessary "that each company should be led to consider itself as a small, distinct body, and [to] exercise in various evolutions independent of the battalion, with every possible view for single companies being taught to depend upon themselves."[55]

Phillips's instructions also made it clear that, even when joined in battalion, each captain would have to exercise considerable tactical latitude in handling his company. This was because the companies were expected to draw up "with small intervals of distance" between them to enable them to exploit good defensive ground (trees, fences, banks, and such), to negotiate obstacles (enclosures, ravines, ditches, marsh, small rises, brushwood, and such), to facilitate changes of position and facing, and to traverse difficult ground. To facilitate command and control and to enable companies to act coherently, Phillips recommended "the commanding officer of a battalion to put himself at the head of one company, and to maneuver that company; while the other companies . . . follow the evolutions so given by the commanding officer." Presumably this unconventional arrangement (which to modern eyes would resemble a cross between "follow my leader" and a "Mexican wave") was intended to address the problem that a field officer at the center of the battalion could hardly have controlled all its companies (spread out over two hundred yards or so) simply by verbal command, particularly on wooded ground.[56]

Although Phillips intended these company-level instructions to confer tactical flexibility on the battalion in action in close country, he acknowledged that even a single company would occasionally be too unwieldy a tactical entity to execute some maneuvers. He therefore indicated that, when it was necessary for the battalion to furcate in order to negotiate multiple obstacles, the officers might have to tell off their companies into even smaller maneuver divisions, each commanded by no less than a sergeant (curiously, Phillips did not simply recommend that the company should break up into two platoons). But as soon as the separated maneuver divisions had negotiated the obstacles in question, and as soon as the ground permitted, they were to reform: first into companies, then into battalion.[57]

Even more explicit evidence as to the degree of tactical autonomy allowed for companies in action in America is provided by a set of tactical instructions that Lieutenant Colonel Henry Hope drew up for the 1st Battalion of Grenadiers in August 1780. These guidelines incorporated the same basic unorthodox, staggered manner of operating in battalion that Phillips had prescribed three years earlier:

> Whatever company or division in the battalion may be first ordered by the commanding officer to perform any movement, the same is always to be immediately followed by the two next on their right and left, and so on through the whole battalion without waiting for further directions—the men receiving the word of command from their own officers. . . . When the battalion is ordered to march in line, the whole is ordered to march by that particular division in front of which the commanding officer marches; the officer of which will give the greatest attention to keep the direction in which he moves, that the same file continue to cover him as when first put in motion.

Like Phillips, Hope clearly envisaged that when the battalion was in line, the various companies could not all be expected to take their dressings from one particular point of the battalion, as was usual in conventional linear warfare. Consequently, each company was to dress itself on one of the two officers posted on its flanks: "In marching by companies or division[s], the officers commanding each should at all times caution his division to which flank he would have his men dress ... remembering always that they should never be required to look in a different direction from that which [it] is intended they should incline to. And to facilitate this still more, there should be always either an officer or sergeant on each flank when the battalion breaks off into companies or divisions (as far at least as the numbers will admit of their being so distributed), [so] that the men may have some superior to look to for regulating their movement and [to] dress by."[58] Although the 1st Battalion of Grenadiers may never have employed Hope's command-and-control method in action (the last occasion on which the grenadier battalions were hotly engaged was the battle of Monmouth), it is interesting that it appears to echo Phillips's instructions to Burgoyne's army. Once again, since it would have been impractical for a field officer to bellow oral commands to the battalion's companies over an extended frontage, particularly in woodland, it is tempting to speculate that Hope's instructions may simply have represented an explicit codification of the method of operating in battalion that was already in widespread use.

If the companies within line battalions often performed as semi-independent tactical entities in action in America, particularly in broken country, then light infantry companies commonly enjoyed even more tactical freedom.[59] For example, as Knyphausen's column approached Chad's Ford at Brandywine, Captain Patrick Ferguson's riflemen cooperated with the companies of the Queen's Rangers in dislodging strong rebel delaying parties from successive prepared positions: "they remained planted like cabbages whilst our parties divided, gained their flanks, [and] turned their breastworks."[60] Once the Queen's Rangers had successfully crossed Chad's Ford, Private Stephen Jarvis's company and one other were detached to occupy an eminence upon the left; from whence "we saw our brave comrades cutting them [i.e., the rebels] up in brave style."[61]

Perhaps the most striking example of the kind of tactical freedom enjoyed by companies of a light battalion was the role of the 1st Battalion of Light Infantry in the attack at Birmingham Meetinghouse, also during the battle of Brandywine.[62] The account that one of the officers who participated in the attack penned later is so dramatic and striking that it deserves to be quoted at length:

As soon as the [first] line [of Cornwallis's division] came to Dilworth Church [i.e., Birmingham Meetinghouse], the enemy opened a fire from five fieldpieces [on Birmingham Hill]. The churchyard wall being opposite the 17th [Regiment's] light company, the captain [William Scott] determined to get over the fence into the road; and calling for the men to follow, ran down the road and lodged the men without loss at the foot of the hill on which the guns were firing. The hedge on the left side of the road [was] much cut with the grape shot. By a bend of the hill, [we] had a view of a part of the enemy's line opposite the [two battalions of] grenadiers [to our right] and opened a fire from about half the company on it, no more being able to form on the space. Presently, [we were] joined by the 38th [Regiment's light] company. Some of their gallant soldiers wanted to ascend the hill immediately; [which was] objected to as too imprudent. The 33rd [Regiment's light] company joined immediately afterwards, and the men of [these] three companies . . . ascended the hill. . . . Their [i.e., the rebels'] line advancing on us, we were compelled to throw ourselves on our knees and bellies, and keep up a fire from the slope of the hill. [The] enemy repeatedly attempted to come on, but were always drove back by our fire, although their General (Lincoln) [*sic,* Major General Sullivan] very much exerted himself. At this time a most tremendous fire of musketry opened from both lines. Looking back to see how far the grenadier line was off, from which alone we could receive immediate support, to my surprise I saw close to me Major [the Honorable Charles] Stuart of the 43rd [Regiment]. . . . Recollecting the 43rd [Regiment's] grenadier company was the left of their line, we persuaded Major Stuart to run down the hill and prevail on that company to hasten to our support. He did so, but before he could return, to my inexpressible joy, [I] saw Captain [Charles] Cochrane of the 4th [Regiment's light] company on my left throw up his cap and cry "Victory!"; and, looking round, [I] saw the 43rd [Regiment's grenadier] company hastening to our relief. We dashed forward,

passed the five pieces of cannon which the enemy had abandoned, and made some few prisoners—the enemy running
away from us with too much speed to be overtaken.[63]

This account makes it perfectly clear that the 1st Battalion of Light
Infantry's companies (totaling together around five hundred men) did
not fight at Brandywine as a single tactical entity under the close
direction of its commanding officer, Lieutenant Colonel Robert Abercrombie. Nor even do they appear to have operated in the staggered
manner laid down by Phillips and Hope (in other words, the individual
companies did not remain loosely coupled and take their tactical cue
from the company at the center). Instead each of the officers commanding the various companies exercised near-total independence in
conducting his men, which enabled the companies to pick their way
forward according to terrain and the strength of the opposition to their
front. Indeed, most tellingly of all, at a moment of crisis the officers of
the 17th Regiment's light company were able to request the immediate support of the 43rd Regiment's grenadier company. This was, of
course, part of another unit altogether, namely, the 2nd Battalion of
Grenadiers (to the right of the 1st Battalion of Light Infantry).[64]

The letters of Captain William Dansey, who commanded the 33rd
Regiment's light company from 1776 to 1778, offer further evidence
that the companies of a light battalion did not keep in formation and
operate in a closely coordinated fashion in combat. Instead Dansey's
references to his company's performance in action (like his verdict on
the affair at Harlem Heights, that this was an engagement "in which
the light infantry were chiefly concerned, and my company among
the first of them") tend to give the impression that the light companies were unleashed against the rebels rather like a pack of savage
dogs.[65] Occasionally one or more other light companies came to
Dansey's assistance when his men were hard pressed. For example, of
the battle of Long Island, Dansey observed: "I led my company into
the very thick of them [i.e., the rebels] and had a most miraculous
escape. In about three minutes I had three men killed and six wounded
out of thirty, [and] Mr. [Richard] Cotton my lieutenant got a graze
upon the shoulder. We were well supported by three companies or
there would not have remained a man to tell the story. I have to thank
God for my safety under the heaviest fire of musketry ever people
escaped from." In his next letter he elaborated on this close scrape: "I

was lucky in my escape, for I had my right hand man wounded and left hand man killed. I had three killed and six wounded in my company in about three minutes, having fallen in with about 400 riflemen unawares. They are not so dreadful as I expected, or they must have destroyed me and my whole company before we were supported by anybody else. Afterwards they were all either killed or taken. My company, though obliged to retreat (not having 20 yards the start and being only thirty men) killed two officers and two men before we gave way. We had got in among them."[66] In other engagements, however, Dansey and his men appear to have maneuvered and fought with almost no support from the rest of the battalion's companies. This appears to have been the case at one point during the battle of Monmouth, of which he recorded: "I have only to tell you I had a very narrow escape from being taken prisoner with my whole company. We were obliged to run up to our middles in a bog to get away from the rebel light horse, and I had only one man taken."[67]

Because light companies appear commonly to have enjoyed near-total tactical independence in action, their captains required a high degree of individual initiative and skill. As might be expected, Dansey's letters give a fascinating insight into his personal role in directing his company in combat. For example, in recounting his part in a major skirmish that developed during a foraging expedition in New Jersey (on 23 February 1777), Dansey explained how he had employed an elementary *ruse de guerre* to induce the enemy to retreat:

I faced two hundred of the rebels with my company only in a wood, for two minutes, myself not twenty yards from some of them, and received all their fire. Our friends thought we were cut to pieces. Another company joined me, and I drove the rebels and had only one man wounded in the arm. We killed six and wounded sixteen of them. I was so near as to call to them, "By God, my lads, we have you now" in the hopes they would be bullied into surrender, but that would not do: they answered me with a heavy fire. However, when I got my men to the trees round about me, and the other company coming up to my support, I bullied them another way. Seeing them snug behind the trees and showing no disposition to run, and too many of them to charge (as we were rather too thin), I cried as loud as I could hollow, that they might be sure to hear

me, "By God, soldiers, they run, have at them my brave boys" which had the desired effect. One thought the other [had] run, and they all set off as if the Devil drove them. We cleared the wood of them and they never [showed?] themselves within shot again that day.[68]

The opportunity to exercise this level of personal initiative and tactical skill in combat made the light company captain's battlefield role markedly different from that of captains of the battalion companies. Indeed, in March 1778, after one of his brother officers was rewarded with the post of aide de camp to Major General William Tryon, Dansey grumbled with obvious frustration about the limited recognition that fell to successful light company officers like himself, especially when they faced the added danger of professional disgrace in the event of mishap:

I am almost wishing for a smug [illegible: berth?] of that kind, for I find there is nothing to be gained by fighting with light infantry but—Lord knows—broken bones. And as to the honor of it, if it was not for self-satisfaction it is all a farce. Merit goes by favor, and we are only tools for the favorites to work with, [so] consequently generally fall into ignorant, unskilful hands. And like the mechanic's tools, we suffer; and if the work does not succeed we are blamed, [while] if it does [succeed] we have no more merit than the carpenter's axe or saw. In short, an officer of the light infantry's character is always at stake; and if he does ever so well, the merit becomes other people's, whose impudence or sycophancy gains them the ears of people in power. But I'll persevere. I may be lucky, [and] therefore will not draw from the lottery of preferment yet.[69]

Other examples can be cited to show the level of initiative that light infantry officers had to display in action. For example, at the action at Spencer's Ordinary, teenaged Lieutenant Charles Dunlop of the Queen's Rangers "led on his division on horseback, without suffering a man to fire, watching the enemy, and giving a signal to his men to lay down whenever a party of theirs was about to fire."[70] Similarly, in September 1776 Lieutenant Loftus Cliffe, a subaltern in the 46th Regiment, marveled at the coolness and flair with which Captain Mathew Johnson conducted the regiment's light company at the affair at Harlem Heights: "Johnson and his . . . company behaved amazingly. He goes through his maneuvers by a whistle, for which he has often been laughed at. They either form to right or left, or squat or rise, by a particular whistle, which his men are as well acquainted with as the battalion [companies of the 46th Regiment are] with the word of command. He (being used to woods fighting, and having a quick eye) had his company down in the moment of the enemy's 'present!,' and up again at the advantageous moment for their fire, killed several, and had not one of his company hurt during the whole time he drove the enemy before him."[71] The 46th Regiment was Howe's own corps, and it may be that the commander in chief himself influenced Johnson to adopt his sensible command-and-control system. Howsoever the case, that Johnson was able to practice such a system, and that his less imaginative brother officers derided him for it, signifies not only how much latitude the light infantry captain exercised in "fighting" his company in action but also that not all officers were fit to be entrusted with so demanding a situation.

In conventional linear combat, the captain and subaltern were likely to be involved in four main activities: motivating their men, keeping them in good order, engaging in personal combat (occasionally), and directing their men. This latter role especially was at a premium in America, where conventional methods of command and control were not always feasible. Because it often proved unnecessary and even impracticable to maintain a well-connected line of battle during the advance, field officers were compelled to exercise a far higher degree of tactical initiative in "fighting" their battalions than was usual in European campaigns. To enable the field officers to synchronize the actions of the battalion's loosely deployed companies in combat, particularly in woody country, some corps appear to have adopted an innovative, staggered method of maneuvering. Finally, in the case of the light battalions, the field officers nominally in command seem commonly to have exercised little overall direction over the companies in action. Once these latter engaged, they appear to have cooperated only loosely, the respective captains enjoying the kind of tactical independence that demanded flair far in excess of that expected of the officers of the line infantry.

# 8

# FIREPOWER

[A] party of our men . . . were met . . . by about the same number of
rebels. When they were about 100 yards from each other, both
parties fired; but I did not see any fall. They still advanced to the
distance of 40 yards or less, and fired again. I then saw a great
number fall on both sides. . . . I never before saw such a shocking
scene: some dead, others dying, death in different shapes. Some of
the wounded [were] making the most pitiful lamentations; others
that were of different parties [were] cursing each other as the author
of their misfortunes.

*Journal of Nicholas Cresswell,* 22 June 1777

In the course of the eighteenth century, the significance of firepower as one of the keys to battlefield success increased greatly.
This chapter discusses the ways in which British commanders in
America provided their troops with artillery support and how and to
what effect the infantry delivered musketry in combat.

## ARTILLERY SUPPORT

A detailed treatment of the training, ordnance, and services of the
late-eighteenth-century Royal Artillery is far beyond the scope of this
work.[1] Nevertheless, it is necessary to say a few words on the subjects
of how and with what success British commanders employed field
artillery against the American rebels.

The Seven Years War marked a dramatic shift in the relationship between the artillery and the other two arms in European land warfare.[2] This shift had its roots in a number of small but cumulative technological advances and in the burgeoning sense of professionalism that had been transforming the various states' artillery corps for some time. In short, in the 1750s and 1760s, the mobility, weight of fire, and accuracy of European field artillery increased significantly. Indeed, according to Christopher Duffy, during the Seven Years War, case shot probably inflicted more battle casualties on the Prussian Army than did any other weapon.[3]

Field artillery's most obvious virtue was its ability to kill and incapacitate at ranges that far outdistanced small arms. Firing roundshot, a light 6-pounder gun was able to destroy men, horses, and guns at a distance of over two-thirds of a mile, though the effective range was much less. When the Second Brigade successfully stormed Chatterton's Hill at the battle of White Plains, Corporal Thomas Sullivan took particular notice of the "horrible" evidence of the preparatory British cannonade: "one [rebel] with his head off and between his feet, and the other with the head and half his breast shot off."[4] Similarly, at Fort Mifflin in 1777, Continental soldier Joseph Plumb Martin saw stooping comrades "split like fish to be broiled" by British roundshot.[5] When artillery played upon a target in enfilade, the results were truly devastating. After the bloody action at the Vigie on St. Lucia (18 December 1778), artilleryman Captain Francis Downman gloated, "I had a fine situation for galling the French army as they marched to the attack in columns." With four 18-pounders, Downman "kept up as heavy a fire as I could on their flank, which was presented to me the greatest part of the action." He graphically conveyed with grim relish the carnage that his guns inflicted: "My shot in this situation swept them off by dozens at a time, and Frenchmen's heads and legs were as plenty and much cheaper than sheep's heads and trotters in Scotland."[6] At shorter ranges showers of case shot carried men off in their dozens. Toward the end of the battle of Bemis Heights, the Crown artillery seems to have done serious execution among the rebel "columns" that attempted to carry the fortifications protecting Burgoyne's camp, particularly the Balcarres Redoubt.[7]

In addition to destroying troops, artillery smashed fieldworks. Indeed, one of the principal tactical lessons of the Seven Years War was that powerful field artillery (particularly howitzers) was indispensable if a commander wished to force the enemy from fortified positions without incurring massive infantry losses.[8] In North America the rolling, wooded topography lent itself well to defensive warfare. Particularly during the war's early campaigns, rebel troops demonstrated an unwelcome ability to supplement nature by quickly throwing up breastworks, entrenchments, and even substantial earthworks. If senior British officers needed to be reminded how costly it was to force such strong positions without decent artillery support, then the carnage at Bunker Hill bloodily underscored the lesson.[9] After that action Burgoyne identified artillery as the key to tactical success against the rebels.[10] In the aftermath of the disaster at Saratoga, he and his supporters were at pains to justify the size of the artillery train that the general's "Canadian army" carried with it on the Albany expedition. Their argument was simple. First, given the various fortified posts along the army's path and given the rebels' predilection for fieldworks, the army needed powerful artillery to be able to batter its way to Albany (and indeed to defend its winter camp once it arrived there). Second, because the army did have this capability, the rebels dared not directly contest its progress until it crossed the Hudson River. Third, once the army was within striking distance of Gates's fortified lines on Bemis Heights, the rebels twice preferred to sally out in strength and confront it in the wooded country beyond (where guns were of less force) before Burgoyne was able to bring his artillery to bear.[11]

If artillery fire was physically destructive, its enervating effect on troops' morale was still more powerful. For infantry or cavalry on the receiving end, artillery killed and maimed in a shockingly impersonal fashion that offered them no immediate way to retaliate. The effect was particularly potent on troops who stood on the defensive because of the frightful way the human evidence of the guns' destructive power tended to accumulate around them. Moreover, artillery fire also tended to have the effect of violently disabusing raw troops of their naive early enthusiasm.[12] These factors gave British commanders further incentive to employ it against the generally unsteady, defensively inclined American rebels. Indeed, during the war's early campaigns, British officers were quick to note that the enemy were (as one officer put it in 1777) "extremely apprehensive" of artillery fire.[13] As an example, on the first day of the war, a few shots from Brigadier General Lord Percy's two 6-pounders on Lexington Heights appear to have saved Lieutenant Colonel Francis Smith's crumbling column from total collapse by temporarily staggering the closing horde of militia.[14]

Given the advantages field artillery promised to confer, Crown troops in America rarely went on campaign without it. The most generously supported force in this respect must have been Burgoyne's 7,500-strong "Canadian army" in 1777, which initially carried 140 pieces (including sixty howitzers and mortars). But the unexpectedly rapid fall of Fort Ticonderoga prompted Burgoyne to leave most of the guns behind, so the train that accompanied his army over the Hudson comprised 42 pieces (including twelve howitzers and mortars) served by 473 artillerymen. Of these, 26 were immediately available (with another 10 guns as "park artillery") on the day the now 6,000-strong army went into battle at Freeman's Farm (approximately one piece per 167 men, if one counts the park artillery).[15] This was a better ratio than was enjoyed by most other royal forces. According to Howe's Hessian aide de camp, the 12,500-strong Crown army at Brandywine had 62 pieces (approximately one per 200 men), of which not more than 20 were fired.[16] By contrast, when Lieutenant Colonel Archibald Campbell was dispatched to seize Savannah in late 1778, he took with him just over 3,000 infantry in eight battalions and 8 field pieces (approximately one per 375 men) served by 36 artillerymen—what the Scotsman called "a miserable proportion for so many regiments of foot."[17] Even less generously supported was Tarleton's 1,100-strong force at Cowpens, which fielded only two 3-pounders.

The organization of the artillery differed from campaign to campaign. When the main army was in the field, the infantry brigades (and some individual units like the *Feldjägerkorps*) were commonly provided with 3-pounders or light 6-pounders as "battalion guns." For example, according to Lieutenant William Hale, at the battle of Monmouth the guns of the 2nd Battalion of Grenadiers fired 160 rounds.[18] Meanwhile, the army's heavier pieces were formed into artillery "brigades" of around six pieces (including howitzers) each. Hence on 25 August 1777, after Howe's army had landed at Head of Elk, Captain Downman was attached with four 3-pounders to the three battalions of the 71st Regiment. Yet on 27 August he was posted to the Second Brigade of Heavy Artillery, which then comprised two medium 12-pounders, two light 12-pounders and two 5.5-inch howitzers.[19] On the day of the battle of Brandywine, this artillery brigade was part of

Knyphausen's division; according to one British diarist, the column carried with it "six medium twelve-pounders, four howitzers, and the light artillery belonging to the [infantry] brigades." Meanwhile, the fire support for Cornwallis's division comprised "four light twelve-pounders, and the artillery of the [infantry] brigades."[20] On the Albany expedition Burgoyne and Major General Phillips declined to give battalion guns to the infantry corps of the "Canadian army." Instead they concentrated the artillery in brigades (what Burgoyne called the recent practice in most services) to ensure that the guns remained under the central direction of artillery officers and that the resulting fire was more formidable than if the pieces were scattered along the line.[21] Nevertheless, at the battles of Freeman's Farm and Bemis Heights, the weapons appear to have operated typically in pairs, much in the style of battalion guns. This was presumably because the broken nature of the rolling, wooded terrain obstructed centralized command and control and made it necessary to parcel out the available fire support between the various hard-pressed units.

Despite the anticipated advantages of field artillery, guns played a significant tactical role in relatively few of the war's engagements. One crucial constraint was the difficulty that campaigning armies experienced in moving their pieces and the accompanying wagons. Part of the problem here was logistical. According to Burgoyne, a 6-pounder needed four horses to draw it, while 3-pounders and 5.5-inch mortars each required three. This was to say nothing of the wagons that carried the artillery's ammunition and stores. Hence, according to artilleryman Captain Thomas Bloomfield, before the army crossed the Hudson, the artillery train alone required four hundred horses.[22] As discussed earlier, to obtain and then to feed these draft animals in what was essentially a hostile country was an enormous challenge.

The problem of mobility extended further than logistics. Once Burgoyne's force left the lakes, it faced severe problems in transporting its pieces overland through the wilderness.[23] Indeed, after the fall of Ticonderoga, when Brigadier General Fraser led the Advanced Corps in pursuit of the retiring rebels, he had to leave behind his guns, "which the road was not capable of receiving."[24] Similarly, Captain Downman recorded the frustratingly slow progress that the Second Brigade of Artillery made on 17 September 1777: "We again set forward about 10 in the morning through dreadful roads. We had advanced about a mile and a half down a hill, when word was brought that the artillery were in the wrong road. We had to turn about in a narrow road, which took up so much time that we could only get about 300 yards from the place we had left when it became quite dark and rain came on."[25]

This lack of mobility was particularly problematic when commanders wished to bring their guns into action. One notable example of this was the way the artillery's slowness in traversing hills delayed the arrival of Cornwallis's division at the battle of Brandywine.[26] While lighter guns like 3-pounders were more mobile, they were of course less powerful. After the action at Trois-Rivières, Major Griffith Williams complained to the American secretary that he wished never again to see "grasshopper" guns or 3-pounders except "in the hands of the enemy or at Woolwich."[27]

Furthermore, once on the field it was not always possible for the artillery to provide the troops with adequate fire support. One reason why this was so was the issue of the ammunition supply. Unless a British field army was operating in conjunction with the fleet, it needed to carry with it everything that it needed. Hence, during the campaigns of the "Canadian army" in 1776 and 1777, Phillips warned his artillery officers that they needed to husband their ammunition carefully to make it last more than one engagement. Indeed, days before the battle of Freeman's Farm, he ordered the gunners not to fire at a retreating enemy and to decline requests for fire support that were not made by Burgoyne, himself, or the officers commanding the various brigades.[28]

A further limitation on the artillery's ability to provide adequate fire support was the speed with which the King's troops maneuvered when on the attack. In 1778 Lieutenant Hale decried the slow-moving Hessians because "[t]hey will not readily fight without being supported by their cannon which we think an useless incumbrance."[29] Hale may have been thinking of the battle of Brandywine, where even the two British 3-pounders that accompanied the Hessian *Jäger* were left far behind during Cornwallis's attack at Birmingham Meetinghouse.[30] The same situation occurred at Cowpens, despite the gunners' best efforts to keep up with Tarleton's rapidly advancing line.[31] Elsewhere, local topography (particularly the abundance of woods and rail fences) severely restricted the artillery's mobility in action.[32]

A related problem, and perhaps the main constraint on the artillery's effectiveness in combat, was the way that the broken, rolling, wooded terrain of North America simultaneously shielded the enemy from the worst effects of the artillery's fire and compelled the gunners to operate within range of the rebels' small arms. The letters of Captain William Congreve of the Royal Artillery illustrate this point. The day after Howe's army landed on Long Island, Congreve observed a party of Hessian *Jäger* use one of his 3-pounders to drive a rebel party into some woods, from where they continued to fire at the Germans. Days later, during the battle of Long Island, the captain was sent with two light 3-pounders to support the advance along the Flatbush Road. By plying the numerous enemy with case shot, he quickly forced them to withdraw their own guns. Yet covered as they were by trees and rocks, the rebel riflemen proved immune to the British fire. Indeed, Congreve quickly lost an artillery captain, a sergeant, and two gunners to small-arms fire, and he believed that only the light infantry's prompt support saved the rest.[33] In the fighting in the center at the battle of Freeman's Farm, Captain Thomas Jones's artillery brigade faced the same predicament. The brigade having divided in half, Lieutenant James Hadden's "company" of two light 6-pounders moved to support the 62nd Regiment (in the angle where the battalion's two left-hand companies formed *en potence*) while Lieutenant George Reid's two light 6-pounders took position between the 9th and 21st Regiments. But the guns failed to silence the fire of the rebels, who took cover in the woods on the far side of the clearing and shot down nineteen of Hadden's twenty-two artillerymen. Although the lieutenant finally succeeded in getting Jones to bring one of Reid's crews to man his guns, the newcomers were all quickly killed or wounded. With the battered 62nd Regiment itself now withdrawing, Hadden had no choice but to abandon his pieces.[34]

This is not to say that the British field artillery did not on occasion provide very effective fire support. For example, Lieutenant Colonel Archibald Campbell clearly felt that his artillery made a decisive contribution to his tactical triumph outside Savannah. At the start of the action, the canny Scotsman concealed his guns behind a swell, from where the gunners ran them up only when they received the signal that Captain Sir James Baird's light infantry had initiated their outflanking march. Campbell's original intention was for the guns to soften up the rebel right in preparation for the impending flank attack and to enfilade any rebel troops who attempted to stand against it. But in the event the guns moved forward so briskly with Campbell's advancing line, and were served so effectively, that the shaken rebel force collapsed before the Crown troops had arrived within a hundred yards.[35]

### The Infantry Contest in Conventional Linear Warfare

Just as most modern narratives of the North American campaigns tend to ignore the global conflict in which Britain was embroiled from 1778, much of what might be called the "battle history" of the American War has been penned by authors with a limited understanding of how eighteenth-century linear warfare was conducted in Europe.[36] This much is clear from the fact that few writers seem to be aware that the heavily shock-orientated tactics that the King's troops employed against the rebels were distinctly at odds with contemporary European practice. Moreover, when British officers in America strove "to inculcate the use of the bayonet, and a total reliance on that weapon," they were turning their backs on a long-standing British tradition of dependence on fire tactics as the primary element of infantry warfare.[37]

By the late seventeenth century, two distinct approaches to infantry tactics had emerged in Europe: one that stressed shock, and one that stressed firepower.[38] The proponents of the former included French theorists who believed that their troops were temperamentally better suited to making lively attacks with the bayonet than to the kind of mechanical volleying in which more "phlegmatic" nations like the Dutch, Germans, and English excelled.[39] Advocates of shock tactics also included those who reasoned that a rapid advance with shouldered or charged firelocks was the quickest and cheapest way to overwhelm enemy infantry. In 1732 Maurice Comte de Saxe argued that it was unnecessary for the battalion to interrupt its advance to trade volleys with the enemy: "The firearm is not so terrible as one thinks; few men are killed in action by fire from the front. I have seen volleys that did not hit four men, and neither I nor anyone else saw an effect sufficient to have prevented us from continuing our advance and revenging ourselves with the bayonets and pursuing fire."[40] Until the early stages of the Seven Years War, Frederick the Great was another firm advocate of infantry shock. In 1748 the Prussian king argued that the advance was likely to stall if attacking infantry stopped to fire. This was fatal because "it is not the number of enemies we kill which gives the victory, but the ground which we gain. To win a battle you must advance proudly and in good order, claiming ground all the time."[41] Here Frederick underlined the misleading implication in Saxe's argument: despite the name, infantry shock tactics were not supposed to bring about actual contact between the contending parties but to shatter the defenders' will to stand their ground and to induce them to break ranks and retreat before the attackers arrived at close quarters. Indeed, infantry melees rarely occurred in eighteenth-century warfare, typically only when opposing battalions struggled for possession of strongpoints or collided accidentally. Consequently, in the vast majority of engagements, bayonets inflicted only a tiny proportion of the total casualties.[42]

Although modern fire tactics appear to have originated with the Dutch, their most conspicuous proponents in the eighteenth century were the Prussians (except for the period 1741–57) and the British.[43] The rationale behind this approach was that a battalion's best means of eroding its opponent's will to stand its ground or to press its attack was to pour musketry fire into it, thereby incapacitating some of its men and sowing disorganization through its ranks. When applied offensively, fire tactics involved the attacking battalion punctuating its advance to trade fire with the defenders. Whether on the offensive or the defensive, however, this tactical approach generally involved the fire divisions of the battalion firing successive volleys in prearranged firings. The point of this cycle was threefold: to keep up a perpetual fusillade (to maintain constant psychological pressure on the enemy), to maintain a loaded "reserve" (with which to repel a sudden enemy advance), and to facilitate fire control by the officers.

Particularly when applied offensively, fire tactics did not entirely discount shock. Generally an infantry firefight endured until one party perceived (from the casualties and trepidation mounting around them and from the intensity of the enemy's fire relative to their own) that they were getting much the worst of the affair. At this point either the worsted battalion's morale collapsed and they withdrew in some confusion or the visible disorder in their ranks and the palpable slackening of their fire triggered an advance with charged bayonets by the ascendant party, which had the same result.

The application of fire tactics in combat was subject to two limitations. One was the gulf between the theoretical and practical effectiveness of infantry long arms. In action a number of factors reduced the accuracy of fire, including stress-related human error, the extra weight of the firelock with the bayonet fixed, the disinclination to aim along the barrel (because of flaring from the touchhole and because of the piece's vicious kick), and limited visibility due to dense powder smoke. Similarly, the rate of fire suffered in combat due to the weapon's idiosyncrasies (the accumulation of carbon deposits, the heating up of the barrel, and the failure of flints), the need to synchronize the loading-and-firing procedure (to prevent jostling and to minimize the risk of injury to the front-rank men), and unfavorable weather conditions (including wind and rain).

The other limitation was that the requirement for strict fire discipline demanded too much of most soldiers amid the noise, confusion, and terror of combat. Consequently, after a few discharges, the sequence of firings almost inevitably broke down.[44] Lieutenant Colonel Charles Russell of the 1st Regiment of Foot Guards described how at Dettingen (1743) the British infantry "were under no command by way of Hyde Park firing, but the whole three ranks made a running fire of their own accord . . . with great judgment and skill, stooping all as low as they could, making almost every ball take place. . . . The French fired in the same manner . . . without waiting for words of command, and Lord Stair did often say he had seen many a battle, and never saw the infantry engage in any other manner."[45] In fact, contrary to the impression given by Russell, this kind of uncontrolled fusillade was more often relatively feeble because the men indulged their natural instinct for self-preservation by frantically blazing away without carefully loading and leveling their pieces.[46] Moreover, once a "running fire" started, it was difficult for the officers to suppress it. This was a particular problem for attackers, whose advance was thereby likely to stall.

Despite the difficulties that officers faced in executing the firings properly in combat, shock-orientated infantry tactics declined in effectiveness during the course of the eighteenth century. Improvements in the quality and quantity of black-powder supplies and design innovations such as the flintlock mechanism, pre-prepared cartridges, and iron ramrods produced a gradual escalation in the volume of musketry that infantrymen were able to deliver. By the time of the Seven Years War, well-disciplined troops could unleash a sustained rate of fire of two to three rounds per minute. This made it increasingly likely that a straightforward frontal assault on steady troops would end in bloody shambles, as the Prussian infantry at Prague (1757) and the French cavalry at Minden (1759) experienced to their cost. Hence in 1768 Frederick the Great—the former arch-proponent of infantry shock—wrote uncompromisingly that "[b]attles are decided by superiority of fire," while in 1782 one British military theorist declared that in modern warfare, "we are dependent on the dexterous use of our firelock."[47]

Although most foreign commentators probably had a modest opinion of the eighteenth-century British Army as a whole, during the course of the War of the Spanish Succession, the War of the Austrian Succession, and the Seven Years War, the redcoats earned a reputation for being among the best infantry in the world. This reputation rested largely upon the relative effectiveness of their musketry. Hence before Ramillies (1706), Louis XIV ordered Marshal Villeroi "to pay special heed to that part of the line that shall sustain the first shock of the English troops."[48] Likewise, after Dettingen (1743), Marshal Noailles observed that the redcoats poured forth "so brisk and well sustained a fire that the oldest officer owned that they had never seen anything like it, incomparably superior to ours."[49] And after Culloden (1746) the Jacobite Colonel John Sullivan asserted that "the English . . . are the troops in the world that fires best."[50] The replacement of the complicated "platoon fire" system that had been used since Marlborough's day by the simpler, Prussian-inspired "alternate fire" system during the early years of the Seven Years War can only have enhanced the effectiveness of British musketry.[51]

### THE EFFECTIVENESS OF BRITISH MUSKETRY IN AMERICA

The reasons why, in combating the American rebels, the British put so much emphasis on what were (by European standards) seemingly outdated shock tactics are explored in detail in the next chapter. Here it is necessary to examine how the redcoats delivered their fire in combat and whether or not it was generally effective.

Strikingly, there is little evidence that British infantry in action in America often employed the regulation firings, whereby volleys were delivered in strict succession by the battalion's fire divisions (whether by the four grand divisions, the eight subdivisions, or the sixteen platoons) in prearranged sequences. This is hardly surprising for three reasons. First (as discussed in the next chapter), throughout the war the British preferred to spurn the firefight wherever possible in favor of putting the rebels quickly to flight at the point of the bayonet. Second (as noted in the last chapter), a combination of broken ground and the battalion's extended frontage often prevented field officers from exerting close control over the whole in action, compelling captains to exercise an unconventional degree of tactical autonomy in handling their companies. It was only natural that this tactical decentralization extended to musketry. Third, because, for most of the war, the rebels lacked good cavalry and most of their infantry were unlikely to adopt the tactical offensive, the British did not need to ensure that a fraction of the battalion was always loaded to repel any sudden, determined enemy advance. These three factors ensured that British battalions on the attack seem commonly to have thrown in a single "general volley" (or "battalion volley") immediately prior to the bayonet charge.

When sustained exchanges of musketry did occur, as at Cowpens or Green Springs, it seems likely that each company loaded and fired independently of the others under the command of its captain or senior subaltern. Evidence of this can be found in George Harris's later account of the action at the Vigie on St. Lucia, where (as major in the 5th Regiment) he commanded the single grenadier battalion: "on my ordering the 35th [Regiment's grenadier] company, commanded by Captain [Hugh] Massey (from a reserve of three companies which I kept under cover of a small eminence) to relieve the 49th [Regiment's grenadier] company, he was in an instant at his post, and as quickly ordered the company to make ready, and had given them the word 'Present!' when I called out, 'Captain Massey, my orders were not to fire; recover!' This was done without a shot, and themselves under a heavy fire."[52] In another possible example, at the battle of Camden, a British officer was "ungenerous enough to direct the fire of his platoon" at the horse of Colonel Otho Williams. The rebel adjutant escaped injury from the British volley only because, as Williams recounted, "I was lucky enough to see and hear him at the instant he gave the word and pointed with his sword."[53] More conclusively, in August 1780 Lieutenant Colonel Henry Hope directed the 1st Battalion of Grenadiers that, when the "Preparative" was beaten in action, the corps was "to begin firing by companies, which is to go on as fast as each is loaded till the first part of the *General,* when not a shot more is ever to be fired."[54]

Although British musketry was supposed to have been quite effective by European standards, contemporary eyewitnesses and modern historians have tended to give the impression that the redcoats were generally no match for the American rebels in the firefight. It is of course impossible to qualify this phenomenon with any degree of precision since, for any given exchange of fire, we cannot precisely document the number of troops engaged on either side, the total rounds discharged, or even the casualties they inflicted. Yet one particularly striking example may serve to indicate how the premise may have had some basis in reality. At Guilford Courthouse Cornwallis's initial attack pitted about 1,100 British and German regulars against roughly 1,600 smoothbore- and rifle-armed militia and light troops, mostly posted behind a rail fence that separated the ploughed farmland to their front from the woods to their rear. Once the British line had advanced to within about 150 yards of the enemy, the rebels opened a general fire that appears to have inflicted numerous casualties. For example, Lieutenant Thomas Saumarez (with the 23rd Regiment, on the left wing) noted that the rebel shooting was "most galling and destructive," while Dugald Stuart (an officer with the 2nd Battalion of the 71st Regiment, on the right) later rued: "In the advance we received a very heavy fire, from the [North Carolina Scotch-] Irish line of the American army, composed of their marksmen lying on the ground behind a rail fence. One half of the Highlanders dropped on that spot, [and] there ought to be a pretty large tumulus where our men were buried."[55]

One participant on the rebel left later recalled that "after they [i.e., the rebels] delivered their first fire (which was a deliberate one) with their rifles, the part of the British line at which they aimed looked like the scattering stalks in a wheat field when the harvest man has passed over it with his cradle."[56] By contrast, the volley that the British battalions delivered at much closer range, immediately prior to their charge, was almost wholly ineffective (rebel returns having indicated that the North Carolina militia sustained only eleven killed and wounded in the course of the whole action). Indeed, Henry Lee later reported of the North Carolina militia (which comprised almost two-thirds of the first rebel line and fled when the British rushed forward) that "not a man of the corps had been killed, or even wounded."[57]

The apparent disparity in the effectiveness of the British and rebel fire in this incident does not appear to have been wholly unrepresentative. To explain this, one is tempted to point to the popularly accepted view that, unlike in Europe, most males in America had access to firearms, which they were very proficient in handling. Although some British participants in the war subscribed to this view,[58] it is likely to have been the case only in the wilder backwoods and on the frontier. Moreover, because the Continental Army and the state regular regiments filled their ranks largely with landless laborers (many of them recent immigrants), it follows that a good proportion of rebel enlisted men were hardly dissimilar to their British and German counterparts.[59]

If most rebel regulars and militia were not inherently skilled in handling firearms, then it is necessary to consider the common assumption that, unlike European regulars (who supposedly simply pointed their muskets in the general direction of the enemy and blazed away on command), the Americans tended to deliver independent, well-aimed fire in combat. This may well have been true of the lively skirmishing that characterized the *petite guerre*, in which individuals typically moved, sought cover, and fired largely at their own initiative. Moreover, rebel militia used rifles more often than is sometimes realized, particularly in the South (as in the case of the North Carolina militia at Guilford Courthouse).[60] For decades historians have been playing down the combat effectiveness of riflemen in America by pointing to their inability either to match the rate of fire of smoothbore-armed troops or to perform bayonet charges.[61] While both of these points are valid, riflemen were undeniably able to do horrifying execution when employed as auxiliaries to smoothbore-armed troops. If thrown forward as a screen, riflemen were able to get off one or two destructive fires at the advancing enemy before retiring to the cover of their musket-armed compatriots in the main line—as occurred at Cowpens and Guilford Courthouse.[62] In addition, riflemen were able to support their fellow infantry during a static firefight by picking off enemy officers, as occurred at Freeman's Farm.

But if smoothbore-armed troops were likely to deliver independent, aimed fire when engaged in the kind of skirmishing that characterized the *petite guerre*, this was not the case in stand-up engagements in the open field, for which rebel regulars and militia alike were trained to employ more or less conventional volleying systems. Indeed, for much of the war, the rebels used the *1764 Regulations* or its British or colonial variants as their standard drill.[63] Because the experience of three years of war showed that the British-style firings were difficult for the relatively inexperienced rebel forces to master, the drill manual that Major General Steuben compiled for them in 1778 prescribed a simpler variant, whereby the different battalions within the line of battle could deliver general volleys in sequence.[64]

The counterpart to the questionable notion that rebel troops generally delivered independent and thus accurate fire in action in America is the widespread assumption that European volleying techniques were ineffective because they were calculated primarily to terrify rather than to kill and maim. Admittedly, by the time of the American War, this kind of "quick-fire" mania appears to have been the hallmark of the Prussian infantry, who reputably were able to loose an astonishing six rounds per minute and whose king wrote in 1768 that "a force of infantry that loads speedily will always get the better of a force which loads more slowly."[65] Interestingly, the subject of speed also figured in contemporary British directives on musketry training. For example, the *1764 Regulations* laid down that, during the performance of the "platoon exercise," the "motions of handling cartridge, to shutting the pans," and "the loading motions" (that is, the fourth to sixth and the eighth to twelfth of the fifteen motions) were "to be done as quick as possible."[66] Similarly, in 1774 Gage reminded the British regiments in Boston that in plying the firelock the soldier "cannot be too quick" in performing the motions, "more particularly so in the priming and loading," and that "there should be no superfluous motions in the platoon exercise, but [it is instead] to be performed with the greatest quickness possible."[67] Strikingly, after the costly Concord expedition, one flank company officer complained that the inexperienced redcoats had "been taught that everything was to be effected by a quick firing" but that the determined harassment they experienced during the return march to Boston had disabused them of the notion that the rebels "would be sufficiently intimidated by a brisk fire."[68]

Nevertheless, it would be wrong to argue that the Prussian quick-fire mania had permeated the British Army by the time of the American War. Significantly, when in 1781 military writer John Williamson decried the "very quick" time adopted for "the performance of the manual," he reasoned that "it does not appear that a battalion can fire oftener in the same space of time since the quick method has taken place, than before it."[69] Another military writer, Lieutenant Colonel William Dalrymple, made the same point in 1782. While he asserted that all motions with the firelock were "to be executed with the utmost celerity," he nevertheless argued that British soldiers should be able to fire three times a minute (in other words, half the best Prussian quick-fire rate) and scarcely ever miss at ranges between fifty and two hundred yards.[70] As Dalrymple's comment suggests, if the British emphasis on rapid priming and loading did not markedly increase the battalion's rate of fire, it certainly was not intended to diminish the accuracy of that fire. Indeed, the leading authority on the performance of British long arms in this period has argued that the eighteenth-century British fire tactics remained consistently and firmly wedded to making the infantryman's musketry as deadly as possible.[71] The dominant perspective probably remained that expressed by Wolfe when in December 1755 he reminded the 20th Regiment that "[t]here is no necessity for firing very fast; a cool and well-leveled fire, with the pieces carefully loaded, is much more destructive and formidable than the quickest fire in confusion."[72] It is instructive to note that Wolfe himself played a significant role in the introduction of the Prussian "alternate fire" volleying system into the British Army.[73]

If the Prussian quick-fire method did not quite permeate into British training in the years before the American War, one might argue instead that volleying was in itself inherently prejudicial to accurate fire. There remains some disagreement on this question. Historians have commonly asserted that, to have had any chance of hitting his target, a man had to choose his moment to pull the trigger. Dr. Robert Jackson, who served in the American War as assistant surgeon to the 71st Regiment, subscribed to this view: "The firelock is an instrument of missile force. It is obvious that the . . . missile ought to be directed by aim, otherwise it will strike only by accident. It is evident that a person cannot take aim with any correctness unless he be free, independent, and clear of all encumbrances; and for this reason, there can be little dependence on the effect of fire that is given by platoons or volleys, and by word of command. Such explosions may intimidate by their noise; it is mere chance if they destroy by their impression."[74]

Although Jackson's argument sounds persuasive, not all contemporaries shared his opinion that volleying was incompatible with accurate, aimed fire. In fact the *1764 Regulations* explicitly directed that, when given the order to present, the soldier should "raise up the butt so high upon the right shoulder, that you may not be obliged to stoop so much with the head (the right cheek [is] to be close to the butt, and the left eye shut), and look along the barrel with the right eye from the breech pin to the muzzle."[75] Military writers likewise commonly advocated that the men should aim carefully before firing. For example, Major General the Earl of Cavan recommended that officers "have at the breech [of the firelock] a small sight-channel made, for the advantage and convenience of occasionally taking better aim."[76] Similarly, in the directions for the training of newly arrived drafts and recruits issued three days before the battle of Bunker Hill, Lieutenant General Gage directed that "[p]roper marksmen [are] to instruct them in taking aim, and the position in which they ought to stand in firing, and to do this man by man before they are suffered to fire together."[77]

Furthermore, if volleying was incompatible with accurate, aimed fire, then it is difficult to understand why the army invested such effort in practicing the men in shooting. As John Houlding has shown, although before 1786 regiments did not receive sufficient quantities of lead in peacetime to fire at marks, in wartime troops spent a good deal of time shooting ball when they were not in the field.[78] In America, shooting at marks was a common element of the feverish training that preceded the opening of each campaign season; indeed, it occurred almost on a daily basis during the tense months before the outbreak of hostilities in 1775.[79] Here two examples of the ingenuity and effort invested in this activity will suffice. At Boston in January 1775, Lieutenant Frederick Mackenzie of the 23rd Regiment wrote:

The regiments are frequently practiced at firing with ball at marks. Six rounds per man at each time is usually allotted for this practice. As our regiment is quartered on a wharf which projects into part of the harbor, and there is a very considerable range without any obstruction, we have fixed figures of men as large as life, made of thin boards, on small stages, which are anchored at a proper distance from the end of the wharf, at which the men fire. Objects afloat, which move up and down with the tide, are frequently pointed out for them to fire at, and premiums are sometimes given for the best shots, by which means some of our men have become excellent marksmen.[80]

While target shooting commonly involved files of men firing successively at marks, and the fire divisions generally practiced volleying with squibs rather than with live ammunition, on occasion both methods were combined. A visitor to Boston witnessed one such session in late March 1775: "I saw a regiment and the body of Marines, each by itself, firing at marks. A target being set up before each company, the soldiers of the regiment stepped out singly, took aim and fired, and the firing was kept up in this manner by the whole regiment till they had all fired ten rounds. The Marines fired by platoons, by companies, and sometimes by files, and made some general discharges, taking aim all the while at targets the same as the regiment."[81] In New Jersey in May 1777, the battalions of the Fourth Brigade were urged to undertake a similar exercise: "Lieutenant Colonel Mawhood recommends to the officers commanding the several regiments of the 4th Brigade to practice the men in firing ball by platoon[s], sub[divisions] and grand-divisions and by battalion; and this [is] to be done by word of command and on uneven ground, so as to accustom the men not to fire but when ordered, and not only to level but to be taught to fire up and downhill."[82]

Frequent target shooting undoubtedly improved soldiers' marksmanship, as David Harding has shown through systematic analysis of the extensive contemporary East India Company test-firing data.[83] Although these impressive test results were unattainable under actual combat conditions, repeated practice with the firelock probably did have the effect of influencing the soldier (even subconsciously) to take more care when shooting in action. This is what Gage probably meant when he observed at Boston in November 1774 "that the men [should] be taught to take good aim, which if they do they will always level well."[84] Moreover, as Houlding has pointed out, practicing with the firelock had other practical benefits than simply enhancing accuracy—such as removing inexperienced men's apprehension at firing live ammunition.[85]

Earlier we noted that the effectiveness of troops' musketry in action tended to deteriorate when orchestrated volleying degenerated into an uncontrollable "running fire." It was therefore essential (as Cuthbertson put it in 1768) for the officers and sergeants "to attend very particularly to the men's behavior during the firings; to observe if they are expert in loading, and to oblige them to perform the whole of their business with a proper spirit."[86] If British musketry was not as deadly in America as on European battlefields, it is possible that the adoption of the formation of two ranks at open files was partly to blame in that the dispersal of the men over a wider frontage weakened the fire control that their officers and sergeants were able to exert over them in combat. This theory gains credence from Thomas Anburey's later account of the scrambling action at Hubbardton (where he participated as a gentleman volunteer with the grenadier battalion), which seems to suggest that, in combat in America, the redcoats did not always load according to the regulation procedure: "In this action I found all manual exercise is but an ornament, and the only object of importance it can boast of was that of loading, firing and charging with bayonets. As to the former, the soldiers should be instructed in the best and most expeditious method. Here I cannot help observing to you, whether it proceeded from an idea of self-preservation, or natural instinct, but the soldiers greatly improved the mode they were taught in, as to expedition. For as soon as they had primed their pieces and put the cartridge into the barrel, instead of ramming it down with their rods, they struck the butt end of the piece upon the ground, and bringing it to the *present,* fired it off."[87] Here Anburey's references to "self-preservation" and "natural instinct," his comment that the men "fired . . . off" their pieces once they brought them to the "present," and the fact that he does not mention verbal commands strongly imply that the grenadiers were loading and firing at will. In the context of the furious, scrambling action at Hubbardton, this is not surprising. But the fact that former sergeant Roger Lamb reproduced Anburey's passage almost verbatim in his memoir (though he participated in Burgoyne's Albany expedition as a corporal in the 9th Regiment, he was not present at Hubbardton) would tend to suggest that he too was familiar with this corner-cutting loading technique.[88]

While both Anburey and Lamb seem to have approved the way in which troops achieved a higher rate of fire by spurning the ramrod and firing at will, Anburey's further comments reveal that at Hubbardton the combination of haste and a lack of supervision had an undesirable side effect: "The confusion of a man's ideas during the time of action, brave as he may be, is undoubtedly great. Several of the men, upon examining their muskets, after all was over, found five or six cartridges which they were positive to the having discharged."[89] Clearly the malfunction of a proportion of the men's weapons reduced the battalion's volume of firepower and had major safety implications. Yet neither Anburey nor Lamb seems to have been aware that the practice of spurning the ramrod also significantly reduced the muzzle velocity of each discharge. As evidence of this one should note that, during a skirmish in New Jersey in February 1780, soldiers of the Queen's Rangers were struck by rebel bullets that did not penetrate their clothes. Simcoe later judged that these rounds had been fired by militiamen "who had not recollection sufficient to ram down their charges."[90]

Inadequate supervision of the loading process in action seems to have been matched on occasion by a failure to ensure that the men directed their fire properly. For example, according to Lieutenant Frederick Mackenzie, during the final leg of the return march from Concord, the panicky redcoats "threw away their fire very inconsiderately, and without being certain of its effect."[91] Similarly, another officer who complained that the redcoats returned the militia's fire "with too much eagerness, so that at first most of it was thrown away" laid the blame for "this improper conduct" largely at the door of the officers, who "did not prevent [it] as they should have done."[92] Significantly, after the battle of Freeman's Farm, Burgoyne's public censure on his troops' unsteady shooting went hand in hand with an avowal of the importance of maintaining fire discipline: "[T]he impetuosity and uncertain aim of the British troops in giving their fire, and the mistake they are still under in preferring it to the bayonet, is much to be lamented. The Lieutenant General is persuaded this error will be corrected in the next engagement, upon the conviction of their own reason and reflection, as well as upon that general precept of discipline, never to fire but by order of an officer."[93] Rebel eyewitnesses frequently observed that the King's troops customarily overshot the enemy in action because, when they brought their pieces to the "present," they did not level them low enough to compensate for the kick and for any difference in elevation between themselves and the target.[94]

Coincidentally, the two most graphic examples of this phenomenon concern the storming of Fort Washington. According to the recollections of one rebel participant, when during the course of the action his militia party discharged a few rounds at two British battalions that were advancing in line against them, the latter

> halted and began to fire on us at not more than eighty yards distance. Their whole battalion on the right of the colors were ordered to fire at once. I heard the words "Battalion, make ready!"; and, as few as we were (notwithstanding their boasted discipline), when the word was given and they came to a "recover" to cock their muskets, a considerable number went off and were fired in the air. When the word PRESENT was given (which means "take aim"), they fired, along the battalion as if it were a *feu de joie;* and when the word FIRE was given, there was but few pieces to fire. The battalion on the left of the colors fired much better than [that on] the right; but I do not recollect of my attending any more of their manner of firing, though it was very brisk for a few rounds. But at least 99 shot out of 100 went a considerable distance over our heads. . . . While we were here engaged with the enemy I saw [Lieutenant] Colonel [Thomas] Bull . . . ride within fifty or sixty yards of the British along their whole front when they were firing briskly, as I supposed to show and demonstrate to the men . . . that there was not so much danger as they might apprehend.[95]

The British corps in question here may have been the 42nd Regiment.[96] Interestingly enough, it was to a party from this corps that Captain Alexander Graydon and a fellow rebel officer attempted to surrender later that day, when they found that the British had cut off their retreat to the fortress. Although ten of the Highlanders discharged their muskets at the pair from various ranges between twenty and fifty yards, Graydon attributed the failure of these *"blunt* shooters" to hit him or his companion to the fact that the pair were ascending a considerable hill. But like Adlum, Graydon also noted significantly, "I observed they took no aim, and that the moment of presenting and firing, was the same."[97]

Nevertheless, any real disparity in the effectiveness of British and rebel musketry in combat in America was almost certainly rooted in other factors. One might argue that the variation in the type and quality of the long arms utilized by the contending armies affected their performance. Rifle-armed regulars and irregulars were to be found on both sides, particularly in the South, where the militia employed the weapon more commonly than is often recognized. But if the focus remains on the smoothbore muskets that the vast majority of troops wielded, there is little evidence that either side enjoyed a significant advantage. Houlding has shown that, while many British regiments' firelocks were in shockingly poor condition in peacetime, the Board of Ordnance often issued ill-armed regiments with new weapons when they went on active service. Indeed, the record for last-minute issues was probably that made to the 52nd Regiment on Boston Common on the morning of 17 June 1775—just hours before the corps fought at Bunker Hill.[98] As for the rebels, both regulars and militia commonly employed old or captured British Land Pattern pieces or locally made imitations (the "Committee of Safety" musket), while from 1777 large numbers of imported French weapons became available. While there is some disagreement as to the respective ballistic qualities of British and French firelocks,[99] it is interesting to note that, when Continental troops at the battle of Monmouth had the opportunity to acquire the muskets of the 2nd Battalion of Grenadiers' dead and wounded, "[t]hey threw away their French pieces, preferring the British."[100]

If probably neither side enjoyed a substantial advantage in terms of the quality of their firelocks, the apparent disparity in the effectiveness of British and rebel musketry may have had something to do with ammunition. In particular, British troops appear to have been supplied with poor-quality flints.[101] Captain the Honorable Colin Lindsay commanded the 55th Regiment's grenadier company in America and during Major General Grant's expedition to St. Lucia, and he later noted that the British musketry at the bloody action at the Vigie would have been even more destructive had it not been for the number of misfires caused by "the badness of a pebble-stone": "In the attack, the bayonet is always a remedy for this deficiency, but to find in a defense that one-third of your men are useless from this cause is indeed extraordinary. . . . It was a common saying among the soldiers in America, that a Yankee flint was as good as a glass of grog. The government flints will often fire five or six shots very well, but they are of a bad sort of flint, and are too thick."[102] As for the propellant, there are hints that the black powder supplied to the army and navy during the American War was also of inferior quality (a problem that was exacerbated by poor storage conditions during the transatlantic voyage), while Henry Lee later asserted that British soldiers commonly overcharged their cartridges.[103] In terms of shot, rebel practice differed from the British in that their musket cartridges customarily included (commonly three) buckshot along with the ball; irregulars sometimes fired these loose.[104] While the redcoats lightheartedly styled these multiple projectiles "Yankee peas,"[105] they were potentially lethal at up to about fifty yards.[106] For example, they probably accounted for a good proportion of the approximately one hundred casualties that Ensign George Inman estimated the 17th Regiment sustained during its first charge at Princeton, he himself having been wounded in the belly by a single buckshot that penetrated his leather shoulder belt.[107]

Leaving aside differences in weaponry, several other factors contributed to give the impression that rebel musketry was superior to that of the redcoats. First, as in the British attack on the first rebel line at Guilford Courthouse, it would often have been the case that the rebels simply had more men involved in an exchange of fire, largely because the British deployed and advanced at open files. The Hessian adjutant general in America made this point explicitly when he reported that, at the action outside Savannah, "the rebels at first withstood the fire of the British, who had opened ranks [sic], but . . . they lost their coolness when the said regiment [von Trümbach] advanced with closed front and effectively answered their disorderly fire."[108] Second, one should not forget that rebel troops on the defensive often knelt or lay down to fire behind trees, rail fences, and walls, which provided stable firing platforms as well as varying degrees of cover.

Finally (and perhaps most significantly), it is well known that in conventional linear warfare a battalion's first fire was the most destructive. This was because the soldiers had carefully loaded this round before the action, their barrels were clean, their flints were sharp, and their field of vision was clear of powder smoke. This is crucial because one should remember that the kind of "heavy though intermitting fire" that the British and rebel centers exchanged "for near three hours" at Freeman's Farm was not typical of most of the war's engagements.[109] Indeed, whenever a genuine firefight of even a few minutes' duration occurred in America (as for instance at Brandywine, Bemis Heights, Monmouth, Cowpens, Green Springs, and Eutaw Springs), participants noted this circumstance with genuine interest.[110] Such prolonged exchanges were comparatively rare because (as discussed in the next chapter) the British tended to spurn them wherever possible in favor of dislodging the enemy quickly at the point of the bayonet. When these bayonet rushes succeeded in their purpose (as they commonly did), rebel troops did not have the opportunity to get off more than one or two rounds. Since these first shots were potentially the most destructive delivered in combat, it may well be that the historical record tends to give an inflated impression of the general effectiveness of rebel musketry. This idea gains strength when one considers, once again, that in the South the militia carried rifles far more commonly than is often realized; clearly the tactic of firing and then retiring played to the rifle's main strength (its accuracy) while negating its principal weakness (the time it took to load).

This idea that the general effectiveness of the rebels' musketry has been overstated tends to gain support from the fact that, when sustained firefights did occur, the redcoats' musketry drew the same kind of praise that it did against European enemies. For example, Tarleton believed that the duel between the British line and the rebel regulars at Cowpens was "well supported" and "equally balanced"; indeed, from an analysis of the rebel casualties, Lawrence Babits has concluded that the 7th Regiment's musketry must have been especially punishing.[111] British troops appear to have shot similarly well at the action at Green Springs. One rebel and one British officer each wrote of the firefight between the Pennsylvania Continentals and Lieutenant Colonel Thomas Dundas's brigade that the latter, "aiming very low kept up a deadly fire," and that many of the rebel casualties "were wounded in the lower extremities, a proof that the young [British] soldiers had taken good aim."[112]

During the eighteenth century, technological advances spawned a significant increase in the volume of musketry that infantry could generate in action. This ensured that fire tactics gradually eclipsed infantry shock as the key to battlefield success. By the end of the Seven Years War, British infantry regiments had cemented their long-standing reputation for being among the most formidable practitioners of fire tactics in Europe. Yet against the shaky American rebels, Crown commanders instead relied overwhelmingly upon shock tactics to deliver quick and cheap tactical decisions. This meant that British musketry was most commonly delivered in combat in America in the form of general volleys, which the troops threw in immediately prior to the bayonet charge (rather than as regulation-style sequenced firings). When British infantry did become involved in sustained firefights, it is most likely that fire control devolved entirely to the officers commanding companies. As at Hubbardton, if these officers and their sergeants did not closely supervise the loading and leveling of weapons, the men probably did not execute these actions well, and the effectiveness of the battalion's fire must almost certainly have suffered accordingly. Despite this, it is difficult to believe that the musketry of the generality of rebel regulars or militiaman significantly outclassed that of the King's troops.

# 9

# THE BAYONET CHARGE

The Highlanders, observing that the rebels would not advance out of the wood, made a charge upon them, which was always a terror to the rebels, and put them to an immediate rout. The enemy could never endure to stand for any time to the bayonet, but if the King's troops kept at a distance, they stood firing with musketry long enough.

Thomas Sullivan, *From Redcoat to Rebel*

The last chapter examined how the European campaigns of the Seven Years War confirmed the British Army's long-standing reliance upon fire tactics as the key to success in infantry contests. In addition, it explored how the evidence does not admit of a firm conclusion that the rebels' musketry was generally superior. Consequently, one needs to ask why the British infantry's minor tactics in America were consistently turned on their head in favor of "the use of the bayonet, and a total reliance on that weapon."[1]

## "A RELIANCE ON THE BAYONET"

In the war's opening campaigns, the most pressing reason for this striking shift from fire to shock tactics was the rebel commanders' predilection for anchoring their ill-trained and unsteady troops behind fieldworks and walls, where they were nearly impervious to

British musketry. The breakdown of Howe's first attack at Bunker Hill underlined for attacking infantry the futility of trading fire with a covered enemy. According to Howe, when he sent the grenadier battalion forward against the lightly fortified rail fence that ran down toward the Mystic River, its defenders opened up "a heavy fire as soon as the line was advanced within distance of their shot."[2] The grenadiers' fire discipline broke down under this sustained enemy musketry, and the attack degenerated into an unauthorized, uncontrolled firefight: "The grenadiers being directed to attack the enemy's left in front, supported by the 5th and 52nd [Regiments], their orders were executed by the grenadiers and two battalions with a laudable perseverance, but not with the greatest share of discipline. For as soon as the order with which they set forward to the attack with bayonets was checked by a difficulty they met with in getting over some very high fences of strong railing, under a heavy fire well kept up by the rebels, they began firing, and by crowding fell into disorder; and in this state the 2nd line mixed with them."[3] It is instructive that the grenadiers succumbed to the temptation to return fire just as they broke ranks to cross one of the fences that obstructed their advance. By doing so, the inexperienced redcoats condemned themselves to an unequal musketry contest with a more numerous and less exposed enemy. Hence one veteran officer later rationalized the heaviness of the losses of the British and French attackers respectively at Bunker Hill and the Vigie on St. Lucia by judging, "Like young soldiers, both halted under the enemy's fire, and both severely suffered for it."[4] Significantly, when Howe planned an assault on the rebel works on Dorchester Heights for the night of 5–6 December 1775, he envisaged that the troops would carry out the attack with unloaded arms.[5]

During the siege of Boston, British officers correctly foresaw that in the course of the 1776 campaign, the rebels would seek at every opportunity to repeat their performance at Bunker Hill. Thus Captain Francis Lord Rawdon observed in August 1775, "As to fighting us in open ground, I believe no advantage of numbers will ever tempt them to do that, but while they have a wall to lie behind be assured they will fight."[6] Lieutenant Francis Laye of the Royal Artillery likewise complained in October that "they will never fight but behind breastworks, entrenched up to their chin, or fences, and they never will meet us on open ground."[7] Burgoyne elaborated on this theme when he wrote soon afterward: "It is not to be expected that the rebel

Americans will risk a general combat or a pitched battle, or even stand at all, except behind entrenchments as at Boston. Accustomed to [the] felling of timber and to grubbing up trees, they are very ready at [raising] earthworks and palisading, and will cover and entrench themselves, wherever they are for a short time left unmolested, with surprising alacrity."[8]

Just over a fortnight after his victory on Long Island, and two days before the landing at Kipp's Bay (15 September 1776), Howe reminded his infantry "of their evident superiority on the 27th August by charging the rebels with their bayonets, even in woods, where they thought themselves invincible." With the successive lines of rebel fortifications on Manhattan presumably in mind, he stressed the need to employ shock rather than fire tactics to overcome an enemy covered by elementary fieldworks: "[T]hey now place their security in slight breastworks of the weakest construction, and which are to be carried with little loss by the same high-spirited mode of attack. He therefore recommends to the troops an entire dependence upon their bayonets, with which they will always command that success which their bravery so well deserves."[9] Before the opening of the Albany expedition, Burgoyne similarly warned his infantry that, although the rebels were "infinitely inferior to the King's troops in open space and hardy combat," British musketry would not drive them from their timber or earthen breastworks: "The officers will take all proper opportunities to inculcate in the men's minds a reliance on the bayonet. Men of their bodily strength and even a coward may be their match in firing; but the bayonet in the hands of the valiant is irresistible. The enemy, convinced of this, will place their whole dependence in entrenchments and rifle pieces. It will be our glory and our preservation to storm when possible."[10] Likewise, in August 1778 Captain Patrick Ferguson theorized that "it is only by vigorous and persevering charges with that weapon [i.e., the bayonet] that an enemy can be dislodged from a strong ground, whither strong by nature or entrenchments."[11]

If troops were to storm fortifications successfully, then it was essential for them to cross the enemy's "killing zone" as quickly as possible. This topic had exercised Wolfe when he composed his well-known tactical instructions for the 20th Regiment in 1755 (first published in 1768). After Bunker Hill one anonymous British officer drew closely on Wolfe's text in criticizing Howe's handling of the engagement, arguing that "[in] advancing, not a shot should have been fired, as it retarded the troops, whose movement should have been as rapid as possible." Instead of being "brought up in line" (the formation that maximized the battalion's firepower), he argued, the troops should have attacked "in columns" (to reduce the time they spent under fire and to lessen the risk that they would break fire discipline). Of course, one serious drawback to this tactic was the crushing weight of fire that resolute defenders would be able to concentrate on the unfortunates in the column's lead maneuver division(s). Indeed, this very situation occurred during the first attack at Bunker Hill, when the militia repulsed the light infantry's columnar advance against the barricade on the Mystic River shoreline. But taking his cue from Wolfe, the aforementioned officer asserted that parties of light infantry advancing in the intervals between his proposed assault columns could have suppressed the rebel fire. "If this had been done," he continued, "their works would have been carried in three minutes, with not a tenth part of our present loss."[12]

Despite Howe and Burgoyne's avowed purpose in recommending a total dependence on shock tactics in 1776 and 1777, after Bunker Hill the redcoats only infrequently stormed rebel fieldworks. During the New York campaign, Howe opted where possible to outflank the enemy's successive fortified lines rather than obligingly dashing his precious regulars against them, while during the Albany expedition, Burgoyne's forces were fought to a standstill by powerful rebel sallies long before they reached Gates's lines. Thereafter the Fabian-style strategy that Washington and his most talented subordinates employed ensured that rebel field armies rarely courted defensive battles in extensively fortified positions. Instead, when rebel regulars and militia engaged the British, whether offensively or defensively, they increasingly formed and fought in the open in a more or less "regular" fashion when there were no convenient walls, fences, and trees behind which to anchor the firing line.

The explanation for why British troops in America did not revert to their traditional fire-orientated offensive tactics after the first campaigns lies in the rebel troops' relative lack of steadiness and discipline throughout the war. As noted in the last chapter, in conventional linear warfare the advance with charged bayonets was a tool with which to force the withdrawal of infantry who had been bloodied and shaken by musket or artillery fire. In May 1777 Hessian officers explained to Admiral Lord Howe's secretary how they looked for visible symptoms of the enemy troops' mounting discomfiture as the signal for launching a bayonet attack: "One observation made by Hessian officers in battle is worth remembering. They watch steadily the arms of the enemy. If they see them moved and waving much about in the ranks, they are sure the men who bear them are dismayed and without courage, and that a vigorous attack will break them."[13] Captain Johann Ewald also highlighted how troops could discern and exploit their opponents' apparent disorder. Of the bold attack that the Queen's Rangers and his *Jäger* made at Spencer's Ordinary, he judged that "had we taken one step back, the courage of the enemy would have redoubled, while that of the soldiers on our side would have forsaken them. . . . It is a principle in war that the party which attacks when the issue is doubtful has already won half the battle."[14] According to one British source, at Camden, two premature bayonet charges by Rawdon's brigade failed to terminate the hour-long firefight with the embattled Continentals. It was only when the rebels vainly attempted "in their turn, *something like it*" that they fell into disorder, giving the King's troops the opportunity to close in and break them.[15] In a similar fashion at Hobkirk's Hill, Crown forces resumed their faltering advance when the 1st Maryland Regiment retired some distance, displaying unmistakable signs of confusion.[16] And at Eutaw Springs the 63rd and 64th Regiments on the British left instinctively ended the firefight with Greene's wavering militia line by launching an impromptu bayonet charge.[17]

The eyewitness account of the battle of Green Springs penned by Samuel Graham (captain lieutenant in the 76th Regiment) provides a fascinating insight into the launching of a bayonet charge. Graham's account indicates that Cornwallis himself initiated the advance, putting to an end the firefight between Lieutenant Colonel Thomas Dundas's brigade and Brigadier General Wayne's Pennsylvania Continentals:

> The enemy kept a good countenance for a short time, returning our fire from their field-pieces and muskets. But the noble earl, coming in the rear of the 76th [Regiment], called out to charge; which order not being heard on account of the noise, he made a motion with his cane, touching a Highlander on the shoulder, which being repeated, they rushed on most rapidly. The 80th [Regiment] in the center still continuing to

fire, Major Gordon, mounted on a very tall horse, dashed out in front and stopped them; when several Edinburgh men of this regiment were heard to cry out, "Brigadier! Will you no luk at the major, we canna get shooting for him; he's aye runnin' in the gate." A general charge took place, which soon put an end to the combat. The enemy disappeared in an instant, as if removed by magic, abandoning their field-pieces and their wounded.[18]

Although Graham's account does not specifically say so, Cornwallis probably ordered the Highlanders to charge because he perceived that the Continentals had fallen into a level of disorder that made them vulnerable to a bayonet rush. As at Camden, it is likely that the breakdown of the rebels' counterattack against the advancing British line was partly responsible for this disorder.

In all of these examples, the redcoats employed the bayonet charge to force the withdrawal of rebel troops who had been visibly shaken by musket fire. Yet in most battlefield encounters it was unnecessary for the King's troops to "soften up" the enemy before attempting to break them with the bayonet. Instead, because most rebel infantry lacked experience and steadiness, it was possible to skip the preliminary firefight and to seek a quick and cheap decision instead at the point of the bayonet. Admiral Lord Howe's secretary made this point explicitly when, in response to the aforementioned observation made by the Hessian officers, he noted that "when the rebels were drawn up to oppose our troops both on Long Island and Fort Washington, I well remember seeing this tremulation [sic] of the arms among them, and that they did not hold them steadily. The consequence was, they ran as soon as they were attacked."[19] Less than a fortnight after the battle of Brandywine, Captain Francis Downman confided in his diary: "I believe there is not an army in the universe better disposed or in better order to fight than this one. The rebels fly before us; they run whenever we advance. They say we are mad or drunk or we would never dash in among them as we do. Our light infantry are the finest set of fellows in the world for this mode of fighting."[20] In short, the speed, vigor, and noise with which the redcoats came on with charged bayonets was often quite enough in itself to send all but the best rebel troops into a panic.

### Rebel Fire Discipline and the Bayonet Attack

Traditionally, historians have explained the consistent success with which the British wielded the bayonet in America by asserting that most rebel troops were incapable of engaging in hand-to-hand fighting because they did not possess bayonets or because they had not been trained to use them.[21] This explanation is misleading. The elementary drill movements for "fixing" and "charging" bayonets (enshrined in the "manual exercise") represented the only bayonet training that British infantry received during this period.[22] Indeed, in 1768 Cuthbertson complained that the infantry should be made "more familiar with the bayonets than is the custom," while in the summer of 1776, Clinton noted with concern that the King's troops handled the weapon clumsily.[23] Admittedly, in 1779 Simcoe instructed the officers of the Queen's Rangers to ensure that the men maintained an upright poise during the charge, asserting that this would aid them in dispatching their intended rebel victims: "The soldier is, particularly, to be taught to keep his head well up and erect: it is graceful, on all occasions, but absolutely necessary if an enemy dare stand the charge; when the British soldier, who fixes with his eye the attention of his opponent, and, at the same instant, pushes with his bayonet without looking down on its point, is certain of conquest."[24] But Simcoe surely intended this training measure more as a confidence-building exercise, much as the Duke of Cumberland foisted an impractical bayonet drill upon his army before the battle of Culloden (1746) to counteract the redcoats' fear of the ferocious Highland charge.[25] This leads to the important point that, more than bayonet drill, troops needed self-assurance and discipline to adopt the tactical offensive. While the King's troops did not lack this (as discussed in chapter 5), by August 1778 Captain Ferguson was still able to observe that "the rebel troops certainly have not as yet attained confidence enough to use bayonets, the favorite arm of our soldiers."[26] In fact it was arguably only during the war's last campaigns that the Continentals began to go onto the attack in this fashion with real success.[27]

British regulars were not trained to "fence" with their bayonets simply because (as noted in the last chapter) there was rarely any call for such a thing. Admittedly, in America some kind of hand-to-hand fighting usually did occur on those occasions when troops stormed fortifications and/or made night attacks with unloaded arms.[28] Attacking troops also got the opportunity to employ cold steel when a broken enemy suddenly found their escape blocked, though this kind of encounter tended to be rather quick and one sided. Such was probably the case at Brandywine, where (according to the journal of Corporal Thomas Sullivan) a party of rebel troops that gave way when Knyphausen's division pushed over Chad's Ford, "being attacked by the [Queen's] Rangers and 71st [Regiment] in a buckwheat field, was totally skivered [i.e., skewered] with the bayonets before they could clear the fence round it."[29]

Yet in stand-up fights on relatively open ground, human nature almost invariably forced one or other body of troops to recoil away from physical contact with the enemy. Hence in most engagements the defenders' resolve to stand their ground usually evaporated if the attackers appeared determined to push through incoming fire and settle the issue with cold steel. According to Admiral Lord Howe's secretary, as Major General Grant began to push his attack at the battle of Long Island, resistance rapidly collapsed when ragged rebel volleys failed to stop the eager redcoats in their tracks: "The rebels abandoned every spot as fast, I should say faster, than the King's troops advanced upon them. One of their officers [Lord Stirling] . . . did indeed make an effort to form a considerable line of them in a ploughed field; but they had scarce formed, when down came the [King's] troops upon the ground, and the [rebel] poltroons ran in the most broken, disgraceful and precipitate manner at the very first fire."[30] Martin Hunter later captured a similar moment in his account of the attack at Birmingham Meetinghouse at Brandywine, where he fought with the 2nd Battalion of Light Infantry: "[T]hey allowed us to advance till within one hundred and fifty yards of their line, when they gave us a volley, which we returned, and [then we] immediately charged. They stood the charge till we came to the last paling. Their line then began to break, and a general retreat took place soon after."[31] Colonel Otho Williams commanded the Maryland Continental Brigade at Eutaw Springs, where the disrupted British line stood the Continentals' bayonet charge almost until the last moment. Williams later mused: "If the two lines on this occasion did not actually come to the mutual thrust of the bayonet, it must be acknowledged that no troops ever came nearer. They are said to have been so near, that their bayonets clashed and the officers sprang at each other with their swords, before the enemy actually broke away."[32] In short, the attackers' purpose in making a bayonet charge was to force the defenders to break ranks and flee before the men came to close quarters. If the defenders did not shatter the attackers' determination to persevere in the attack by sowing destruction and chaos into their ranks with musket fire or by making them shrink from the threat of this fire, those defenders invariably broke and ran.

Rebel troops had it in their power to repel a British charge, provided they exploited their firepower correctly. To understand why they generally failed to do this, at least until late in the war, one must recall the moral factors that were at work during the course of an attack, in particular the psychological advantages that the King's troops generally enjoyed when on the offensive. First, throughout the war British soldiers maintained a potent moral ascendancy over the rebels, whom they generally held in low regard. Second, during the advance, the redcoats cheered repeatedly to bolster their spirits and to intimidate the enemy. Third, they came on at alarming speed: from 1776, British soldiers in America seem commonly to have advanced at the quickstep (over 100 yards per minute), broke into a trot or a jog (over 150 yards per minute) once they entered the killing zone of the enemy's small arms, and then accelerated to a full run for the charge (over 200 yards per minute). Fourth, troops derived a powerful moral boost from the act of moving forward. Major General William Heath made this clear when he judged that, in the question of how well a battalion would behave under fire, "the point of decision is in the mind": "While advancing, although galled by the fire of their opponents, the dead and wounded are left behind them as they fall; and the troops feel an ardor for arriving in a few minutes at a point where they can use their own arms to retaliate for the injury they sustain." Conversely, Heath added, when troops stood enemy fire at the halt, "the dead and wounded fall and lie among them or are drawn away, and every groan they make is heard."[33]

Throughout the war, furious bayonet rushes proved highly effective against unsupported rebel riflemen. While the rifle's maximum effective range was something like three hundred yards, stationary riflemen could get off no more than two shots at rapidly advancing troops because of the time it took to reload. Indeed, if the contending parties came within view of each other at a considerably shorter distance, an immediate charge almost invariably scattered the riflemen "before they are able to make a second discharge" (as one naval officer put it after the battle of Long Island).[34] Additionally, the sight (and sound) of the furiously advancing British troops was likely to ruffle the composure and spoil the aim of all but the most hardened rebel troops, as Simcoe later pointed out when he explained how the Queen's Rangers had dealt with rebel riflemen, "whose object it was to fire a single shot with effect": "The principle which Lieutenant Colonel Simcoe always inculcated and acted on against the riflemen . . . was to rush upon them. . . . [T]he position of an advancing soldier was calculated to lessen the true aim of the first shot, and his rapidity to prevent the rifleman, who requires some time to load, from giving a second; or at least to render his aim uncertain, and his fire by no means formidable."[35]

The success of this vigorous tactic can be gauged from George Hanger's later account of how Lieutenant Colonel Robert Abercrombie's 1st Battalion of Light Infantry dispersed the vaunted rebel sharpshooters in a brief brush on 7 December 1777, during Howe's Whitemarsh expedition: "When [Colonel Daniel] Morgan's riflemen came down to Pennsylvania . . . they marched to attack our light infantry. . . . The moment they appeared before him [i.e., Abercrombie], he ordered his troops to charge them with the bayonet. Not one man out of four had time to fire, and those that did had no time given them to load again: the light infantry not only dispersed them instantly but drove them for miles over the country. They never attacked, or even looked at, our light infantry again, without a regular force to support them."[36] Simcoe echoed Hanger's implication that rebel riflemen were ineffective without the support of disciplined and confident bayonet-armed regulars: "if each separate [British] company kept itself compact, there was little danger, even should it be surrounded, from troops who were without bayonets."[37] The suggestion that the attacking British troops were vulnerable to counterattack, and Simcoe's point that they needed to remain "compact" during the charge, are particularly noteworthy. (We will return to this theme later in this chapter while examining the reasons why the British bayonet charge became gradually less effective as the war progressed.)

Our attention must now turn to the manner in which the King's troops generally attacked rebel regulars or militia armed predominantly with smoothbores. In theory, because the common musket had a maximum effective range of about two hundred yards and because well-trained troops could sustain a rate of fire of between two and three rounds per minute, rebel infantry might have shot any advancing British battalion to pieces. In practice, however, (for reasons examined in the last chapter) the defenders' best chances of halting the attackers lay rather in hitting them with a single, well-delivered, close-range volley. For example, early in the battle of Princeton, a heavy rebel discharge at forty yards brought down seven of Lieutenant William Hale's thirty-strong advancing grenadier platoon and forced the rest to recoil some distance before he could rally them and renew the attack.[38] Likewise, a crashing volley loosed by the Virginia and Maryland Continentals at a range of around twenty to twenty-five yards abruptly halted the premature advance of the 33rd Regiment, Guards light infantry, and *Jäger* at Guilford Courthouse.[39] Even more stunning was the murderous blast with which the retiring Continentals overturned the pursuing 1st Battalion of the 71st Regiment at Cowpens, a volley that Lawrence Babits has estimated may have been delivered when the Highlanders were as little as ten to fifteen yards away.[40]

While in each of these cases, the King's troops were rebuffed by the effects of a destructive, close-range volley, one should note that it was also possible for the attackers to balk at the prospect of such a fire. According to Roger Lamb's vivid personal account, something like this happened during the attack on the rebel first line at Guilford Courthouse, after Lieutenant Colonel James Webster's brigade had thrown in its fire at about fifty to seventy-five yards from the enemy:

> [T]he colonel rode on to the front, and gave the word, *"Charge."* Instantly, the movement was made, in excellent order, in a smart run, with arms charged. When arrived within forty yards of the enemy's line, it was perceived that their whole force had their arms presented, and resting on a rail fence, the common partitions in America. They were taking aim with the nicest precision. . . . At this awful period a general pause took place: both parties surveyed each other for the moment with the most anxious suspense. Nothing speaks the general more than seizing on decisive moments: Colonel Webster rode forward in the front of the 23rd Regiment, and said, with more than even his usual commanding voice (which was well known to his brigade) *"Come on, my brave Fusiliers."* This operated like an inspiring voice, [and] they rushed on forward among the en-

emy's fire; dreadful was the havoc on both sides. . . . At last the Americans gave way, and the brigade advanced to the attack of their second line.[41]

According to Lamb then, Webster's inspirational intervention was critical—without it the British advance would have faltered in front of the rebel line.

Because rebel infantry needed to maximize the effectiveness of their fire if they were to stop any British attack in its tracks, the officers perennially entreated the men not to shoot prematurely. For example, in late October 1776, toward the end of the British offensive from Canada, Gates announced to his rebel Northern Army: "As the enemy's attack will probably be rash and sudden, the General earnestly recommends to every commanding officer of a regiment, party, post, or detachment to be deliberate and cool in suffering his men to fire, never allowing them to throw away their shot in a random, unsoldierlike manner. One close, well-directed fire, at the distance of eight or ten rods [forty-four to fifty-five yards], will do more towards defeating the enemy than all the scattered, random shot, fired in a whole day."[42] In combat rebel officers commonly attempted to restrain their unsteady troops' understandable inclination to shoot early. Militiaman Thomas Young later recorded how, as the British line advanced at Cowpens, Brigadier General Morgan "galloped along the lines, cheering the men and telling them not to fire until we could see the whites of their eyes. Every officer was crying, 'Don't fire!' for it was a hard matter to keep us from it."[43]

Despite these efforts, in action it was common for rebel infantry to open fire prematurely at ranges up to and exceeding 150 yards. Sometimes this happened simply because their officers gave the command to fire too early. At the affair at Harlem Heights, one of the rebel companies sent to demonstrate in the front of the light infantry and Highlanders opened fire too soon, when the British were still between 250 and 300 yards away. As Captain John Chilton of the 3rd Virginia Regiment explained, "Our orders were not to fire until they came near, but a young officer (of whom we have too many) on the right fired, and it was taken [up] from right to left."[44]

Premature shooting most often occurred because rebel soldiers anticipated the command to fire. Five decades after the war, a former North Carolina militiaman named Garret Watts provided striking evidence for why rebel troops commonly yielded to this temptation. Watts confessed that, in the early stages of the battle of Camden, the psychological strain of the sight (and doubtless the sound) of Webster's brigade coming on confidently had panicked him into firing early in order (as it appeared to him) to preserve his own life: "I well remember everything that occurred that morning. I remember that I was among the nearest to the enemy; that a man names John Summers was my file leader; [and] that we had orders to wait for the word to commence firing. . . . I can state on oath that I believe my gun was the first gun fired, notwithstanding the orders; for we were close to the enemy, who appeared to maneuver in contempt of us, and I fired without thinking except that I might prevent the man opposite from killing me. The discharge and loud roar soon became general from one end of the lines to the other."[45] In scenarios like Webster's advance at Camden, the natural instinct for self-preservation must have produced a situation where the rebel defenders were collectively willing their officers to release them from the obligation to hold their fire. This urge must have intensified as the advancing redcoats came ever closer. When individuals like Watts succumbed to it and pulled the trigger, the resulting "popping shots" were likely to overwhelm the officers' efforts to maintain fire control and trigger a premature, ragged volley from the whole unit—even from the entire line. One of the redcoats who advanced so briskly and menacingly toward the North Carolina militia was Private John Robert Shaw of the 33rd Regiment. Interestingly, Shaw later claimed that the militia loosed their first fire when the opposing lines had "approached within 100 yards of each other."[46]

The rebel defenders' chances of repelling the attack were much reduced if they loosed their first volley early. Such long-range fire was unlikely to inflict the level of damage and disorder required to stop disciplined and determined attackers. Indeed, the limited execution wrought by this premature fire was likely to boost the attackers' confidence, as Major General Massey noted in the tactical instructions that he issued to a field force drawn from the Halifax garrison in September 1777: "[N]othing can more strongly mark the want of discipline and indeed of resolution and firmness, than firing wantonly without effect. . . . A body of men wasting injudiciously their ammunition soon becomes insignificant to a discerning enemy."[47] By contrast, as the smoke from this premature fire cleared, the sight of the undaunted redcoats still closing in remorselessly must sorely have dented the rebel defenders' collective will to stand. If the attackers immediately accelerated into the charge, the temporarily defenseless defenders were very likely to break ranks and flee. Howe's infantry seem to have employed this tactic at the battle of Long Island; its success may be judged from the cursory British accounts of the short, sharp, fluid combats that occurred as the outflanking column sliced though the rebel rear toward Brooklyn. For example, General Lord Percy (who accompanied the Guards in Howe's column) wrote that the cheapness of the victory "was entirely owing to our men attacking them the proper way. The moment the rebels fired, our men rushed on them with their bayonets and never gave them time to load again."[48] The testimony of another officer confirms Percy's point: "It was the General's orders that the [King's] troops should receive the rebels' first fire, and then rush on them (before they [i.e., the rebels] had recovered their arms) with their bayonets; which threw them into the utmost disorder and confusion, they being unacquainted with such a manoeuvre."[49] Indeed, rebel troops often broke and ran almost immediately after this first volley. As one anonymous flank company officer put it after the battle of Monmouth (with some exaggeration), "Their behavior, Sir, during this war [has] been uniform; they never having done more than give a fire and retreat, never daring to wait the shock of our bayonets."[50]

Even if the defenders did not immediately break ranks when the redcoats accelerated into the charge but instead managed frantically to reload and get off another round or two (as the North Carolina militia did at Guilford Courthouse), then this fire was likely to become less rather than more effective. This was largely because (as noted in the last chapter) the first volley was always the most effective: the men had carefully loaded their pieces before the action, their barrels were clean, their flints were sharp, and their field of vision was clear. Another reason was that (as discussed earlier) the sight and sound of British troops dashing toward them was likely to ruffle the defenders' composure and spoil their aim—and doubtless to hinder careful reloading. A third reason was the reassuring point that Simcoe made to the loyalist soldiers of the Queen's Rangers: "that, in the position of running, their bodies afforded a less and more uncertain mark to their antagonists."[51]

As noted in the last chapter, if the advancing troops halted to fire, there was a danger that the attack would degenerate into an indecisive and uncontrolled firefight. Alternatively, if the attackers continued to advance without firing, this put yet more pressure on the defenders to break ranks and flee. Massey's tactical instructions and Simcoe's description of the Queen's Rangers' training regimen help explain why. In 1777 Massey's infantry was instructed that the bayonet charge would commence without a preparatory volley, "the whole advances briskly in an extended [order] of two ranks, charging the enemy with fixed bayonets, but on no account to commence firing till ordered." Likewise, Simcoe later wrote that the Queen's Rangers "were particularly trained to attack a supposed enemy, posted behind railing, the common position of the rebels. They were instructed not to fire, but to charge their bayonets with their muskets loaded." As he put it, the defenders' "minds also must be perturbed by the rapidity of their approach with undischarged arms." Massey made the same observation: "the soldier who possesses his firearms loaded and ready for execution is ever formidable and his approach is dreaded." Simcoe assumed that the rebels would turn and run before the Queen's Rangers arrived at close quarters: "upon their arrival at the fence, each soldier [was] to take his aim at their opponents, who were then supposed to have been driven from it." Even if the rebels managed to stand the charge until then, the devastating impact of a close-range British volley must have overwhelmed them utterly. In Massey's words this fire was to be unleashed "so near as to be sure of not missing the object before them, that there may be no doubt of their doing certain and serious execution."[52]

The tactic of charging without stopping to shoot (or doing so only once the troops had reached their objective) was not typical British practice in America. Regardless of enemy fire, the redcoats seem generally to have halted to unleash a volley at a point about fifty to seventy-five yards from the defenders before resuming the advance, typically at a run, with charged bayonets. Charles Noël Romand de Lisle, a French officer who served as a rebel major of artillery, noted after Germantown that "the principal advantage of General Howe's army over General Washington's . . . must be ascribed to their being more trained to the use of the bayonet. The American army know their superior dexterity in firing well, and rely entirely upon it. The British army know it likewise, and dread it. Hence in all engagements the British soldiers rush on with the bayonet after one fire, and seldom fail of throwing the Americans into confusion."[53] A tactical directive issued to the expeditionary force sent against Savannah in December 1778 outlines what would appear to have been the most common sequence for the attack: "On every occasion where it is possible to approach the enemy, it is Lieutenant Colonel [Archibald] Campbell's orders that the troops destined for the attack shall, with their usual intrepidity, march briskly up to the distance of 60 yards, without regarding their [i.e., the rebels'] fire, throw in a general volley, give a military cheer, and rush upon them with their bayonets. The superior prowess of British and Hessian troops in every attack of this nature will crown their arms with glory and success."[54] The tactic of unleashing a single "general volley" at medium range before rushing forward had several purposes. If the rebel defenders had not yet fired, then the British volley was likely to draw their fire. Alternatively, if the rebels had fired, this volley repaid some of the punishment that the rebels must have inflicted. Either way, the volley delivered a psychological punch that, when followed by an immediate charge, was expected to shatter the enemy's will to stand.

The battle of Camden provides the best-documented example of how unsteady rebel battalions dissolved into flight when the British loosed their volley and launched into the charge. Colonel Otho Williams served on Gates's staff during the campaign. When Webster's brigade began to advance, Williams led forward parties from Brigadier General Edward Stevens's Virginia militia brigade (on the rebel left) "to take trees and keep up as brisk a fire as possible . . . to extort the enemy's fire at some distance in order to the rendering it less terrible to the militia." Williams's ploy failed to deter the advancing redcoats (the light infantry, on the extreme right flank, and the 23rd Regiment) as his account makes clear:

> [T]he impetuosity with which they advanced, *firing* and *huzzaing*, threw the whole body of the [Virginia] militia into such a panic that they generally threw down their *loaded* arms and fled in the utmost consternation. . . . The unworthy example of the Virginians was almost instantly followed by the North Carolinians; only a small part of the brigade . . . made a short pause. A part . . . next in the line to the Second Maryland Brigade fired two or three rounds of cartridge. But a great majority of the militia (at least two-thirds of the army) fled with-

out firing a shot. . . . He who has never seen the effect of a panic upon a multitude can have but an imperfect idea of such a thing. The best-disciplined troops have been enervated and made cowards by it. Armies have been routed by it, even where no enemy appeared to furnish an excuse. Like electricity, it operates instantaneously—like sympathy, it is irresistible where it touches.[55]

As Williams indicates, although Major General Richard Caswell's North Carolina militia brigade (which comprised the right of the militia wing) got off a premature and ragged volley at the incoming 33rd Regiment, they too broke and ran when the latter launched into the charge. Once again, Garret Watts was disarmingly candid about his own part in the rout: "Amongst other things, I confess that I was amongst the first that fled. The cause of that I cannot tell, except that everyone I saw was about to do the same. It was instantaneous. There was no effort to rally, no encouragement to fight. Officers and men joined in the flight. I threw away my gun, and, reflecting I might be punished for being found without arms, I picked up a drum, which gave forth such sounds when touched by the twigs [that] I cast it away."[56] Just as a few premature "popping shots" often had the effect of triggering an unauthorized general fire, it would appear that when a few men broke ranks and fled in the face of a British charge, their example somehow released the rest of their comrades from the unwelcome obligation to stand their ground.

### Ruthlessness in Combat

As discussed earlier, British troops appear to have viewed the rebels with considerable hostility. This antipathy probably contributed to the grim reputation for ruthlessness that the redcoats earned in America because of the frequency with which they seem to have killed enemy combatants attempting to surrender in the heat of the action and finished off the wounded.

Although Martin Hunter (who served in America as a light company officer) later admitted that, during Howe's Pennsylvania campaign, "the whole army were so inveterate against the Americans that they seldom gave any quarter," most British sources are understandably quiet about this dark phenomenon.[57] For more detail of supposed atrocities, one must therefore turn to rebel sources. Here a few examples will suffice. For instance, when Lieutenant Colonel Charles Mawhood's 17th Regiment broke Brigadier General Hugh Mercer's brigade with a furious bayonet rush at Princeton, the redcoats repeatedly skewered or bludgeoned the handful of abandoned wounded. One rebel sergeant took particular notice that a comrade with a broken leg had been dragged from under a wagon in William Clark's barnyard, where he was later found "dead, having received several wounds from a British bayonet."[58] In a similar fashion, when rebel officers returned to the scene of a skirmish with a British foraging party near New Brunswick on 1 February 1777, they found that "the [rebel] men that was wounded in the thigh or leg, they [i.e., the redcoats] [had] dash[ed] out their brains with their muskets and run them through with their bayonets, [and] made them like sieves. This was barbarity to the utmost."[59] Lawrence Babits has speculated that the nature of the wounds that some rebel riflemen sustained at Cowpens implies similar ruthlessness. According to Babits, as the Highlanders of the 1st Battalion of the 71st Regiment moved up from their reserve position to turn the enemy's main line, they must have bayoneted writhing rebels in their path who had been cut down earlier by British Legion dragoons.[60] Indeed, when the Highlanders surrendered, the apprehensive Captain Robert Duncanson tellingly sought the protection of Lieutenant Colonel John Eager Howard, warning "that they [i.e., the Highlanders] had orders to give no quarter, and they did not expect any."[61] Had the rebels won more battlefield actions and thus obtained possession of all the dead and wounded at the end of the fighting, they undoubtedly would have recorded more evidence of this kind of bloody behavior.

The claim that the Highlanders had instructions to give no quarter at Cowpens reminds us that ruthlessness was sometimes not spontaneous but was instead (allegedly) put into effect on the direct orders of officers. Perhaps the best example of this was the "Baylor Massacre" (27 September 1778), when Major General Charles Grey repeated his earlier coup at the "Paoli Massacre" (21 September 1777) by leading the 2nd Battalion of Light Infantry in a successful night attack on Lieutenant Colonel George Baylor's 3rd Regiment of Continental Dragoons.[62] According to rebel survivors' accounts, the light infantrymen who set about bayoneting the dazed dragoons (with the exception of one troop) in the various barns in which they had been sleeping rejected calls for mercy with cries of *"Skiver him,"* *"there is no quarter for you,"* and *"run him through"* or coldly warded them off with assertions "that their captain had ordered them to stab all and take no prisoners."[63] Considering the confusion and risk inherent in a night attack, this does not sound particularly controversial. Indeed, according to the report of rebel surgeon Dr. David Griffith, only 28 of the 104 dragoons were killed or so badly wounded that they had to be left behind, while another 33 were carried off as prisoners of war (8 of them wounded) and the rest evaded capture.[64] What does make the incident contentious is that in several cases the survivors testified that British officers ordered their men to kill the rebel dragoons after they had been captured. For example, Southward Cullency of 1st Troop claimed "that the British captain ([Bent] Ball of the 2nd Light Infantry) asked his men how many of the rebels were actually dead; and, on being told the number, he ordered all the rest to be knocked on the head—that the soldiers muttered about it, and asked why they had not been made to kill them at all once, and why they need have two spells about it?"[65] Griffith singled out Major Turner Straubenzee (17th Regiment), Captain Bent Ball (63rd Regiment), and Captain Sir James Baird (71st Regiment) as having been "the principal agents . . . in this bloody business."[66] Baird in particular appears to have been a ferocious individual. According to one loyalist civilian, after the incident Baird allegedly "walked through the streets with his bayonet hanging at his back, stained with the blood of Lady Washington's Life Guards."[67] Later that year, after the victory at Briar Creek, another loyalist was appalled when the captain "vaunted of having put to death nearly a dozen . . . supplicants with his own hands, and eventually showed their blood oozing out of the touchhole of his fusee."[68] Doubtless, Baird was one of those officers who viewed the employment of "severity" against the rebels as the only way to win the war.[69]

Even if incidents like the night attack on Baylor's dragoons are set aside as untypical, it is probably significant that the perpetrators of these alleged atrocities were light infantrymen. History shows that the officers and enlisted men of supposed elite formations, intoxicated by a well-developed sense of martial superiority, have often been particularly liable to employ what might be interpreted as excessive force both in and out of combat. Here one should remember that the King's troops typically held the American rebels in contempt and that the lion's share of the fighting was often done by elite corps such as the flank battalions—and especially by the light infantry, which attracted the most active officers and men. It should therefore be little surprise that the redcoats sometimes proved less than generous in action. Indeed, in America British light infantry gained particular notoriety for alleged brutality, especially in the northern campaigns. For example, after rebel captain Alexander Graydon was captured at Fort Washington, he and his fellow prisoners were subjected to degrading abuse by British light company officers. Graydon later dismissed his tormentors as "for the most part young and insolent puppies, whose worthlessness was apparently their recommendation to a service, which placed them in the post of danger, and in the way of becoming food for powder, their most appropriate destination next to that of the gallows."[70] As discussed below, not for nothing did the rebels learn to call the British light infantry "the bloodhounds."

Some of the atrocities that British soldiers allegedly committed in action can probably be explained more easily. That the redcoats were repeatedly ordered to view their bayonets as the weapon of choice against the rebels must surely have made it more likely that they would ply them whenever the fleeting opportunity arose. Indeed, when one considers the mechanics of the bayonet charge, it is hardly remarkable that blood was sometimes spilled unnecessarily. Men who rushed forward with charged bayonets, renting the air with cheers, and who saw rebel musketry pluck down their comrades around them were keyed up into a state of acute stress. They were hardly liable to halt calmly and accept the surrender of enemies who, shrouded in their own powder smoke, belatedly threw down their empty weapons now this appeared a more promising means of self-preservation than further resistance or flight. In such circumstances the unhappy supplicants were almost inevitably going to receive short shrift—as indeed has probably been the case in most conflicts throughout history.

The redcoats' tendency to be ruthless when they got to grips with their elusive foes becomes even more understandable when we remember that many Crown officers and men were exasperated by the nature of the opposition that they frequently faced in America and considered that the rebels were prone to fighting what we might today call a "dirty war." In April 1777, after Howe's troops in hostile New Jersey had spent a miserable winter almost besieged in their cramped cantonments, Captain John Bowater reported that the men were eager to take revenge: "I am certain that our troops will act with less humanity this campaign than they did in the last, as they have been very much irritated by the most wanton cruelties committed by the rebels in the Jerseys, by which we lost a number of very fine fellows, both officers and men, and in a manner too horrid to describe."[71] One incident probably encapsulates the attitude of many British soldiers to rebel irregulars. When on the morning of 28 September 1778 (in the aftermath of the "Baylor Massacre"), light infantrymen cornered a rebel captain of the Orange County militia, the redcoats reacted to his attempt to surrender by shooting and then bayoneting him, swearing "that they would give no quarter to no militiaman."[72]

Whether regulars or irregulars, rebel combatants risked immediate vengeance if they contravened the conventions of acceptable military conduct as understood by most European soldiers. Thomas Anbury later recorded one such instance at the action at Hubbardton, in which he participated as a gentleman volunteer with the 29th Regiment's grenadiers:

> During the battle the Americans were guilty of such a breach of all military rules, as could not fail to exasperate our soldiers. . . . Two companies of grenadiers . . . observed a number of the Americans, to the amount of near sixty, coming across the field, with their arms clubbed, which is always considered to be a surrender as prisoners of war. The grenadiers were restrained from firing, [and] commanded to stand with their arms, and show no hostility. When the Americans had got within ten yards, they in an instant turned round their muskets, fired upon the grenadiers, and run as fast as they could into the woods. Their fire killed and wounded a great number of men, and those who escaped immediately pursued them, and gave no quarter.[73]

The incident was not an isolated one, for Howe's Hessian aide de camp noted in April 1778 that British troops patrolling near Philadelphia had butchered a party of rebels "because, as they commonly do, they had first asked for pardon and then fired on our men after they had come close."[74] The events of the return march from Concord paint a similar picture. Disturbed perhaps by rumors that the militia had mutilated wounded British soldiers at the North Bridge,[75] and "enraged at suffering from an unseen enemy" who sniped at them from cover, the maddened redcoats "forced open many of the houses from which the fire proceeded, and put to death all those found in them."[76] A similar episode occurred in February 1779, when Major General Lincoln declined to punish the rebel irregulars who had killed and mutilated a light infantryman from the 71st Regiment guarding a captured rebel major's family in Augusta. Lieutenant Colonel Archibald Campbell confided in his diary that "[t]he British troops . . . were greatly exasperated by this shameful act of injustice; especially the light infantry, who had determined to revenge Mac-Alister's murder on the first favorable occasion." According to Campbell, the embittered redcoats got their chance weeks later during the action at Briar Creek: "[W]hen the Light Infantry were running up in line to charge the rebels, one of the Highlanders called out, 'Now my boys, remember poor MacAlister'; in consequence of which, this corps spared very few that came within their reach."[77]

## The Bayonet Charge: Disorder

Ideally, the bayonet charge was executed as a swift but disciplined forward movement in which the men remained under the full command of their officers. For instance, Howe reported of the maneuvers performed by the 33rd Regiment at its 1774 review: "The regiment made a most formidable charge in battalion, running upward of two hundred yards, in the best order."[78] In his tactical instructions to the 1st Battalion of Grenadiers in August 1780, Lieutenant Colonel Henry Hope explained why it was necessary for the officers not to lose control of their men during the bayonet attack: "When the line is ordered to charge, either by word of command from the commanding officer or by signal of drum, each officer will repeat the word to his own company, and will endeavor as much as possible in rushing forward to prevent his men from breaking their order, [so] that, either upon being ordered to halt, or after coming up with and forcing the first body of the enemy, the line may be reformed again with as little confusion and loss of time as possible; so as to throw in a fire upon such of the broken, flying enemy as they can't come up with, or [else] to be in order to charge any second body that may present itself."[79] Likewise, Major General Massey reminded his small field force in September 1777 that "[w]hen ordered to charge, it must be done with that steady and animated coolness which is the criterion of discipline and denotes the genuine medium which distinguishes intrepid vivacity from unbridled confusion and rash precipitation."[80] Significantly, Roger Lamb later wrote that the bayonet charge executed by Cornwallis's line against the North Carolina militia at Guilford Courthouse "was made, in excellent order, in a smart run, with arms charged."[81]

Attacks conducted in this disciplined and restrained manner would arguably have had the mere effect of dislodging the enemy from one point to another. In March 1778 Lieutenant William Hale gave the rebels' "chief qualification" as "agility in running from fence to fence and thence keeping up an irregular, but galling fire."[82] Here Hale had in mind their performance at Brandywine. There Cornwallis's attack at Birmingham Meetinghouse caught and routed Major General Sullivan's division (on the left) while it was still redeploying and dislodged the divisions of Major Generals Stirling and Stephen (in the center and on the right) after more sustained fighting. Thereafter Cornwallis's battalions closely followed up the disorganized and intermixed rebel forces. To prevent the enemy from renewing their stand, the British punctuated their brisk advance with vigorous bayonet rushes. Howe's Hessian aide de camp reported that the redcoats "drove them back three miles with their bayonets without firing a shot, in spite of the fact that the rebel fire was heavy," while Captain Ewald later wrote that the enemy line was driven back as far as Dilworth "after a steady, stubborn fight from hill to hill and from wall to wall."[83] Likewise, Lieutenants John Peebles and Hale, both with the 2nd Battalion of Grenadiers, recorded that the grenadiers "pursued the fugitives through woods and over fences for about three miles" and "drove them from six successive railings under an exceeding heavy fire . . . the battle continued for three miles."[84] While the distance over which the shattered divisions were pursued was more like one or two miles rather than three, it is difficult to imagine that Cornwallis's battalions can have traversed this uneven and partially wooded ground in anything other than the loosest order. Nor can they have paused long to reform after each charge.

When the King's troops succeeded in breaking enemy units, they sometimes gave immediate chase—in other words, they maintained the full momentum of the advance, sometimes for considerable distances, nipping at the rebels' heels like a pack of hunting dogs. In fact, this metaphor is peculiarly appropriate. During the early stages of the affair at Harlem Heights, jubilant British light companies "in the most insulting manner sounded their bugle horns as is usual after a fox chase," while after their brilliant nocturnal attack at Paoli, the men of the 2nd Battalion of Light Infantry were dubbed "the blood-hounds" because they pursued stragglers from Brigadier General Wayne's shattered division for up to two miles through the night.[85] Perhaps the most vivid description of the chronic level of disorder into which the redcoats sometimes fell in attempting to come up with broken or retiring enemy troops is Lieutenant Hale's colorful account of his experience with the 2nd Battalion of Grenadiers at the battle of Monmouth:

At length we came within reach of the enemy, who cannon-aded us very briskly without doing much damage; and, after-wards, marching through a cornfield, [we] saw them drawn up behind a morass on a hill, with a rail fence in front and a thick wood on their left filled with their chosen light troops. We rose on a small hill, commanded by that on which they were posted, in excellent order, notwithstanding a very heavy fire of grape; when, judge of my inexpressible surprise, General Clinton himself appeared at the head of our left wing, accom-panied by Lord Cornwallis, and crying out "Charge, Grena-diers, never heed forming!" We rushed on amidst the heaviest fire I have yet felt. It was no longer a contest for bringing up our respective companies in the best order, but all officers as well as soldiers strove who could be foremost, to my shame I speak it. I had the fortune to find myself after crossing the swamp with three officers only, in the midst of a large body of rebels who had been driven out of the wood by the 1st Bat-talion of Grenadiers, accompanied by not more than a dozen men who had been able to keep up with us. Luckily the rebels were too intent on their own safety to regard our destruction. Lieutenant [Joseph] Bunbury of the [illegible: 49th Regiment's grenadiers?] killed one of them with his sword, as we all might have done. But seeing a battalion running away with their colors, I pushed for them with the few fellows I had; but to my unutterable disappointment they outran us in a second.[86]

While the tone of Hale's narrative would tend to indicate that the grenadiers' tumultuous dash at Monmouth was an aberration, it was untypical only in the degree to which the battalion's order and discipline broke down.

The disarray in which British battalions commonly rushed on in action against the rebels was one key theme in a curious collection of short literary pieces published together after the war by the former major of the 35th Regiment, Edward Drewe. In one satire Drewe borrowed the thick-skulled villain Ensign Northerton from Fielding's *Tom Jones*, promoted him to the command of a battalion in America, and let him explain the regimental commanding officer's role during the attack:

> "[D]amn me, all I do is to halloo my men to the enemy, and he that gets up first is the best man; and I believe I am as good an officer as my neighbors." "Aye, by God are you, sir, says the lieutenant," (who had been listening with admiration) "for the devil a man in our regiment can run with you. By God, I have often seen you, in a charge, twenty yards ahead of Jack Thomas, the long fifer; and if your men had not always been knocked up, I'll be sworn you would often have beat the enemy." Here the colonel called out, with great ecstasy, "Follow me; come on, come on—stop for no-one"—concluding with that harmonious sound, which in the hunting phrase is termed a view halloo.[87]

Here Drewe pointed to a potentially dangerous paradox in British tactics: the physical effort of such a furious charge was likely to exhaust the redcoats before they came to close quarters with the enemy.

Another of Drewe's satirical pieces (probably written as a reaction to the somewhat ragged British performance at the battle of Monmouth) purported to be a South American Indian warrior's war speech to his tribe. In reality this apparent historical curiosity was a biting denunciation of the operational and tactical complacency into which the main British army had lapsed during three years' fighting against an essentially second-rate opponent—a state of affairs that the author believed would prove fatal if the redcoats found themselves confronting disciplined Bourbon forces in America. Once again, among his complaints was the disorderly and headlong manner in which the King's troops typically dashed on in combat. Drewe dismissed the notion that any given body of British troops could overwhelm superior rebel forces in an indiscriminate encounter, asserting instead that "it is only as a firm collected body that you can be formidable to undisciplined numbers." In considering what induced officers and men typically "to forego the aid of discipline, and rush on the enemy with a precipitance and confusion which would dishonor even a popular tumult," he speculated that it proceeded "from eagerness to be signalized, and a fear lest the enemy should escape you," and not from a desire "to shorten danger, rather than await its regular approach" or "from a consciousness that you are incapable of preserving order, and so wish to hide the defect under the mask of valor." Nevertheless, he reasoned that such impetuous and debilitating rushes were futile if the enemy was determined not to make a stand (because the rebels could run away fully as fast as the redcoats could advance) and unnecessary if they did: "How often have you seen by much the greater part of your fellow warriors panting, dying, dead, scattered through a very long line of march, that a few of the most vigorous might reach the enemy with expedition? Have they reached them? Seldom. Have they had strength to pursue the advantage? I will venture to say never. Of what use then was this celerity? Of none. And yet a few minutes delay would have brought you up regular, in breath, and ensured you every advantage." In fact, Drewe continued, precipitate and scattered attacks were positively dangerous should the enemy ever be in a position to take advantage of the charging troops' fatigue and disorder:

> [H]ave we not often found ourselves in so defenseless a state as to afford an easy prey to those we pursued, should they have had resolution to turn on us? The Tucumans [i.e., the French] never think themselves beaten until their ranks are broke. What would be their astonishment to hear that we began the battle by breaking them; and what fatal advantages would they not reap from it? You now have a foe [i.e., the French] that will stand you at bay. Conceive the horrors of these [British] soldiers who, in our usual exhausted state, should come up with an enemy who stood firm, and [who] charged in their turn, fresh, and in regular order? In vain would they look back for assistance on their numerous companions. These, almost exhausted, can only behold their fate with unavailing eye, expecting the stroke which soon must

fall on themselves. You may call this a picture of the fancy, but I dread the hour when it may prove a true one.[88]

Captain Ewald likewise predicted that the British would "come out dirty" in their first combat against the French in America, arguing that it was impossible for troops advancing two deep and at open files to maintain good order.[89]

Ultimately it was the American rebels rather than French regulars who delivered this blow. Throughout the war, the impetuous and loose manner in which the redcoats dashed on in action had exposed them to the risk of a check whenever they encountered fresh rebel forces. For instance, at Brandywine, after having beaten and driven three divisions for two miles from Birmingham Hill, Cornwallis's troops ("much fatigued with a long march and a rapid pursuit") unexpectedly found their advance barred by Greene's division, which had hurriedly redeployed as a second line at Dilworth.[90] Likewise, Otho Williams later wrote that at Camden, after Webster's brigade had put the militia to a precipitate rout, the presence of the First Maryland Brigade in reserve two hundred yards in the rear "abated the fury of their assault, and obliged them to assume a more deliberate manner of acting."[91] And at Cowpens, after Tarleton's troops had forced the militia line to withdraw, the vigorous pursuit was curtailed when the British infantry spotted the rebel main line, one Continental officer noting that "[t]he enemy, seeing us standing in such good order, halted for some time to dress the line."[92]

In all of these incidents, however, the officers managed to regain full control over their troops, halt them, and reform them before renewing the attack in a more concerted and regular fashion. Here one should recall Lieutenant Colonel Henry Hope's aforementioned direction that the officers of the 1st Battalion of Grenadiers needed to prevent their men from slipping into disorder during the charge. Significantly, Hope's stated concern was to ensure that the battalion was able to resume offensive action as quickly as possible. Indeed, he does not openly appear to have entertained the suggestion that, if it dashed forward impetuously, the battalion would make itself vulnerable to counterattack by a fresh enemy force.

Yet by this late stage in the war, well-disciplined Continentals were certainly capable of dealing this kind of stunning counterblow to fatigued and disordered British troops. At Cowpens the collapse of

Tarleton's line occurred because the flank attack delivered by the 1st Battalion of the 71st Regiment triggered the accidental staggered withdrawal of the entire rebel main line, which in turn prompted the Highlanders, the 7th Regiment, the infantry of the British Legion, and the light infantry to rush forward in pursuit. In Henry Lee's words, "the British line rushed on with impetuosity and disorder; but, as it drew near, [Lieutenant Colonel John Eager] Howard faced about, and gave it a close and murderous fire. Stunned by this unexpected shock, the most advanced of the enemy recoiled in confusion. Howard seized the happy moment, and followed his advantage with the bayonet."[93] As Lawrence Babits has related in detail, although parties of Highlanders stubbornly put up some brief resistance, the majority of Tarleton's physically and mentally exhausted troops dropped their weapons in shock and either surrendered or attempted to escape.[94] It was doubtless this catastrophe that George Hanger had in mind when he later wrote that allowing "victorious troops in a broken and irregular manner to pursue the enemy" had "in cases I could mention . . . proved fatal where British valor, intoxicated with a momentary success, has lost sight of discipline, regularity and order; which neglect of regularity may in future wars, if not corrected, be more severely felt." Hanger supported his assertion by pointing approvingly to Lieutenant Colonel Thomas Dundas's conduct in the minor victory at Green Springs, where his brigade (the 43rd, 76th, and 80th Regiments) played a leading role: "After repulsing the first line of the enemy, instead of permitting his men, elated with the mere appearance of victory, to pursue *á la debandade* the flying foe, this able officer ordered his men to halt, formed them in regular order, and then moved on in a collected body. He was presently opposed by a fresh body of Continentals in reserve, whom he repulsed, because he was ready to receive them; and he gained all the advantages which were the natural consequences of his judicious conduct."[95] The rebel infantry in question were probably part of Brigadier General Wayne's brigade of three battalions of Pennsylvania Continentals.

Early in the war the rebels' predilection for fighting behind hard cover triggered a shift in British infantry tactics from the traditional reliance on fire to speed and shock. Although as the conflict unfolded, British troops were rarely called upon to storm rebel fieldworks, they nevertheless retained their dependence on the bayonet. They did not do this because they believed themselves qualitatively inferior in the firefight or because rebel troops lacked the bayonets or the training for hand-to-hand combat. Instead it usually proved unnecessary to engage in costly firefights to "soften up" rebel troops, most of whom lacked the discipline and confidence to repel bayonet rushes with firepower. Although the evidence is limited, once the rebels were put to flight, quarter was sometimes denied to surrendering and wounded enemy combatants. This grim phenomenon stemmed from various factors, including some British officers' hard-line attitude toward the rebellion, the heavy emphasis given to the bayonet in British tactics, the mechanics of the bayonet charge, and the soldiery's hostility to the rebels (particularly irregulars). But as one French adventurer noted, in time experienced Continentals became "as firm at the approaches of a bayonet, as the whistling of a musket ball."[96] Against such troops British bayonet rushes proved expensive and fruitless. Moreover, the disorder into which the redcoats often descended during the charge left them dangerously vulnerable to counterattack. Again, for most of the war, few rebel troops were disciplined enough to exploit this. Yet the catastrophic overturning of Tarleton's line at Cowpens indicates that, by this late stage in the conflict, it was unwise for the British to treat the Continentals with anything other than the respect that they would ordinarily have reserved for European regulars.

# 10

# "Bushfighting"

The woods here are immense, and a European can hardly get an
idea of their extent without having seen them. They are marshy,
full of underbrush and almost impassable, large trees having fallen
down, barring the way. . . . Each soldier must do his best to seek
cover behind a tree and advance without command, keeping an eye
only on the movements of the whole body of soldiers, to which our
regular troops are not accustomed.

*Journal of Du Roi the Elder*

Perhaps the most important tactical lesson that British officers
learned in North America during the French and Indian War was
that "bushfighting," or skirmishing in wooded country, was the preserve of specially constituted, trained, and equipped regular light infantry. To recapitulate the story of the temporary introduction of
these light companies and their permanent restoration on an armywide basis in 1771–72 is not the intention here,[1] nor to trespass on
the story of the evolution of a genuine British light infantry arm from
the 1790s.[2] The aim instead is to sketch the tactical role that by 1775
the newly restored light infantry was expected to play, and to examine how and with what success British troops combated the rebels in
the woods of North America.

### British Light Infantry Training in 1775

At annual regimental reviews in Britain and Ireland during the 1770s, it was common for the light company (sometimes augmented by the grenadier company) to deploy as skirmishers, operating as a screen for the battalion's front or flanks.[3] Indeed, no other role was practical, given that infantry regiments rarely exercised together, never mind in collaboration with the other service arms. More important, British light infantry received no armywide operational or tactical discipline until the appearance of a rather inadequate section on the subject in Major General David Dundas's celebrated *Rules and Regulations for the Formations, Field-Exercise, and Movements, of His Majesty's Forces* (1792). This is not to say (as some historians have censoriously pronounced) that the army "forgot" everything about bushfighting that it had learned so painfully against the Canadians and Indians during the French and Indian War; the unwritten living body of "customary" expertise that endured within the service undoubtedly included much valuable guidance on the employment of light troops.[4] Yet for some concrete indication of the newly reintroduced light infantry's expected combat role, one must look to two semi-official sources: the instructions that Lieutenant General Lord George Townshend (as lord lieutenant of Ireland) issued in May 1772 to regiments then serving in Ireland on the subject of the training and equipping of the new light companies; and Major General Howe's light infantry drill of 1774.

Townshend's instructions incorporated sound advice on a number of themes, including the responsibilities of light infantry in the field, the adoption of specific equipment, and the mastering of certain fieldcraft skills.[5] Most important from our perspective, however, were the purely tactical elements. These were designed to enable the light company to skirmish in "strong" terrain like woodlands, whether operating independently, in cooperation with its parent regiment, or in concert with other light companies as part of a composite light battalion. One departure in Townshend's instructions from the orthodox "heavy" infantry drill laid down in the *1764 Regulations* was the adoption of the two-deep firing line at open file intervals. Another was the practice of maneuvering and forming by files.[6] A third was the employment of new command methods designed to enable officers to maintain control over the loosely deployed light infantrymen in action. Townshend required officers commanding companies or battalions of light infantry to establish particular signals (which the "stoutest of the drummers" was to convey via a whistle or horn) for particular maneuvers, such as advancing, retiring, or extending or contracting the frontage. The fourth and most crucial departure was the manner of giving fire in pairs rather than in volleys. This devolution of fire control required each file to work together so that one man remained loaded at all times. Ideally the two men were expected to share a tree from behind which they would alternately fire and retire a few feet to reload. To excel in this kind of unsupervised, irregular style of firing, Townshend recommended that the soldier should seek, through target shooting, to discover the best measure of powder for his firelock and to make up his own cartridges accordingly.

While Townshend's tactical instructions focused on how a single light company might operate in action, Howe's Salisbury drill was by contrast designed for maneuvering a number of light companies in concert as a composite light battalion.[7] Although historians have commonly saluted Howe as godfather to the developing British light infantry arm, his drill was neither particularly comprehensive nor especially innovative. It composed three sections: a set of maneuvers for a light battalion operating in broken country in two ranks and at open file intervals, a "platoon exercise" that diverged only marginally from that of the 1764 Regulations (to reflect the light infantry's two-deep formation), and an account of the training exercise performed for the King at Richmond.[8] Curiously, there was little in Howe's drill concerning firepower, which was central to light infantry's primary tactical role. Despite the modified "platoon exercise," it is difficult to believe that Howe expected the light battalion always to give its fire by means of volleys; more likely in close country the troops would have reverted to something like Townshend's method of firing in pairs.

On the subject of Howe's light infantry maneuvers (of which there were too many permutations to catalogue here), a few simple observations will suffice. First, the only maneuver divisions utilized were wings, companies, and platoons, with the emphasis firmly on companies. Second, most of the maneuvers enabled the battalion to change its formation and/or facing, with the troops maneuvering and forming by files instead of marching and wheeling by ranks. Third, although Howe did not prescribe exact cadences, he distinguished three different paces: "slow," "quick," and "run."[9] Fourth, the format of the exercise at Richmond gives some indication of the role that light infantry would play in action. Not only did Howe expect individual companies to detach themselves from the light battalion during combat to act semi-independently, but he also expected the battalion to maneuver and alter its formation and/or facing faster than its opponents so that it could (for example) outflank and roll up the enemy line.

Howe's drill does appear to have gained some currency within the army beyond the seven companies that practiced it at Salisbury in 1774. Toward the end of the conflict, John Williamson reproduced a portion of the general's light infantry maneuvers in his military treatise.[10] A simple table catalogued sixty different maneuvers (those in which the battalion line deployed into columns of double files from the center of each maneuver division before redeploying back into line to front, flank, or rear), half a dozen of which were expounded as illustrative examples. Yet in an important way Howe's original instructions were different from those that Williamson presented. While Howe's were designed for a composite light battalion comprising an unspecified number of light companies, Williamson's were intended for a hatman battalion divided conventionally into two wings, four grand divisions, eight subdivisions, and sixteen platoons. This was significant (as we shall shortly see).

Roger Lamb's semi-autobiographical writings provide further evidence for the possible spread of Howe's light infantry drill beyond the seven Salisbury companies.[11] Decades after the American War, the Irishman recalled that his corps, the 9th Regiment, marched to Dublin early in 1775. Having been promoted to corporal, he and several other noncommissioned officers were sent to what one might call a camp of instruction, where "the non-commissioned officers of the 33rd Regiment" taught them Howe's "new exercise," which "consisted of a set of maneuvers for light infantry" and which (according to Lamb) the King had ordered the army to adopt. Unfortunately, Lamb's text does not make it clear whether he taught the exercise to the "squad of our regiment" to which he was appointed on his return.[12] Similarly, while he correctly asserted that the army was not using Howe's drill at the time he was writing (1811), his statement that it was "well adapted for the service in America" does not tell us whether it was in fact utilized against the rebels. Furthermore, the characteristics that the Irishman recorded about the maneuvers he claimed to have learned in 1775 tie them closely to those that Williamson printed in 1781 rather than to those in the original Howe drill. For instance, here is Lamb's description of what he believed to be the Howe system: "The maneuvers were chiefly intended for woody and intricate districts, with which North America abounds, where an army cannot act in line. The light infantry maneuvers . . . were done from center of battalions, grand-divisions, and sub-divisions, by double Indian files." Compare this with Williamson's own explanatory text: "These maneuvers are principally calculated for a close or woody country. They are all done from the center, and the two center files of battalion, grand- and sub-divisions must be told off for the purpose."[13] More conclusive was Lamb's erroneous claim that Howe's maneuvers "were six in number." As we have already seen, Williamson's text expounded six permutations from a given total of sixty; these sixty in turn represented only a fraction of the maneuvers in the original Howe drill. Lamb was surely writing here with the aid of Williamson's treatise and pretending to remember more of the events at Dublin in 1775 than he really did. This should hardly surprise anyone familiar with his two works, which he compiled late in life and with obvious access to a rich vein of published sources from which he borrowed freely.

Whether or not the details of Lamb's testimony are wholly reliable, his claim that the 33rd Regiment taught the Howe maneuvers at Dublin in 1775 is very interesting.[14] While the 33rd Regiment's light company had not attended the Salisbury camp, two of the corps whose light companies had done so were in Ireland at this time.[15] More importantly, Lamb's testimony indicates that the camp was not just a transfer of specialist tactical doctrine between the 33rd Regiment's light company and the light companies of the other regiments in the Irish garrison; Lamb, for instance, was a corporal in one of the 9th Regiment's hatman companies. This suggests that at least some of Howe's light infantry maneuvers potentially had a wider use within the army and probably explains why Williamson's versions were seemingly designed for a battalion of eight companies. Regiments were able to perform a much wider repertoire of "customary" maneuvers than the dozen or so "core" ones laid down in the *1764 Regulations*, so it should be no surprise that Howe's maneuvers had gained notice beyond the companies for which they were devised. Nor indeed should it surprise us that Cornwallis's 33rd Regiment was apparently in the position to teach (at least a portion of) Howe's drill by 1775, given that it was undoubtedly the best-disciplined corps in the army during the last three decades of the eighteenth century.[16] How exactly the 33rd Regiment first learned the maneuvers that it taught at Dublin is unclear. Possibly Lamb's testimony provides part of the answer, the Irishman having stated that "his Lordship's exertations [sic] contributed to give it [i.e., the Howe drill] the desired extension and effect."[17] The nobleman referred to here was Charles Stanhope, who (as Lord Viscount Petersham) had attended Howe's Salisbury camp as captain of the 29th Regiment's light company and served as aide de camp to Burgoyne on the Albany expedition.[18] It was in this very regiment in Canada that John Williamson himself served as a hatman company ensign between 1775 and 1779—and crucially, it was to Stanhope (by then the 3rd Earl of Harrington) that Williamson dedicated his treatise in 1781.[19]

As John Houlding has written, the outbreak of the American War overtook Howe's effort to provide the light infantry with a uniform system of drill.[20] None of Gage's corps at Boston in 1775 had attended the Salisbury or Dublin camps.[21] Nevertheless, we do have some fragmentary evidence of the kind of specialized training that their light companies were undergoing shortly before the war. Less than a month before the outbreak of hostilities, a Scotch immigrant visiting Boston (who took a particular interest in the redcoats' drilling and considered some of the regiments to be "extremely expert in their exercise") recorded what he saw of the light infantry's performance on the Common: "Every regiment here has a company of light infantry, young active fellows; and they are trained in the regular manner, and likewise in a peculiar discipline of irregular and bush fighting. They run out in parties on the wings of the regiment where they keep up a constant and irregular fire. They secure their retreat and defend their front while they are forming. In one part of the exercise they lie on their backs and charge their pieces and fire lying on their bellies. They have powder horns and no cartouche boxes."[22] Yet only days before the ill-fated Concord expedition, Gage issued a tantalizing instruction at Boston that seems to suggest that a new set of light infantry maneuvers were to be taught imminently: "As the grenadiers and light infantry will be ordered out, to learn grenadier exercise, and some new evolutions for the light infantry, they are to be off all duty till further orders. . . . The majors and adjutants will begin to instruct the grenadiers of their own corps in the grenadier exercise tomorrow at the most convenient place near their own barracks. The light companies will be instructed in the new maneuvers by Lieutenant Mackenzie, Adjutant of the 23rd Regiment, who will fix a time of assembling with the respective captains tomorrow morning at guard mounting."[23] Lieutenant John Barker assumed that this instruction was a "blind" designed to free the flank companies from routine garrison duties to carry out some important project.[24] This may well have been the case: there is no evidence that any such training took place (or even that the supposed new light infantry maneuvers existed), and the column that Gage secretly sent against the rebel stores at Concord days later was indeed drawn exclusively from the grenadiers and light infantry. But that Mackenzie himself recorded Gage's order in his own diary without suspicion or comment of any kind might be regarded as significant.[25] Howsoever the case, in the aftermath of the Concord expedition, the flank companies returned to their parent regiments, so nothing more appears to have come of this mysterious business.[26]

The performance of British light companies during the opening clashes of the war does not suggest that they were particularly proficient in the skills of woodland skirmishing. In 1781 Colonel Edward Winslow, the muster master general of provincial forces, declared: "When the British Light Infantry began their operations in this country they were almost compact in their movements, regular in their marching and from habit and general instructions they appeared averse to every attempt to screen or cover themselves from danger however imminent. Hence many of them were picked off in all the first skirmishes."[27] Winslow was speaking from personal experience —he had accompanied Brigadier General Lord Percy's relief column to Lexington and had witnessed the battle of Bunker Hill. Moreover, his comments echoed more contemporaneous judgments. On the very day that Howe's battalions were decimated at Bunker Hill, Townshend wrote to Amherst from London commenting on the reports from America of the light infantry's failure to protect Lieutenant Colonel Francis Smith's column during the return march from Concord: "[A]s to the loss of the flanking parties I do not wonder at it—for it is not a short coat or half gaiters that makes a light infantryman, but as you know, Sir, a confidence in his aim, and that stratagem in a personal conflict, which is derived from experience. This is still to learn, the Americans have it."[28] In July Clinton likewise despaired from Boston, "Perhaps in all America there is not a worse spot than this we are in for a regular army without light troops . . . for I cannot call our light companies such, nor would you if I were to converse with you for five minutes."[29]

## The Light Infantry's Combat Role in America

Lieutenant General von Heister's advance at Flatbush during the battle of Long Island provides a good example of true light infantry work. There the German advance was spearheaded by knots of skirmishing *Jäger* and grenadiers, with light field guns providing fire support. Picked volunteers from the line battalions followed in open order, acting as a screen for the close-order battalions, which came on steadily, hardly firing a shot.[30] Unfortunately, British light infantry were arguably incapable of performing in such a tactical role when hostilities commenced in 1775, nor did they adopt this method of fighting as the war progressed. Instead the British flank battalions generally fought in the line of battle, employing much the same open and shallow linear formations and the same aggressive bayonet-orientated tactics as the rest of the infantry. On the battlefield the principal tactical distinctions between the flank battalions and the line infantry were that the former developed as elite formations, while the latter acted almost as auxiliaries to the former rather than the other way round (see chapter 3).

From 1776 onward, many British officers in America professed to believe that these shock-orientated tactics were fully as effective in close country as in the open and congratulated themselves that the light infantry in particular had achieved tactical superiority in any conditions over any troops that the rebels dared bring against them. Of the battle of Long Island, Major the Honorable Charles Stuart boasted that "[t]he enemy thought they were invincible in the woods, and they were amazed to see that we were bold enough to attack them in their own way, in defiance of redoubts, woods or anything," while Captain Sir James Murray likewise wrote that "[t]he light infantry (who were first engaged) dashed in as fast as foot could carry. The scoundrels [i.e., the rebels] were driven into the wood and out of the wood, where they had supposed that we should never venture to engage them."[31] Similarly, Ensign Thomas Hughes considered that the minor victory of Brigadier General Fraser's Advanced Corps at Hubbardton "did our troops the greatest honor, as the enemy were vastly superior in numbers, and it was performed in a thick wood, in the very style that the Americans think themselves superior to regular troops."[32] Of the same action Burgoyne's aide de camp, Captain Francis-Carr Clarke, wrote, "The enemy that prided themselves in the woods, were taught to know that even there the British bayonet will ever make its way."[33] The letters of light company officer Captain William Dansey give the impression that he had full confidence in his men's ability to best the rebels in bushfighting, he having written "that a day's Yankee hunting is no more minded than a day's fox hunting," and "it is very good fun fighting when all the killed and wounded are on the side of the enemy. I like it prodigiously, it is better than a fox chase."[34] By August 1778 Captain Patrick Ferguson could assert that British light troops had "gained that superiority in the woods over the rebels which they once claimed."[35]

There is some evidence that early British tactical successes against the rebels in the woods derived in part from improvised training in elementary bushfighting tactics. For example, prior to the New York campaign, Major Thomas Musgrave oversaw some unspecified specialist tactical training for the flank battalions of Howe's army at Halifax (see chapter 7). Likewise, in the summer of 1776, during the pause in Carleton's offensive from Canada, his troops "were trained to the exercise calculated for the woody country of America, with which they were totally unacquainted."[36] Similarly, at Boucherville in May 1777, Fraser's Advanced Corps formed a line of battle a mile long and "performed, exclusive of the common maneuvers, several new ones calculated for defense in this woody country."[37] More than a year later, in the course of Burgoyne's overland march to Fort Edward during his Albany expedition, the British commander sought to improve the troops "in the very essential point of wood service."[38]

What this all seems to mean is that the troops were encouraged in combat to take the basic precaution of breaking ranks and seeking cover when it presented itself instead of remaining inert and vulnerable to enemy fire. In September 1777 Major General Massey informed a small field force drawn from the Halifax garrison that "[t]he troops when halted [are] to be always drawn up in open order and never unnecessarily to expose themselves."[39] One way the troops could have done this was to go prone, like the men of the 1st Battalion of Light Infantry who threw themselves on their knees and bellies during the heavy fighting at Birmingham Meetinghouse at the battle of Brandywine (see chapter 7). In a similar manner George Harris related that, after the affair at Harlem Heights, a man "in the battalion on our left" was shot dead while the troops were lying on the ground, while in later years he recorded that, during the action at the Vigie, "Captain Shawe, with the 4th [Regiment's grenadier] company, was ordered by me to make his men lie down, and cover themselves in the brushwood as much as possible, to prevent them being seen as marks."[40]

When fighting in the woods, the most obvious way that the troops could protect themselves from enemy fire was to take refuge behind the trees. According to Winslow, in the war's early skirmishes, "the enemy placed themselves behind trees and walls, etc., and it was apparently necessary to take them in their own way. In consequence a new word was adopted and the flank corps were on subsequent occasions ordered 'to tree'—a word of command as well known to them now as any other."[41] In July 1776 Major General Baron Riedesel reported to the Duke of Brunswick his intention to teach the Brunswick infantry in America to secure the protection of the trees while advancing so they could meet the rebels in the woods on equal terms (see chapter 6). His journal gives some indication of what he desired his soldiers to be able to do: "As soon as the first line has jumped into the supposed ditch, the command 'fire' is given, when the first line fires, reloads its guns, gets up out of the ditch, and hides behind a tree, rock, shrub or whatever is at hand, at the same time firing off four cartridges in such a manner that the line is kept as straight as possible. As soon as the first line has fired off the four cartridges, the second line advances and fires off the same number in the same manner. While this is taking place, the woods have been thoroughly ransacked by the sharpshooters who have thus become familiar with every part of it."[42]

British light infantrymen seem to have been particularly encouraged to employ trees as cover during combat in the woods—like the men of the flank companies of the Guards Brigade at the affair at Young's House, who "scattered, taking the advantage of the ground and trees in the orchard."[43] Similarly, after a mishandled skirmish in New Jersey on 23 February 1777, Captain Sir James Murray claimed that, though his company received a heavy fire, it sustained small loss by "favor of some pretty large trees, which by a good deal of practice we have learnt to make a proper use of."[44] Captain William Dansey explained that "the light infantry are in the most danger . . . of being wounded in the arms, for we have learned from the rebels to cover our bodies if there's a tree or a rail near us."[45] And in March 1778 grenadier Lieutenant William Hale characterized the tactics that the redcoats had adopted "in a country almost covered with woods, and against an enemy whose chief qualification is agility in running from fence to fence and thence keeping up an irregular but galling fire": "Light infantry accustomed to fight from tree to tree, or charge even in woods; and grenadiers, who after the first fire lose no time in loading again, but rush on, trusting entirely to that most decisive of weapons the bayonet, will ever be superior to any troops the rebels can ever bring against them. Such are the British, and such the method of fighting which has been attended with constant success."[46] As Hale suggests, the flank battalions were not the only British troops who had learned to fight in the woods. As the 24th Regiment was Brigadier General Fraser's own unit, it formed part of his elite Advanced Corps during Burgoyne's Albany expedition. One of the regiment's battalion company officers, Joshua Pell, later recorded that, during the battle of Freeman's Farm, the battalion attempted to outflank the rebel forces assailing the British center: "The 24th Battalion received orders to file off by the left. They took the wood before them, firing after them [their?] own manner from behind trees, and twice repulsed their repeated reinforcements without any assistance."[47]

## "THE . . . WOODS RENDERED OUR BAYONETS OF LITTLE USE"

If British and German regulars in America do not seem to have been as helpless in bushfighting and in the *petite guerre* as historians have commonly implied, one must nevertheless not exaggerate their proficiency. In particular, Crown troops' shock-orientated tactics did not always meet with success during engagements fought in heavily timbered terrain like the northern wilderness or the southern backwoods. One crucial factor in this failure was the nature of the opposition that the King's troops faced in these confrontations. If the vast majority of the colonial population can hardly have been as proficient in woodcraft and marksmanship as American mythology suggests, the hardy individuals who lived on the wilder fringes of the colonies were altogether more formidable bushfighters. Few Crown officers deluded themselves that British regulars could match these men in their own element. In October 1778, when a party of 400 British and Provincial regulars and Indians under Major Christopher Carleton ranged across Lake Champlain, Lieutenant John Enys accompanied the redcoats as they "went into the woods a little way to practice 'treeing,' as they call it; that is to say, the manner of hiding ourselves behind tree stumps, etc., etc., etc. And at our return the major was pleased to say the men had exceeded his expectations; though I could see very plainly our awkwardness diverted the Indians and royalists, who are far better hands at this work, being bred in the woods from their infancy and accustomed to this manner of hiding themselves in order to shoot deer and other wild beasts."[48] After the heavy defeat of a detachment of Brunswick troops under Lieutenant Colonel Friedrich Baum at Bennington, artilleryman Lieutenant James Hadden likewise deprecated the inclusion of the heavily accoutered German dragoons in the ill-fated enterprise, when "treeing or bush fighting was a task the British light infantry of this army are not fully equal to."[49] Another veteran of the Albany expedition, Thomas Anburey, later judged, "our European discipline is of little avail in the woods" and that "the Americans are by much our superiors at wood fighting, being habituated to the woods from their infancy."[50] Lastly, Henry Lee later ascribed the disproportionate casualties suffered by the two armies at Guilford Courthouse partly to the fact that "[w]e were acquainted with wood- and tree-fighting; he [i.e., the British soldier] [was] ignorant of both."[51]

One of the most notable examples of the inefficacy of British bayonet charges against an enemy in dense woodland is the four-hour seesaw struggle in the center at the battle of Freeman's Farm. There Brigadier General Hamilton's brigade (the 20th, 21st, and 62nd Regiments, supported by the 9th Regiment), posted in the clearing around Freeman's Farm, repeatedly resorted to bayonet charges to drive away Brigadier General Enoch Poor's brigade, Colonel Daniel Morgan's riflemen, and Lieutenant Colonel Henry Dearborn's light infantry. Contemporary accounts make it clear that the dense woods around the clearing provided the rebels with cover from which to shoot at the exposed British troops and a rallying point when they had to fall back to evade enemy bayonets.[52] Captain John Money (Burgoyne's deputy quartermaster general) later related that "the 62nd Regiment charged four times . . . quitting their position each time. . . . [T]he rebels fled at every charge deeper still into the woods; but when the British troops returned to their position, they were slowly followed, and those who had been the most forward in the pursuit were the first to fall."[53] Burgoyne later stressed the cost of this bitter and unequal struggle: "Few actions have been characterized by more obstinacy in attack or defense. The British bayonet was repeatedly tried ineffectually. Eleven hundred British soldiers, foiled in these trials, bore incessant fire from a succession of fresh troops in superior numbers, for above four hours; and after a loss of above a third of their numbers (and in one of the regiments above, two-thirds), forced the enemy at last. Of a detachment of a captain and forty-eight artillerymen, the captain and thirty-six were killed or wounded."[54] Hamilton's embattled corps did not just have to contend with fire from their front. According to Lieutenant Hadden, swarming rebel parties exploited the thick woods to work their way onto the flanks and even into the rear of the 62nd Regiment.[55]

Comparable to the struggle for the clearing at Freeman's Farm was the destruction of Major Patrick Ferguson's mixed force of Provincial regulars and loyalist militia at King's Mountain. Loyalist captain Alexander Chesney described how the terrain (which Henry Lee aptly described as "more assailable with the rifle than defensible with the bayonet"[56]) proved ideal for the ferocious "over-mountain-men": "Kings Mountain from its height would have enabled us to oppose a superior force with advantage, had it not been covered with wood which sheltered the Americans and enabled them to fight in their favorite manner. In fact, after driving in our pickets they were able to advance in three divisions under separate leaders to the crest of the hill in perfect safety until they took post and opened an irregular but destructive fire from behind trees and other cover." Although loyalist bayonet charges drove back each of the rebel "divisions" in turn, it soon became clear that this was an imperfect tactical antidote to the frontiersmen's way of fighting. As Chesney explained, "by this time the Americans who had been repulsed had regained their former stations and, sheltered behind trees, poured in an irregular destructive fire. In this manner the engagement was maintained near an hour, the mountaineers flying whenever there was danger of being charged by the bayonet, and returning again so soon as the British detachment had faced about to repel another of their parties."[57] One of the principal rebel officers at the battle, Colonel Isaac Shelby, later echoed Chesney's evaluation: "Ferguson's men were drawn up in close column [sic] on the summit and thus presented fair marks for the mountaineers, who approached them under cover of the trees. As either [rebel] column would approach the summit, Ferguson would order out a charge with fixed bayonet, which was always successful, for the riflemen retreated before the charging column slowly, still firing as they retired. When Ferguson's men returned to regain their position on the mountain, the patriots would again rally and pursue them."[58] Once it became clear that his loyalists were doomed, Ferguson appears to have attempted to break through the closing ring of menacing rebel irregulars, who blasted him from the saddle. When a teen-aged rebel rifleman, James Collins, examined the corpse of the "great chief," he found that "seven rifle balls had passed through his body, both of his arms were broken, and his hat and clothing were literally shot to pieces."[59]

A similar pattern occurred at Guilford Courthouse during the attack on the second rebel line, where, as Cornwallis put it, "the excessive thickness of the woods rendered our bayonets of little use and enabled the broken enemy to make frequent stands with an irregular fire."[60] This was particularly true of the struggle on the British right, where Colonel William Campbell's riflemen and the light troops of Lieutenant Colonel Henry Lee's Legion fought on after the flight of most of the Virginia militia. Tarleton later described how the Hessian Regiment von Bose and the 1st Battalion of Guards became drawn into a private battle against Campbell and Lee:

> The [British] right wing, from the thickness of the woods and a jealousy for its flank, had imperceptibly inclined to the right, by which movement it had a kind of separate action after the front line of the Americans gave way, and was now engaged with several bodies of militia and riflemen above a mile distant from the center of the British army. The 1st Battalion of the Guards, commanded by Lieutenant Colonel [the Honorable Chapel] Norton, and the Regiment of Bose, under Major [Johann Christian] Du Buy, had their share of the difficulties of the day, and, owing to the nature of the light troops opposed to them, could never make any decisive impression.

As they advanced, the Americans gave ground in front, and inclined to the flanks.[61]

As Stedman's later account indicates, the thickness of the woods enabled knots of determined rebels to attack the Crown troops from all directions: "No sooner had the Guards and Hessians defeated the enemy in front, than they found it necessary to return and attack another body of them that appeared in the rear; and in this manner they were obliged to traverse the same ground in various directions, before the enemy were completely put to the rout."[62] Sergeant Berthold Koch was with the Regiment von Bose. His later recollections of the confused fighting against Campbell and Lee illustrates how difficult it was for formed bodies of troops to catch, or even to drive off, the determined rebel parties that harried them from all sides: "[T]he von Bose Regiment pulled out of the battle line and pursued the enemy, but before we knew it, the enemy attacked us again, in the rear. The regiment therefore had to divide into two parts. The second, commanded by Major [Friedrich Heinrich] Scheer, had to attack toward the rear against the enemy who were behind us, and forced them once again to take flight. Lord [sic] Tarleton came with his light cavalry and pursued the enemy. During this time Colonel Du Buy advanced with the first part of the regiment and Major Scheer returned with the second part of the regiment and rejoined the first part."[63] By the time Tarleton's cavalry appeared to disperse the remaining riflemen, the action elsewhere was effectively over. In this private struggle less than a tenth of Greene's initial force had effectively kept busy almost a third of Cornwallis's heavily outnumbered army. Had these Crown troops been available at the climax of the action at the third rebel line, the outcome of the battle might have been more favorable.

These three examples show quite clearly that, for most rebel troops, fighting in thick woods neutralized the principal tactical weakness that separated them from their British opponents—their limited ability to maneuver and fight in the ordered formations that provided such a powerful sense of psychological "security" to disciplined regulars. In short, all but the rebels' best troops were probably most effective when they operated in loosely directed swarms in broken terrain. Early in the war Burgoyne touched on this factor: "Composed as the American army is, together with the strength of the country (full of woods, swamps, stone walls, and other enclosures and hiding places), it may be said of it that every private man will in action be his own general, who will turn every tree and bush into a kind of temporary fortress; from whence, when he hath fired his shot with all [the] deliberation, coolness, and certainty which hidden safety inspires, he will skip (as it were) to the next, and so on, for a long time."[64] Burgoyne was speaking here about the Continentals as well as the militia. Moreover, if the latter were, in his estimation, inferior to the former in "method and movement," they were nevertheless "not a jot less serviceable in woods."[65] It hardly needs to be added here that the kind of ungovernable, unforgiving, half-wild frontiersmen who at King's Mountain urinated upon Ferguson's naked corpse, and who could hardly be restrained from murdering all his surviving men, were unlikely to have been able to practice any other kind of warfare than the bushfighting in which they proved such deadly opponents.[66]

The counterpart to this phenomenon of course was that bushfighting deprived trained British soldiers of the advantages that their regular-military discipline conferred upon them "on the plain, where veteran and well-appointed forces must always prevail over soldiers such as the colonial regiments were composed of." What Roger Lamb (an experienced former sergeant) meant by this comment was that, under the control of capable officers and noncommissioned officers, confident professional soldiers like the redcoats possessed a level of cohesion that enabled them to brush aside much larger bodies of inadequately trained, inexperienced, and unsteady enemy troops, at least in the open. But this regular discipline and subordination was a positive disadvantage in "wood fighting and skirmishing among intersected and intricate grounds." As Lamb explained, in this kind of confused combat, "experienced generals and old soldiers are left at a loss and obliged to encounter unforeseen obstacles and accidents which demand new movements and momentary measures; in the execution whereof, every officer ought to be an excellent general, and every company ably disposed for whatever the passing minute of time might bring about. It is therefore plain that the best army, so circumstanced, cannot co-operate or concentrate itself with effect or advantage."[67] Lieutenant William Digby, who also served on the Albany expedition, put Lamb's point more succinctly when he observed that "it has always been the wish of the Americans to avoid a general engagement, except they have a great superiority, and to surround small parties of ours, and get them into a wood, where the discipline of our troops is not of such force."[68] A third veteran of the Albany expedition, Thomas Anburey, later encapsulated the impossibility of maintaining regular troops' discipline and order in the woods when he related his experience at the action at Hubbardton, in which he participated as a gentleman volunteer with the grenadiers. In that engagement the inability of the British troops to exploit their "military skill and discipline" meant that "[p]ersonal courage and intrepidy [sic]" became the most important factor: "It was a trial of the activity, strength and valor of every man that fought. . . . Both parties engaged in separate detachments unconnected with each other, and the numbers of the enemy empowered them to front, flank and rear."[69]

Importantly, the redcoats' shock-orientated tactics were hardly compatible with the mechanics of bushfighting. Thick woods defused the power of British bayonet charges at battles like Freeman's Farm, King's Mountain, and Guilford Courthouse because the trees provided the rebels with valuable tactical advantages that they would not have enjoyed by fighting in the open. The most obvious of these was cover against British fire, including case shot. Another advantage was concealment. This enabled troops to lay in ambush or to bypass Crown forces in order to attack them from the flank or rear. Even more importantly, the ability to melt into the woods gave the rebels the chance to shake off pursuit and rally in security before returning to the attack. In short, the British could not attack, rout, and drive away rebel troops that they could not maintain in view. A third advantage was that the attackers were hidden from sight save at close range, which effectively prevented nervous troops from giving their fire prematurely and leaving themselves vulnerable to a sudden bayonet rush while they were unloaded. A fourth advantage was that trees provided a stable firing platform, which facilitated careful aiming. Last (and as noted earlier), the fact that British bayonet charges were of limited potency in the woods meant that the combat was likely to degenerate into a sustained firefight. This not only precluded the British from cheaply dislodging the enemy and hustling them into flight but also gave rebel riflemen more time to practice their deadly art.

Anburey's comments on the action at Hubbardton suggest another factor that was of crucial importance in at least some combats in the woods: numerical superiority. For example, in the struggle for the center at Freeman's Farm, the 1,100 British soldiers of Brigadier

General Hamilton's brigade were assailed for four hours by something approaching twice their number of Continentals and militia. At Guilford Courthouse Cornwallis's advancing line of battle faced similar odds in attacking the second rebel line. That the rebels enjoyed such a clear numerical advantage in such actions was of enormous significance when one considers how difficult it was in heavily timbered country for the British to beat enemy troops and to prevent them from rallying and returning to the fray. In such circumstances, displacing individual parties of rebels was akin to cutting off the heads of the Hydra.

No effective tactical doctrine existed for the newly restored British light infantry when hostilities commenced in America. When in 1776 the British infantry in America adopted two ranks and open file intervals as the standard formation and switched to shock as the primary element of offensive infantry tactics, the light companies took on the role of elite corps. Although light infantrymen were sometimes trained to use trees as cover, on the battlefield they did not commonly perform as genuine skirmishers by utilizing their initiative to exploit the terrain to their advantage and to overcome the enemy by means of accurate, independently delivered fire. Instead, like the grenadiers and line infantry, the light battalions' primary tactic was to hustle the unsteady rebels into flight with vigorous bayonet rushes. On open or lightly wooded ground, these shock-orientated tactics enabled British infantry to overthrow all but the best rebel troops. But in thickly timbered country, regular military discipline was at a discount, and the irregular-style tactics that hardy backwoodsmen and inexperienced but enthusiastic levies favored were at a premium. In this bush-fighting, British bayonet rushes lost their potency; instead combats degenerated into the kind of indecisive and costly firefights in which numerical superiority told and in which rebel riflemen could operate to greatest effect. Consequently, even where the British succeeded in defeating the rebels in thick woods, they usually did so at disproportionate cost.

# 11

# HOLLOW VICTORIES

[W]henever the rebel army is said to have been cut to pieces, it
would be more consonant with truth to say that they have been
dispersed, determined to join again upon the first favorable
opportunity; and in the meantime they take the oaths of allegiance,
and live comfortably at home and among us, to drain us of our
monies, get acquainted with our numbers, and learn our
intentions, the better to deceive and avail themselves of every
occasion that may present itself.

Brigadier General Charles O'Hara to the Duke of Grafton,
1 November 1780

The first chapter discussed how British soldiers and statesmen
identified "decisive actions" against the Continental Army as
the most effectual way to terminate the rebellion. By inflicting seriously disproportionate losses on Congress's forces and compelling
them to withdraw and disperse, the British expected to establish their
troops in garrisons that would secure control over territory, to persuade the armed population to withdraw its support for the rebellion,
and to bring key opposition figures to the negotiating table.

## CASUALTIES

Nevertheless, Crown commanders did not expect to "destroy" the
Continental Army on the battlefield itself. Indeed, the many histo-

rians who have castigated the British for having failed to achieve this result have judged them by standards simply inappropriate before the French Revolutionary and Napoleonic wars. Field commanders in these later conflicts were able to pursue a "strategy of annihilation" because they benefited from significant later-eighteenth-century improvements in European land communications and agriculture as well as the advent of mass conscription during the 1790s. These three developments enabled commanders to campaign with armies of up to (and sometimes more than) 100,000 men, organized in semi-autonomous *corps d'armée*. These corps maneuvered along separate and parallel lines of march; the men extracted most of their food from the countryside they traversed and made do without impediments like tents. The articulation and maneuverability that the corps system conferred upon these massive field armies enabled the skillful commander to overwhelm the enemy's forces by unbalancing them and bringing them to action on terms unfavorable to them, ideally beating their adversaries piecemeal—a feat most famously achieved by Napoleon against the Austrians and Russians during the Ulm-Austerlitz campaign (1805). To confirm the defeat of enemy forces on the battlefield, and to harry them to disintegration in the hours, days, and weeks following the battle, the successful commander turned to his powerful cavalry reserves—again, as Napoleon did after beating the Prussians at Jena-Auerstädt (1806). The destruction of the enemy's military forces ideally paved the way for the occupation of his capital and the imposition of peace terms.[1]

In the American War, while significant forces surrendered at Fort Washington, Saratoga, Charleston, and Yorktown, in very few major battlefield engagements did the casualties of the defeated force approach 50 percent. Of these defeats, the destruction of Ferguson's 1,000 militia and Provincial regulars at King's Mountain was clearly the most comprehensive. The second-most complete victory would appear to have been Cornwallis's triumph at Camden over Gates's 3,000-strong "Grand Army," of which only a few hundred Continentals appear to have regrouped at Hillsboro days later. Cowpens would place third: less than a quarter of Tarleton's 1,100-strong detachment escaped the field. If a fourth action is added to the list, it should be Long Island. If one ignores those rebel troops who remained unengaged within the lines on Brooklyn Heights, more than 40 percent of the 3,500 rebels posted along the heavily wooded, three-mile long Heights of Guan were killed or captured.

But when dealing with rebel battlefield losses, one must be particularly wary of the casualties that the rebel militia reportedly incurred. For instance, only a small number of Gates's militiamen were killed or taken at Camden, the vast majority simply declined to rejoin the remnants of his army after they were routed from the field. Crucially, these fugitives were not permanently lost to the rebel cause. Former militiamen Garrett Watts and Guilford Dudley, for example, were later candid enough to admit that they returned to their homes in North Carolina after the battle, Dudley having pointed out that "it is well known that everybody, after this disastrous battle was over or during the conflict, discharged himself." Yet both men—and doubtless many others like them—joined Greene before the battle of Guilford Courthouse and fought at Hobkirk's Hill.[2] Ignoring the fugitive militia then, it would be more realistic to estimate that Gates's army sustained casualties of over 50 percent at Camden—still probably the most successful British battlefield performance of the war.

As in those European battlefield actions in which over half of the vanquished army was destroyed, the defeated forces' casualties at Long Island, King's Mountain, Camden, and Cowpens were so high because, once the battle swung away from them, escape from the battlefield was seriously obstructed. At King's Mountain this was because Ferguson took a defensive position that allowed the rebels to assail his force from all sides. Faulty dispositions were likewise to blame at both Long Island and Camden. Howe's nine-mile flank march through the Jamaica Pass at Long Island put 10,000 redcoats squarely in the rear of the rebels on the Heights of Guan, leaving the perilous Gowanus Marsh as the only avenue of retreat to the safety of the Brooklyn Heights. At Camden smoke and dust hid the militia's precipitate flight from the view of the Continentals on the right. This denied the latter the chance to disengage and enabled the British to hit them from front, flank, and rear, leaving the swampland that bordered the battlefield as the only viable escape route. The second main factor behind the scale of Cornwallis's victory there was that his two hundred British Legion dragoons ruthlessly pursued the flying rebels along the road to Rugeley's Mills for over twenty miles. At Cowpens two factors prevented the routed British infantry from escaping: first, the hundreds of militia, many of them mounted, who swept back onto the field from behind the cover of the Continentals; and second, extreme mental and physical exhaustion. Before the battle the King's troops had endured four days' hard marching without proper rest, rations, or shelter against the January weather. Once the battle commenced, they had advanced at speed over several hundred yards, losing more than a third of their numbers to musket and rifle fire even before they had reached the third defensive line. In the face of the rebel regulars' unexpected counterattack, many British soldiers instantly "threw down their arms and fell on their faces"—a clear symptom of chronic battle fatigue (as Lawrence Babits has demonstrated in his revisionist account of the battle).[3]

Having established that the primary factor in the completeness of the four victories outlined above was the inability of the defeated troops, for whatever reason, either to disengage, to make a fighting withdrawal, or even to escape as individual fugitives, one must ask why nearly all British battlefield successes fell short of these standards.

The simple answer is that rebel commanders were generally successful in avoiding major confrontations under disadvantageous conditions. Indeed, throughout the war only twice did the British have the opportunity to destroy if not the whole, then a significant portion of Washington's main rebel army. The first occasion was during the period between the battle of Long Island on 27 August 1776 and Washington's evacuation to Manhattan on the night of 29–30 August (while the rebel forces on Long Island had the East River to their backs).[4] The second was between 30 August and 18 October, when Washington evacuated Manhattan (save for the garrison of Fort Washington) to prevent the British from bottling up his forces by seizing Kingsbridge.

As discussed earlier, after the disasters of 1776, Washington and his most-talented subordinates adopted a Fabian-style strategy, which dictated that they should not take up positions from whence their troops could not withdraw. Nor did they knowingly offer or seek battle on ground that would inevitably have spelled disaster in the event of defeat. At Camden and Cowpens it was the unusual fitness of the field for the very superior numbers of British cavalry that posed the critical threat. At Monmouth, Cowpens, and Green Springs, the rebels chose to engage despite the fact that the Middle and West Ravines, the Broad River, and swampland passable only via a narrow causeway promised to hinder a withdrawal in the event of a reverse. Yet none of the rebel commanders rushed into these engagements with their eyes shut. At

Monmouth and Green Springs, Major Generals Lee and Lafayette committed their respective forces to an attack because they mistakenly judged that they had the chance to isolate and destroy vastly outnumbered British rearguards. At Camden Gates fought Cornwallis very much against his will: both commanders had resolved to surprise each other by a nocturnal march and stumbled into each other on the road between Rugeley's Mills and Camden on the night before the battle. When Gates requested his officers' advice at a council of war, Brigadier General Stevens allegedly responded by rhetorically questioning whether it was "not too late *now* to do anything but fight?"[5] By this he doubtless meant that Gates could not have turned his back on Cornwallis and attempted to march away without infecting his troops (especially the militia) with panic. With Tarleton's cavalry snapping aggressively at the rebels' heels, a panicky retreat inevitably would have ended in the disintegration of the rebel army. Similarly, although Brigadier General Morgan was almost as reluctant to give battle at Cowpens, he feared that, "[h]ad I crossed the [Broad] river, one half of the militia would immediately have abandoned me."[6]

If it was difficult enough for the British to bring the rebels to battle in the first place, then it was still possible for the rebels to escape the worst consequences of a probable defeat even after the opposing forces had come into contact. First, even as the preliminaries of an engagement commenced, a rebel commander was able to order a general withdrawal if he was dissatisfied with his position, without the British having been able to do much about it. This happened at the "Battle of the Clouds" (16 September 1777), where Washington cheated the British columns converging on his still-deploying army by retiring to a new position two miles across the waterlogged valley to his rear.[7] Second, even if an action did commence in earnest, it was usually still possible for the rebel commander to disengage from an unpromising situation rather than to play the game out to its end. In the South much of the rebel militia campaigned on horseback; although they fought on foot, they kept their mounts close in the rear to facilitate flight or pursuit.[8] Not only parties of mounted militia, however, but also entire rebel armies were capable of disengaging once a British victory appeared likely. As Brigadier General O'Hara put it in late 1780, "in all our victories, where we are said to have cut them to pieces, they very wisely never stayed long enough to expose themselves to those desperate extremities."[9] The best example of this phenomenon is the last phase of the battle of Guilford Courthouse, when the collapse of the 2nd Maryland Regiment prompted Greene to order the immediate withdrawal of his army, covered by Lieutenant Colonel John Green's Virginia Regiment, to prevent the British from repeating their coup at Camden by taking his Continentals simultaneously in flank and rear.[10] Because rebel commanders exhibited such pragmatism at defeats such as Brandywine, Germantown, and Hobkirk's Hill, their beaten armies rarely left the field as a torrent of vulnerable, panic-stricken fugitives, each man intent on self-preservation and heedless of his officers. Instead they all too commonly marched away in tolerable order, with their morale surprisingly unimpaired—as Greene himself famously put it after Hobkirk's Hill, "We fight, get beat, rise and fight again."[11]

### THE FAILURE TO PURSUE

If it was very difficult for a British commander to induce his rebel counterpart both to commit his army to action under disadvantageous conditions and to see that engagement through to its bitter end, then it was no easier to exploit combat successes. Without remorseless pressure, a victory meant—in effect—only displacing and possibly temporarily scattering enemy troops. Indeed, one of the commonest accusations that historians have leveled against British commanders in America is that they failed to demonstrate appropriate aggressiveness in pursuing defeated rebel forces.

Here one should recognize that "pursuit" might have taken two forms in eighteenth-century and Napoleonic warfare. In an operational sense, pursuit meant that the victorious army shadowed the remnants of the defeated forces in the days and weeks following an engagement. Unless the unsuccessful commander was willing to expose his battered forces to another (probably more disadvantageous) engagement, it was necessary for him to withdraw in the face of the enemy advance. In theory, the enervating effect that repeated, forced retreats exerted on a defeated army's physical and moral fabric would have made a further action an even less attractive option to the unsuccessful commander. Indeed, if the cycle of pursuit and retreat continued long enough, the victorious commander could realistically have expected it to lead to the disintegration of the defeated forces.

In America factors beyond Crown commanders' control generally precluded the British from mounting this kind of operational pursuit. For example, after Brandywine Howe could not transport the army's provisions and his sick and wounded simultaneously; he therefore spent five days evacuating the latter to Wilmington, from whence his brother's fleet was able to embark them.[12] Similarly, after Lieutenant Colonel Archibald Campbell's expeditionary force landed and beat a southern rebel army outside Savannah, he had to spend the next two days acquiring wagons and horses to carry his provisions and ammunition before he could resume operations.[13] On some occasions British commanders chose not to pursue retreating rebel armies because they considered that other strategic objectives were of more immediate importance, as in November 1776, when Howe turned to seize Fort Washington rather than follow Washington's main army, which had avoided battle by withdrawing from White Plains. Alternatively, a further action was not always a desirable course for British commanders. Cornwallis averred that, after Guilford Courthouse, "[t]he care of our wounded and the total want of provisions in an exhausted country made it equally impossible for me to follow the blow next day."[14] In reality, it is hardly conceivable that Cornwallis's battered army was up to another major clash. The same was true of other costly British victories, such as Bunker Hill, Freeman's Farm, Hobkirk's Hill, and Eutaw Springs.

The second type of pursuit that successful eighteenth-century and Napoleonic commanders were able to mount was the tactical pursuit. This refers to the manner in which, in the engagement's last phase and immediate aftermath, elements of the victorious army ruthlessly harried the retreating enemy troops as the latter attempted to escape. If this kind of pressure was not maintained, even a torrent of terrified men eventually stopped running, and their officers regained control over them, as Major General William Heath explained: "When an enemy is routed, and panic-struck are flying before the assailants, the best (if not the only way) is to follow them, if the ground will permit of it, close at their heels; taking care not to fall into ambuscades. Thus the panic of fear continues to multiply; but if the pursuers stop . . . [t]his immediately recovers them from their panic."[15] In America Tarleton's dragoons succeeded in mounting this kind of tactical pursuit at the battle of Camden, where they cut down defenseless, fleeing rebels from behind, provoked the disintegration of retiring units into mobs of panicky fugitives who failed to rejoin their army, and captured the cumbersome artillery and baggage.

Fortunately for the rebels, their experience at Camden was not representative. Just as British commanders typically failed to pursue defeated enemy armies in an operational sense, they generally did not mount effective tactical pursuits. Again this failure stemmed largely from factors beyond British commanders' control, of which the most important was the inability to commit the military resources that were most appropriate to the task. The fittest troops for converting a disorderly retreat into a bloody rout were of course cavalry, for the obvious reason that (as Otho Williams later made clear) they could easily outpace even running men: "A pursuing army is always impeded by the effort that is necessary to maintain its own order; while, whether from terror, for safety, or for rallying, the speed of the fugitive is unrestrained. Hence, cavalry are the military means for rendering disorder irretrievable."[16] Thus British dragoons had enormous battlefield potential in America. The emotive manner in which rebel propagandists (and later, historians) portrayed the British Legion's annihilation of Colonel Abraham Buford's command at the Waxhaws conveniently ignores the fact that, in warfare of any age, prodigious slaughter was inevitable once cavalry got in among disordered enemy infantry.[17] In fact, the shallow and open linear formations that the infantry of both sides commonly employed in America rendered well-handled cavalry charges doubly dangerous, and the rebels generally feared the red- or green-coated dragoons much more than they did British infantry.[18]

British cavalry in America rarely lived up to their battlefield potential, partly because of the modest numbers in which they served. Although some independent troops and even a few small units of loyalist horse were raised and equipped locally (particularly after 1777),[19] only two regular cavalry corps were dispatched from the British Isles, and one of these was drafted in late 1778.[20] Particularly during the campaigns in the middle colonies, what little horse was available was usually parceled out between the different divisions or columns. This meant that general officers often had negligible mounted forces with which to improve an advantage, if they had any at all. For example, Cornwallis's division at Brandywine (which did the lion's share of the fighting) included only two squadrons, or less than a hundred dragoons—hardly an appropriate number with which to confirm the rout of a single battalion, never mind an entire army.[21] Likewise, Lieutenant Colonel Alexander Stewart lamented (with considerable exaggeration) of his Pyrrhic victory at Eutaw Springs, "[t]he glory of the day would have been more complete had not the want of cavalry prevented me from taking the advantage which the gallantry of my infantry threw in my way."[22]

The two main factors responsible for this usual paucity of mounted troops were the difficulty of procuring suitable horses and the problems of feeding them. Of these, procurement was the most pressing. For example, when Howe asked for three hundred dragoon remounts from Britain in late 1776, he was promised only one hundred and told to find the rest locally.[23] The inevitable losses that were incurred whenever horses were transported by sea prevented large numbers being sent out from the British Isles and had serious consequences when the main army moved from New York to Pennsylvania in 1777 and to Charleston in 1780.[24] From 1777 onward, the development of an increasingly effective rebel cavalry arm exacerbated the British shortfall in mounted troops—a factor that became increasingly significant during the southern campaigns, in which the rebel dragoons of Colonels Henry Lee and William Washington played a vital and distinguished operational and tactical role. In the Carolinas Cornwallis's dragoons often found themselves at a distinct disadvantage to their rebel counterparts due to the difficulty of obtaining suitable mounts. The earl's decision to take his army off to Virginia in 1781 enabled him to mount his cavalry properly for the first time by drawing on the excellent horseflesh available in that province. Yet if Cornwallis enjoyed total cavalry superiority over the meager rebel forces that opposed him during his brief summer campaign in Virginia, then Greene enjoyed a similar advantage when he returned to South Carolina to pick off the embattled British garrisons during the remainder of the contest there.[25]

Even on those battlefields where numbers of British dragoons were available, it was often not possible to employ them with success. In eighteenth-century warfare cavalry was generally only effective against unbroken, formed infantry if they were able to pounce upon an exposed flank. Steady infantry could defend themselves against horsemen by forming impenetrable, bristling squares, as Russian and Austrian infantry commonly did when they campaigned against the ferocious Turks.[26] When attacked by cavalry from the front, steady infantry could defend themselves with volleys of musketry, as the British and Hanoverian forces did most famously at Minden (1759). Henry Lee later noted that infantry's best response to a frontal charge was to close up, and for the front rank to charge bayonets while the rear rank fired—a tactic that the 1st Battalion of the 71st Regiment successfully utilized against Brigadier General Count Pulaski's dragoons after the action at Stono Ferry.[27] Alternatively, Tarleton asserted that the Continentals would have repulsed his British Legion dragoons at the Waxhaws had they not reserved their fire for too long and instead employed "a successive fire of platoons or divisions, commenced at the distance of three or four hundred paces."[28] There are numerous actual examples of infantry fire having repelled frontal attacks by cavalry in America—as for instance at Monmouth, where charges by two or three troops of the 16th Light Dragoons were beaten off on at least two separate occasions during the battle.[29]

As already suggested, cavalry were most effective against unsteady, disordered, unformed infantry—specifically in converting a confused, scattered, irregular retreat into a bloody, panic-stricken rout. As Greene put it with reference to operations in the South in 1781, the commander who possessed "a superior cavalry" was able to improve "a disorder . . . into a defeat, and a defeat into a rout."[30] When, in April 1781, Major General Phillips outlined the roles that each of the corps under his command should play in the event of an action at Petersburg, he specifically prescribed that "the cavalry will watch the moment for charging a broken enemy."[31] If, however, the enemy infantry left the field in good order, under the control of their officers (as at Guilford Courthouse and Hobkirk's Hill), or if they were well covered by rebel horse during their retirement (as at the New Garden skirmish, Guilford Courthouse, and Eutaw Springs), then this precluded the Crown cavalry from galloping madly after them.[32] After Hobkirk's Hill Lieutenant Colonel Francis Lord Rawdon reported to Cornwallis that his victorious army had pursued Greene for three miles, "but the enemy's cavalry greatly surpassing ours as to number, horses and appointments, our dragoons could not risk much, nor could I suffer the infantry to break their order in hopes of overtaking the fugitives."[33] Militia officer St. George Tucker, who was among the last of Greene's troops to leave the field at Guilford Courthouse, described what happened when the British Legion dragoons attempted to dispute the rebel withdrawal: "We were soon after ordered to retreat. Whilst we were doing so, Tarleton advanced to attack us with his horse; but a party of Continentals, who were fortunately close behind us, gave him so warm a reception that he retreated with some degree of precipitation. A few minutes after we halted by the side of an old field fence, and observed him surveying us at the distance of two or three hundred yards. He did not think it proper to attack us again, as we were advantageously posted; and the Continentals, who had encountered him just before, were still in our rear."[34] In the opinion of Continental veteran Joseph Plumb Martin, British cavalry rarely pursued defeated rebel troops from the battlefield because "they dared not do it."[35]

Even when rebel troops did retreat in confusion and were therefore vulnerable to a mounted charge, the broken and restrictive nature of America's topography usually thwarted the British cavalry's ability to exploit their opportunity. As Major General Grey put it in 1779, "A defeat of the Americans can hardly be decisive; the country renders a retreat in general so very secure."[36] On one level, close terrain helped obscure the retreating troops from the sight of their pursuers; on another, it offered enemy rearguards or knots of more-indomitable rebels the opportunity to rally around, take cover behind, and offer renewed resistance from obstacles like walls, fences, hedges, and trees. In these conditions an incautious advance risked a severe check, as Brunswick officer Lieutenant Du Roi pointed out after the failure of the Albany expedition: "Whenever the attack proves too serious, they [i.e., the rebels] retreat, and to follow them is of little value. It is impossible on account of the thick woods, to get around them, cutting them off from a pass, or to force them to fight. Never are they so much to be feared as when retreating. Covered by the woods, the number of enemies with which we have to deal can never be defined. A hundred men approaching may be taken for a corps. The same are attacked, they retreat fighting. We think ourselves victors and follow them; they flee to an ambush, surround and attack us with a superior number of men and we are the defeated."[37] As one example of how this could happen, Henry Lee later claimed that Major John Coffin's loyalist horsemen were ambushed and routed by Colonel William Washington's dragoons as the result of an incautious pursuit after Hobkirk's Hill.[38]

Another reason why topography made pursuit so difficult was that the ubiquitous woods and high rail fences or walls proved effective barriers to mounted troops. As Washington tried to reassure his army in general orders issued on the day before the battle of White Plains, "in such a broken country, full of stone walls, there is no enemy more to be despised [than cavalry], as they cannot leave the road; so that any party attacking them may be always sure of doing it to advantage, by taking post in the woods by the roads, or along the stone walls, where they will not venture to follow them."[39] Like Washington, Greene felt that "[t]o the northward, cavalry is nothing from the numerous fences," and many officers would have agreed with the Hessian officer who wrote from Pennsylvania that fences "make this country so cut-up that one cannot maneuver with cavalry, even where it is level."[40] Nevertheless, even in many southern actions, topography rendered Tarleton's British Legion dragoons largely impotent. For example, at the Alamance River skirmish, rail fences and woods prevented the troopers from charging. At Guilford Courthouse the thickness of the woods compelled them to remain in column on the road for most of the action. Similarly, at Green Springs a combination of woods, boggy ground, and growing darkness prevented Cornwallis from unleashing the dragoons against the retiring enemy.[41] Seen in this respect, it becomes clear quite why the result of the battle of Cowpens seemed so extraordinary to contemporaries when the lightly wooded field was apparently such an unusually favorable arena for Tarleton's very superior numbers of cavalry.[42]

With cavalry either unavailable or unable to ride down retiring rebel troops, the prospect of pursuit dimmed, for, as British officer Martin Hunter later put it, "it is always very difficult to come up with a retreating army with infantry."[43] By this Hunter meant that victorious infantry battalions, even when fresh, were unable simultaneously to maintain their order and to keep pace with a flying enemy, nevermind overtaking one with a head start. In the experience of Joseph Plumb Martin, the redcoats were no longer any threat once the retiring rebels were out of range of their musketry: "There was one thing . . . that always galled my feelings, and that was, whenever I was forced to a quick retreat, to be obliged to run till I was worried down. . . . Some of our men at this time seemed to think that they could never run fast or far enough. I never wanted to run, if I was forced to run, further than to be beyond the reach of the enemy's shot, after which I had no more fear of their overtaking me than I should have of an army of lobsters doing it."[44] At Brandywine Sergeant Major

John Hawkins of Congress's Own Regiment was able to evade his pursuers by casting away his knapsack: "had I not done so [I] would have been grabbed by one of the ill-looking Highlanders, a number of whom were firing and advancing very brisk towards our rear."[45] Similarly, after Germantown both Cornwallis's and Major General Grant's troops (none of whom had been much engaged, though Cornwallis's grenadiers had run all the way from Philadelphia) marched after the rebels for some miles without being able to catch them.[46] This was despite Grant's redcoats having moved, as the Scotsman later put it, "as fast as men could trot."[47]

That the ordinary line infantry in America were unsuited to the pursuit role was one of the subjects of a memorandum penned by Captain Patrick Ferguson soon after the battle of Monmouth. Ferguson argued that, as things currently were, the line brigades were fit only for employment as a reserve, they having been "totally unfit for courses [i.e., swift movements], detachment, [or] pursuit." In particular, the latter role was "an employment from which two-thirds of the soldiers are incapacitated by nature, and all of them from their discipline, equipment, and want of exercise, were they not at any rate blown and disabled for the time by the exertions of the previous attack." Indeed, Ferguson asserted, when British line infantry advanced at speed for just a few hundred yards, they were "thoroughly knocked up and thrown into general disorder." Unfortunately, he continued, the army's light battalions were no more capable of fulfilling this role: "being employed to flank [the column of march], scour the country, and skirmish with every body that interrupts the way before a serious attack, and afterwards [being] pushed in the front of the attack itself, [the light infantry] are generally too exhausted to be able to pursue with effect." As a solution to this problem, Ferguson called for a fourfold or fivefold increase in the light infantry's numbers to the point where they would have composed around half of any field army. To achieve this he suggested that the establishment of each British light company should be doubled and that each regiment in garrison at New York and Rhode Island should organize and donate a second light company for field service. Additionally, he recommended that all Provincial regulars should be disciplined and armed specifically for light service and that the Highlanders should be relieved of "firelocks and ammunition" in favor of "their beloved swords and pistols" —a measure that would, he predicted, not only increase the Scots' fleetness and "flatter their natural taste" but also terrify the rebels. According to Ferguson, this augmentation of the army's light troops not only would have facilitated the various duties currently performed largely by the overworked light battalions but also would have provided a field commander with a substantial reserve of wholly fresh light troops with which to exploit success on the battlefield. Such men could have been deployed both on the flanks ("where they would be . . . the only substitutes in this impracticable country for cavalry") and in the rear of the brigades of line infantry (where they would have been able to sustain the line in the event of miscarriage). Once the main British line had compelled the rebels to give way, the commander might have instructed the hatmen "to half-regain their order and follow at leisure." Meanwhile, the fresh light troops in the hatmen's rear would have been able to "dart through the intervals and, being certain of support from the line in good order, push on at full speed without any caution or hesitation, so as to prevent all possibility of an enemy's rallying or escaping."[48]

Occasionally, other determinants were to blame for the British inability to disrupt a rebel retreat. At some actions the onset of darkness covered the rebel withdrawal, as at Green Springs.[49] But British participants most commonly blamed sheer physical and mental exhaustion for the lack of any serious pursuit. This is hardly surprising when one considers that, in order to reach the field, British troops usually had to break camp early and march many miles, often through rough country and without nourishment. Light infantry captain Sir James Murray recounted the exacting experience of Howe's outflanking march at Long Island: "It was well that the fortune of the day repaid us for the labors of the night, which was to me at least, as disagreeable a one as I remember to have passed in the course of my campaigning. I had been up three out of the five preceding nights. We dragged on at the most tedious pace from sunset till 3 o'clock in the morning, halting every minute just long enough to drop asleep, and to be disturbed again in the same manner. The night was colder than I remember to have felt it, so that by daybreak my stock of patience began to run very low."[50] Likewise, in concluding his account of the fatiguing and nerve-racking nocturnal march that Major General Grant's column undertook over on the British left, Captain the Honorable William Leslie bluntly asserted, "I never wish to be concerned in a night attack a second time."[51] At Brandywine Cornwallis's outflanking division marched at 5:00 A.M., halted to eat at 1:00 P.M., and finally engaged at about 4:00 P.M. They then fought a furious action that lasted about two hours. By the time the fighting concluded, the redcoats were spent and the light was giving way.[52] As Lieutenant Loftus Cliffe put it: "The fatigues of this day were excessive: some of our best of men were obliged to yield, one of 33 dropped dead, nor had we even daylight, [so] we could not make anything of a pursuit. If you knew the weight a poor soldier carries, the length of time he is obliged to be on foot for a train of artillery to move 17 miles, the duties he goes through when near an enemy, [and] that the whole night of the 9th we were marching, [then] you would say we had done our duty on the 11th to beat an army strongly posted, numerous and unfatigued."[53] On the mornings of the battles of Cowpens and Guilford Courthouse, the respective British forces moved off at 3:00 A.M. and at daybreak. Henry Lee later judged that, in contrast with the relative freshness of the rested and fed rebels, the hunger and fatigue of the King's troops was a key factor at both actions.[54]

## The Resilience of the Rebellion

Even when the British did win victories against less wary and able rebel commanders, these proved ultimately unimpressive because of the resilience of the rebels' military forces. For example, in New Jersey in November and December 1776, in Georgia in December 1778 and January 1779, and in South Carolina in May and June 1780, the British managed to defeat, drive off, disperse, or capture the enemy's forces; they then detached troops to fortify and garrison posts to tie down the occupied territory. Yet in each case the battered rebels recovered remarkably quickly. In the North the unexpected blows that Washington's dwindling, tattered band delivered at Trenton and Princeton compelled Howe to evacuate almost all of occupied New Jersey. In Georgia and South Carolina, despite shattering British victories at Savannah, Briar Creek, Charleston, and Camden, the rebels were able to keep putting regular and militia forces in the field to contest the reestablishment of royal authority in the backcountry. In such circumstances British commanders must have felt that they were engaged in a never-ending struggle to cut off the heads of a Hydra-like enemy.

As the war progressed, the rebels' military forces gradually gained experience and discipline, despite the Continental Army's continued dependence on short-service drafts. In part, this was the result of Washington's deliberate strategy of exposing his regulars to small doses of combat in the *petite guerre*. As Major the Honorable Charles Stuart put it in 1777: "The rebel soldiers, from being accustomed to peril in their skirmishes, begin to have more confidence, and their officers seldom meet with our foraging parties, but they try every ruse to entrap them. And though they do not always succeed, yet the following our people as they return, and the wounding and killing many of our rearguards, gives them the notion of victory, and habituates them to the profession."[55] Colonel Allan MacLean was of the same mind: "The rebels have the whole winter gone upon a very prudent plan of constantly harassing our quarters with skirmishes and small parties, and always attacking our foraging parties. By this means they gradually accustom their men to look us in the face, and stand fire which they never have dared to attempt in the field. But this is a plan which we ought to avoid most earnestly, since it will certainly make soldiers of the Americans."[56]

The winter at Valley Forge in 1777–78 marked a major milestone in the tactical effectiveness of the Continental Army, largely due to the efforts of the rebels' Prussian drillmaster, Major General Friedrich von Steuben. Despite a shaky start, Washington's regulars performed better at Monmouth Courthouse than in most previous engagements, and the rebel coup against Stony Point the next year was particularly impressive. In January 1780 captive British ensign Thomas Hughes saw a battalion of Continentals marching southward who "had good clothing, were well armed and showed more of the military in their appearance than I ever conceived American troops had yet attained."[57] Months later Captain John Peebles made a similar observation on the surrendered rebel troops at Charleston: "They are a ragged, dirty-looking sort of people as usual, but [they have] more appearance of discipline than what we have seen formerly, and some of their officers [are] decent-looking men."[58]

During the southern campaigns, disciplined Continental Army corps like the 1st Maryland Regiment demonstrated their increasing ability to repulse British bayonet rushes. Hence the Hessian adjutant general in America expressed surprise at Clinton's displeasure at the expense of Cornwallis's hollow victory at Guilford Courthouse: "I myself do not see anything extraordinary in it, for since we made no effort to smother the rebellion at the beginning, when it could have been done at a small cost, the rebels couldn't help but become soldiers."[59] After his capture at Yorktown, the sight of rebel troops at exercise particularly impressed captive Captain Johann Ewald: "Concerning the American army, one should not think that it can be compared to a motley crowd of farmers. The so-called Continental, or standing, regiments are under good discipline and drill in the English style as well as the English themselves. I have seen the Rhode Island Regiment march and perform several mountings of the guard which left nothing to criticize. The men were complete masters of their legs, carried their weapons well, held their heads straight, faced right without moving an eye, and wheeled so excellently without their officers having to shout much, that the regiment looked like it was dressed in line with a string."[60]

As the war dragged on, an increasing number of those who were drafted into the Continental Army or called out for militia service, or who offered themselves as paid substitutes for such men, were themselves veterans of previous campaigns.[61] In short, it is difficult to avoid the conclusion that, by the end of the war, the best of the rebels' regular corps were tactically every bit the equals of their British counterparts.

The resilience of the Continental Army was central to Britain's eventual failure in America. Eighteenth-century military convention dictated that the army that held the field at the end of an engagement had gained the victory. By this standard Crown troops won the great majority of the engagements of the American War. Yet while battles like Bunker Hill, Freeman's Farm, Guilford Courthouse, Hobkirk's Hill, and Eutaw Springs were all unquestionably British tactical victories, they were simultaneously strategic reverses on three counts. First, they cut deeply into Britain's limited military manpower. Second, they did not neutralize the rebels' field armies. Third, they failed to convince colonial public opinion that Crown forces were invincible. For example, if Cornwallis had intended that a victory at Guilford Courthouse would prove the superiority of His Majesty's arms and thereby rally the people of North Carolina to the royal cause, then the result impressed few. As the earl sadly reported, in the aftermath of the action, barely one hundred locals were willing to come out in arms in his support: "Many of the inhabitants rode into camp, shook me by the hand, said they were glad to see us and to hear that we had beat Greene, and then rode home again."[62]

Furthermore, as the war unfolded, the political dividend that Crown forces gained from clear operational or tactical successes against the rebels proved less and less potent. Probably the best example of this was Cornwallis's triumph at Camden. In the first flush of his victory, the earl optimistically predicted, "The rebel forces being at present dispersed, the internal commotions and insurrections in the province will now subside." But when (as Lord Rawdon put it) "the dispersion of that force did not extinguish the ferment which the hope of its support had raised," Cornwallis rationalized the failure of his prediction by suggesting that "[t]he disaffection . . . in the country east of [the] Santee [River] is so great that the account of our victory could not penetrate into it, any person daring to speak of it being threatened with instant death." Rawdon's assessment was more straightforward: "The approach of General Gates's army unveiled to us a fund of disaffection in this province of which we could have formed no idea. . . . A numerous enemy now appears on the frontiers drawn from Nolachucki and other settlements beyond the mountains whose very names have been unknown to us."[63] Rawdon's admission that the British had simply been oblivious to the scale, intensity, and persistence of popular hostility to royal authority in South Carolina was reminiscent of Burgoyne's obvious alarm three years earlier, when he reported from New England that "[t]he great bulk of the country is undoubtedly with the Congress in principle and in zeal" and that New Hampshire, "a country unpeopled and almost unknown in the last war, now abounds in the most active and most rebellious race of the continent and hangs like a gathering storm on my left."[64] In short, if British military successes impressed the undecided, they did not intimidate inveterate rebels, whose numbers and determination Crown commanders gradually came to realize they had drastically underestimated.

If British commanders ultimately did not reap the expected political fruits from their military successes, their armies' unhappy interaction with the population at large certainly wrought massive political damage. Among the leading causes of this alienation were the unauthorized employment of "fire and sword" methods by some hard-line officers and the nefarious misdemeanors committed by the rank and file, including theft and rape.[65] In some ways British soldiers proved excellent recruiting agents for the rebel cause.

Even if British military successes had encouraged the rebel leadership to sue for peace and the majority of the population to acquiesce in the restoration of royal government, it is far from clear that this would have signaled the end of the conflict. Instead, it is quite possible that the British would have found their authority still contested at a local level by inveterately hostile sections of the population (much as occurred over a century later during the guerrilla phase of the Second Boer War). The lawlessness that wracked the "no-man's-land" around New York City for much of the conflict, and the bloody civil war that ravaged Georgia and the Carolinas when the strategic focus shifted to the South, were surely a foretaste of what must have happened had the British succeeded in defeating organized rebel resistance across the continent. It is difficult to see how Britain's limited military resources could have successfully overcome such a state of universal anarchy.

While Crown forces won the great majority of the battlefield engagements of the American War, the fruits of these victories were too limited to decide the outcome. Certainly it was beyond the powers of the British to "destroy" rebel field armies on the battlefield. This was because rebel commanders generally succeeded either in evading battle under unfavorable conditions or in escaping the worst consequences of a defeat. They managed the latter feat because the British were generally incapable of mounting an effective pursuit to disrupt or interdict the flight of the vanquished from the battlefield. As Major General the Chevalier de Chastellux put it, "it is not in intersected countries, and without cavalry, that great battles are gained, which destroy or disperse armies."[66] As the struggle dragged on, and despite repeated reverses, the rebels' military forces gradually gained in experience and discipline to the point that, by the end of the war, the Continental Army's best corps were able to meet the King's troops on the open field on more or less equal terms. This made British victories all the more difficult and costly. Additionally, the British appear simply to have overestimated the political worth of military success. While their Pyrrhic tactical victories predictably failed to convince many Americans that Congress was doomed to defeat, neither did great victories like Camden persuade inveterate rebels to abandon the cause. Had the rebel leadership given up the struggle, and had the mass of the population resigned themselves to the restoration of royal authority, it is likely that these incorrigibles would simply have made America ungovernable.

# Notes

## ABBREVIATIONS

| | |
|---|---|
| *1764 Regulations* | *The Manual Exercise, as Ordered by His Majesty, in 1764. Together with Plans and Explanations of the Method Generally Practis'd at Reviews and Field-Days, &c.* (New York: H. Gaine, 1775) |
| APSL | American Philosophical Society Library, Sol Feinstone Manuscripts Collection, Philadelphia |
| *DAR* | K. G. Davies, ed., *Documents of the American Revolution*, 21 vols. (Dublin: Irish University Press, 1972–81) |
| HMC | Historical Manuscripts Commission |
| HSD | Historical Society of Delaware |
| *JSAHR* | *Journal of the Society for Army Historical Research* |
| LOC | Library of Congress, Washington, D.C. |
| NAM | National Army Museum, Chelsea |
| NAS | National Archives of Scotland, Edinburgh (formerly the Scottish Record Office) |
| NYHS | New-York Historical Society |
| *PNG* | Nathanael Greene, *The Papers of Nathanael Greene*, ed. R. K. Showman and D. M. Conrad, 13 vols. (Chapel Hill: University of North Carolina Press, 1976–2005) |
| PRO | The National Archives, Kew (formerly the Public Record Office) |
| WLCL | William L. Clements Library, Ann Arbor, Mich. |
| WO | War Office Papers, The National Archives, Kew (formerly the Public Record Office) |

## PREFACE

1. For surveys of the most important material, see J. Black, "Bibliographical Review: Some Recent Work on the American War of Independence in Bibliographical Context," *War in History* 1 (1994): 337–54; and D. Syrett, "The British Armed Forces in the American Revolutionary War: Publications, 1875–1998," *Journal of Military History* 63 (1999): 147–64.

2. Perhaps the very best example of these works to date is Babits, *Devil of a Whipping*.

3. See Caruana, "Dress of the Royal Artillery," 124–29; Burke and Bass, "Preparing a British Unit for Service in America," 2–11; Embleton and Haythornwaite, "British Troops on Campaign," 24–28; S. Gilbert, "Analysis of the Xavier della Gatta Paintings," 46 (1994): 98–108, and 47 (1995): 146–62; Haarmann, "Royal Artillery and 62nd Regiment," 134–35.

4. H. Pyle, *The Battle of Bunker Hill*, in H. C. Lodge, *Scribner's Magazine*, Feb. 1898.

5. For these topics, see Conway, "British Army Officers and the American War," 265–76; Conway, "To Subdue America," 381–407; Syrett, "Methodology of British Amphibious Operations," 269–80.

6. For example, much of the material in Anburey, *Travels*, and Lamb, *Journal*, was in fact lifted from earlier works. Compare, for instance, Lamb's oft-quoted account of the battle of Guilford Courthouse with that in Stedman, *History*.

## ACKNOWLEDGMENTS

1. Matthew H. Spring, " 'With Zeal and with Bayonets Only': The British Army on Campaign in North America, 1775–83" (Ph.D. thesis, University of Leeds, 2001).

## 1. THE ARMY'S TASK

*Epigraph. PNG*, 8:75.

1. For the rebels' confidence in the inevitability of British defeat, see, for instance, Lenman, *Britain's Colonial Wars*, 202–205, 211–12.

2. Quoted in Conway, *War of American Independence*, 219.

3. For the failure of British peace overtures in 1776 and 1778, see Gruber, *Howe Brothers*, 116–20, 298, 301–302.

4. See Black, *War for America*, 44–46.

5. For the abortive European negotiations to secure such a peace in 1781, see R. B. Morris, *The Peacemakers: The Great Powers and American Independence* (New York: Harper & Row, 1965), 153–90.

6. *DAR*, 12:47, Howe to Dartmouth, 16 Jan. 1776.

7. For the efforts of John Houston and John Glen, respectively former rebel governor and former chief justice of Georgia, to secure royal pardons after the collapse of rebel authority in that colony, see *DAR*, 20:124, Commissioners for Restoring Peace to Germain, 30 Apr. 1781.

8. Washington, *Papers*, 6:249, Washington to John Hancock, 8 Sept. 1776.

9. Washington, *Writings,* 20:267, Washington to Lafayette, 30 Oct. 1780.

10. *PNG,* 8:75, Greene to Sumter, 8 Jan. 1781.

11. The best overall study of the militia's role in the war is Kwasny, *Washington's Partisan War.*

12. *PNG,* 8:251, Greene to Huntington, 14 May 1781.

13. *DAR,* 18:214, Arnold to Germain, 28 Oct. 1780.

14. For the main themes of eighteenth-century warfare, see Strachan, *European Armies and the Conduct of War,* chaps. 2–3; Chandler, *Warfare in the Age of Marlborough,* 12–21; Paret, *Makers of Modern Strategy,* chap. 4; and Black, *European Warfare,* chap. 3.

15. One exception would be the charge of the Bayreuth dragoons at Hohenfriedberg (1745), which foreshadowed the later Napoleonic grand-tactical use of cavalry reserves to confirm the enemy's defeat. Duffy, *Frederick the Great,* 65.

16. For a discussion of the Austrian success in Bohemia, see ibid., 54–57; and Browning, *War of the Austrian Succession,* 182–85.

17. Quoted in Black, *European Warfare,* 84.

18. *DAR,* 12:46, Howe to Dartmouth, 16 Jan. 1776; ibid., 157, Howe to Germain, 7 July 1776. For the extensiveness of the rebel fortifications on Manhattan, see Kemble, "Papers," 1:88–89.

19. HMC, *Rawdon Hastings,* 3:180, Rawdon to Lord Huntingdon, 5 Aug. 1776.

20. Ibid., 186, unknown to Lord Huntingdon, 25 Sept. 1776.

21. F. Mackenzie, *Diary,* 1:42.

22. Cohen, "Captain William Leslie's Paths to Glory," 67, Leslie to his father, 22 Nov. 1776.

23. Muenchhausen, *At General Howe's Side,* 30.

24. Ibid., 16.

25. Fortescue, *Correspondence of King George the Third,* 4:546, "A Plan for reducing the Colonies . . . ," c.1779.

26. F. Mackenzie, *Diary,* 2:525.

27. Most historians have ignored Tarleton's claim that his 1,100-strong force at Cowpens faced almost 2,000 rebels (including 1,000 militia), preferring to believe Morgan's claim that he had only 800 men. But Lawrence Babits has demonstrated that this latter figure excluded the militia and that the rebel force actually totaled something between 1,800 and 2,400 men. Tarleton, *History,* 215–16; Babits, *Devil of a Whipping,* 150–52.

28. *DAR,* 18:227, Germain to Sir James Wright, 9 Nov. 1780.

29. Ibid., 20:188, Clinton to Cornwallis, 15 July 1781.

30. Ibid., 17:44, Germain to Clinton, 23 Jan. 1779.

31. Ibid., 14:33, Howe to Germain, 20 Jan. 1777; Howe, *Narrative,* 19; Clinton quoted in Willcox, *Portrait of a General,* 270.

32. Quoted in S. Frey, "British Armed Forces and the American Victory," in Ferling, *World Turned Upside Down,* 179.

33. Bolton, *Letters of Hugh, Earl Percy,* 38, Percy to his father, 12 Sept. 1774.

34. See Nelson, "Citizen Soldiers or Regulars," 126–32.

35. *DAR*, 14:166, Burgoyne to Germain, 20 Aug. 1777.

36. Hanger, *Address*, 82n.

37. Tarleton, "New War Letters," 76, 5 July 1777.

38. *DAR*, 20:166, Cornwallis to Clinton, 30 June 1781.

39. See, for instance, Shy, *People Numerous and Armed*, 176–77, 236–37.

40. *PNG*, 2:244, Greene to Jacob Greene, 3 Jan. 1778.

41. See Mackesy, *War for America*, 35, 38–39.

42. See Conway, "To Subdue America," 381–407.

43. *PNG*, 8:131, Greene to Samuel Huntington, 22 Apr. 1781.

44. WO 3/5, fo. 37, Harvey to Lt. Gen. Irwin, 30 June 1775. See also ibid., fo. 49, Harvey to Lt. Col. Smith, 31 July 1775. The secretary at war agreed, warning "that the Americans may be reduced by the fleet, but never can be by the army." Barrington, *Political Life of William Wildman, Viscount Barrington*, 159, Barrington to Lord North, 8 Aug. 1775. See also Stedman, *History*, 1:234.

45. Gruber, "The American Revolution as a Conspiracy," 360–72.

46. For one relatively modern expression of this traditional interpretation, see Royster, *Revolutionary People*.

47. Shy, *People Numerous and Armed*, esp. chaps. 5, 7, 9, 10.

48. Quoted in Conway, "To Subdue America," 381.

49. Howe, *Narrative*, 27.

50. *DAR*, 18:245, Cornwallis to Clinton, 3 Dec. 1780.

51. *PNG*, 7:51, 153, Morgan to Greene, 4 Jan. 1781, 19 Jan. 1781.

52. J. Sparks, *Correspondence of the American Revolution; Being Letters of Eminent Men to George Washington, from the Time of His Taking Command of the Army to the End of His Presidency. . . .* 4 vols. (Boston: Little, Brown, 1853), 3:304, Lafayette to Washington, 4 May 1781.

53. Lafayette, *Memoirs, Correspondence, and Manuscripts*, 1:417, Lafayette to Washington, 24 May 1781.

54. HMC, *Stopford-Sackville*, 2:44, Germain to Lord Howe, 18 Oct. 1776.

55. De Fonblanque, *Political and Military Episodes*, 192–93, Burgoyne to Germain, 20 Aug. 1775. About eight days after the battle, Burgoyne had written that the action "must be of important assistance by the impression it will make all over America." He warned, however, that "it must be good policy to support that impression to the utmost." Fortescue, *Correspondence of King George the Third*, 3:225, Abstract of a letter from Major General Burgoyne, 25 June 1775.

56. HMC, *Stopford-Sackville*, 2:30, Howe to Germain, 26 Apr. 1776; *DAR*, 12:145–46, Howe to Germain, 7 June 1776.

57. *DAR*, 12:159, 158, Howe to Germain, 7 July 1776.

58. McDonald, "Letter-Book," 283, July 1776.

59. Quoted in McGuire, *Philadelphia Campaign. Volume Two*, 27–28.

60. HMC, *Stopford-Sackville*, 2:30, Howe to Germain, 26 Apr. 1776.

61. Baxter, *British Invasion*, 269.

62. The best overall treatment remains P. H. Smith, *Loyalists and Redcoats*.

63. For the development, implementation, and eventual failure of the

"southern strategy," see especially P. H. Smith, *Loyalists and Redcoats*, chaps. 6–9; Gruber, "Britain's Southern Strategy," 205–38; and Shy, *People Numerous and Armed*, chap. 9.

64. Robertson, *Twilight of British Rule*, 40.

65. *DAR*, 20:89–90, Cornwallis to Germain (No. 7), 17 Mar. 1781.

66. T. Jefferson, *The Papers of Thomas Jefferson*, ed. J. P. Boyd, 33 vols. to date (Princeton, N.J., 1951–), 3:558–59, Stevens to Jefferson, 20 Aug. 1780.

67. Johnson, *Sketches*, 1:497.

## 2. OPERATIONAL CONSTRAINTS

*Epigraph.* O'Hara, "Letters," 174.

1. Willcox, *Portrait of a General*, 109–11, 121–22.

2. Clinton, *American Rebellion*, 46n12.

3. *DAR*, 12:232, Howe to Germain, 25 Sept. 1776.

4. Corsar, "Letters from America," 134–35, Stuart to his brother, 7 Jan. 1781. The Guards Brigade was with Major General Leslie's force marching from Charleston to reinforce Cornwallis's army.

5. Howe, *Narrative*, 32–33.

6. Stedman, *History*, 2:334. Rawdon's intelligence had similarly collapsed when Gates crossed the Pee Dee River in early August 1780. See *DAR*, 18:140, Gov. Martin to Germain, 18 Aug. 1780.

7. J. Burgoyne, *State of the Expedition*, 17.

8. *DAR*, 18:149, Cornwallis to Germain, 21 Aug. 1780.

9. Ibid., 20:123, Rawdon to Cornwallis, 26 Apr. 1781. Ironically, two days later Greene instructed Lee to "undeceive the people" about the battle's "consequences." *PNG*, 8:169, Greene to Lee, 28 Apr. 1781.

10. O'Hara, "Letters," 159, O'Hara to Grafton, 1 Nov. 1780.

11. For these and related statistics, see Boatner, *Encyclopedia*, 263–64; Higginbotham, *War of American Independence*, 389; Conway, *War of American Independence*, 30; Conway, *British Isles and the American War*, 26; Peckham, *Toll of Independence*, xiii; Neimeyer, *America Goes to War*, 138, 165; Bowman, *Morale of the American Revolutionary Army*, 70, 72.

12. This is one historian's estimate, based on a painstaking study of the manpower wastage of the 22nd and 33rd Regiments in America. Lamb, *British Soldier's Story*, i, xxxvii n1.

13. For rebel recruitment, see Martin and Lender, *Respectable Army*; Shy, *People Numerous and Armed*, chaps. 2, 5; Neimeyer, *America Goes to War*; and H. M. Ward, *War for Independence and the Transformation of American Society*, chap. 7.

14. Ewald, *Diary of the American War*, 341.

15. For British recruitment, see Conway, "British Mobilization in the American War," 58–76; Conway, "Recruitment of Criminals," 46–58; Frey, *British Soldier in America*, chaps. 1–2; Curtis, *Organization of the British Army*, chap. 3; Robson, "Raising a Regiment," 107–15; A. N. Gilbert, "Charles Jenkinson," 7–11; and Houlding, *Fit for Service*, 134–37.

16. *Considerations upon the Different Modes of Finding Recruits*, 3–4. For the horror that a party of recruits displayed when they unexpectedly

found themselves destined for America in 1778, see *John Robert Shaw*, 17–18.

17. Quoted in Frey, *British Soldier in America*, 27. Frey shows that it was not uncommon for recruits sent out from the British Isles to be returned as unfit for service.

18. Robson, "Raising a Regiment," 110, 113.

19. Blanchard, *Journal*, 153.

20. Luvaas, *Frederick the Great on the Art of War*, 77.

21. Pausch, *Journal and Reports*, 47, 76.

22. Pattison, "Official Letters," 27, 104–105, 107, 119, 122, 124.

23. Quoted in Mackesy, *War for America*, 85.

24. Howe, *Narrative*, 5, 19, 27, 32.

25. HMC, *Rawdon Hastings*, 3:186, unknown to Lord Huntingdon, 25 Sept. 1776. See also WLCL, Loftus Cliffe Papers, Cliffe to Jack, 21 Sept. 1776; and F. Mackenzie, *Diary*, 1:89.

26. Howe, *Narrative*, 5.

27. Ewald, *Diary of the American War*, 18.

28. Closen, *Revolutionary Journal*, 75.

29. Ewald, *Diary of the American War*, 340–41. See also "A Frenchman's Comments," 366; and Lafayette, *Memoirs, Correspondence, and Manuscripts*, 1:376, 386–87, Lafayette to Vergennes, 30 Jan. 1781, and to Mme. de Lafayette, 2 Feb. 1781.

30. Frey, *British Soldier in America*, 72–73.

31. The respective works are Baker, *Government and Contractors*; Syrett, *Shipping and the American War*; Bowler, *Logistics*; and Bowler, "Logistics and Operations," 54–71.

32. See especially Perjés, "Army Provisioning, Logistics, and Strategy," 1–51; J. Lynn, "Food, Funds, and Fortresses," 137–59.

33. Chandler, *Art of Warfare*, 17; Van Creveld, *Supplying War*, 24, 34; J. Lynn, "Food, Funds, and Fortresses," 141–42.

34. Lynderberg, *Archibald Robertson*, 159.

35. For the length of the campaigning season in America, see Galloway, *Letters to a Nobleman*, 36–38; Howe, *Narrative*, 47–49; and Fortescue, *Correspondence of King George the Third*, 3:215, "Letter of Intelligence," Boston, 12 June 1775. See also Bowler, *Logistics*, 58–59; and Curtis, *Organization of the British Army*, 115–18.

36. For Burgoyne's foraging difficulties, see Baxter, *British Invasion*, 259, 266, 269–70, 275–76, 284–86, 303–304. For evidence of two "grand forages" around Philadelphia in December 1777, after Howe's army had gone into winter quarters there, see Abbatt, *Major André's Journal*, 71–73.

37. Bowler, *Logistics*, 8–9, 52n37, 56n49, 99, 252. For the difference between garrison and field rations, see De Krafft, "Journal," 32, 48.

38. Stanley, *For Want of a Horse*, 105, General Orders, 24 June 1777. The Hessians in America preferred "zwieback" (biscuit) to bread, once they got used to it. Ewald, *Treatise*, 79. Apparently neither Lieutenant General the Comte de Rochambeau in America nor even Frederick the Great in Europe brought his troops to acquiesce in the same measure. Tarleton, *History*, 382–83; Luvaas, *Frederick the Great on the Art of War*, 109.

39. Kopperman, " 'Cheapest Pay,' " 445–70; Frey, *British Soldier in America*, 63–65, 78; Conway, " 'Great Mischief Complain'd Of,' " 382–83; Bowler, *Logistics*, 8, 171–72.

40. *The [New York] Royal Gazette*, 24 Feb. 1781, Anthony Allaire, letter, 30 Jan. 1781.

41. Bowler, *Logistics*, esp. 93–95, 260–63. For a critique of this thesis, see R. H. Kohn, "Feeding the War Machine, Eighteenth-Century Style," *Reviews in American History* 4 (1976): 178–83.

42. See, however, *PNG*, 7:88, 89, Greene to Col. Alexander Hamilton, 10 Jan. 1781, and 8:200, Greene to Joseph Reed, 4 May 1781. Greene's handling of logistics is examined in L. E. Babits, "Supplying the Southern Continental Army, March 1780 to September 1781," *Military Collector and Historian* 47 (1995): 163–71.

43. Quoted in Mackesy, *War for America*, 252.

44. See Beattie, "Adaptation of the British Army to Wilderness Warfare," 56–83.

45. *DAR*, 11:80, Gage to Dartmouth (Secret), 20 Aug. 1775. See also Muenchhausen, *At General Howe's Side*, 14; and De Fonblanque, *Political and Military Episodes*, 148.

46. *DAR*, 14:207, Howe to Germain, 10 Oct. 1777; Abbatt, *Major André's Journal*, 67.

47. *DAR*, 14:127–29, Howe to Germain, 5 July 1777; Howe, *Narrative*, 16; [Montagu-Stuart-Wortley], *Prime Minister and His Son*, 113, Stuart to his father, 10 July 1777. See also Alexander Hamilton, *The Works of Alexander Hamilton in Twelve Volumes*, ed. H. C. Lodge, 12 vols. (New York: G. P. Putnam's Sons, 1904), 9:50–51, Hamilton to the New York Convention, 5 Apr. 1777.

48. *DAR*, 14:64, Howe to Germain, 2 Apr. 1777.

49. As Major General Grey declared before a House of Commons Committee in 1779, "It is impossible to carry on any very important operation at a distance from the fleet, unless you have a navigable river, and are masters of both sides of it, with vessels to carry the stores." *Detail and Conduct of the American War*, 71, Testimony of Major General Charles Grey before a House of Commons Committee, 6 May 1779.

50. Bowler, *Logistics*, 57n51; [Montagu-Stuart-Wortley], *Prime Minister and His Son*, 113, Maj. the Hon. Charles Stuart to his father, 10 July 1777.

51. For the post at Wilmington, established in preparation for Cornwallis's second invasion of North Carolina, see Massey, "British Expedition to Wilmington," 387–411.

52. Fortescue, *Correspondence of King George the Third*, 4:546, "A Plan for reducing the Colonies . . . ," c. 1779.

53. *Detail and Conduct of the American War*, 69, Cornwallis's testimony, 6 May 1779.

54. Bowler, *Logistics*, 159–60.

55. Baxter, *British Invasion*, 154, 165, 240; Abbatt, *Major André's Journal*, 37, 38, 39–40, 41, 42.

56. Howe, *Narrative*, 65.

57. Corsar, "Letters from America," 134, Stuart to his brother, 7 Jan.

1781. See also *PNG*, 7:21, Greene to Gen. Ezekiel Cornell, 29 Dec. 1780, and 111–12, Greene to Washington, 13 Jan. 1781.

58. Lamb, *Journal*, 381.

59. *John Robert Shaw*, 36.

60. Stedman, *History*, 2:224–25.

61. *DAR*, 20:86, Cornwallis to Germain (No. 7), 17 Mar. 1781; O'Hara, "Letters," 174, O'Hara to the Duke of Grafton, 20 Apr. 1781; Tarleton, *History*, 223; Stedman, *History*, 2:326; Lee, *Revolutionary War Memoirs*, 232. Some of the baggage was destroyed at Buffalo Creek on 21 January 1781; most of the rest went up in smoke at Ramseur's Mills four days later. See Wickwire and Wickwire, *Cornwallis*, 274–75.

62. Stedman, *History*, 2:334–35.

63. *John Robert Shaw*, 40.

64. Lamb, *Journal*, 357.

65. See, for instance, Kemble, "Papers," 1:478–79; and Abbatt, *Major André's Journal*, 39–40. Provisions issued in advance were not always carefully husbanded. See Barker, *British in Boston*, 31–32, 37; Kemble, "Papers," 1:391, After Orders, 16 Oct. 1776; and J. Burgoyne, *State of the Expedition*, 149–50.

66. *Detail and Conduct of the American War*, 69, Cornwallis's testimony, 6 May 1779.

67. Bowler, *Logistics*, 56–57.

68. J. Burgoyne, *State of the Expedition*, app., lxxiii.

69. Muenchhausen, *At General Howe's Side*, 32; Howe, *Narrative*, 26.

70. *DAR*, 20:86, Cornwallis to Germain (No. 7), 17 Mar. 1781.

71. For the pontoons, see Muenchhausen, *At General Howe's Side*, 11; Abbatt, *Major André's Journal*, 78; and Hadden, *Journal and Orderly Books*, 144, 150.

72. Hadden, *Journal and Orderly Books*, 142, 244–45, 263; Anburey, *Travels*, 1:379; Baxter, *British Invasion*, 271–72; Kemble, "Papers," 1:311; F. Mackenzie, *Diary*, 1:29, 31, 2:649; Gruber, *John Peebles' American War*, 94; Sullivan, *From Redcoat to Rebel*, 102–103; Campbell, *Journal of an Expedition*, 7–8, 18, 19, 20.

73. For British troops' field shelters, see Muenchhausen, *At General Howe's Side*, 46; Gruber, *John Peebles' American War*, 189, 340; Hunter, *Journal*, 27, 32; Kemble, "Papers," 1:486; Scull, "Montresor Journals," 442; Schmidt, *Hesse-Cassel Mirbach Regiment*, 15, 16; and S. Graham, "An English Officer's Account," 269.

74. G. Smith, *Universal Military Dictionary*, 45.

75. J. Burgoyne, *State of the Expedition*, 148n. Lamb and Anburey later drew on Burgoyne's estimate without acknowledgement, while Stedman inexplicably came up with a total of 125 pounds for the same gear. See Lamb, *Memoir*, 178–79; Anburey, *Travels*, 1:378–79; and Stedman, *History*, 1:128, 129. For a contemporary definition of the term "camp equipage," see G. Smith, *Universal Military Dictionary*, 45.

76. Döhla, *Hessian Diary*, 71. See also Campbell, *Journal of an Expedition*, 18; and Heath, *Memoirs*, 214.

77. Townshend, "Some Account of the British Army," 23.

78. Ewald, *Diary of the American War*, 108; Lowell, *Hessians and the Other German Auxiliaries*, 226–27.

79. Contrary to generations of scandalized American writers, however, Burgoyne did not bring thirty wagons of his personal gear from Canada. This absurd fallacy originated in a misreading of Major General Phillips's brigade order of 19 August 1777 in which he complained that officers had individually withdrawn around thirty different carts from the provisions train by passing off their personal baggage as that of the commander in chief! In fact Burgoyne allocated himself just six horses for his baggage. Hadden, *Journal and Orderly Books*, 313–15; J. Burgoyne, *State of the Expedition*, 146n.

80. Burgoyne later reiterated at Fort Edward that officers would have to use their bat and forage money to arrange for the carriage of their baggage overland. See J. Burgoyne, *Supplement*, 17, General Orders, 5 Aug. 1777.

81. J. Burgoyne, *State of the Expedition*, 95–96, General Orders, 30 May 1777; Pausch, *Journal and Reports*, 69–70, 72.

82. J. Burgoyne, *State of the Expedition*, 145–46n; Baxter, *British Invasion*, 227; Pettengill, *Letters from America*, 83, anonymous letter, 20 July 1777.

83. See, for instance, Baxter, *British Invasion*, 227; and Anburey, *Travels*, 1:354. See also J. Burgoyne, *State of the Expedition*, 113–14; and Atkinson, "Some Evidence for Burgoyne's Expedition," 141.

84. J. Burgoyne, *Supplement*, 16, General Orders, 12 July 1777. Some officers complied with Burgoyne's wishes, leaving them in a sorry state after the Convention. See J. Burgoyne, *State of the Expedition*, 96; Pettengill, *Letters from America*, 83, 98, 140; Pausch, *Journal and Reports*, 66; and Baxter, *British Invasion*, 227.

85. For these injunctions, see Hadden, *Journal and Orderly Books*, 137, 148, 309, 310–12, 313–14, 314–15; and J. Burgoyne, *Supplement*, 17–18.

86. See Kemble, "Papers," 1:455–56, 481, 487–88, 591, 601; Princeton University Library, Glyn Journal, General Orders, 23 Sept. 1776, 5 June 1777; NYHS, British HQ Orderly Book, 26 Sept. 1776–2 June 1777, General Orders, 27 Sept. 1776; De Krafft, "Journal," 50; and Wilkin, *Some British Soldiers*, 220, Lt. William Hale to unknown, 19 Dec. 1776.

87. Princeton University Library, Glyn Journal, General Orders, 23 Sept. 1776; Kemble, "Papers," 1:456, General Orders, 1 Jul. 1777.

88. For wagon allotments, see, for instance, *Orderly Book of the Three Battalions of Loyalists*, 19–20; and Kemble, "Papers," 1:344, 403, 404, 486, 497, 501, 528, 544.

89. Gruber, *John Peebles' American War*, 89, 184, 196, 261; "Memorandum of Clothing lost at Brandywine," reproduced in McGuire, *Battle of Paoli*, 49. For officers' baggage in conventional European operations, see especially Duffy, *Military Experience in the Age of Reason*, 84–86; Duffy, *Army of Frederick the Great*, 61–62; and M. S. Anderson, *War of the Austrian Succession*, 28.

90. See, for instance, Drake, *Bunker Hill*, 29; Baxter, *British Invasion*, 266; Lushington, *Life and Services of General Lord Harris*, 75, Capt. George Harris to his cousin, n.d.; Gruber, *John Peebles' American War*, 339, 340; and WLCL, Loftus Cliffe Papers, Cliffe to Jack, 21 Sept. 1776.

91. Cohen, "Captain William Leslie's Paths to Glory," 63, Leslie to his parents, 2 Sept. 1776. Interestingly, after the battle of Princeton (where Leslie was killed), one rebel sergeant noted that he had acquired a knapsack, "which had belonged to a British officer, and [which] was well furnished." "Battle of Princeton, by Sergeant R——," 518.

92. WLCL, Loftus Cliffe Papers, Cliffe to Jack, 24 Oct. 1777. See Schmidt, *Hesse-Cassel Mirbach Regiment*, 87, 4 Sept. 1777.

93. Wilkin, *Some British Soldiers*, 219, 227–29, 233, 234–35, 246–47.

94. Bowler, *Logistics*, 25, 183; Curtis, *Organization of the British Army*, 139; Mackesy, "Redcoat Revived," 176.

95. Cresswell, *Journal*, 242; *DAR*, 15:160–61, Clinton to Germain, 5 July 1778.

96. Babits, *Devil of a Whipping*, 132. When, in January 1779, Lieutenant Colonel Archibald Campbell marched against Augusta, his 1,044-strong force took with it only one month's supplies loaded onto six wagons and two tumbrels. Campbell, *Journal of an Expedition*, 48.

97. For which see Bowler, *Logistics*, 225–30; and Mackesy, *War for America*, 133–36.

98. See Seybolt, "A Contemporary British Account," 71, 80–81; Muenchhausen, *At General Howe's Side*, 28, 32, 34; and Ewald, *Diary of the American War*, 89.

99. Fortescue, *Correspondence of King George the Third*, 4:546, "A Plan for reducing the Colonies . . . ," c. 1779. Howe made the same point in early 1777 but unfairly blamed the Germans. *DAR*, 14:33, Howe to Germain, 20 Jan. 1777; Atwood, *The Hessians*, 107.

100. Lawrence Babits has upheld Tarleton's version, disproving the traditional interpretation that the plunderers were opportunistic loyalists. Tarleton, *History*, 214, 218; Babits, *Devil of a Whipping*, 131–33.

101. For the dangers that Clinton's swollen baggage train posed during the march from Philadelphia to New York, see Ewald, *Diary of the American War*, 136.

102. Corsar, "Letters from America," 135, Stuart to his brother, 7 Jan. 1781. See also Baxter, *British Invasion*, 221, 216.

103. Scull, "Montresor Journals," 453–55. See also Clinton, *American Rebellion*, 71.

104. For low morale and sickness as a consequence of short rations during the siege of Boston and at New York during the winter of 1778–79, see Clinton, *American Rebellion*, 23; De Krafft, "Journal," 70, 74–78; and Kemble, "Papers," 1:170. For hunger as a cause of plundering, see Conway, " 'Great Mischief Complain'd Of,' " 383–85.

105. WLCL, Loftus Cliffe Papers, Cliffe to Jack, 24 Oct. 1777.

106. O'Hara, "Letters," 177, 178, O'Hara to Duke of Grafton, 20 Apr. 1781.

107. These returns are reproduced in Hatch, *Battle of Guilford Courthouse*, 137.

108. *John Robert Shaw*, 42.

109. Lee, *Revolutionary War Memoirs*, 132.

110. Campbell, *Journal of an Expedition*, 31.

111. Howe, *Narrative*, 6, 26.

112. Burgoyne and Burgoyne, *Journal of the Hesse-Cassel Jaeger Corps*, 6.

113. Simcoe, *Military Journal*, 66–67.

114. Fonblanque, *Political and Military Episodes*, 149, Burgoyne to Lord Rochford, 1775.

115. See, for instance, Stedman, *History*, 2:334, 448–49; and Ewald, *Treatise*, 93.

116. Quoted in Wickwire, *Cornwallis*, 243. The collapse of Cornwallis's intelligence system in November–December 1780 is discussed in ibid., 242–44.

117. Harcourt, *Papers*, 11:208, Harcourt to Earl Harcourt, 17 Mar. 1777.

118. *DAR*, 20:227, Stewart to Cornwallis, 9 Sept. 1781.

119. Quoted in Nelson, *Sir Charles Grey*, 37. See also Baurmeister, *Revolution in America*, 226–27; and Burgoyne and Burgoyne, *Journal of the Hesse-Cassel Jaeger Corps*, 121, 137, 179.

120. Allaire, *Diary*, 6, 7, 8, 28; Anburey, *Travels*, 1:424; Biddulph, "Letters," 96; Baxter, *British Invasion*, 240–41, 256; Hanger, *Address*, 68–69; T. Hughes, *Journal*, 14–15, 19.

121. For a selection of observations on the topography of the eastern seaboard, see Kipping, *Hessian View of America*, 14; Lamb, *Journal*, 361; Hunter, *Journal*, 29; Anburey, *Travels*, 2:323–24; Pettengill, *Letters from America*, 184–85; Cresswell, *Journal*, 264–65; Clinton, *American Rebellion*, 10–12, 325; Willcox, *Portrait of a General*, 55; and *PNG*, 8:131–32, 200.

122. Major the Honorable Charles Stuart wrote of Long Island that "this place . . . is very like the wooded parts of England. . . . The country is in general flat, and there are large plains highly cultivated." [Montagu-Stuart-Wortley], *Prime Minister and His Son*, 84, Stuart to his father, 3 Sept. 1776. See also Serle, *American Journal*, 249.

123. See Gates, *British Light Infantry*, 22–24, 29–32, 58–59.

124. The rebel Delaware Continental Regiment famously marched more than 5,000 miles between April 1780 and April 1782. Royster, *Revolutionary People*, 241.

125. For the rebels' use of terrain during the "Race to the Dan," see Lee, *Revolutionary War Memoirs*, 237–46.

126. Howe, *Narrative*, 38. See also Stedman, *History*, 1:240. For a contrary assessment by a fellow Pennsylvanian loyalist, see Galloway, *Letters to a Nobleman*, 2–6. Most of the latter's argument is rebutted in Howe, *Narrative*, 37–38.

127. Simcoe, *Military Journal*, 15.

128. Lee, *Revolutionary War Memoirs*, 232.

## 3. GRAND TACTICS

*Epigraph.* Murray, *Letters from America*, 36. Murray was referring to the battle of Long Island.

1. Howe, *Narrative*, 25.

2. In 1779 Howe claimed to have gone to Pennsylvania in 1777 because "the defense of Philadelphia was an object which I justly concluded would

engage the whole of his [i.e., Washington's] attention. It was incumbent on him to risk a battle to preserve that capital." Yet in July 1777, at the second of the two meetings in which Clinton frantically tried to persuade Howe to go up the Hudson instead of cooperating with Burgoyne, the commander in chief allegedly agreed with his testy second in command that Washington would not fight to save Philadelphia. Although Washington's stand at Brandywine invalidated this alleged admission, Howe's original avowed interest in going to Pennsylvania was to draw on the support of the supposed loyalist majority of the population. Howe, *Narrative*, 19; Willcox, *Portrait of a General*, 149–50, 155; Clinton, *American Rebellion*, 64n11; *DAR*, 14:65, Howe to Germain, 2 Apr. 1777.

3. *DAR*, 18:214, Arnold to Germain, 28 Oct. 1780; ibid., 248, Germain to Clinton, 7 Dec. 1780.

4. Wilcox, *Portrait*, 70, 152, 154–59, 162, 164, 175–77, 232, 271, 276–77, 339–42.

5. Ibid., 139–40.

6. Clinton, *American Rebellion*, 92–98; Willcox, *Portrait of a General*, 233–37.

7. The best modern account of the short campaign is Vivian, "A Defence of Sir William Howe," 63–83.

8. Willcox, *Portrait of a General*, 46–48, 51.

9. *Detail and Conduct of the American War*, 14, unknown to unknown, 5 July 1775. The Honorable Charles Stuart later recalled that, "[h]ad General Howe recollected a military maxim that cutting off a retreat is half a victory he in all probability would have possessed Charlestown Neck with a considerable corps of troops." Quoted in Murdock, *Bunker Hill*, 10n.

10. See, for instance, Higginbotham, *War of American Independence*, 155; and Gallagher, *Battle of Brooklyn*, 97.

11. Gruber, *Howe Brothers*, 105–106; Willcox, *Portrait of a General*, 70, 102–104, 108–109.

12. The first proposal was for Clinton to attack Philadelphia via the Chesapeake while Howe advanced across New Jersey and the fleet and a supporting corps cleared the Delaware River. The second proposal was for Clinton to land on the New Jersey coast with the aim of retarding Washington's retreat until Cornwallis came up from the rear. The third proposal was for Clinton to go up the Delaware to Philadelphia and disperse Congress, raising havoc in Washington's rear. Willcox, *Portrait of a General*, 115–16.

13. Clinton, *American Rebellion*, 160–71; Willcox, *Portrait of a General*, 302–309.

14. In 1779 Howe dismissed the ill-considered criticism that he had "lost an opportunity of destroying the rebel army" at White Plains in October 1776 by failing to send a detachment to seize the bridge over the Croton River (four miles in Washington's rear) by marveling, "I cannot conceive the foundation of such an idea." Howe, *Narrative*, 7.

15. G. Smith, *Universal Military Dictionary*, 24. Frederick the Great gave a slightly different definition: "Combats are affairs in which small units are engaged or only a portion of the army is involved. Battles are general

actions where all are engaged equally on both sides." Luvaas, *Frederick the Great on the Art of War*, 141.

16. Dundas, *Principles*, 51.

17. See, for instance, Newlin, *Battle of New Garden*. Newlin argued for the elevation of this skirmish, which preceded the battle of Guilford Courthouse, to the status of a "battle."

18. *The Annual Register, or View of the History, Politics and Literature for the Year 1781* (London, 1782), 65, quoted in Newlin, *Battle of New Garden*, 68.

19. Chastellux, *Travels in North America*, 1:249, 412.

20. Stedman, *History*, 1:237.

21. Wilkin, *Some British Soldiers*, 268, Hale to his parents, 21 July 1778.

22. Muenchhausen, *At General Howe's Side*, 32; WO 34/111, fo. 71, unknown to Lord Amherst, n.d.

23. Peckham, *Sources of American Independence*, 2:302, Ferguson to Clinton, 1 Aug. 1778.

24. See for instance Gates, *British Light Infantry*, 65–66.

25. Quoted in Robson, "British Light Infantry," 221–22.

26. Stedman, *History*, 2:325. At Cowpens Tarleton lost four light companies and the infantry component of the British Legion, generally considered a light corps.

27. The grenadier battalions remained at New York while the 1st and 2nd Battalions of Light Infantry were dispatched to Virginia with Major General Phillips in 1781.

28. "Letters of British Officers in America," 69, Lindsay [?] to William Pitt, Philadelphia, 23 Oct. 1777.

29. NAM, Laye Letters, Laye to his father, 12 Dec. 1778. The grenadiers were then quartered with the light infantry at Jamaica on Long Island.

30. Peckham, *Sources of American Independence*, 2:303, Ferguson to Clinton, 1 Aug. 1778.

31. Permanent concentration in London would have facilitated the Guards' training, though it seems unlikely that they obtained socially or physically "better" recruits than the line regiments. I am most grateful to Dr. John Houlding for his comments on this theme.

32. [Montagu-Stuart-Wortley], *Prime Minister and His Son*, 69, Capt. the Hon. Charles Stuart to his father, 24 July 1775. One rebel newspaper gloated that British casualties at the battle of Monmouth were heaviest among the grenadiers and light infantry, "which renders their loss still more important." Moore, *Diary of the American Revolution*, 2:68, extract from *The New York Journal*, 13 July 1778.

33. It is probably no coincidence that the majority of the British-officer diaries and correspondence that survive were penned by flank company officers.

34. Wilkin, *Some British Soldiers*, 217–18, 255–56, Hale to his parents, 19 Dec. 1776, 15 June 1778.

35. Hunter, *Journal*, 27, 29.

36. Sullivan, *From Redcoat to Rebel*, 161, 163–64. For an illustration of

the barracks, which were one story high and covered a half-mile perimeter, built around three sides of a square, see Jackson, *British Army in Philadelphia*, 21.

37. Murray, *Letters from America*, 37, Murray to his sister, 31 Aug. 1776.

38. Williamson, *Elements*, 5–6 and n.

39. WO 27/31.

40. Cuthbertson, *System*, 16–17, 190.

41. Simes, *Military Course*, 211.

42. See for instance Kemble, "Papers," 1:497, General Orders, 17 Sept. 1777. Hatmen may have been able to apply to join a flank company. For instance, having been grossly abused, reduced from corporal, and apparently deprived of his post as regimental clerk over a misunderstanding about some plundered mutton, disgruntled Private Thomas Sullivan of the 49th Regiment recorded in his journal on 10 October 1777: "After the ill-treatment [that] I received from Lieutenant Colonel [Sir Henry] Calder . . . I would not stay in the battalion. Therefore I joined the light company, then in the 2nd Battalion of those corps." Sullivan, *From Redcoat to Rebel*, 136, 147. The date of Sullivan's transfer from the major's company to the light company is confirmed in WO 12/6032/1, item 88.

43. Before Howe's 1776 campaign, one Staten Island woman supposedly alleged that seven grenadiers had violated her. When General Lord Percy queried how she could have known them to be such in the dark, the woman retorted saucily that "they could be nothing else, and if your Lordship will examine I am sure you will find it so." Presumably, as in the case of the young "horse grenadier" in one popular contemporary work of erotic fiction, it was not the assailants' height that betrayed them. HMC, *Rawdon-Hastings*, 3:179, Capt. Francis Lord Rawdon to Lord Huntingdon, 5 Aug. 1776; John Cleland, *Fanny Hill or Memoirs of a Woman of Pleasure* (Penguin Popular Classics, n.d.), 40–41. I am most grateful to Dr. Stephen Brumwell for having brought the latter source to my attention. For the selection of tall hatmen for the grenadiers in America, see also McDonald, "Letter-Book," 398–40; and J. Smith, "Diary," 261, 262.

44. Ewald sought out experienced soldiers over thirty years old to fill his *Jäger* company for its first campaign in America, which proved a mistake: "The young people of sixteen to eighteen years of age were those who best withstood the climate and the strain, while the older ones, who had already been worn out during previous campaigns, had to be sent to the hospital." Ewald, *Treatise*, 68–69.

45. LOC, Washington Papers, British 40th Regt. Orderly Book, Regimental Orders, 8 June 1777. See also Kemble, "Papers," 1:456, General Orders, 1 July 1777; and NYHS, British HQ Orderly Book, 1 Aug. 1781–20 Feb. 1782, General Orders, 21 Aug. 1781.

46. Surviving muster lists do not support Ewald's later claim that British light battalions suffered heavily from desertion. They do demonstrate, however, significant wastage due to enemy action, sickness, and transfers back to the parent corps. Ewald, *Treatise*, 71. See for example WO 12/2750, 4803/1, 6240 (muster lists of the 10th, 33rd, and 52nd Regiments).

47. The commander in chief regretted that the regiment was obliged to receive men "so stigmatized" but trusted that peer pressure would "reform these perverse members." Quoted in Frey, "Courts and Cats," 9. For another case, see WO 36/5, General Orders, 9 July 1776.

48. Lushington, *Life and Services of General Lord Harris*, 79, Capt. George Harris to his uncle, n.d.; second quote from McGuire, *Surprise of Germantown*, 113n127; WO 34/111, fo. 71, unknown to Lord Amherst, n.d.

49. Stanley, *For Want of a Horse*, 75.

50. Quoted in Lawrence, "Howe and the British Capture of Savannah," 320.

51. Hunter, *Journal*, 40–41. Simcoe also believed "the vast advantages of the Philadelphia marches" explained the vigorous performance of his Queen's Rangers at the battle of Monmouth. There they accompanied the 1st Battalion of Light Infantry in a breakneck advance to turn the rebel left without a single man dropping out, despite having been under arms all the preceding night. Simcoe, *Military Journal*, 72.

52. WLCL, Loftus Cliffe Papers, Cliffe to Jack, 21 Sept. 1776.

53. Howe, *Narrative*, 7.

54. The storming of Fort Washington also involved a turning movement: the 42nd Regiment landed on the east side of Manhattan to get behind and render untenable the rebels' extensive lines to the south of the fortress, which General Lord Percy attacked frontally. For the clearest contemporary expression of the entire British plan, see Lynderberg, *Archibald Robertson*, 109–12.

55. See for instance Duffy, *Frederick the Great*, 312.

56. Heath, *Memoirs*, 185.

57. Serle, *American Journal*, 88.

58. Commager and Morris, *Spirit of 'Seventy-Six*, 630, Lt. Col. T. Will Heth to Col. John Lamb, 12 Oct. 1777.

59. Coleman, "Southern Campaign," 40, Judge St. John Tucker to Fanny, 18 Mar. 1781.

60. Ewald, *Treatise*, 80.

61. Lee, *Revolutionary War Memoirs*, 131. See also Bland, *Treatise*, 164–65.

62. NYSC, British Guards Brigade Orderly Book, 14 Aug. 1776–28 Jan. 1777, Brigade Orders, 11 Aug. 1776.

63. Ewald, *Treatise*, 113.

64. The withdrawal and its aftermath are brilliantly explained in Babits, *Devil of a Whipping*, 109–23, 154–55.

65. The major exception was the storming of Chatterton's Hill at White Plains, which was executed by troops from Lieutenant General von Heister's Second Division (Brigadier General Leslie's Second Brigade and a number of Hessian corps). Presumably the attack (on the rebel right) was conducted by troops from Heister's division because it comprised the left-hand British column during the approach march. Had Howe known more of the rebel position beforehand, he would probably have arranged the march differently.

66. Atwood, *The Hessians*, 71–72.

67. Elting, *Battle of Bunker's Hill*, 9, 18, 22, 28.

68. Ewald, *Diary of the American War*, 84. Authorities variously iden-

tify the most important British guide at Brandywine as a Chester County loyalist named Curtis Lewis or as the better-known Joseph Galloway. Ibid., 392n56; S. S. Smith, *Battle of Brandywine*, 13.

69. Campbell, *Journal of an Expedition*, 25–26; *DAR*, 17:35–36, Campbell to Germain, 16 Jan. 1779. For the rebel view of this action, see Lawrence, "Howe and the British Capture of Savannah," 303–27.

70. See S. S. Smith, *Battle of Brandywine*, 12–13; and McGuire, *Philadelphia Campaign. Volume One*, 190–93.

71. Scull, "Montresor Journals," 138.

72. Willcox, *Portrait of a General*, 105–107 and nn; Clinton, *American Rebellion*, 41–43.

73. Elting argued that the rebels had around 7,000 men on the Charlestown peninsula at one point or another. Of these, between 2,500 and 4,000 were directly involved in the fighting. Elting, *Battle of Bunker's Hill*, 30.

74. Willcox, *Portrait of a General*, 48, 105.

75. This interpretation of the initial British plan was first coherently argued in Murdock, *Bunker Hill*, 9–12 and nn. For a convincing modern analysis of the options discussed at this council, see Elting, *Battle of Bunker's Hill*, 21–22.

76. T. S. Anderson, *Command of the Howe Brothers*, 77. Anderson nevertheless wrongly argued that a bold frontal assault was always the intention. Ibid., 73–78 and nn.

77. For the rebel response to the British landing, see Elting, *Battle of Bunker's Hill*, 27.

78. See Murdock, *Bunker Hill*, 24–25; and Elting, *Battle of Bunker's Hill*, 30–31. While Elting styled Howe's plan an "envelopment," a turning movement was more likely what Howe intended.

79. Howard Murdock challenged the traditional interpretation that the rebels repulsed two separate attacks before the third succeeded. Instead, pointing to the action's short duration and drawing on the (especially British) contemporary accounts, he suggested that only two distinct attacks occurred and that when eyewitnesses wrote of the British having been twice repulsed, they in fact were describing the failure of each British wing in the initial attack. Predictably, subsequent writers have generally ignored Murdock's theory. Murdock, *Bunker Hill*, 69–72.

80. For this successful attack, see Elting, *Battle of Bunker's Hill*, 34–35.

81. De Fonblanque, *Political and Military Episodes*, 247, Burgoyne to Gen. Harvey, 11 July 1777.

82. *DAR*, 14:231–32, Burgoyne to Germain, 20 Oct. 1777; Baxter, *British Invasion*, 291.

83. See S. S. Smith, *Battle of Princeton*, 18–27.

84. The fruitless attempt by the 2nd Battalion of Light Infantry and the Queen's Rangers to turn Washington's left was not ordered by Clinton, who later complained that "the usual gallantry and impetuosity" of these light corps "had engaged them too forward." Clinton, *American Rebellion*, 95; Peckham, "Clinton's Review of Simcoe's Journal," 363–64, 368. For an account of the light infantry's vain dash, see WO 34/111, fo. 71, unknown to Lord Amherst, n.d.

85. See S. S. Smith, *Battle of Monmouth*, 9–26.

86. Quoted in Johnson, *Sketches*, 1: 376.

87. See Babits, *Devil of a Whipping*, 81–83.

88. *DAR*, 20:90–91, Cornwallis to Germain (No. 8), 17 Mar. 1781; Tarleton, *History*, 272.

89. For the outflanking attempt at Cowpens, see Babits, *Devil of a Whipping*, 62–65, 82.

90. Townshend, "Some Account of the British Army," 25.

91. Hadden, *Journal and Orderly Books*, 161, General Orders, 18 Sept. 1777. True to these instructions, during the action, when Brigadier General Hamilton referred Hadden's request for extra hands for the guns to Brigadier General Phillips, that officer was found with Burgoyne near two log huts behind the British center. Ibid., 165.

92. See Duffy, *Military Experience in the Age of Reason*, 238–39.

93. Lamb, *Journal*, 362.

94. HMC, *Rawdon Hastings*, 3:167, Rawdon to Lord Huntington, 13 Jan. 1776.

95. Biddulph, "Letters," 95, 96–97, Biddulph to his parents, 27 Aug. 1780, 17 Mar. 1781.

96. Lamb, *Journal*, 381. See also Stedman, *History*, 2:225.

97. Stedman, *History*, 2:326.

98. A disgraced marine officer who was not present at Bunker Hill dubiously related that Howe assured the attacking troops there, "I shall not desire one of you to go a step farther than where I go myself at your head." British deserter John Robert Shaw later claimed that Cornwallis delivered an equally fanciful address before the battle of Camden. Clarke, *Impartial and Authentic Narrative*, 3–4; *John Robert Shaw*, 31.

99. Sullivan, *From Redcoat to Rebel*, 69.

100. APSL, Anonymous British Journal, 1776–78, 11 Sept. 1777.

101. Townshend, "Some Account of the British Army," 23.

102. Baxter, *British Invasion*, 274.

103. Kemble, "Papers," 1:154.

104. Wilkin, *Some British Soldiers*, 258, 268, Hale to his parents, 4, 14 July 1778.

105. Muenchhausen, *At General Howe's Side*, 32. Germain told Howe that the King himself had taken notice of the commander in chief's tendency to expose his person in action and warned "how much the public would suffer by the loss of a general who had gained the affection of the troops, and the confidence of his country." HMC, *Stopford-Sackville*, 2:42, Germain to Howe, 18 Oct. 1776.

106. Baxter, *British Invasion*, 287–88.

## 4. MARCH AND DEPLOYMENT

*Epigraph.* Lee, *Revolutionary War Memoirs*, 277.

1. The 60th Regiment ("Royal Americans") had an establishment of four battalions. Other regular corps were divided into battalions in America on an ad-hoc basis. On arrival in 1776 the Brigade of Guards (specially formed

for American service) was divided into two battalions, each of five companies. The 42nd ("Royal Highland") Regiment also divided into two battalions, while the 71st Regiment (despite having lost several companies in June 1776 when a number of transports were captured at Boston) was rearranged from two into three battalions. These local reorganizations presumably facilitated command-and-control arrangements for what were, initially at least, relatively large corps. Hard campaigning thereafter produced further revisions. On the day after the battle of Brandywine, the 71st Regiment was reduced to two battalions. Similarly, by the time Cornwallis left the Carolinas in 1781, the Brigade of Guards had dwindled to a single four-company battalion. To complicate matters, during the war, the 42nd Regiment raised a second battalion in Britain, which served in India.

2. WO 34/116, Return of British Forces in North America, 15 July 1779. For the muster lists for the regiment's service in America, see WO 12 4803/1, 4803/2.

3. See Conway, "British Army Officers and the American War," 268-70. For the ebbing of enthusiasm for service in America, especially from 1778 onward, see Robson, *American Revolution in its Political and Military Aspects*, 123-25.

4. Tarleton, *History*, 136. This figure included three staff officers (adjutant, surgeon, and mate) but excluded Cornwallis, the colonel.

5. Specifically for the firings and maneuvers. For the review, file intervals of four inches were prescribed. *1764 Regulations*, 13, 35.

6. Cavan, *New System*, 32-33, 61, 200; Dalrymple, *Tacticks* 39, 39n; Dundas, *Principles*, 56.

7. Cuthbertson, *System*, 177-78. For criticism of these file intervals, see Pickering, *Easy Plan*, 13-15.

8. *1764 Regulations*, 13.

9. As the colonel was a proprietary absentee, the captain lieutenant (ranked as the battalion's junior captain from 1772 onward) administered and commanded his company in his absence. One of the subalterns commonly filled the adjutant's post.

10. *1764 Regulations*, 19-22, plate 1, fig. 1; plate 2, fig. 1. Each company had two sergeants until August 1775, and three thereafter. Each company's three (four, from 1779 onward) corporals served in the ranks, acting as models for the privates rather than exercising authority. See Williamson, *Elements*, 31; and Cavan, *New System*, 217. For alternative dispositions for the companies in battalion line, see Bland, *Treatise*, 3; Cavan, *New System*, 221, 222; Pickering, *Easy Plan*, 108-10, 125-26; Simes, *Military Course*, 260; and Williamson, *Elements*, 31, 35-38.

11. Tarleton, *History*, 136. These figures include adjutants but exclude other staff officers who were present. The figure for the 33rd Regiment excludes Cornwallis, its colonel.

12. Corsar, "Letters from America," 134, Stuart to his brother, 7 Jan. 1781. The Guards Brigade in America labored under a particularly unfavorable officer-to-man ratio, for its 100-man companies had only two or three officers each, and inadequate replacements came out from Britain. *DAR*,

12:265, Howe to Germain (No. 32, Separate), 30 Nov. 1776; Corsar, "Letters from America," 134, Stuart to Lord Blantyre, 23 Sept. 1780.

13. Simcoe, *Military Journal*, 21.

14. Sullivan, *From Redcoat to Rebel*, 69; WO 12/6032/1, item 64.

15. Collection of the Fort Ticonderoga Museum, British 47th Regt. Orderly Book, Regimental Morning Orders, 9 Sept. 1777. I am most grateful to Mr. Eric H. Schnitzer, park ranger/historian at Saratoga National Historical Park, for having brought this extract to my attention and for having provided crucial information on the seniority and whereabouts of the 47th Regiment's officers during the Albany expedition.

16. R. Mackenzie, *Strictures on Lt.-Col. Tarleton's History*, 97; Hanger, *Address*, 102–103. Mackenzie fought at Cowpens as a lieutenant in the 1st Battalion of the 71st Regiment. Hanger was a major in the British Legion but was not present at the battle.

17. NAS, GD 174/2106, 2107, Orders, 11 Sept. 1777.

18. The raid is related in Nelson, *William Tryon*, 167–68.

19. Jervis, *Three Centuries of Robinsons*, Frederick Robinson autobiography, 78, 79.

20. Anburey embarked at Cork for Quebec in August 1776 with some recruits for the 47th Regiment. During the Saratoga campaign, he served as a "gentleman volunteer" with the 29th Regiment's grenadier company, with which he fought at Hubbardton. On 10 August 1777 he received an ensigncy in the 24th Regiment with which he fought at Freeman's Farm and Bemis Heights. Hadden, *Journal and Orderly Books*, xcvii.

21. Smith and Elting, "British Light Infantry," 88. The author may have been William Scott, who captained the 17th Regiment's light company at Brandywine.

22. J. Burgoyne, *Supplement*, 6, General Orders, 1 May 1777.

23. Burgoyne and Burgoyne, *Journal of the Hesse-Cassel Jaeger Corps*, 5–6. At this time the First Division comprised the *Jäger*, the two battalions of light infantry, and the two battalions of grenadiers.

24. Smith and Elting, "British Light Infantry," 88.

25. Bland, *Treatise*, 2; Cavan, *New System*, 60–61; Williamson, *Elements*, 35. Once the company had been "sized," the sergeants drew up a "size roll" that they could check when the men formed on the company parade.

26. Cuthbertson, *System*, 176; Simcoe, *Military Journal*, 21.

27. Smith and Elting, "British Light Infantry," 88.

28. NYSC, British Orderly Book kept by Capt. Frederick DePeyster, Detachment Orders, 23 Jan. 1780.

29. Dalrymple, *Tacticks*, vii–viii.

30. Quoted in Downman, *Services*, 65.

31. NAS, GD 21/492, Papers of Lt., later Capt., John Peebles of the 42nd Foot, 1776–82, book 11, 16–21.

32. As the battalions of the Fourth Brigade were reminded in May 1777, "In marching by sub- or grand-divisions, it is expected that the officers be very attentive to preserve their exact distance from the front rank of the preceding

division." LOC, Washington Papers, British 40th Regt. Orderly Book, Brigade Orders, 10 May 1777.

33. See for instance Ewald, *Diary of the American War*, 279. See also Clinton, *American Rebellion*, 42. In the latter the published text states that Clinton's advanced guard at Long Island marched "in one column by half-battalions, ranks and files close," though "half companies" makes more military sense and agrees with WO 36/5, After Orders, 5 P.M., 26 Aug. 1776.

34. Clinton, *American Rebellion*, 95n16. Dundas took up the complaint in 1788. Dundas, *Principles*, 190.

35. Baurmeister, *Revolution in America*, 36. On the night-march before the battle of Long Island, the 17th Regiment advanced in the van of the Fourth and Sixth Brigades by files. Cohen, "Captain William Leslie's Paths to Glory," 61, Leslie to his father, 2 Sept. 1776.

36. This was the method advocated in the tactical instructions issued in 1772 to the newly raised light infantry in Ireland. Smythies, *Historical Records*, 549–52, "Rules and Orders for the Discipline of the Light Infantry Companies in His Majesty's Army in Ireland," 15 May 1772.

37. Sullivan, *From Redcoat to Rebel*, 51. Two months later at White Plains, the Second Brigade was ordered to move up from the rear in preparation for the attack. Sullivan, with the 49th Regiment, noted, "Accordingly *we faced to the left*, and marched up to an eminence, where the field pieces . . . were placed." Ibid., 67 (my emphasis). More specifically, when the expeditionary force sent to Savannah in late December 1778 had landed and formed up, "The corps destined for action marched from the right by files." Campbell, *Journal of an Expedition*, 25.

38. Campbell, *Journal of an Expedition*, 32, 48.

39. Newsome, "A British Orderly Book," 366, General Orders, 10 Feb. 1781.

40. See for instance Hadden, *Journal and Orderly Books*, 75–78; and Abbatt, *Major André's Journal*, 47.

41. See for instance the tactical instructions issued to the battalions of the Fourth Brigade in May 1777: LOC, Washington Papers, British 40th Regt. Orderly Book, Brigade Orders, 10 May 1777.

42. Dundas, *Principles*, 191.

43. Ewald, *Diary of the American War*, 83–85.

44. Bland, *Treatise*, 143.

45. Morristown National Historical Park, British HQ Orderly Book, General After Orders, 5 P.M., 26 Aug. 1776.

46. Kemble, "Papers," 1:451, Morning Orders, 27 June 1777.

47. The composition and activities of the British flanking parties during the march both to and from Concord are reconstructed in impressive detail in Galvin, *The Minute Men*, 114, 118–19, 123–25, 130, 168–69, 178–81, 208–11, 215, 222–23.

48. Sullivan, *From Redcoat to Rebel*, 51; Schmidt, *Hesse-Cassel Mirbach Regiment*, 90.

49. Atwood, *The Hessians*, 105. See also Muenchhausen, *At General Howe's Side*, 18; B. E. Burgoyne, *Defeat, Disaster, and Dedication*, 65, 66–68;

Kemble, "Papers," 1:97; Abbatt, *Major André's Journal*, 26-27, 30-31, 44, 71; [Montagu-Stuart-Wortley], *Prime Minister and His Son*, 115-16; and Huth, "Letters from a Hessian Mercenary," 499-500.

50. Dalrymple, *Tacticks*, ix.

51. Cuthbertson, *System*, 175. In 1788 Colonel David Dundas similarly complained that "filing, which was formerly little known or practiced in the infantry, is now general and often misapplied where division-marching should take place." Dundas, *Principles*, 11.

52. Atwood, *The Hessians*, 105. See also Baurmeister, *Revolution in America*, 63; and Ewald, *Diary of the American War*, 12.

53. Duffy, *Army of Frederick the Great*, 122.

54. Gibbes, *Documentary History of the American Revolution*, 2:139, Col. William Campbell to Rev. Cumming, n.d. The editor mistakenly dated this letter to September 1780.

55. Heath, *Memoirs*, 70.

56. Campbell, *Journal of an Expedition*, 17, "General Orders, on Board the *Phoenix* off Wassabaw Island," 23 Dec. 1778. If necessary, the front- and rear-rank men would simply have exchanged places to preserve their proper stations in the line.

57. LOC, Washington Papers, British 40th Regt. Orderly Book, Brigade Orders, 10 May 1777.

58. Ibid.

59. Campbell, *Journal of an Expedition*, 17-18, "General Orders, on Board the *Phoenix* off Wassabaw Island," 23 Dec. 1778.

60. Quoted in Ashmore and Olmstead, "Battles of Kettle Creek and Briar Creek," 114. Lieutenant Colonel Mark Prevost's 900-strong army at Briar Creek comprised a small force of light infantry, the 2nd Battalion of the 71st Regiment, three grenadier companies from the 60th Regiment, a small troop of dragoons, and "about 150 provincials, rangers and militia." *DAR*, 17:78, Maj. Gen. Prevost to Germain, 5 Mar. 1779.

61. Muenchhausen, *At General Howe's Side*, 31, 53 (map). See also *DAR*, 14:203, Howe to Germain, 10 Oct. 1777; Scull, "Montresor Journals," 449-50, diagram; and APSL, Anonymous British Journal, 1776-78, 11 Sept. 1777.

62. NAS, GD 21/492, Peebles papers, book 11, 16-21.

63. G. Smith, *Universal Military Dictionary*, 28.

64. For an explanation of the drawing up of the line of battle and the allocation of commands to the general officers, see Bland, *Treatise*, 297-301. See also Nosworthy, *Anatomy of Victory*, 81-82; and Kennett, *French Armies in the Seven Years' War*, 62-63.

65. Kemble, "Papers," 1:355; Cumming and Rankin, *Fate of a Nation*, manuscript plan facing 57; Campbell, *Journal of an Expedition*, 16-17, plate 2, General Orders, 23 Dec. 1778.

66. Simcoe, *Military Journal*, 194, General Orders, 23 or 24 Apr. 1781.

67. For the battle of Savannah, see Campbell, *Journal of an Expedition*, 25-29; and *DAR*, 17:35-36, Campbell to Germain, 16 Jan. 1779. For the affair at Petersburg (the largest skirmish in which Phillips's army was involved dur-

ing its operations), see Simcoe, *Military Journal*, 195–98; and Davis, *Where a Man Can Go*, 149–62.

68. Howe, *Narrative*, 8.

69. Sullivan, *From Redcoat to Rebel*, 133–34. For Howe's dispatch, on which Sullivan drew heavily, see *DAR*, 14:202–204, Howe to Germain, 10 Oct. 1777. The First and Second Brigades at Brandywine respectively comprised the 4th, 23rd, 28th, and 49th Regiments, and the 5th, 10th, 27th, 40th, and 55th Regiments.

70. Lee, *Revolutionary War Memoirs*, 130, 183, 183n. Lee was not present at either action.

71. LOC, Washington Papers, British 40th Regt. Orderly Book, Brigade Orders, 10 May 1777.

72. Tarleton, *History*, 221.

73. Simcoe, *Military Journal*, 188.

74. Abbatt, *Major André's Journal*, 46; Muenchhausen, *At General Howe's Side*, 31.

75. *DAR*, 20:184, Cornwallis to Clinton, 8 July 1781; S. Graham, "An English Officer's Account," 270.

76. *DAR*, 14:199, Clinton to Howe, 9 Oct. 1777.

77. Clinton, *American Rebellion*, 94, 95, 95n16.

78. R. Mackenzie, *Strictures on Lt.-Col. Tarleton's History*, 115–17.

79. Stedman, *History*, 2:340. Stedman was writing of Cornwallis's dispositions at Guilford Courthouse.

80. Lee, *Revolutionary War Memoirs*, 337. See also *DAR*, 20:123, Rawdon to Cornwallis, 26 Apr. 1781.

81. *DAR*, 20:91, Cornwallis to Germain, 17 Mar. 1781.

82. Washington, *Papers*, 6:160, Stirling to Washington, 29 Aug. 1776. In the published letter Stirling's poor use of punctuation makes his description of Grant's deployment ambiguous. As reproduced here with modern punctuation, the passage reflects my interpretation of his meaning.

83. Sullivan, *From Redcoat to Rebel*, 67–70.

84. Ibid., 72.

85. Tarleton, *History*, 214–15, 216.

86. Hanger, *Address*, 104–105.

87. Babits, *Devil of a Whipping*, 45–46 and nn.

88. Lawrence Babits has questioned Tarleton's claim that his infantry fought "loosely formed" at Cowpens, citing the narrowness of the field. Indeed, Babits's map of the initial British dispositions shows the light infantry, British Legion infantry, and 7th Regiment deployed on a frontage of only about 200 yards—a distance that would have been barely wide enough for the three units even had they deployed with files closed up. The latter appears very unlikely. Significantly, in his biting attack on Tarleton's account of the action, Roderick Mackenzie (who was present with the 1st Battalion of the 71st Regiment) did not question the veracity of his assertion that the troops were "loosely formed," but its relevance: "If his files were too extensive, why did he not contract them?" Babits, *Devil of a Whipping*, 153–54, map 10, 85; R. Mackenzie, *Strictures on Lt.-Col. Tarleton's History*, 114–15.

## 5. MOTIVATION

*Epigraph.* Simcoe, *Military Journal,* 15.

1. See for instance M. Howard, *War in European History* (Oxford: Oxford University Press, 1976), 66; and M. S. Anderson, *War of the Austrian Succession,* 33. For a dissenting view on the nature of voluntary recruits, see Duffy, *Military Experience in the Age of Reason,* 89–91.

2. Blanning, *French Revolutionary Wars,* 119.

3. Frey, *British Soldier in America,* 128–29. See also Martin and Lender, *Respectable Army,* 38.

4. WLCL, Loftus Cliffe Papers, Cliffe to Jack, 21 Sept. 1776.

5. See for instance Cohen, "Captain William Leslie's Paths to Glory," 65; Abbatt, *Major André's Journal,* 42–43; Pell, "Diary," 109; and Wasmus, *Eyewitness Account,* 72.

6. Frey, *British Soldier in America,* 118–22.

7. Interestingly, none of the evidence that Mark Odintz has cited for the development of regimental traditions by the 1770s directly relates to the period before the 1790s. Odintz, "British Officer Corps," 21–22.

8. We may safely discount the suggestion that one satirist proffered to British officers—that the colors supplied an excellent covering for the gaming table—to prevent its being soiled. [Grose], *Advice to the Officers,* 81–82.

9. For instance, the broadswords and iron-stocked pistols that were issued to the 42nd ("Royal Highland") Regiment before it went to America were put into store upon its arrival. Stewart, *Sketches,* 1:367, 399.

10. Houlding, *Fit for Service,* 23–90, 391–92.

11. According to Houlding's survey, three-quarters of the officers with eight sample regiments in 1775 were no longer with them by 1783. Ibid., 107n23.

12. For the practice of drafting, see ibid., 120–25. For the transfer of men between corps in America before the war, see Shy, *Toward Lexington,* 359–63.

13. Compiled from review data in WO 27/31, 32, 35.

14. Duffy, *Military Experience in the Age of Reason,* 95. For an analysis of the manpower problems that regiments faced in the British Isles—too few recruits to complete establishments, yet too many recruits in the ranks to maintain efficiency—see Houlding, *Fit for Service,* 116–37.

15. WO 27/35, 12/4803/1, 12/5478.

16. Frey, *British Soldier in America,* 23–26.

17. See for instance Odintz, "British Officer Corps," esp. 391–92.

18. Duffy, *Military Experience in the Age of Reason,* 101–103. See also J. C. R. Childs, *The British Army of William III, 1698–1702* (Manchester: Manchester University Press, 1987), 127; and N. A. M. Rodger, *The Wooden World: An Anatomy of the Georgian Navy* (London: Collins, 1986), 118, 198–200.

19. B. Rush, *Letters of Benjamin Rush,* ed. L. H. Butterfield, 2 vols. (Princeton, N.J.: Princeton University Press, 1951), 1:155, Rush to John Adams, 1 Oct. 1777.

20. Uhlendorf, *Siege of Charleston*, 297, 299; Allaire, *Diary*, 16; Gruber, *John Peebles' American War*, 374.

21. *John Robert Shaw*, 41–42.

22. T. Hughes, *Journal*, 14–15.

23. A. Hulton, *Letters of a Loyalist Lady, being the Letters of A. Hulton, Sister of Henry Hulton, Commissioner of Customs at Boston, 1767–1776* (Cambridge, Mass.: Harvard University Press, 1927), 98, Henry Hulton to unknown, 20 June 1775. According to Lieutenant William Fielding, the marines mourned Pitcairn for six weeks. Balderston and Syrett, *The Lost War*, 33, Fielding to Lord Denbigh, 18 July 1775.

24. Hayes, *Stephen Jarvis*, 33, 34–35.

25. Tarleton, *History*, 30–31.

26. Anburey, *Travels*, 2:508–509.

27. Conway, " 'Great Mischief Complain'd Of,' " 387–89.

28. Gruber, *John Peebles' American War*, 368.

29. Ibid., 507.

30. In barracks or billets, the "mess" comprised six to eight soldiers. In the field the mess group probably corresponded with the tent group of five men. G. Smith, *Universal Military Dictionary*, 175, 243. For a summary of the importance of the "primary group" in warfare, see J. A. Lynn, *Bayonets of the Republic*, chap. 2, esp. 30–35.

31. Duffy, *Military Experience in the Age of Reason*, 135; M. S. Anderson, *War of the Austrian Succession*, 35.

32. Cuthbertson, *System*, 17–18.

33. Sullivan, *From Redcoat to Rebel*, 7–8.

34. NYSC, British Orderly Book kept by Capt. Frederick DePeyster, Detachment Orders, 23 Jan. 1780.

35. Simes, *Military Course*, 210n.

36. For example, in 1781 the 42nd Regiment's pipers and band of music played alternately at a St. Andrew's Day celebratory event attended by Prince William at New York. Gruber, *John Peebles' American War*, 497. For the tendency of regimental officers to congregate with their ethnic peers, see Odintz, "British Officer Corps," 556–66.

37. For the lyrics, sung to the jaunty tune "Langolee," see Moore, *Diary of the American Revolution*, 2:261–62.

38. Cuthbertson, *System*, 66–67.

39. *Considerations upon the Different Modes of Finding Recruits*, 5–6.

40. S. Graham, "An English Officer's Account," 244.

41. *Considerations upon the Different Modes of Finding Recruits*, 11–12. See also Simes, *Military Course*, 162.

42. "A Frenchman's Comments," 365. See also HMC, *Rawdon Hastings*, 3:167, Rawdon to Lord Huntingdon, 13 Jan. 1776. For rivalry between the attacking British and Hessian corps at Chatterton's Hill, see Atwood, *The Hessians*, 74.

43. For review reports for 1775, see WO 27/35.

44. The regiment shared with the Queen's Rangers and Roman Catholic Volunteers a monopoly on the recruitment of Irish deserters from the

rebels. See *DAR*, 15:227–29, Clinton to Germain, 23 Oct. 1778; Clinton, *American Rebellion*, 110–11; and Kemble, "Papers," 1:588.

45. Records of recruits' county of origin exist for the 2nd ("Coldstream") Regiment of Foot Guards and the 58th Regiment. These show that the northwest and southwest of England provided a disproportionate number of the English-born recruits. Frey, *British Soldier in America*, 10–11, table 1. For an analysis of the composition of the 58th Regiment during the Seven Years War, see Brumwell, "Rank and File," 3–24.

46. Quoted in Lunt, *Duke of Wellington's Regiment*, 13.

47. *John Robert Shaw*, 15–16.

48. WO 27/35. See also Frey, *British Soldier in America*, 10–11.

49. Odintz, "British Officer Corps," 383–84.

50. See for instance Hadden, *Journal and Orderly Books*, 230, 234; and Kemble, "Papers," 1:555. In August 1781, when the weakened 40th Regiment returned to New York (after three years in Florida, the West Indies, and with the fleet), it recovered those of its recruits who had been drafted into other corps during its absence and received drafts of men from other units, including recently exchanged men from the Convention Army. Gruber, *John Peebles' American War*, 469; NYHS, British HQ Orderly Book, 1 Aug. 1781–20 Feb. 1782, General Orders, 30 Aug., 15 Sept., 15 Nov., 27 Oct. 1781.

51. British Library, St. Pancras, Burley Collection of Early English Newspapers (microfilm), 691b, *The London Chronicle*, 133 vols. (London, 1757–1823), vol. 48, no. 3729, 26 Oct. 1780, 398, extract from a letter written by an officer of the Volunteers of Ireland to his friend in Glasgow, Camden, 25 Aug. 1780.

52. Lamb, *Journal*, 361.

53. "Extracts from the Letterbook of Captain Hinrichs," 168, Hinrichs to his brother, 4 July 1780.

54. S. Graham, "An English Officer's Account," 269. The "two Scotch regiments" were the 76th ("MacDonnell's Highlanders") and 80th ("Royal Edinburgh Volunteers") Regiments, which were raised in Britain in 1777–78 and dispatched to America in 1779.

55. Lamb, *Memoir*, 90–91.

56. Royal Artillery Institute, Royal Artillery Brigade Orderly Book, Brigade Orders, Philadelphia, 1 Jan. 1778.

57. Pattison, "Official Letters," 211, Pattison to Lt. Col. Martin, 31 Aug. 1780.

58. Hunter, *Journal*, 27.

59. Lushington, *Life and Services of General Lord Harris*, 86, Harris to his uncle, 16 Jan. 1777 (my emphasis).

60. See for instance Gruber, *John Peebles' American War*, 70.

61. For the history of both tunes, and for a song composed during the American War for the light infantry (published in New York in the loyalist newspaper *The Royal Gazette*), see Winstock, *Songs and Music of the Redcoats*, 29–36, 75–76. One British military writer asserted in 1759 that "The Grenadiers' March" "should never be beat but with the grenadiers; or when the whole advance to charge an enemy." In 1772, when the King noticed that

the 23rd Regiment played it on all occasions, he insisted "that the same march must be beat by the Welch Fusiliers as is observed by the other corps on the same establishment." Camus, *Military Music*, 109–11.

62. Hunter, *Journal*, 29.

63. Wilkin, *Some British Soldiers*, 231, Hale to his parents, 21 Oct. 1777. At Brandywine the 1st Battalion of Grenadiers may have fielded fifty-two fifers and drummers, the battalion probably having comprised the grenadier companies of the 4th, 5th, 10th, 15th, 17th, 22nd, 23rd, 27th, 28th, 33rd, 35th, 37th, and 38th Regiments. The three battalions of Hessian grenadiers, in the second line, also put on their heavy brass-fronted caps prior to the attack and beat their own march as they advanced. Ibid., 245–46, Hale to his parents, 23 Mar. 1778; Heath, *Memoirs*, 117.

64. Hunter, *Journal*, 34–35.

65. WLCL, Loftus Cliffe Papers, Cliffe to Jack, 24 Oct. 1777.

66. J. Burgoyne, *State of the Expedition*, 58–59.

67. Atwood, *The Hessians*, 118–19. Shortly before, at the Carpenters Island battery, Matross Donald MacLean of the elite Royal Artillery repeatedly pulled down the white handkerchief raised by Captain Blackmore of the 10th Regiment, attempting to prevent what artilleryman Captain Francis Downman described as "one of the most disgraceful events that has attended us." Downman, *Services*, 45. The affair is related in McGuire, *Philadelphia Campaign. Volume Two*, 187–90.

68. Houlding, *Fit for Service*, 160–62, 257–66. As Houlding has explained, the "evolutions" (which originally composed a distinct fifth element of drill) had by this time been absorbed into the "manual."

69. Ibid., chaps. 5–7.

70. WO 36/1, fo. 15, General Orders, 18 July 1774.

71. See for instance Kemble, "Papers," 1:605, 609; De Krafft, "Journal," 83, 108, 111, 132, 180–84; and Bardeleben, *Diary*, 88–89, 90, 91, 92, 94, 98–99, 100. Summer heat limited the New York garrison's training, Captain John Peebles of the 1st Battalion of Grenadiers writing in August 1780: "We march and maneuver through the adjoining fields every evening and morning, when it is not too hot." Gruber, *John Peebles' American War*, 402.

72. *DAR*, 11:192, Howe to Dartmouth, 26 Nov. 1775. Major General Phillips's verdict on the regiments that arrived in Canada from Ireland in 1776 was: "The troops are raw." Atkinson, "Some Evidence for Burgoyne's Expedition," 135, Phillips to Brig. Gen. Fraser, 7 Sept. 1776.

73. Sullivan, *From Redcoat to Rebel*, 3, 7. For the similar experience of Private Roger Lamb in 1773, see Lamb, *Memoir*, 61–62.

74. Houlding, *Fit for Service*, 274; *John Robert Shaw*, 11–17, 121; Kemble, "Papers," 1:472, 555.

75. Massachusetts Historical Society, British 40th Regt. Orderly Book, Regimental Orders, 22 Oct., 13 Nov. 1776. The 40th Regiment was part of the detachment with which General Lord Percy was ordered to defend New York City.

76. Hadden, *Journal and Orderly Books*, 140, 141.

77. Sullivan, *From Redcoat to Rebel*, 50. That these men had not yet received their regimentals probably means that they still wore the jackets and

trousers with which eighteenth-century recruits seem to have been issued at British depots like Chatham, Stirling Castle, and Kinsale. It was there that recruits for corps serving outside the British Isles were concentrated and where they began their training prior to embarking overseas. See Reid and Hook, *British Redcoat*, 35, plate C, 50–51.

78. Gruber, *John Peebles' American War*, 25.

79. Stewart, *Sketches*, 2:50–51.

80. Simcoe, *Military Journal*, 21, 107.

81. Quoted in McGuire, *Philadelphia Campaign. Volume Two*, 20. In a letter dated 20 October 1777, Major General Grant reminded General Harvey that Erskine had made this comment at a dinner in London at which (according to Cornwallis) Harvey had made Erskine repeat it.

82. Lamb, *Journal*, 143.

83. See for instance Sullivan, *From Redcoat to Rebel*, 50; Tarleton, *History*, 354; Baurmeister, *Revolution in America*, 445–47; and Lee, *Revolutionary War Memoirs*, 467n.

84. See for instance Stedman, *History*, 2:378–79; Lee, *Revolutionary War Memoirs*, 389, 389n; Hanger, *Address*, 102; Tarleton, *History*, 212, 216.

85. Moore, *Diary of the American Revolution*, 1:326, extract from anonymous letter, 23 Oct. 1776, published in *Freeman's Journal*, 12 Nov. 1776.

86. Barker, *British in Boston*, 32, 39.

87. WO 36/1, fo. 43, General Orders, 22 Apr. 1775. For the concern over indiscipline at Bunker Hill, see HMC, *Rawdon Hastings*, 3:157; and De Fonblanque, *Political and Military Episodes*, 147.

88. F. Mackenzie, *Diary*, 1:25–26. This eyewitness account, which Mackenzie copied into his own diary, was penned by a flank company officer.

89. *Discord and Civil Wars*, 21–22.

90. See Duffy, *Military Experience in the Age of Reason*, 196–97, 252–534.

91. *Considerations upon the Different Modes of Finding Recruits*, 18.

92. Ewald, *Treatise*, 69.

93. Quoted in Fuller, *British Light Infantry*, 146. Although Fuller wrote that this incident occurred on 26 October 1776, Ewald almost certainly was referring to an affair on 23 October 1776 near La Rochelle in which "a handful of my *Jäger* engaged with several battalions of Americans." See Ewald, *Diary of the American War*, 9–10.

94. Lamb, *Memoir*, 175–76. For similar sentiments, see Anburey, *Travels*, 1:337–38.

95. See for instance Adlum, *Memoirs*, 82; Balderston and Syrett, *The Lost War*, 33.

96. Lamb, *Journal*, 107.

97. Stedman, *History*, 1:222–23.

98. Peckham, *Sources of American Independence*, 2:301–302, Ferguson to Clinton, 1 Aug. 1778.

99. Murdoch, *Rebellion in America*, 385.

100. Simcoe, *Military Journal*, 17–18.

101. "Extracts from the Letterbook of Captain Hinrichs," 146, Hinrichs

to Herr H., 14 June 1778. See also Muenchhausen, *At General Howe's Side*, 52; Pausch, *Journal and Reports*, 59, 60–63; Pettengill, *Letters from America*, 153–54; and Döhla, *Hessian Diary*, 71.

102. See for instance Duffy, *Military Experience in the Age of Reason*, 31.

103. Quoted in ibid., 31–32.

104. Drewe, *Military Sketches*, 45. Not all senior British military figures necessarily approved of this independent spirit. See Willcox, *Portrait of a General*, 80.

105. Impressive British victories like Camden were occasionally celebrated in a similar fashion. See for instance Gruber, *John Peebles' American War*, 408; and De Krafft, "Journal," 120.

106. F. C. L. Riedesel, *Baroness von Riedesel*, 110. Because the servicemen were sailors and described their destination as "an excellent naval hospital near London," the baroness clearly meant the Royal Naval Hospital at Greenwich rather than the Royal Military Hospital at Chelsea.

107. Quoted in McGuire, *Philadelphia Campaign. Volume One*, 245; *Papers of the Continental Congress, 1774–1789*, National Archives Microfilm Publications M247 (Washington, D.C., 1958), reel 94, 387, Alexander Dow to the President of Congress, 23 May 1781. I am most grateful to Mr. Don H. Hagist for supplying this extract.

108. Lawrence's diary is reproduced in G. A. Wheeler, *History of Castine, Penobscot, and Brooksville, Maine* (Bangor, Maine: Burr and Robinson, 1875), 314–20.

109. Sampson, *Escape in America*, chap. 11, app. 5.

110. Ibid., 65–73, 96; Frey, *British Soldier in America*, 131.

111. Frey, *British Soldier in America*, 129–32.

112. Lamb, *Memoir*, 249, 270.

113. See for instance Gruber, "For King and Country," 21–40.

114. Conway, "British Army Officers and the American War," 265–76; Conway, "To Subdue America," 396–97; Conway, *War of American Independence*, 39–40.

115. Townshend, "Some Account of the British Army," 23.

116. Sullivan, *From Redcoat to Rebel*, 221–22. Sullivan claimed to have attempted unsuccessfully to desert at Boston in September 1775, soon after the 49th Regiment arrived in America. His journal gives the date of his successful desertion as 25 June 1778. The muster list for Captain Nicholas Wade's light company gives the date as 26 June 1778. WO 12/6032/1, item 98.

117. For Sullivan, the army was "a repository for all manner of vice" in which a man who endeavored "to maintain and practice his duty before GOD . . . will be derided and laughed at, and hated by some, while others load him with reproaches." Sullivan, *From Redcoat to Rebel*, 222–23. Sullivan's education and intelligence are evident from his writing a lengthy and detailed journal as well as acting as battalion clerk successively for the 49th Regiment and the 2nd Battalion of Light Infantry. Ibid., 136, 150. His change in unit stemmed from an incident on 14 September 1777, when his commanding officer, Lieutenant Colonel Sir Henry Calder, "abused [him] very grossly," reduced him from corporal, and apparently deprived him of his post as battalion clerk over a misunderstanding about some plundered mutton. This

"ill-treatment" not only led the disgruntled Sullivan to transfer to the 2nd Battalion of Light Infantry on 10 October but also, he later claimed, roused his lingering desire for freedom. See Ibid., 136, 147, 222.

118. Quoted in Murdock, *Bunker Hill*, 35.

119. De Fonblanque, *Political and Military Episodes*, 147, Burgoyne to Lord Rochford, n.d. See also Willcox, *Portrait of a General*, 80–81.

120. Sullivan, *From Redcoat to Rebel*, 26.

121. See for instance Adlum, *Memoirs*, 82, 84–85; and [Graydon], *Memoirs*, 183, 188.

122. Moore, *Diary of the American Revolution*, 1:289, anonymous letter, 17 Aug. 1776.

123. Muenchhausen, *At General Howe's Side*, 38. The resolution was passed on 20 February 1778, and news of it reached the army in Philadelphia by express frigate on 14 April.

124. B. Willson, *The Life and Letters of James Wolfe* (London: W. Heinemann, 1909), 392, Wolfe to Sackville, 7 Aug. 1758. For an analysis of the disastrous British misjudgment of the colonial militia, see Shy, *People Numerous and Armed*, 29–41.

125. HMC, *Rawdon Hastings*, 3:167, Rawdon to his uncle, 13 Jan. 1776. See also Bolton, *Letters of Hugh, Earl Percy*, 31, 44; Evelyn, *Memoir and Letters*, 27, 36, 49–50, 51–52, 53; Barker, *British in Boston*, 45; Pell, "Diary," 44; Serle, *American Journal*, 106; Wilkin, *Some British Soldiers*, 242–43; and Commager and Morris, *Spirit of 'Seventy-Six*, 61–62, 150, 152–53. See also Conway, "To Subdue America," 395–96.

126. Biddulph, "Letters," 90, letter, 4 Sept. 1781.

127. Adlum, *Memoirs*, 84–85.

128. *Orderly Book of the Three Battalions of Loyalists*, 30, After Orders, 24 Aug. 1777. See also Kemble, "Papers," 1:398, 409–10, 434–35, 451, 493, 501, 510, 602.

129. Murray, *Letters from America*, 36, Murray to his sister, 31 Aug. 1776. Captain Murray was writing in the aftermath of the British victory at Long Island.

130. Simcoe, *Military Journal*, 15.

131. WLCL, Loftus Cliffe Papers, Cliffe to Jack, 21 Sept. 1776.

132. Hunter, *Journal*, 34.

133. Muenchhausen, *At General Howe's Side*, 18.

134. Cresswell, *Journal*, 242.

135. *Detail and Conduct of the American War*, 32, anonymous letter, 16 Dec. 1777.

136. "Battle of Princeton, by Sergeant R——," 517.

137. Bradford, "Lord Francis Napier's Journal," 324.

138. Moore, *Diary of the American Revolution*, 2:508n, extract from a letter published in *The New Jersey Gazette*, 7 Nov. 1781.

139. [MacDowell], "Journal," 303; Thacher, *Military Journal*, 280; Denny, "Military Journal," 248; Martin, *Private Yankee Doodle*, 240–41.

140. Thacher, *Military Journal*, 280.

141. S. Graham, "An English Officer's Account," 273. Even the supposedly phlegmatic German mercenaries were affected by the defeat. Private

Johann Conrad Döhla of the Bayreuth Regiment wrote that, when his colonel gave the order to ground arms, "we executed the command, but not without his and our tears." Döhla, *Hessian Diary*, 178.

142. Blanchard, *Journal*, 152, 153.

143. See Mathieu Dumas, *Memoirs of His Own Time*, 2 vols. (Philadelphia: Lea & Blanchard, 1839), 1:52n–53n.

144. Lushington, *Life and Services of General Lord Harris*, 101, Reserve Orders, 25 Dec. 1778.

145. Lindsay, *Lives of the Lindsays*, 3:343n, 350, "Narrative of the Occupation and Defence of the Island of St. Lucie against the French, 1779."

146. Blanchard, *Journal*, 125–26, 154. See also Ewald, *Diary of the American War*, 342.

147. See for instance [Graydon], *Memoirs*, 186–87; Cresswell, *Journal*, 160; Pettengill, *Letters from America*, 81, 132; F. C. L. Riedesel, *Baroness von Riedesel*, 67; and "Diary of a French Officer," 6 (1880): 209. For Continental Army officers' increasing jealousy for their status, see Royster, *Revolutionary People*, esp. 86–96.

148. Adlum, *Memoirs*, 82–83.

149. Cuthbertson, *System*, 107.

150. Hence, before the newly raised Royal Highland Emigrants received their regimentals, the regulars of the Halifax garrison taunted them as "ragged rascals." McDonald, "Letter-Book," 259, 296–97, letter, 24 Mar. 1776.

151. Quoted in Willcox, *Portrait of a General*, 81.

152. In October Cresswell dismissed the 6th Virginia Regiment as "[a] set of dirty, ragged people, badly clothed, badly disciplined and badly armed." Cresswell, *Journal*, 159, 163–64.

153. F. Mackenzie, *Diary*, 1:111–12.

154. See for example Serle, *American Journal*, 88; Tarleton, "New War Letters," 64; Bardeleben, *Diary*, 57; Schmidt, *Hesse-Cassel Mirbach Regiment*, 54; Ewald, *Diary of the American War*, 238, 340–41, 355; Baurmeister, *Revolution in America*, 156; Pettengill, *Letters from America*, 105; Hunter, *Journal*, 19; Wilkin, *Some British Soldiers*, 241–42; Gruber, *John Peebles' American War*, 372; and *John Robert Shaw*, 42.

155. See for instance Wilkin, *Some British Soldiers*, 249–50, anonymous letter, 20 Apr. 1778.

156. Kemble, "Papers," 1:429, General Orders, 12 Dec. 1776.

157. Ewald, *Treatise*, 115.

158. Barker, *British in Boston*, 35–36. Another officer observed, "When we got to Charlestown Neck the rebels' fire ceased, they not having it in their power to pursue us any further in their skulking way behind hedges and walls." Innes, "Jeremy Lister," 66.

159. Bolton, *Letters of Hugh, Earl Percy*, 52, 53, Percy to General Harvey, 20 Apr. 1775. See also Fortescue, *Correspondence of King George the Third*, 3:215.

160. Cresswell, *Journal*, 258; NAS, GD 174/2106, 2107, Orders, 15 Sept. 1777.

161. Force, *American Archives: Fourth Series*, 2:440, anonymous letter, 28 Apr. 1775.

162. Lamb, *Memoir*, 174.

163. See Anburey, *Travels*, 1:330–31; Muenchhausen, *At General Howe's Side*, 50; Bardeleben, *Diary*, 63–64; F. Mackenzie, *Diary*, 1:48; Baurmeister, *Revolution in America*, 49; and Sullivan, *From Redcoat to Rebel*, 130.

164. Anburey, *Travels*, 1:331.

165. Carter, *Genuine Detail*, 7, Carter to unknown, 2 July 1775.

166. Serle, *American Journal*, 36, 47, 72.

167. Author's possession, Diary of Thompson Forster, 72, 91n(a).

168. Döhla, *Hessian Diary*, 15, 71–72.

169. Quoted in McGuire, *Philadelphia Campaign. Volume One*, 15.

170. Serle, *American Journal*, 95; Martin, *Private Yankee Doodle*, 33. In similar circumstances almost exactly one year later, during the clandestine evacuation of Fort Mifflin, the rebels heard voices from a British sloop eagerly anticipating the next day's planned assault on the fortress: "We will give it to the damned rebels in the morning." Martin, *Private Yankee Doodle*, 93.

171. HMC, *Rawdon Hastings*, 3:183–84, Rawdon to Lord Huntingdon, 23 Sept. 1776.

172. Martin, *Private Yankee Doodle*, 215.

173. [Graydon], *Memoirs*, 182–85, 201.

174. See also Adlum, *Memoirs*, 78; and Force, *American Archives: Fifth Series*, 1:1254, "Journal of the Transactions of August 27, 1776 . . . by Colonel Samuel J. Atlee."

## 6. THE ADVANCE

*Epigraph*. Dundas, *Principles*, 12.

1. Ibid., 51–53.

2. See for instance Duffy, *Army of Frederick the Great*, 119; Nosworthy, *Battle Tactics*, 193–94; Harding, *Smallarms*, 357; and Nafziger, *Imperial Bayonets*, 44–46. Nafziger has calculated that most Peninsular War British battalions would have been too weak to comply with the regulation company frontage (a minimum of twenty files) while in three ranks.

3. Dundas, *Principles*, 11–13, 50–51, 53. For a good modern treatment of this tactical shift, see Brumwell, *Redcoats*, 245–63.

4. Smythies, *Historical Records*, 549–52, "Townshend's Rules and Orders for the Discipline of the Light Infantry Companies in His Majesty's Army in Ireland," 15 May 1772; NAM, Howe's Light Infantry Discipline.

5. WO 36/1, fo. 19, General Orders, 14 Aug. 1774.

6. F. Mackenzie, *Diary*, 1:19. See also *Discord and Civil Wars*, 11.

7. WO 36/1, fo. 53, General Orders, After Orders, 3 June 1775.

8. [Montagu-Stuart-Wortley], *Prime Minister and His Son*, 69, Stuart to his father, 24 July 1775; Clinton quoted in French, *First Year of the American Revolution*, 235. Although Stuart arrived in America after the battle, Clinton watched the initial attack from the Copp's Hill Battery in Boston.

9. Dundas, *Principles*, 50–51.

10. Scheer and Rankin, *Rebels and Redcoats*, 59, extract from Robert Steele to William Sumner, 10 July 1825; Heath, *Memoirs*, 12; Commager and Morris, *Spirit of 'Seventy-Six*, 127, Rev. Peter Thacher's narrative. The grena-

dier battalion and the battalion companies of the 5th, 38th, 43rd, and 52nd Regiments made this initial attack.

11. HMC, *Stopford-Sackville*, 2:5, Howe to Adm. Lord Howe, 22 June 1775. See also Fortescue, *Correspondence of King George the Third*, 3:221–22, Howe to Gen. Harvey, 22/24 June 1775; *DAR*, 9:198, Gage to Dartmouth (No. 33), 25 June 1775; Hunter, *Journal*, 10–11; and Force, *American Archives: Fourth Series*, 2:1094–95, Burgoyne to Lord Stanley, 25 June 1775.

12. Boston Public Library, Stanley Letters, Stanley to unknown, 7 Aug. 1775.

13. Commager and Morris, *Spirit of 'Seventy-Six*, 629, Lt. Col. T. Will Heth to Col. John Lamb, 12 Oct. 1777. Heth's corps was the 3rd Virginia Regiment, in Brigadier General George Weedon's division. The right wing, advancing down the Germantown High Road, fared similarly, according to its commanding officer, Major General Sullivan: "we were compelled to remove every fence as we passed, which delayed us much." Quoted in McGuire, *Philadelphia Campaign. Volume Two*, 73. For a similar comment on the rebel advance at Eutaw Springs, see Gibbes, *Documentary History of the American Revolution*, 3:146, "Account furnished by Col. Otho Williams. . . ."

14. Hunt, *Fragments of Revolutionary History*, 50, Lt. Col. Mercer to Col. Simms, c.1809–17. See also Lee, *Revolutionary War Memoirs*, 435.

15. Stevens, *Howe's Orderly Book*, 222, General Orders, 29 Feb. 1776. This is the published version of what appears to be the original manuscript headquarters order book, preserved as PRO 30/55/106 and 30/55/107.

16. Ibid., 294, General Orders, 26 May 1776. This published version of the text corresponds precisely with its manuscript source (PRO 30/55/107, fo. 273). But an alternative manuscript copy of Howe's headquarters order book records the instruction with a significant textual variation: "The grenadiers and battalions in the line, are to form in future *in the ranks* with the file as formerly ordered, at eighteen inches interval." WO 36/5, General Orders, 26 May 1776 (my emphasis). This variation makes little sense, given that the grenadiers and line battalions were already forming in this fashion (since 29 February) and that the wording of Howe's next order on the subject of infantry formations (on 22 July, which fails to mention files) strongly implies that some of his infantry were not at that time forming in two ranks, as he now wanted them to do. This variation was therefore almost certainly a transcription error.

17. For the exercises at Halifax, see chap. 7.

18. WO 36/5, General Orders, 22 July 1776. This was not the exact wording of Howe's original instruction, which was ambiguous: two days later he ordered that "[t]he words 'in line' [are] to be erased out of the orders of the 22nd instant relative to the troops forming two deep." Ibid., General Orders, 24 July 1776. That the text of the 22 July order appears in this particular manuscript without the errant words "in line" must prove that it is a later duplication of Howe's original headquarters order book. Unfortunately, the manuscript version (PRO 30/55/106 and 30/55/107) runs only from 17 June 1775 to 26 May 1776, making comparison difficult.

19. WO 36/5, General Orders, 1 Aug. 1776.

20. Author's possession, Diary of Thompson Forster, 94.

21. Hadden, *Journal and Orderly Books*, 198, General Orders, 29 June 1776.

22. Stanley, *For Want of a Horse*, 69. The 47th Regiment left Halifax in April 1776 for Quebec, where it arrived in time to participate in the relief of the city on 6 May.

23. Hadden, *Journal and Orderly Books*, 75, General Orders, 20 June 1777.

24. Wilkinson, *Memoirs of My Own Times*, 1:267.

25. Quoted in Clinton, *American Rebellion*, 95n16.

26. Campbell, *Journal of an Expedition*, 16–17, and plate 2, General Orders, 23 Dec. 1778. One of Campbell's maneuvers enabled an army, battalion, or detachment formed in line to change its front to the rear. To achieve this, "the soldiers of the front rank go immediately to the right about, and spring one pace into the intervals of the rear rank" while "the men of the rear rank step one pace forward, turn to the right about and cover their former file leaders." This tells us that Campbell's infantry deployed in two ranks with one pace between the ranks and intervals between the files at least as wide as a man. Campbell's orders of battle indicated the precise number of rank and file that each line of battle comprised and how much frontage it required. From these one can calculate that he allowed an interval of eight yards between battalions for a single gun (or no gun) and sixteen yards for a pair of guns. Given that, in his third order of battle, Campbell's total of 1,172 rank and file for the first line should read 1,772; it is clear that in each case he allowed one yard per file, or eighteen inches per man and eighteen inches per file interval. Interestingly, Campbell's plan assumed that the two Hessian regiments in his force would also deploy with open files. I am most grateful to my fiancée, Sarah Day, for having unraveled Campbell's calculations.

27. Ibid., 51.

28. Clinton, *American Rebellion*, 247; Tarleton, *History*, 221.

29. Simcoe, *Military Journal*, 188, Maj. Gen. Phillips's General Orders, Apr. 1781.

30. F. Mackenzie, *Diary*, 2:660.

31. See Atwood, *The Hessians*, 61, 68, 82–83, 243–44. For evidence that the Hessians fought two deep in close order in the South, see Baurmeister, *Revolution in America*, 169, 253–54; and Lamb, *Journal*, 354.

32. In July Major General Baron Riedesel wrote that he was ashamed when the ranks of the Brunswick regiments were open and the middle-rank men became visible and that, when practicing the firings, Lieutenant Colonel Friedrich Breymann's grenadiers "get down on their knees better" than Riedesel's own corps did. Both statements clearly imply a three-rank formation. F. A. Riedesel, *Memoirs, Letters, and Journals*, 1:233, 245, letters to the Hereditary Prince Charles William Ferdinand, July 1776.

33. Eelking, *German Allied Troops*, 270–71 (see also 93).

34. F. A. Riedesel, *Memoirs, Letters, and Journals*, 1:58, 64.

35. Papet, *Canada during the American Revolutionary War*, 66.

36. Eelking, *German Allied Troops*, 129, 272–73.

37. F. A. Riedesel, *Memoirs, Letters, and Journals*, 1:204. The corps concerned were the Regiment von Riedesel and two companies from the Regiment von Rhetz.

38. Pettengill, *Letters from America*, 70–71, anonymous letter, n.d.

39. Ewald, *Treatise*, 73.

40. Duffy, *Military Experience in the Age of Reason*, 110–11, 201, 203.

41. Bland, *Treatise*, 156–57.

42. Duffy, *Army of Frederick the Great*, 118.

43. Houlding, *Fit for Service*, 259–60 and n8. Contemporary military treatises tended to define one pace as 2.5 feet. See Cavan, *New System*, 41; G. Smith, *Universal Military Dictionary*, 198; and Pickering, *Easy Plan*, 41.

44. Cuthbertson, *System*, 173. See also Simes, *Military Course*, 195.

45. Dalrymple, *Tacticks*, 22–24.

46. Pickering, *Easy Plan*, 160.

47. Simcoe, *Military Journal*, 98.

48. Tarleton, *History*, 273. Stedman's account was clearly closely based on Tarleton's narrative. See Stedman, *History*, 2:339.

49. See for instance Tarleton, *History*, map facing 276; and Hatch, *Battle of Guilford Courthouse*, maps 1–5.

50. Simcoe, *Military Journal*, 96–97.

51. Lushington, *Life and Services of General Lord Harris*, 76, Capt. George Harris to his uncle, n.d.; Heath, *Memoirs*, 70; Muenchhausen, *At General Howe's Side*, 31; Commager and Morris, *Spirit of 'Seventy-Six*, 595, account of Ebenezer Mattoon; Stedman, *History*, 1:361; Gruber, *John Peebles' American War*, 193.

52. Quotes from Lawrence, "Howe and the British Capture of Savannah," 320; Dann, *The Revolution Remembered*, 179, deposition of James Fergus; Simcoe, *Military Journal*, 231, 232.

53. Scheer and Rankin, *Rebels and Redcoats*, 430, Thomas Young's memoir; James Collins, *Autobiography of a Revolutionary Soldier*, ed. J. M. Roberts (Clinton, La.: Feliciana Democrat, 1859), 264.

54. Balderston and Syrett, *The Lost War*, 126, Bowater to Lord Denbigh, 22 May 1777.

55. Gruber, *John Peebles' American War*, 63.

56. *Some British Soldiers*, 245–46, Hale to his parents, 23 Mar. 1778. For another denunciation of the Hessian grenadiers' slowness at Brandywine, see Seybolt, "A Contemporary British Account," 79.

57. Quoted in McGuire, *Philadelphia Campaign. Volume Two*, 75.

58. The quick step was reserved for wheeling. See *Order Book of the Hesse-Cassel von Mirbach Regiment*, 26–27, order, 10 May 1777.

59. Atwood, *The Hessians*, 66, 243–44 and n59.

60. J. Burgoyne, *Supplement*, 7, General Orders, 30 May 1777.

61. Hadden, *Journal and Orderly Books*, 77, General Orders, 20 June 1777.

62. Pausch, *Journal and Reports*, 49–50, 52, 59.

63. WO 36/1, General Morning Orders, 10 A.M., 17 June 1775. Captain George Harris was wounded in the head leading the 5th Regiment's grenadier company at Bunker Hill, and later described his waterborne evacuation to Boston: "[O]ur blankets had been flung away during the engagement; luckily there was one belonging to a man in the boat, in which wrapping me up, and laying me in the bottom, they conveyed me safely to my quarters." Lushing-

ton, *Life and Services of General Lord Harris*, 55, memo by Lord Harris [?], n.d.For the root of the erroneous historical tradition that the redcoats fought in full kit, see Stedman, *History*, 1:128, 129.

64. Lushington, *Life and Services of General Lord Harris*, 78, Harris to his uncle, n.d. Harris meant that the grenadiers had cast off their blankets at the battle of Long Island as they chased the fleeing rebels into the Brooklyn lines.

65. Tarleton, *History*, 216.

66. Townshend, "Some Account of the British Army," 25.

67. Gruber, *John Peebles' American War*, 194. The Third Brigade comprised the 15th, 17th, 42nd, and 44th Regiments. Joseph Plumb Martin, a private in the 8th Connecticut Regiment, noticed that the retiring Highlanders of the 42nd Regiment with whom he skirmished in the Sutfin Farm orchard toward the end of the battle were "divested of their packs." Martin, *Private Yankee Doodle*, 130.

68. Collins, *Brief Narrative of the Ravages of the British and Hessians*, 32–33.

69. "Battle of Princeton, by Sergeant R——," 517.

70. Collins, *Brief Narrative of the Ravages of the British and Hessians*, 37.

71. Denny, "Military Journal," 241.

72. Meaning the men of the other two ranks held their firelocks at the position called "the recover." *1764 Regulations*, 33.

73. Pickering, *Easy Plan*, 9. By "*carry them in their right hands*," Pickering meant "trail arms."

74. Adlum, *Memoirs*, 66; Commager and Morris, *Spirit of 'Seventy-Six*, 595, account of Ebenezer Mattoon. After the war Johann Ewald advised that light troops should trail arms, "the men hold[ing] their rifles in the middle with their right hand and carry[ing] them on their right side, so that the branches of the trees do not impede their march." Ewald, *Treatise*, 73.

75. Simcoe, *Military Journal*, 65. The English military treatise in question was Cavan, *New System*, 90.

76. Wilkin, *Some British Soldiers*, 223, 258, Hale to his parents, 15 Jan., 4 July 1777.

77. Sullivan, *From Redcoat to Rebel*, 70.

78. Ewald, *Diary of the American War*, 340.

79. Dundas, *Principles*, 52.

80. Tarleton, *History*, 216.

81. R. Mackenzie, *Strictures on Lt.-Col. Tarleton's History*, 114–15.

82. Lamb, *Journal*, 142.

83. Huth, "Letters from a Hessian Mercenary," 499, Donop to the Prince of Prussia, 2 Sept. 1777.

84. Smith and Elting, "British Light Infantry," 88.

85. NYSC, British Orderly Book kept by Capt. Frederick DePeyster, Detachment Orders, 21 Jan. 1780.

86. Simcoe, *Military Journal*, 229, 231.

87. Ibid., 187–89; Ewald, *Diary of the American War*, 297.

88. Simcoe, *Military Journal*, 194–95.

89. Phillips died on 13 May 1781 at Petersburg, where Cornwallis's army arrived a week later.

90. Baurmeister, *Revolution in America,* 443, 445. Uhlendorf's translation has Baurmeister referring to "three files and closed squads" when he surely meant "three ranks and closed files."

91. Hunt, *Fragments of Revolutionary History,* 50, Lt. Col. Mercer to Col. Simms, c.1809–17; Linn and Egle, "Diary of the Pennsylvania Line," 713–14.

92. Denny, "Military Journal," 241.

93. Cornwallis's first line at Green Springs appears to have comprised, from right to left, the 1st and 2nd Battalions of Light Infantry, the Guards, and the 43rd, 80th, and 76th Regiments while his second line comprised, from right to left, the 82nd Regiment's light company, the 23rd and 33rd Regiments, the *Jäger,* the Regiment von Bose, and the 2nd Battalion of the 71st Regiment. Tarleton's British Legion dragoons remained in the rear.

94. Muenchhausen, *At General Howe's Side,* 52; Uhlendorf, *Siege of Charleston,* 151, 253; T. Hughes, *Journal,* 7.

95. For references to the heavy baggage having remained in regimental stores at New York, see Gruber, *John Peebles' American War,* 89, 261.

96. Quoted in Ketchum, *Winter Soldiers,* 382.

97. WLCL, Freiherr von Jungkenn Papers, letters, 6 Jan., 6 Dec. 1778. I am most grateful to Mr. Don H. Hagist for supplying these extracts (translated here from the original German).

98. Surtees, "British Colours at Saratoga," 103. Michael Glover defended Burgoyne's claim, pointing to this statement made by an anonymous Brunswick officer: "Our standards bother us a lot, and no English regiment brought any along." Yet this letter was clearly composed in winter quarters at the parish of St. Anne (between Quebec and Trois-Rivières on the St. Lawrence River) sometime in March or April 1777—i.e., two months or more before the actual outset of Burgoyne's expedition in June. See M. Glover, "Note 1667," *JSAHR* 54 (1976): 177; and Pettengill, *Letters from America,* 71, anonymous letter, n.d.

99. Hadden, *Journal and Orderly Books,* 309, General Orders, 18 July 1777. See also Stanley, *For Want of a Horse,* 120. The "eldest" British corps would have been the 9th Regiment.

100. F. C. L. Riedesel, *Baroness von Riedesel,* 72–73.

101. Surtees, "British Colours at Saratoga," 102. Apparently, only the regimental color of the 9th Regiment (now at Sandhurst), both colors of the 53rd Regiment, and a King's color of the 62nd Regiment (said to be of the period c.1772–81) have survived. See Richardson, *Standards and Colours,* 166–67; M. E. Jones, "Note 1658," *JSAHR* 54 (1976): 55; and E. W. Geddes, "Note 1638," *JSAHR* 53 (1975): 124. Burgoyne's force included all ten companies (each) of the 9th, 20th, 21st, 24th, 47th, 53rd, and 62nd Regiments but only the flank companies of the 29th, 31st, and 34th Regiments. The colors of these latter three units undoubtedly would have remained with the battalion companies in Canada. Likewise, the 53rd Regiment's colors would have accompanied the battalion companies when these moved back to garrison Fort George and Fort Ticonderoga in August.

102. Cornwallis's regular British forces comprised the Guards Brigade; the 1st and 2nd Battalions of Light Infantry; the 82nd Regiment's light company; the battalion companies of the 17th, 23rd, 33rd, 43rd, 71st (2nd Battalion), 76th, and 80th Regiments; and detachments from both the Royal Artillery and the 17th Light Dragoons. His Provincials were almost all from the British Legion, the Queen's Rangers, and the North Carolina Volunteers. The six British colors handed over appear to have been those of the 43rd, 76th, and 80th Regiments. Probably ten of the eighteen German colors belonged to the two Anspach-Bayreuth regiments (each of five companies), while the other eight belonged to the two Hessian regiments (each of four companies). Four "British Union flags" were also surrendered, but these may not have been colors. Tarleton, *History*, 453.

103. Geddes, "Note 1638," *JSAHR* 53 (1975): 123, 124.

104. For evidence that the German mercenaries carried their colors into action in America, see for instance Sullivan, *From Redcoat to Rebel*, 70; and Schmidt, *Hesse-Cassel Mirbach Regiment*, 61.

105. Quoted in Wilkin, *Some British Soldiers*, 200. Medows's contingency orders in the event of a French breakthrough seem to have involved a final rallying around the 5th Regiment's colors, from which a final, desperate bayonet charge might have been attempted. See Lushington, *Life and Services of General Lord Harris*, 99, memo by Lord Harris, c.1824.

106. Lushington, *Life and Services of General Lord Harris*, 102, Reserve Orders, 25 Dec. 1778.

107. Adlum, *Memoirs*, 68. Because Adlum claimed that the colors were carried between two battalions, the regiment in question may well have been the 42nd Regiment, which was organized in two battalions for the 1776 campaign and attacked westward across the Harlem River.

108. Lamb, *Journal*, 305; Piecuch, *Battle of Camden*, 93–94, "Extract of a letter of Lord Rawdon's regiment" and "Extract of a letter of the Volunteers of Ireland," published in *The [New York] Royal Gazette*, 20 Sept. 1780.

109. Stedman, *History*, 2:381. When the 64th Regiment was inspected in Jamaica soon after the war, it was reported to have lost one color. Since part of the centerpiece of the regimental color supposedly survives, the missing standard must have been the King's color. H. C. B. Cook, "Note 1658," *JSAHR* 54 (1976): 55.

110. Geddes, "Note 1638," *JSAHR* 53 (1975): 123; Tarleton, *History*, 136, 218; *DAR*, 20:33, Cornwallis to Clinton, 18 Jan. 1781. The unlucky 7th Regiment previously had been captured at Fort Chambly in October 1775.

111. The 7th Regiment had been on its way to garrison Ninety-Six when it was incorporated into Tarleton's detachment. Tarleton's other infantry corps were the 1st Battalion of the 71st Regiment, the infantry of the British Legion, and three or four light companies. One rebel officer later falsely claimed to have captured the 71st Regiment's colors at Cowpens. Tarleton, *History*, 212; Babits, *Devil of a Whipping*, 122, 197n100.

112. According to regulations, a color reserve of six files (three men from each of the two center companies and two from each of the other six companies) was to station itself in the rear of the color party. *1764 Regulations*, 13.

113. Williamson, *Elements*, 7n. One satirist advised colonels and lieutenant colonels to raise bands because, while they reaped the many advantages, the expense fell entirely to the captains. [Grose], *Advice to the Officers*, 34–35.

114. *DAR*, 20:123, Rawdon to Cornwallis, 26 Apr. 1781.

115. Milborne, "British Military Lodges." I am most grateful to Mr. Jay Callaham for having provided me with this information.

116. Anburey, *Travels*, 2:228.

117. This extended to the military's social occasions. See Hadden, *Journal and Orderly Books*, 35; Muenchhausen, *At General Howe's Side*, 51, 52; T. Hughes, *Journal*, 52; and Gruber, *John Peebles' American War*, 497.

118. Seybolt, "A Contemporary British Account," 83; Uhlendorf, *Siege of Charleston*, 291, 293. See also Baurmeister, *Revolution in America*, 350. Howe's Hessian aide de camp wrote that the troops "passed in review to the accompaniment of martial and other music," which included "fifes and drums," while Captain Francis Downman recorded that "we entered the town with drums and music." Muenchhausen, *At General Howe's Side*, 36; Downman, *Services*, 36.

119. Each company had one authorized drummer before the augmentation of 25 August 1775 and two thereafter. Sullivan, *From Redcoat to Rebel*, 28.

120. As a single example, when the 63rd Regiment's grenadier and light companies (commanded by Captains Edward Drury and Henry Lysaght) were respectively mustered at Philadelphia on 9 and 24 February 1778, the former had four drummers and fifers, of whom two were marked absent "on duty with regiment," while the latter had only a single drummer, who was marked as absent, "prisoner with rebels." WO 12/7241, items 2, 9.

121. See Williamson, *Elements*, 7n; and Pattison, "Official Letters," 7, 36.

122. Gruber, *John Peebles' American War*, 229–30. For the drum salutes beaten to general and field officers in garrison or in camp, see *Orderly Book of the Three Battalions of Loyalists*, 97–98, General Orders, 16 June 1778.

123. Moore, *Diary of the American Revolution*, 1:35, letter by "A Spectator," published in *The New York Gazetteer*, 16 Mar. 1775.

124. Gruber, *John Peebles' American War*, 104, 105. The officer in question was apparently Major General James Grant.

125. Stanley, *For Want of a Horse*, 74. Similarly, as Burgoyne's army passed down the South River from Ticonderoga toward Skenesboro on 6 July 1777, "the music and drums of the different regiments were continually playing and contributed to make the scene and passage extremely pleasant." Hadden, *Journal and Orderly Books*, 85. See also Moore, *Diary of the American Revolution*, 1:329; Hunter, *Journal*, 18; and Serle, *American Journal*, 127.

126. J. A. Stevens, "The Battle of Harlem Plains," *Magazine of American History* 4 (1880): 370, Adj. Gen. Joseph Reed to his wife, 17 Sept. 1776, quoted in Scheer and Rankin, *Rebels and Redcoats*, 184.

127. Quoted in Lawrence, *Storm over Savannah*, 70.

128. Houlding, *Fit for Service*, 259–61 and n8, 277–79. For an explana-

tion of why the speed of sound obstructed efforts to provide a musical cadence, see Nosworthy, *Battle Tactics*, 61–62. John Adams later complained that the Boston garrison's "spirit stirring drums and the ear-piercing fife" had daily interrupted his sleep. Frey, *British Soldier in America*, 98.

129. *1764 Regulations*, 19.

130. Cuthbertson, *System*, 169.

131. WO 3/26, fo. 32, circular, June 1779.

132. Williamson, *Elements*, 24–25; Wolfe, *Instructions to Young Officers*, 48. See also Simes, *Military Course*, 422. This was common practice in the Prussian army even before the Seven Years War. Luvaas, *Frederick the Great on the Art of War*, 147.

133. Stevens, *Howe's Orderly Book*, 209, General Orders, 6 Feb. 1776. Similarly, among Lieutenant Colonel Charles Mawhood's tactical instructions to the Fourth Brigade in May 1777 was the blunt directive, "No fifing or drumming but when ordered." LOC, Washington Papers, British 40th Regt. Orderly Book, Brigade Orders, 10 May 1777.

134. Baurmeister, *Revolution in America*, 37–38.

135. NAS, GD 21/492, Peebles papers, book 11, 16–21. For Lieutenant Colonel Patrick Ferguson's "Signals for the Drum, Bugle, or Whistle" for the American Volunteers, see NYSC, British Orderly Book kept by Capt. Frederick DePeyster, Detachment Orders, 1 Jan. 1780.

136. APSL, Anonymous British Journal, 1776–78, 11 Sept. 1777. See also Hunter, *Journal*, 29.

137. Duffy, *Military Experience in the Age of Reason*, 243.

138. Bland, *Treatise*, 156. See also Nosworthy, *Battle Tactics*, 59.

139. Wolfe, *Instructions to Young Officers*, 47.

140. De Krafft, "Journal," 136. For British cheering in action, see Sullivan, *From Redcoat to Rebel*, 70; Pettengill, *Letters from America*, 101; Hunter, *Journal*, 31; Heath, *Memoirs*, 213; Tarleton, *History*, 107, 114; Lee, *Revolutionary War Memoirs*, 183–84, 228, 277, 337–38; Hunt, *Fragments of Revolutionary History*, 49; Scheer and Rankin, *Rebels and Redcoats*, 408; Commager and Morris, *Spirit of 'Seventy-Six*, 77, 81, 82; and Hatch, " 'Affair near James Island,' " 189–90. Alternatively, in August 1778, light infantrymen of the 23rd Regiment (serving temporarily as marines) conveyed their eagerness to board a French warship by giving "the Indian war [w]hoop." Similarly, when Cornwallis's and Gates's armies blundered into one another in the early hours of 16 August 1780 at Camden, Tarleton's dragoons galloped forward, "every officer and soldier with the yell of an Indian savage . . . crying out, 'charge, charge, charge,' so that their own voices and the echoes resounded in every direction through the pine forest." Wilkin, *Some British Soldiers*, 270, Lt. William Hale to unknown, n.d.; Piecuch, *Battle of Camden*, 74.

141. Lushington, *Life and Services of General Lord Harris*, 101, Reserve Orders, 25 Dec. 1778.

142. *PNG*, 7:154, Morgan to Greene, 19 Jan. 1781.

143. For these and other quotes, see Babits, *Devil of a Whipping*, 89. Babits rightly highlights the psychological significance of the cheering.

## 7. COMMANDING THE BATTALION

*Epigraph.* NAM, Services and letters of James Green, "Account of Green's Services," 8.

1. Wolfe, *Instructions to Young Officers*, 47, 48. Similarly, at Guilford Courthouse, to prevent a repetition of the rebel Virginia militia's ignominious flight at Camden, Brigadier General Stevens "placed a line of sentinels in his rear, with orders to shoot every man that flinched." Lee, *Revolutionary War Memoirs*, 277.

2. Lamb, *Memoir*, 175.

3. [De Berniere], "Narrative," 29. Since it was at this point that the hard-pressed grenadiers and light infantry saw Brigadier General Lord Percy's relief force drawn up on Lexington Heights, the incident must have occurred before the battered column reached Lexington rather than afterward, as De Berniere had it.

4. Tarleton, *History*, 217.

5. Bland, *Treatise*, 170. See also Simes, *Military Course*, 238–39n.

6. Duffy, *Military Experience in the Age of Reason*, 76–78; Frey, *British Soldier in America*, 125–26.

7. Duffy, *Military Experience in the Age of Reason*, 213, 220.

8. Hayes, *Stephen Jarvis*, 99–100.

9. Anburey, *Travels*, 1:423–24.

10. [Montagu-Stuart-Wortley], *Prime Minister and His Son*, 69, Stuart to his father, 24 July 1775. Stuart was not present at the action.

11. See Duffy, *Military Experience in the Age of Reason*, 221; M. S. Anderson, *War of the Austrian Succession*, 28.

12. "Original Letter of Major Patrick Ferguson," *The Gentleman's Magazine and Historical Review*, 40 (1853): 128, Ferguson to a friend, n.d. Ferguson was later informed that the officer was Washington, but the circumstances make this unlikely. For a similar incident at Richmond in May 1781, when Lafayette "excited great dissatisfaction" by refusing to allow his riflemen to "pick off" the reconnoitering Major General Phillips and Brigadier General Arnold, see Dann, *The Revolution Remembered*, 405–406, deposition of James Johnston.

13. In July 1776 English adventurer Nicholas Cresswell noted in his journal with obvious distaste that the rebels were enlisting the best riflemen in the Pennsylvania backcountry "for the humane purpose of killing the English officers." Cresswell, *Journal*, 97.

14. [S. Graham], "Recollection," 210–11.

15. John Almon, ed., *The Remembrancer; or Impartial Repository of Public Events*, 17 vols. (London, 1775–84), 2(pt. 1, 1776):366, 19 Mar. 1776. For a detailed analysis of the modifications made to the Guards' clothing and equipment, see Burke and Bass, "Preparing a British Unit for Service in America," 2–11.

16. Schmidt, *Hesse-Cassel Mirbach Regiment*, 51, 16 Aug. 1776; Bardeleben, *Diary*, 52, 17 Aug. 1776.

17. See, for instance, Stevens, *Howe's Orderly Book*, 210, 214; Kemble, "Papers," 1:303, 305, 375; Hadden, *Journal and Orderly Books*, 210; Eelking,

*German Allied Troops,* 34; and Atwood, *The Hessians,* 81. How long this practice persisted after 1776 is unclear. Clinton's later account of Howe's New York campaign mentions that it "was then and had been the general practice on the American service." Clinton, *American Rebellion,* 51.

18. HSD, Dansey Letters, W. Dansey to his mother, 3 Sept. 1776, 10 Jan. 1777.

19. Simcoe, *Military Journal,* 264.

20. *Papers of the Continental Congress, 1774–1789,* National Archives Microfilm Publications M247 (Washington, D.C., 1958), reel 94, 387, Alexander Dow to the President of Congress, 23 May 1781. Dow mistakenly believed the British officer in question was Lieutenant Colonel the Honorable Henry Monckton, who in fact had been killed at the head of the 2nd Battalion of Grenadiers much earlier in the battle. I am most grateful to Mr. Don H. Hagist for bringing this item to my attention.

21. Sullivan, *From Redcoat to Rebel,* 69–70.

22. J. Burgoyne, *State of the Expedition,* 163–64. See also Anburey, *Travels,* 1:429; Lamb, *Journal,* 159; and Lamb, *Memoir,* 199.

23. R. Mackenzie, *Strictures on Lt.-Col. Tarleton's History,* 99. According to Morgan, ten British officers were killed and twenty-nine captured (the number of wounded among these was not specified). Babits, *Devil of a Whipping,* 142, 143.

24. Hunter, *Journal,* 42. Captains William Davison (or Davidson), Andrew Neilson, Thomas Williamson, and John Powell were killed or mortally wounded respectively at the battles of Bunker Hill, Long Island, Princeton, and Monmouth. In this same period the company lost one subaltern, Lieutenant Henry D'Oyley, at Brandywine. WO 12/6240.

25. Odintz, "British Officer Corps," 461–64.

26. Quoted in ibid., 462.

27. Wilkin, *Some British Soldiers,* 258–59, 261, Hale to his parents, 4 July 1778.

28. Dalrymple, *Tacticks,* 16. For examples where German and British officers actually used rifles or fusils in the American *petite guerre,* see Schmidt, *Hesse-Cassel Mirbach Regiment,* 52; B. E. Burgoyne, *Defeat, Disaster, and Dedication,* 65; and HSD, Dansey Letters, W. Dansey to his mother, 15 Mar. 1777.

29. Hadden, *Journal and Orderly Books,* 74–75, General Orders, 20 June 1777.

30. Quoted in Willcox, *Portrait of a General,* 80.

31. Clinton, *American Rebellion,* 51–52 and n27. The officer in question at Chatterton's Hill may have been the 35th Regiment's Lieutenant Colonel Robert Carr , who was mortally wounded.

32. See, for instance, Dalrymple, *Tacticks,* 115–16. One former officer with the 1st Battalion of Light Infantry put the case succinctly by noting that "[i]n danger, men—like all animals—crowd together." Smith and Elting, "British Light Infantry," 88.

33. Drake, *Bunker Hill,* 29–30, Waller to his brother, 22 June 1775.

34. Wilkin, *Some British Soldiers,* 223, Hale to his parents, 15 Jan. 1777. Hale's "platoon" comprised assorted recruits and drafts from the parent regi-

ments, whom he and other officers had been escorting to the flank battalions with Cornwallis at Trenton. He indicated that "15 out of 30 grenadiers and a captain" were lost in the course of the action. The dead officer was Captain Thomas Williamson of the 52nd Regiment's grenadier company. See WO 12/6240, item 91.

35. Innes, "Jeremy Lister," 65. According to Lister, even then only the 10th and 43rd Regiment's light companies reformed; that of the 4th Regiment remained scattered for the rest of the day.

36. *DAR*, 20:228, Stewart to Cornwallis, 9 Sept. 1781. Henry Lee confirmed that Stewart did "restore his broken line, which being accomplished, he instantly advanced, and the action was renewed." Lee, *Revolutionary War Memoirs*, 472.

37. For the maneuvers and firings, see *1764 Regulations*. Some of the firings were marginally more elaborate, particularly those performed while the battalion was advancing or retiring.

38. Bland, *Treatise*, 158, 159, 164.

39. Quoted in Houlding, *Fit for Service*, 351.

40. See Kemble, "Papers," 1:335–77. Howe recommended that the officers commanding battalions should take the latter out individually for drill at their own initiative, though not in the enclosed fields adjacent to the town because of the risk of damage to crops. Ibid., 344, 366.

41. Howe, *Narrative*, 4. Even before the outbreak of hostilities, this would have been difficult to do at Boston.

42. Significantly, the case was similar with the enemy. One French officer, in commenting in 1781 on Major General Steuben's drill, noted that rebel battalions were able to form together in line and to advance simultaneously "but without the least idea of alignment." "Diary of a French Officer," 7 (1881): 294.

43. Burgoyne and Burgoyne, *Journal of the Hesse-Cassel Jaeger Corps*, 14.

44. Abbatt, *Major André's Journal*, 46. André was aide de camp to Major General Grey, who commanded the Third Brigade.

45. Muenchhausen, *At General Howe's Side*, 31.

46. Burgoyne and Burgoyne, *Journal of the Hesse-Cassel Jaeger Corps*, 15.

47. Anburey, *Travels*, 1:336.

48. Pettengill, *Letters from America*, 92, anonymous letter, 18 Aug. 1777.

49. Stedman, *History*, 2:340.

50. Quoted in Hatch, *Battle of Guilford Courthouse*, 58.

51. Tarleton, *History*, 273–76.

52. Simcoe, *Military Journal*, 194–95, General Orders, 23 or 24 Apr. 1781.

53. Cohen, "Captain William Leslie's Paths to Glory," 61, Leslie to his parents, 2 Sept. 1776.

54. Lamb, *Journal*, 362. The company in question was probably from the 2nd Battalion of Guards.

55. J. Burgoyne, *Supplement*, 5, 6, General Orders, 1 May 1777.

56. Ibid.

57. Ibid., 6.

58. NAS, GD 21/492, Peebles papers, book 11, 16–21.

59. This theme is touched upon in Odintz, "British Officer Corps," 448–55.

60. Peckham, *Sources of American Independence*, 2:299, Ferguson to Dr. Adam Ferguson, 31 Jan. 1778.

61. Hayes, *Stephen Jarvis*, 99.

62. At Brandywine the 1st Battalion of Light Infantry probably comprised the light companies of the 4th, 5th, 10th, 15th, 17th, 22nd, 23rd, 27th, 28th, 33rd, 35th, 38th, and 42nd Regiments. The 2nd Battalion of Light Infantry probably comprised the light companies of the 37th, 40th, 43rd, 44th, 45th, 46th, 49th, 52nd, 55th, 57th, 63rd, 64th, and 71st Regiments. I am most grateful to Mr. Stephen Gilbert for having shared the fruits of his research on the makeup of the flank battalions.

63. APSL, Memo Battle of Brandywine. The account is published in full in McGuire, *Philadelphia Campaign. Volume Two*, 289–91. McGuire has identified the author as Captain William Scott of the 17th Regiment's light company. Ibid., 295.

64. At Brandywine the 2nd Battalion of Grenadiers probably comprised the grenadier companies of the 40th, 42nd, 43rd, 44th, 45th, 46th, 49th, Marines, 52nd, 55th, 57th, 63rd, and 64th Regiments. The 1st Battalion of Grenadiers probably comprised the grenadier companies of the 4th, 5th, 10th, 15th, 17th, 22nd, 23rd, 27th, 28th, 33rd, 35th, 37th, and 38th Regiments.

65. HSD, Dansey Letters, W. Dansey to his mother, 20 Sept. 1776.

66. Ibid., W. Dansey to Miss. M., 30 Aug. 1776, W. Dansey to his mother, 3 Sept. 1776.

67. Ibid., W. Dansey to his mother, 28 July 1778.

68. Ibid., W. Dansey to his mother, 20 Apr. 1777. This costly skirmish was recounted in detail by Lieutenant John Peebles of the 42nd Regiment, whose grenadier company fared less well than Dansey's light company. Peebles characterized the affair as one of several "shabby, ill-managed occasions." See Gruber, *John Peebles' American War*, 95–98.

69. HSD, Dansey Letters, W. Dansey to his mother, 20 Mar. 1778.

70. Simcoe, *Military Journal*, 233–34.

71. WLCL, Loftus Cliffe Papers, Cliffe to Jack, 21 Sept. 1776. At this date the 3rd Battalion of Light Infantry comprised the light companies of the 15th, 28th, 33rd, 37th, 46th, 54th, and 57th Regiments.

## 8. FIREPOWER

*Epigraph.* Cresswell, *Journal*, 241.

1. The best works on this topic are by Adrian B. Caruana: *The Light Six-Pounder Battalion Gun of 1776* (Bloomfield, Ont.: Museum Restoration Service, 1977); *Grasshoppers and Butterflies: The Light 3-Pounders of Pattison and Townshend* (Bloomfield, Ont.: Museum Restoration Service, 1979); *British Artillery Ammunition, 1780* (Bloomfield, Ont.: Museum Restoration Service, 1979); and "Dress of the Royal Artillery," 124–29. He also wrote numerous articles on the subject in the magazine *Arms Collecting*, of which the most relevant here are "The British 8-inch Howitzer," 26, no. 2 (May 1988):

65–68; "British Artillery Drill of the 18th Century," 16, no. 2 (May 1978): 46–60; "The Light 3-Pounder of William Congreve," 18, no. 2 (May 1980): 66–70; and "Tin Case Shot in the 18th Century," 28, no. 1 (Feb. 1990): 11–17.

2. For a brief survey of the use of field artillery in eighteenth-century warfare, see Duffy, *Military Experience in the Age of Reason*, 216–19, 230–36.

3. Ibid., 217, 234, 265. American sources more commonly call case shot "canister."

4. Sullivan, *From Redcoat to Rebel*, 71.

5. Martin, *Private Yankee Doodle*, 92.

6. Downman, *Services*, 105.

7. J. Burgoyne, *State of the Expedition*, 43; Baxter, *British Invasion*, 288.

8. For the swelling train of field artillery that Frederick the Great reluctantly employed, though with increasing success, during the Seven Years War, see Duffy, *Frederick the Great*, 108, 165, 185, 238–39, 312–13. For the problems that Frederick's artillery train caused him during the War of the Bavarian Succession (1778–79), see ibid., 268–69, 274.

9. Howe's four light 12-pounders, four light 6-pounders, and four 5.5-inch howitzers proved less useful than they should have done. Some bogged down when they were advanced, and twelve-pound roundshot was somehow supplied erroneously for the 6-pounders. The Royal Artillery's commanding officer, Lieutenant Colonel Samuel Cleaveland, defended himself by claiming that not half of the sixty-six rounds supplied to each gun had been fired and that the men detailed to carry ammunition had wandered off. Murdock, *Bunker Hill*, 21, 27–28.

10. In his letter "Reflections upon the War in America" (1776), Burgoyne wrote that rebel irregulars would invariably exploit woods "till dislodged either by cannon or by a resolute attack by light infantry." In his letter "Thoughts for Conducting the War from the Side of Canada" (1777), he predicted that, by "fortifying the strong ground at different places," the rebels would oblige "the King's army to carry a weight of artillery with it." De Fonblanque, *Political and Military Episodes*, 209, 483.

11. J. Burgoyne, *State of the Expedition*, 15–16, 39–40, 60, 79, 89–91, 125. Thomas Anburey, who also served on the Albany expedition, later asserted that 500 militiamen planted behind abatis could have held off 5,000 of the bravest men if the latter had no artillery support. Anburey, *Letters*, 1:383.

12. Duffy, *Military Experience in the Age of Reason*, 217–18.

13. Harcourt, *Papers*, 11:208, Lt. Col. the Hon. William Harcourt to Earl Harcourt, 17 Mar. 1777. See also *DAR*, 12:265, Howe to Germain (No. 32, Separate), 30 Nov. 1776.

14. Barker, *British in Boston*, 35–36.

15. J. Burgoyne, *State of the Expedition*, 13–16. Burgoyne and his supporters denied that the two light 24-pounders were too cumbersome to accompany the army, pointing out that these guns (taken from the rebels at Quebec) were lighter than the British medium 12-pounders and therefore fell into the category of field artillery. Ibid., 14, 79, 89. Burgoyne's breakdown conflicts slightly with the order of battle that Hadden recorded on 17 September 1777. Hadden, *Journal and Orderly Books*, 153–59.

16. Muenchhausen, *At General Howe's Side*, 32, 65n24.

17. Campbell, *Journal of an Expedition*, 4.

18. This was probably a pair of light 6-pounders. Hale wrote that they stopped firing "only lest ammunition should be wanting for case shot." *Some British Soldiers*, 262, Hale to his parents, 14 July 1778.

19. Downman, *Services*, 30.

20. Sullivan, *From Redcoat to Rebel*, 129-30.

21. J. Burgoyne, *State of the Expedition*, 14-15.

22. Ibid., 92. The Advanced Corps and artillery park required respectively 85 and 237 horses. Ibid., 94.

23. Baxter, *British Invasion*, 239, 247.

24. Hadden, *Journal and Orderly Books*, 85.

25. Downman, *Services*, 34.

26. Burgoyne and Burgoyne, *Journal of the Hesse-Cassel Jaeger Corps*, 5-6.

27. Fortescue, *Correspondence of King George the Third*, 3:384, Williams to Germain, 23 June 1776.

28. Hadden, *Journal and Orderly Books*, 180, 150-51.

29. Wilkin, *Some British Soldiers*, 246, Hale to unknown, 23 Mar. 1778.

30. Burgoyne and Burgoyne, *Journal of the Hesse-Cassel Jaeger Corps*, 13.

31. R. Mackenzie, *Strictures on Lt.-Col. Tarleton's History*, 100.

32. See for instance Baurmeister, *Revolution in America*, 64-65.

33. [Congreve], "Battle of Long Island," 202-203, Congreve to Rev. Richard Congreve, 4 Sept. 1776.

34. Hadden, *Journal and Orderly Books*, 164-65. The guns were recovered toward the end of the action.

35. Campbell, *Journal of an Expedition*, 27.

36. For straightforward analysis of eighteenth-century infantry warfare, see Duffy, *Military Experience in the Age of Reason*, 204-14; Chandler, *Art of Warfare*, chap. 8; and Nosworthy, *Battle Tactics*, 49-58, 219-44.

37. Simcoe, *Military Journal*, 21. Simcoe here refers to the training of his Queen's Rangers.

38. This theme is clearly explored in Nosworthy, *Battle Tactics*, 50-58.

39. Duffy, *Military Experience in the Age of Reason*, 18, 20-21.

40. Quoted in Rogers, *British Army of the Eighteenth Century*, 68.

41. Quoted in Duffy, *Army of Frederick the Great*, 130.

42. Duffy, *Military Experience in the Age of Reason*, 204-206.

43. Eighteenth-century British fire tactics are summarized in Nosworthy, *Anatomy of Victory*, 55-58, 229-35.

44. See Houlding, *Fit for Service*, 350-52; Duffy, *Military Experience in the Age of Reason*, 213-14; Nosworthy, *Battle Tactics*, 73, 193-94; Duffy, *Army of Frederick the Great*, 119; S. Ross, *From Flintlock to Rifle*, 27.

45. Quoted in Houlding, *Fit for Service*, 351.

46. Duffy, *Military Experience in the Age of Reason*, 210.

47. Quoted in Duffy, *Army of Frederick the Great*, 130; Dalrymple, *Tacticks*, 113-14.

48. Quoted in D. Chandler, "The Great Captain General, 1702-14," in *The Oxford Illustrated History of the British Army*, ed. D. Chandler (Oxford: Oxford University Press, 1995), 85.

49. Quoted in Chandler, *Art of Warfare*, 127.

50. Quoted in Reid, *Wolfe*, 111.

51. For the change to the Prussian-style volley system, see Houlding, *Fit for Service*, 318–21, 370–73.

52. Lushington, *Life and Services of General Lord Harris*, 98, memo by Lord Harris, c.1824. I have here amended Harris's erroneous reference to the 45th Regiment's grenadier company to that of the 35th Regiment.

53. Extract from Williams to his sister, 24 Nov. 1780, reproduced in Piecuch, *Battle of Camden*, 26.

54. NAS, GD 21/492, Peebles papers, book 11, 16–21.

55. Quoted in Hatch, *Battle of Guilford Courthouse*, 48, 52. As 63 (or less than a quarter) of the 244 or so Highlanders who went into action were killed and wounded at Guilford Courthouse, Stuart may have meant that half of these total casualties were sustained from the first fire. See ibid., 124, 136–77.

56. Quoted in ibid., 53.

57. Tarleton, *History*, 273, 315, 319–20; Lee, *Revolutionary War Memoirs*, 277–78.

58. See for instance Lamb, *Journal*, 32; F. Mackenzie, *Diary*, 1:27; HMC, *Stopford-Sackville*, 2:6; Simcoe, *Military Journal*, 75; Ewald, *Diary of the American War*, 182; and Stedman, *History*, 1:120. See also Higginbotham, *War of American Independence*, 4–5; and Black, *War for America*, 48.

59. For the likely similarities between the common soldiers on both sides, see Shy, *People Numerous and Armed*, esp. chap. 7; Martin and Lender, *Respectable Army*; Papenfuse and Stiverson, "Smallwood's Recruits," 117–32; and Neimeyer, *America Goes to War*.

60. Weller, "Irregular but Effective," 118–31.

61. See for instance Wright, "The Rifle in the American Revolution," 293–99; and Starkey, "Paoli to Stony Point," 13–14.

62. For the deadliness of the riflemen's one or two rounds at Cowpens, see Babits, *Devil of a Whipping*, 92–93.

63. See for instance Martin, *Private Yankee Doodle*, 28.

64. Steuben, *Revolutionary War Drill Manual*, 64–65. According to Lawrence Babits, the rebel militia and regulars at Cowpens utilized both the "older" and "newer" volleying techniques. Babits, *Devil of a Whipping*, 17, 91–92, 102–103.

65. Duffy, *Frederick the Great*, 318; Duffy, *Army of Frederick the Great*, 128, 130.

66. *1764 Regulations*, 10.

67. WO 36/1, fos. 19, 32, Orders, 14 Aug., 21 Nov. 1774.

68. F. Mackenzie, *Diary*, 1:26. This eyewitness account, which Mackenzie copied into his own diary, was penned by a flank company officer.

69. Williamson, *Elements*, 56.

70. Dalrymple, *Tacticks*, 38.

71. Harding, *Smallarms*, 280.

72. Wolfe, *Instructions to Young Officers*, 49.

73. For Wolfe and the adoption of the "alternate fire" system, see Reid, *Wolfe*, 111–12, 132–35, 168.

74. R. Jackson, *A Systematic View of the Formation, Discipline, and Economy of Armies*, 3rd rev. ed. (London: Parker, Furnivall, and Parker, 1845), 258. In the original edition Jackson was more succinct: "If it be meant to kill the enemy, it is common sense that soldiers be taught to fire with aim; if it be meant to frighten by noise and appearance, general level, in platoon firings, will serve the purpose." Jackson, *A Systematic View of the Formation, Discipline, and Economy of Armies* (London: John Stockdale, 1804), 163.

75. *1764 Regulations*, 11.

76. Cavan, *New System*, 23. Interestingly, surviving British Land Pattern muskets from this period sometimes exhibit unmistakable signs of Cavan's recommendation. I am most grateful to Mr. Mark Tully for having brought this phenomenon to my attention.

77. WO 36/1, fo. 57, order, Boston, 14 June 1775.

78. Houlding, *Fit for Service*, 144–45, 262–63, 279–80, 335–36, 366–68, 375.

79. For target practice and shooting with squibs at Boston in 1774 and 1775, see for instance WO 36/1, fos. 9, 31, 32, 53, 57; Evelyn, *Memoir and Letters*, 30; Lushington, *Life and Services of General Lord Harris*, 47; and Barker, *British in Boston*, 7, 8, 9–10. For shooting thereafter within the main army, see for instance Kemble, "Papers," 1:298, 300, 329, 440, 606–608, 610, 611, 613–16, 618–21, 623; and Gruber, *John Peebles' American War*, 185, 256, 429, 430, 436.

80. F. Mackenzie, *Diary*, 1:4.

81. Honyman, *Colonial Panorama*, 44, entry for 22 Mar. 1775 (see also 50, entry for 25 Mar. 1775).

82. LOC, Washington Papers, British 40th Regt. Orderly Book, Brigade Orders, 13 May 1777.

83. Harding, *Smallarms*, chap. 25, esp. 291–329.

84. WO 36/1, fo. 32, After Orders, Boston, 21 Nov. 1774.

85. Houlding, *Fit for Service*, 280.

86. Cuthbertson, *System*, 171.

87. Anburey, *Travels*, 1:333.

88. Lamb, *Memoir*, 175.

89. Anburey, *Travels*, 1:333–34.

90. Simcoe, *Military Journal*, 134.

91. F. Mackenzie, *Diary*, 1:21.

92. Ibid., 1:26. This eyewitness account, which Mackenzie copied into his own diary, was penned by a flank company officer.

93. J. Burgoyne, *Supplement*, 25, General Orders, 21 Sept. 1777.

94. See for instance Lee, *Revolutionary War Memoirs*, 275n, 285n; Scheer and Rankin, *Rebels and Redcoats*, 34; Commager and Morris, *Spirit of 'Seventy-Six*, 620; Dann, *The Revolution Remembered*, 179; and Heath, *Memoirs*, 383. See also Babits, *Devil of a Whipping*, 14–15, 73, 93. One rebel veteran later recalled how his colonel expressly advised the men against this error: "Take care now and fire low, bring down your pieces, fire at their legs, one man wounded in the leg is better [than] a dead one, for it takes two more to carry him off and there is three gone—leg 'em, I say, leg them." Bostwick, "Connecticut Soldier," 94–107.

95. Adlum, *Memoirs*, 68–69.

96. Because the 42nd Regiment comprised around nine hundred men, it was organized into two battalions before the 1776 campaign to facilitate command and control.

97. [Graydon], *Memoirs*, 182.

98. Houlding, *Fit for Service*, 137–43, 141n86. One officer with the corps later recalled: "It was very extraordinary, but that morning . . . the 52nd had received an entire new set of arms, and were trying them at marks when they received orders to march immediately to Charlestown Ferry. . . . I may add that, singularly enough, not a firelock had missed fire." Hunter, *Journal*, 10. At Halifax in 1776, those British corps that still possessed older firelocks with wooden ramrods exchanged them for newer models with steel ones, though the process took longer in the case of the Provincial units. Kemble, "Papers," 1:369; *Orderly Book of the Three Battalions of Loyalists*, 77, 99, 110.

99. Houlding, *Fit for Service*, 139–40; Nosworthy, *Battle Tactics*, 196–98.

100. Dann, *The Revolution Remembered*, 124–25, deposition of William Lloyd.

101. Houlding, *Fit for Service*, 145–46; Harding, *Smallarms*, 201–204.

102. Lindsay, *Lives of the Lindsays*, 3:351–52 and n, "Narrative of the Occupation and Defence of the Island of St. Lucie against the French, 1779."

103. Harding, *Smallarms*, 56, 77; Lee, *Revolutionary War Memoirs*, 285n, 275n. Interestingly, months before the outbreak of hostilities, Gage warned that "forty or forty-two cartridges to a pound of powder will carry a ball truer than thirty-two cartridges, which is the number usually made up with a pound of powder." WO 36/1, fo. 31, After Orders, 21 Nov. 1774. See also Atkinson, "Some Evidence for Burgoyne's Expedition," 134–35, Brig. Gen. Fraser, "Memorandum relative to a Company of Marksmen," 30 Aug. 1776.

104. See McGuire, *Philadelphia Campaign. Volume Two*, 130–31; Babits, *Devil of a Whipping*, 13; and Weller, "Irregular but Effective," 122, 126.

105. Martin, *Private Yankee Doodle*, 205.

106. See for example Pettengill, *Letters from America*, 80–81; Baxter, *British Invasion*, 209–10; Wilkin, *Some British Soldiers*, 216.

107. "George Inman's Narrative," 240.

108. Baurmeister, *Revolution in America*, 254. For a similar incident that occurred toward the end of the battle of Freeman's Farm, see Baxter, *British Invasion*, 213; and J. Burgoyne, *State of the Expedition*, 70.

109. Hadden, *Journal and Orderly Books*, 164.

110. See for instance Lee, *Revolutionary War Memoirs*, 89; Anburey, *Travels*, 1:442; Baurmeister, *Revolution in America*, 186; Denny, "Military Journal," 241, 242; and Tarleton, *History*, 216–17, 354.

111. Tarleton, *History*, 216–17; Babits, *Devil of a Whipping*, 106.

112. Hunt, *Fragments of Revolutionary History*, 50, Lt. Col. Mercer to Col. Simms, c.1809–17; S. Graham, "An English Officer's Account," 270.

## 9. THE BAYONET CHARGE

*Epigraph.* Sullivan, *From Redcoat to Rebel*, 103.

1. Simcoe, *Military Journal*, 21.

2. HMC, *Stopford-Sackville*, 2:5, Howe to Adm. Lord Howe, 22 June 1775.

3. Fortescue, *Correspondence of King George the Third*, 3:221–22, Howe to General Harvey, 22/24 June 1775. A similar situation occurred at the rebel assault on Lieutenant Colonel the Honorable John Maitland's fortified line at Stono Ferry. See Lee, *Revolutionary War Memoirs*, 131.

4. Lindsay, *Lives of the Lindsays*, 3:349, "Narrative of the Occupation and Defence of the Island of St. Lucie against the French, 1779."

5. Barker, *British in Boston*, 70. For the same precaution prior to Major General Grey's night attack at Paoli, see Abbatt, *Major André's Journal*, 49–50.

6. HMC, *Rawdon Hastings*, 3:157, Rawdon to Lord Huntingdon, 3 Aug. 1775.

7. NAM, Laye Letters, Laye to his father, 12 Oct. 1775.

8. Quoted in De Fonblanque, *Political and Military Episodes*, 208–209.

9. F. Mackenzie, *Diary*, 1:44–45. The order can be found with minor textual variations in WO 36/5, General Orders, 13 Sept. 1776.

10. Hadden, *Journal and Orderly Books*, 74, General Orders, 20 June 1777. See also Stanley, *For Want of a Horse*, 100–101; and Anburey, *Travels*, 1:212–13. Anburey added, "Our success in any engagement must greatly rely on the bayonet." That his letters in fact were composed after the war (rather than contemporaneously with events, as the reader was intended to believe) explains how Burgoyne's order of 20 June could have found its way into a letter supposedly dated 20 May 1777 from Montreal.

11. Peckham, *Sources of American Independence*, 2:302, 306, Ferguson to Clinton, 1 Aug. 1778.

12. *Detail and Conduct of the American War*, 13–15, anonymous letter, 5 July 1775; Wolfe, *Instructions to Young Officers*, 51.

13. Serle, *American Journal*, 220–21. Interestingly, Simcoe believed that when soldiers carried their arms at the advance rather than shouldered, it "took off the appearance of wavering from a column more than any other mode of carrying them." Simcoe, *Military Journal*, 65.

14. Ewald, *Diary of the American War*, 312.

15. Moore, *Diary of the American Revolution*, 2:314–15, excerpt from *The [New York] Royal Gazette*, 3 Jan. 1781.

16. Lee, *Revolutionary War Memoirs*, 338. Lee was not present at the battle.

17. DAR, 20:228, Stewart to Cornwallis, 9 Sept. 1781; Gibbes, *Documentary History of the American Revolution*, 3:149, "Account furnished by Col. Otho Williams. . . ."; Lee, *Revolutionary War Memoirs*, 468.

18. S. Graham, "An English Officer's Account," 270.

19. Serle, *American Journal*, 220–21.

20. Downman, *Services*, 35.

21. For an early example of this explanation, see Murdoch, *Rebellion in America*, 430.

22. Houlding, *Fit for Service*, 261n10, 369; Brumwell, *Redcoats*, 246; Glover, *Peninsular Preparation*, 142.

23. Cuthbertson, *System*, 170–71; Willcox, *Portrait of a General*, 81. One contemporary satirist mocked that the bayonet's only uses were as a tool

for foraging, cooking, and plundering or as a screwdriver with which to replace worn flints. [Grose], *Advice to the Officers*, 111, 131-32.

24. Simcoe, *Military Journal*, 98-99.

25. See Alan J. Guy, "King George's Army," in *1745: Charles Edward Stuart and the Jacobites*, ed. R. C. Woosnam-Savage (Edinburgh: HMSO, 1995), 49, 54n15.

26. Peckham, *Sources of American Independence*, 2:302, 306, Ferguson to Clinton, 1 Aug. 1778.

27. According to Joseph Plumb Martin, during the march to Yorktown, Washington instructed his infantry that, "in case the enemy should come out to meet us, we should exchange but one round with them and then decide the conflict with the bayonet, as they valued themselves at that implement." Martin, *Private Yankee Doodle*, 229.

28. Significantly, one Brunswick officer observed of the storming of Lieutenant Colonel Friedrich Baum's fieldworks at Bennington, "The bayonet, the butt of the rifle, the sabre, the pike were in full play; and men fell, as they rarely fall in modern war, under the direct blows of their enemies." Scheer and Rankin, *Rebels and Redcoats*, 264, "Account of the Battle of Bennington."

29. Sullivan, *From Redcoat to Rebel*, 135. Since Sullivan's 49th Regiment crossed Chad's Ford as part of the First Brigade, it is possible that he witnessed this incident.

30. Serle, *American Journal*, 78-79.

31. Hunter, *Journal*, 29.

32. Gibbes, *Documentary History of the American Revolution*, 3:150, "Account furnished by Col. Otho Williams. . . ." Henry Lee later claimed that individuals from the Maryland Continentals and 3rd Regiment were found on the field mutually transfixed. Lee, *Revolutionary War Memoirs*, 469. That Williams witnessed the rebuff of the 2nd Battalion of Guards at Guilford Courthouse suggests that historians have erred in portraying that incident as an epic melee. For three contemporary accounts of the Guards' repulse, see *DAR*, 20:91-92, Cornwallis to Germain (No. 8), 17 Mar. 1781; Tarleton, *History*, 274; and Lee, *Revolutionary War Memoirs*, 279-80.

33. Heath, *Memoirs*, 172. Heath's comments were made with particular reference to artillery fire.

34. Moore, *Diary of the American Revolution*, 1:350, excerpt from *The Middlesex Journal*, 31 Dec. 1776. Likewise, Hessian colonel Henrich Anton von Heeringen wrote (with some exaggeration): "The greater part of the riflemen were pierced with the bayonet to the trees. These dreadful people ought rather to be pitied than feared; they always require a quarter of an hour's time to load a rifle, and in the meantime they feel the effects of our balls and bayonets." Quoted in Field, *Battle of Long Island*, 433.

35. Simcoe, *Military Journal*, 229-30.

36. Hanger quoted in Babits, *Devil of a Whipping*, 18. This encounter is mentioned in Lynderberg, *Archibald Robertson*, 160.

37. Simcoe, *Military Journal*, 229.

38. Wilkin, *Some British Soldiers*, 223, Hale to unknown, 15 Jan. 1777.

39. Tarleton, *History*, 274; Stedman, *History*, 2:377; Lee, *Revolutionary War Memoirs*, 279.

40. Babits, *Devil of a Whipping*, 115–17.

41. Lamb, *Journal*, 350, 361.

42. Force, *American Archives: Fifth Series*, 3:532, General Orders, 27 Oct. 1776. See also Washington, *Papers*, 6:110, General Orders, 23 Aug. 1776.

43. Scheer and Rankin, *Rebels and Redcoats*, 430, Thomas Young's memoir.

44. Ibid., 185, anonymous letter, 17 Sept. 1776.

45. Dann, *The Revolution Remembered*, 194–95, deposition of Garret Watts.

46. *John Robert Shaw*, 31. Shaw's comment that this fire "killed and wounded nearly one half our number" was a gross exaggeration.

47. NAS, GD 174/2106, 2107, Orders, 15 Sept. 1777.

48. Bolton, *Letters of Hugh, Earl Percy*, 68, Percy to his father, 1 Sept. 1776.

49. Force, *American Archives: Fifth Series*, 2:168, anonymous letter, 4 Sept. 1776.

50. WO 34/111, fo. 71, unknown to Lord Amherst, n.d.

51. Simcoe, *Military Journal*, 98.

52. Ibid.; NAS, GD 174/2106, 2107, Orders, 15 Sept. 1777.

53. "A Frenchman's Comments," 366.

54. Campbell, *Journal of an Expedition*, 19, 20, General Orders, 24 Dec. 1778.

55. Johnson, *Sketches*, 1:495–96.

56. Dann, *The Revolution Remembered*, 195.

57. Hunter, *Journal*, 29.

58. "Battle of Princeton, by Sergeant R——," 517. For details of the redcoats' fury, see Dwyer, *The Day Is Ours*, 344–45, 342n; and S. S. Smith, *Battle of Princeton*, 23.

59. McCarty, "Revolutionary War Journal," 45. The same incident, or another very much like it, is recounted in Bostwick, "Connecticut Soldier," 105.

60. Babits, *Devil of a Whipping*, 107–109.

61. Quoted in ibid., 122.

62. The written and archaeological evidence relating to the incident is examined in Demarest, "The Baylor Massacre," 28–93.

63. These depositions are reproduced in ibid., 44–45.

64. Ibid., 43.

65. Cullency quoted in ibid., 44.

66. Ibid., 43.

67. Louisa Susannah Wells, *The Journal of a Voyage from Charlestown to London* (New York, 1968), 53, quoted in Odintz, "British Officer Corps," 464.

68. Quoted in Howard, " 'Things Here Wear a Melancholy Appearance,' " 495–96.

69. See Conway, "To Subdue America," 381–407.

70. [Graydon], *Memoirs*, 184.

71. Balderston and Syrett, *The Lost War*, 122, Bowater to Lord Denbigh, 4 Apr. 1777.

72. Quoted in Demarest, "The Baylor Massacre," 45.

73. Anburey, *Travels*, 1:330-31.

74. Muenchhausen, *At General Howe's Side*, 50. For similar incidents at Kipp's Bay and Brandywine, see Bardeleben, *Diary*, 63-64; F. Mackenzie, *Diary*, 1:48; Baurmeister, *Revolution in America*, 49; and Sullivan, *From Redcoat to Rebel*, 130.

75. For the rumored atrocities at the North Bridge, see Bolton, *Letters of Hugh, Earl Percy*, 51; and Innes, "Jeremy Lister," 65. The incident is examined in Galvin, *The Minute Men*, 161.

76. F. Mackenzie, *Diary*, 1:20-21; Barker, *British in Boston*, 36; Evelyn, *Memoir and Letters*, 54; Bolton, *Letters of Hugh, Earl Percy*, 50; *Discord and Civil Wars*, 12-13. For similar incidents later in the war, see Sullivan, *From Redcoat to Rebel*, 108; Scull, "Montresor Journals," 477; Morton, "Diary," 28-29; and Simcoe, *Military Journal*, 52, 92-93.

77. Campbell, *Journal of an Expedition*, 57-58, 77.

78. WO 27/30, fo. 175.

79. NAS, GD 21/492, Peebles papers, book 11, 16-21.

80. NAS, GD 174/2106, 2107, Orders, 15 Sept. 1777.

81. Lamb, *Journal*, 350, 361.

82. Wilkin, *Some British Soldiers*, 245, Hale to his parents, 23 Mar. 1778.

83. Muenchhausen, *At General Howe's Side*, 31; Ewald, *Diary of the American War*, 86.

84. Gruber, *John Peebles' American War*, 133; Wilkin, *Some British Soldiers*, 230, 231, Hale to his parents, 21 Oct. 1777.

85. Commager and Morris, *Spirit of 'Seventy-Six*, 468, Adj. Gen. Joseph Reed to his wife, 17 Sept. 1776; Hunter, *Journal*, 31-32, 34.

86. Wilkin, *Some British Soldiers*, 258-59, Hale to his parents, 4 July 1778.

87. Drewe, *Military Sketches*, 84-85.

88. Ibid., 72-74.

89. Ewald, *Diary of the American War*, 340.

90. Gruber, *John Peebles' American War*, 133.

91. Johnson, *Sketches*, 1:496.

92. T. Anderson, "Journal," 209.

93. Lee, *Revolutionary War Memoirs*, 228-29. Lee was not present at Cowpens.

94. Babits, *Devil of a Whipping*, 116-23.

95. Hanger, *Address*, 29-30, 30n. Hanger was not present at Cowpens.

96. "A Frenchman's Comments," 366.

## 10. "BUSHFIGHTING"

*Epigraph. Journal of Du Roi the Elder*, 7-8.

1. For the beginnings of the light infantry arm, see particularly Robson, "British Light Infantry," 209-22; P. E. Russell, "Redcoats in the Wilderness," 629-52; M. C. Ward, "'European Method of Warring Is Not Practiced Here,'"

249-63; Brumwell, "British Army and Warfare with the North American Indians," 147-75; and Brumwell, *Redcoats*, 191-263.

2. For the evolution of the light infantry, see especially Gates, *British Light Infantry*; and Glover, *Peninsular Preparation*.

3. Houlding, *Fit for Service*, 287-88, 304-306.

4. Ibid., 251.

5. Smythies, *Historical Records*, 549-52, "Townshend's Rules and Orders for the Discipline of the Light Infantry Companies in His Majesty's Army in Ireland," 15 May 1772.

6. To deploy from a two-deep line into a column of double files, or vice versa, Townshend recommended that the men should simply face to the left or right. To change the line's facing, he envisaged that the men would break ranks and run up obliquely to their proper place in the new formation, arriving on their ground successively rather than wheeling by ranks (in which the maneuver division maintained an unbroken front). This echoed the regulation instruction: "In all evolutions where the wheelings [sic] are long, and cannot be easily and expeditiously effected by reason of . . . broken ground . . . not admitting of it, forming the battalion and all similar evolutions may be performed by wheeling and facing briskly by files." *1764 Regulations*, 27. See also Young, *Manoeuvres*; and Pickering, *Easy Plan*, 139-59.

7. NAM, Howe's Light Infantry Discipline. Between 6 August and 22 September 1774, Howe held a training camp on Salisbury Plain, where the assembled light companies of the 3rd, 11th, 21st, 29th, 32nd, 36th, and 70th Regiments practiced his maneuvers. Afterward the light companies departed for Richmond Park in London, where on 3 October they performed for the King. Among the officers was Lieutenant Patrick Ferguson of the 70th Regiment's light company, whom Howe particularly commended to the King. Gilchrist, *Patrick Ferguson*, 24, 29.

8. The three sections occupy pages 1-11, 13, 15-17, and 19-22 of Howe's Light Infantry Discipline (12, 14, and 18 are blank). John Houlding has lauded the performance at Richmond as one of the most realistic military exercises staged anywhere in the later eighteenth century. Houlding, *Fit for Service*, 337n31.

9. The commanding officer signified the pace at which he required the battalion to perform a maneuver by adding to his oral command the imperative *"March!" "March, March!"* or *"Advance!"*

10. Williamson, *Elements*, 111-17. This particular selection of Williamson's work was later excerpted, without explanation, in Fuller, *British Light Infantry*, app. 1, 247-50. Yet along with the Howe maneuvers, Fuller reproduced an unrelated chunk of Williamson's evaluation of the various drill systems that he had surveyed throughout that entire chapter of his treatise. As reproduced therein, these comments (Fuller, *British Light Infantry*, 250-52, commencing "Thus we have taken a view . . .") appear to be a part of, and to deal solely with, Howe's drill. In this context they are unintelligible.

11. Lamb, *Memoir*, 89-91. Lamb wrongly stated that the King saw the light infantry perform at Salisbury; in fact he watched them at Richmond.

12. The squad was an administrative rather than a tactical unit, and

though Lamb mentioned "the necessary business of the drill," it is difficult to see how so few men could have profitably practiced much from Howe's maneuvers.

13. Williamson, *Elements*, 111–12.

14. Despite Lamb's unambiguous statement that he learned the drill at Dublin in 1775, two modern writers have wrongly asserted that the Irishman attended Howe's Salisbury camp. Yet the 9th Regiment was in Ireland at the time, and Lamb was a hatman corporal. See Robson, "British Light Infantry," 209; and Gates, *British Light Infantry*, 50.

15. The two units were the 3rd and 11th Regiments. Howe's own corps, the 46th Regiment, was also in Ireland, though its light company had not attended the Salisbury camp. The "old" Dublin garrison, which rotated out of the city in the spring of 1775, consisted of the 24th, 35th, 40th, 49th, 53rd, and 57th Regiments; the "new" garrison was made up of the 9th, 15th, 33rd, 34th, 37th, and 46th Regiments. I am most grateful to Dr. John Houlding for having provided me with this information.

16. Such is the verdict of the leading authority on the training of the eighteenth-century British army. See Houlding, *Fit for Service*, 316–17.

17. Lamb, *Memoir*, 91.

18. Charles Stanhope (1753–1829) became the 3rd Earl of Harrington in 1779, attained the rank of general in 1802, and from 1805 to 1812 was commander in chief in Ireland.

19. The 29th Regiment's flank companies served on the Saratoga expedition, but the battalion companies remained in Canada. I am most grateful to Dr. John Houlding for having kindly supplied me with service data on both Stanhope and Williamson.

20. Houlding, *Fit for Service*, 336n30. In his study of the light infantry on Burgoyne's Albany expedition of 1777, Brian Hubner has dissented from this view. Hubner has claimed that only two of the ten light companies serving under Carleton and Burgoyne in 1776–77 can have had no opportunity of learning Howe's drill before departing the British Isles for North America. Additionally, he has pointed to Stanhope and to Brigadier General Fraser as light infantry enthusiasts who were in an excellent position to promote the drill within the Canadian army. He has also highlighted a number of hints that Burgoyne's troops learned some unorthodox maneuvers for operating in woods. See Hubner, "Formation of the British Light Infantry Companies," esp. 72–76, 82, 89–91.

21. Gage's units were the 4th, 5th, 10th, 23rd, 38th, 43rd, 47th, 52nd, 59th, and 64th Regiments and part of the 18th and 65th Regiments. None of these corps arrived in America later than October 1774.

22. Honyman, *Colonial Panorama*, 43–44.

23. WO 36/1, fo. 42, General Orders, c.15 Apr. 1775.

24. Barker, *British in Boston*, 29.

25. Mackenzie recorded the gist of the order on 15 April and elaborated a little the next day. F. Mackenzie, *Diary*, 1:48, 50.

26. After the outbreak of hostilities, Gage curtly announced that "[t]he grenadiers and light infantry [are] to do duty with their corps till further orders." WO 36/1, fo. 42, General Orders, n.d.

27. Raymond, *Winslow Papers*, 68, Edward Winslow to Gov. John Wentworth, [1781].

28. Kent Record Office, Amherst MSS, 073/21, fo. 1, Lord Townshend to Lord Amherst, 17 June 1775. I am most grateful to Dr. John Houlding for having provided me with this extract.

29. Clinton quoted in Odintz, "British Officer Corps," 134.

30. Atwood, *The Hessians*, 68. For brief accounts of the attack penned by Hessian participants, see Bardeleben, *Diary*, 56; B. E. Burgoyne, *Defeat, Disaster, and Dedication*, 17; and Schmidt, *Hesse-Cassel Mirbach Regiment*, 53–54.

31. [Montagu-Stuart-Wortley], *Prime Minister and His Son*, 84, Stuart to his father, 3 Sept. 1776; Murray, *Letters from America*, 33, Murray to Mrs. Smith, 31 Aug. 1776.

32. T. Hughes, *Journal*, 10.

33. Kingsley, "Letters to Lord Polwarth from Sir Francis-Carr Clarke," 420, 17 July 1777.

34. HSD, Dansey Letters, W. Dansey to mother, 15 Mar. 1777, 19 Jan. 1778.

35. Peckham, *Sources of American Independence*, 2307, Ferguson to Clinton, 1 Aug. 1778.

36. T. Hughes, *Journal*, 5–6.

37. Anburey, *Travels*, 1:205.

38. J. Burgoyne, *State of the Expedition*, 17.

39. NAS, GD 174/2106, 2107, Orders, 15 Sept. 1777.

40. Lushington, *Life and Services of General Lord Harris*, 79-80, Capt. Harris to his uncle, n.d.; 97, memo by Lord Harris, c.1824.

41. Raymond, *Winslow Papers*, 68, Edward Winslow to Gov. John Wentworth, [1781].

42. F. A. Riedesel, *Memoirs, Letters, and Journals*, 1:64 (see also 58).

43. Heath, *Memoirs*, 213. Heath himself was not present at the affair.

44. Murray, *Letters from America*, 40, Murray to Mrs. Smith, 25 Feb. 1777.

45. HSD, Dansey Letters, W. Dansey to mother, Piscataway, 20 Apr. 1777.

46. Wilkin, *Some British Soldiers*, 245, Hale to his parents, 23 Mar. 1778.

47. Pell, "Diary," 109. See also Hadden, *Journal and Orderly Books*, 164.

48. Enys, *American Journals*, 24.

49. Hadden, *Journal and Orderly Books*, 132.

50. Anburey, *Travels*, 1:297.

51. Lee, *Revolutionary War Memoirs*, 285n.

52. J. Burgoyne, *State of the Expedition*, 70. Burgoyne regretted that his troops had never been able to deliver "a charge upon an open plain." Ibid., 176.

53. Money quoted in Gates, *British Light Infantry*, 57.

54. J. Burgoyne, *State of the Expedition*, 162.

55. Hadden, *Journal and Orderly Books*, 164–66.

56. Lee, *Revolutionary War Memoirs*, 200. Lee was not present at the action.

57. Chesney, *Journal*, 17–18.

58. Commager and Morris, *Spirit of 'Seventy-Six*, 1141, account of Col. Isaac Shelby of North Carolina.

59. Ibid., 1144, account of James P. Collins.

60. *DAR*, 20: 91, Cornwallis to Germain (No. 8), 17 Mar. 1781.

61. Tarleton, *History*, 275.

62. Stedman, *History*, 2:341–42.

63. B. E. Burgoyne, *Enemy Views*, 448–49, excerpted from Koch's account of Guilford Courthouse. Koch had enlisted in 1742 and was a veteran of the Seven Years' War. See also Atwood, *The Hessians*, 41, 140–41.

64. De Fonblanque, *Political and Military Episodes*, 209, from a letter by Burgoyne dated late 1775 or early 1776.

65. J. Burgoyne, *State of the Expedition*, app., xcvii.

66. Gilchrist, *Patrick Ferguson*, 69.

67. Lamb, *Memoir*, 200. Lamb's comments were prompted by a similar passage in Anburey, *Travels* (1:446–47). See also Fuller, *British Light Infantry*, 180.

68. Baxter, *British Invasion*, 221.

69. Anburey, *Travels*, 1:336–37.

## 11. HOLLOW VICTORIES

*Epigraph*. O'Hara, "Letters," 159.

1. See Black, *European Warfare*, chap. 3.

2. Dann, *The Revolution Remembered*, 194–96, 216–20, depositions of Garret Watts and Guilford Dudley.

3. Babits, *Devil of a Whipping*, 117, 155–59. The collapse of Tarleton's stunned infantry echoed that of the Russian Observation Corps on the Mühl-Berge salient at the battle of Kunersdorf (1759). Having suffered a concentric bombardment by three Prussian batteries, the stupefied Russians were simply slaughtered where they stood or lay during the subsequent assault. See Duffy, *Frederick the Great*, 185; and Duffy, *Military Experience in the Age of Reason*, 205.

4. Only about 10,000 of Washington's men were on Long Island on the day of the battle (the rest were on or around Manhattan). This figure rose to perhaps 12,000 the next day, when Washington temporarily reinforced the doomed Brooklyn lines.

5. Johnson, *Sketches*, 1:494–95.

6. Quoted in ibid., 376. See also Babits, *Devil of a Whipping*, 53–54.

7. See McGuire, *Battle of Paoli*, 31–36; and McGuire, *Philadelphia Campaign. Volume One*, 287–92. In this instance Washington was seeking not to avoid an action, but to fight on better ground. In the event, a violent deluge (blowing toward the British) transformed the low ground between the two armies into a quagmire and ruined the troops' ammunition. This halted Howe's advance and prevented the affair from developing into a major engagement on the scale of Brandywine.

8. Hanger, *Address*, 82n; Lee, *Revolutionary War Memoirs*, 175.

9. O'Hara, "Letters," 159, O'Hara to Duke of Grafton, 1 Nov. 1780.

10. *PNG*, 7:434, Greene to Samuel Huntington, 16 Mar. 1781; Lee, *Revolutionary War Memoirs*, 281–82.

11. *PNG*, 8:168, Greene to the Chevalier de La Luzerne, 28 Apr. 1781.

12. Muenchhausen, *At General Howe's Side*, 32; Howe, *Narrative*, 26.

13. Campbell, *Journal of an Expedition*, 31.

14. *DAR*, 20:92, Cornwallis to Germain (No. 8), 17 Mar. 1781.

15. Heath, *Memoirs*, 121–22. Heath postulated that routed troops who were allowed to rally would renew their resistance with more obstinacy than before.

16. Gibbes, *Documentary History of the American Revolution*, 3:151, "Account furnished by Col. Otho Williams. . . ."

17. See for instance Duffy, *Military Experience in the Age of Reason*, 216, 228, 257.

18. *DAR*, 12:265–66, Howe to Germain (No. 32, Separate), 30 Nov. 1776; Lee, *Revolutionary War Memoirs*, 260; Lushington, *Life and Services of General Lord Harris*, 87, Capt. George Harris to his uncle, 16 Jan. 1777; Lafayette, *Memoirs, Correspondence, and Manuscripts*, 1:417, Lafayette to Washington, 24 May 1781.

19. The best-known loyalist cavalry units—such as the mounted elements of the British Legion and the Queen's Rangers and the King's American Dragoons—were created by amalgamating independent troops like the Caledonian Volunteers, the Bucks County Volunteers, and the Philadelphia Light Dragoons. See Katcher, *King George's Army.*

20. The two units from Britain were the 16th and 17th Light Dragoons. The latter regiment arrived at Boston in June 1775, while the former arrived at New York in September 1776 and was drafted there in December 1778.

21. Sullivan, *From Redcoat to Rebel*, 130.

22. *DAR*, 20:228, Stewart to Cornwallis, 9 Sept. 1781.

23. Ibid., 12:265–66, Howe to Germain (No. 32, Separate), 30 Nov. 1776; ibid., 14:32, Germain to Howe, 14 Jan. 1777.

24. See for instance Clinton, *American Rebellion*, 159–60, 165–66, 169; Baurmeister, *Revolution in America*, 55, 98; Kemble, "Papers," 1:91; Muenchhausen, *At General Howe's Side*, 23, 24, 26, 28; Scull, "Montresor Journals," 440; and Seybolt, "A Contemporary British Account," 75–76.

25. Lee, *Revolutionary War Memoirs*, 236, 241–42, 255, 260, 265, 265n, 269–70, 274n, 321, 379; Tarleton, *History*, 377, 382–83.

26. Although elements of the hard-pressed loyalist garrison appear to have formed an irregular square at the hotly contested action at Hanging Rock, it seems unlikely that they did so primarily to fend off Major William Davie's handful of mounted militia.

27. Lee, *Revolutionary War Memoirs*, 131, 389n.

28. Tarleton, *History*, 31.

29. Abbatt, *Major André's Journal*, 79; Clinton, *American Rebellion*, 94; WO 34/111, fo. 71, anonymous to Lord Amherst, n.d.

30. *PNG*, 8:441, Greene to Washington, 22 June 1781. See also ibid., 367, Greene to Lafayette, 9 June 1781.

31. Simcoe, *Military Journal*, 194–95, General Orders, 23 or 24 April 1781. The cavalry in question were the Queen's Rangers dragoons (who were in reserve) and hussars (who formed part of the advanced guard).

32. Tarleton, *History*, 275, 463–64, 511; Lee, *Revolutionary War Memoirs*, 275, 338–39; *DAR*, 20:92, Cornwallis to Germain (No. 8), 17 Mar. 1781.

33. *DAR*, 20:123, Rawdon to Cornwallis, 26 Apr. 1781.

34. Coleman, "Southern Campaign," 41, Judge St. John Tucker to Fanny, 18 Mar. 1781.

35. Martin, *Private Yankee Doodle*, 74.

36. *Detail and Conduct of the American War*, 71, "Testimony of Major General Charles Grey before a House of Commons Committee," 6 May 1779.

37. *Journal of Du Roi the Elder*, 108.

38. Lee, *Revolutionary War Memoirs*, 338–39, 339n.

39. Washington, *Papers*, 7:36, General Orders, 27 Oct. 1776. When in late 1776 Howe requested that the government send out three hundred dragoon remounts in time for the next campaign, he added that he would prefer Irish horses, for they were not only hardier but "more accustomed to get over fences than the horses from England." *DAR*, 12:265–66, Howe to Germain (No. 32, Separate), 30 Nov. 1776.

40. *PNG*, 8:441, Greene to Washington, 22 June 1781; Pettengill, *Letters from America*, 184–85, Capt. Johann Hinrichs to unknown, 18 Jan. 1778. See also Pettengill, *Letters from America*, 70–71; J. Burgoyne, *State of the Expedition*, 115; Clinton, *American Rebellion*, 42–43; and Lynderberg, *Archibald Robertson*, 93. By contrast, Captain Patrick Ferguson judged that "cavalry could be generally employed with effect" in New England, where the fences were lower and slighter and would not stop a horse. Peckham, *Sources of American Independence*, 2:308, Ferguson to Clinton, 1 Aug. 1778.

41. Tarleton, *History*, 235, 273–74, 354. For other good examples of British inability to exploit cavalry tactically, see *DAR*, 14:208, Howe to Germain, 10 Oct. 1777; Clinton, *American Rebellion*, 42–43; Abbatt, *Major André's Journal*, 78–79; and Hayes, *Stephen Jarvis*, 25–26.

42. Tarleton, *History*, 221; Lee, *Revolutionary War Memoirs*, 226.

43. Hunter, *Journal*, 30.

44. Martin, *Private Yankee Doodle*, 74.

45. Hawkins, "Journal," 421. These Highlanders were probably from the light company of either the 42nd or 71st Regiment. At Brandywine those companies were respectively part of the 1st and 2nd Battalions of Light Infantry.

46. *DAR*, 14:208, Howe to Germain, 10 Oct. 1777; Abbatt, *Major André's Journal*, 56–57; Muenchhausen, *At General Howe's Side*, 39.

47. Quoted in Nelson, *General James Grant*, 123.

48. Peckham, *Sources of American Independence*, 2:303–305, Ferguson to Clinton, 1 Aug. 1778.

49. *DAR*, 20:184, Cornwallis to Clinton, 8 July 1781; Tarleton, *History*, 354; Stedman, *History*, 2:395.

50. Murray, *Letters from America*, 33, Murray to his sister, 31 Aug. 1776.

51. Cohen, "Captain William Leslie's Paths to Glory," 61.

52. Abbatt, *Major André's Journal*, 46–47; Gruber, *John Peebles' Amer-*

*ican War,* 132–33; Hunter, *Journal,* 30; Muenchhausen, *At General Howe's Side,* 31–32; Seybolt, "A Contemporary British Account," 79.

53. WLCL, Loftus Cliffe Papers, Cliffe to Jack, 24 Oct. 1777.

54. Tarleton, *History,* 214; *DAR,* 20:90, Cornwallis to Germain (No. 8), 17 Mar. 1781; Lee, *Revolutionary War Memoirs,* 226, 230–31, 285n, 286n.

55. [Montagu-Stuart-Wortley], *Prime Minister and His Son,* 101–102, Stuart to his father, 29 Mar. 1777.

56. Ibid., 104–105, MacLean to Alexander Cummings, 19 Feb. 1777.

57. T. Hughes, *Journal,* 79.

58. Gruber, *John Peebles' American War,* 372.

59. Baurmeister, *Revolution in America,* 426.

60. Ewald, *Diary of the American War,* 340.

61. See for example Lafayette, *Memoirs, Correspondence, and Manuscripts,* 1:376, Lafayette to Vergennes, 30 Jan. 1781.

62. *DAR,* 20:107, Cornwallis to Clinton, 10 Apr. 1781.

63. Ibid., 18:151, Cornwallis to Germain, 21 Aug. 1780; ibid., 170, Cornwallis to Germain, 19 Sept. 1780, 189–90, Rawdon to Leslie, 24 Oct. 1780.

64. Ibid., 14:166, Burgoyne to Germain, 20 Aug. 1777.

65. See for instance Conway, "To Subdue America," 381–407; Conway, "'Great Mischief Complain'd Of,'" 370–90; Tiedemann, "Patriots by Default," 35–63; and Shy, *People Numerous and Armed,* 225–26, 232–34.

66. Chastellux, *Travels in North America,* 1:215.

# Bibliography

PRIMARY SOURCES

*Manuscripts*

American Philosophical Society Library, Sol Feinstone Manuscripts Collection, Philadelphia
Memo Battle of Brandywine, #111.
Anonymous British Journal, 1776–78, #409.
Author's possession
Diary of Thompson Forster, Staff Surgeon to his Majesty's Detached Hospital in North America, Oct. 19, 1775–Oct. 23, 1777. Transcribed in 1938 from the original in the possession of Robert Ethelstone Thompson Forster.
Boston Public Library
Thomas Stanley Letters.
British Library, London
British 43rd Regt. Orderly Books Add. Mss. 42,449–50.
Claydon House, Buckinghamshire
Sir Harry Calvert Diary, 16 August 1780–19 October 1781, 9/102/1.
Collection of the Fort Ticonderoga Museum, New York
British 47th Regt. Orderly Book, 16 July–6 Oct. 1777.
Historical Society of Delaware, Dover
William Dansey Letters.
Library of Congress, Washington, D.C.
Peter Force Collection
Richard Augustus Wywill Journal.

George Washington Papers
British 40th Regt. Orderly Book, 20 Apr.–28 Aug. 1777.
British 64th Regt. Light Company Orderly Book, 14 Sept.–3 Oct. 1777.
British 2nd Bn. Grenadiers Orderly Book, 1–27 June 1778.
British 1st Bn. Light Infantry Orderly Book, 4 Aug.–13 Oct. 1778.
Massachusetts Historical Society, Boston
British 40th Regt. Orderly Book, 6 Oct.–27 Dec. 1776.
John Waller Orderly Book (British 1st Bn. Marines), 25 Mar. 1775–26 Jan. 1776.
Morristown National Historical Park, New Jersey
British HQ Orderly Book, 30 June–4 Oct. 1776.
The National Archives, Kew, London (formerly the Public Records Office)
Colonial Office Papers
5: America and West Indies.
War Office Papers
3: Office of the Commander in Chief: Out Letters.
12: General Muster Books and Pay Lists.
27: Inspection Returns.
28: Records of Military Headquarters.
34: Baron Jeffrey Amherst, Commander in Chief, Papers.
36: Military Headquarters, North America, Entry Books, American Revolution.
National Archives of Scotland, Edinburgh (formerly the Scottish Records Office)
GD 21: Cunninghame of Thourtoun Papers.
GD 174: MacLaine Papers.
National Army Museum, Chelsea
Howe's Light Infantry Discipline, 6807/157/6.
Francis Laye Letters, 6807/154.
Services and letters of James Green, 7201/36/1–2.
New-York Historical Society
British HQ Orderly Book, 26 Sept. 1776–2 June 1777.
British HQ Orderly Book, 11 Sept.–24 Oct. 1778.
British HQ Orderly Book, 25 Apr.–2 Aug. 1781.
British HQ Orderly Book, 1 Aug. 1781–20 Feb. 1782.
British Guards Brigade Orderly Book, 14 Aug. 1776–28 Jan. 1777.
British 17th Regt. Orderly Book, 11 Oct.–28 Dec. 1776.
British Bn. of Grenadiers Orderly Book, 7 June–3 July 1777.
British Orderly Book kept by Capt. Frederick DePeyster, 1 Jan.–23 Aug. 1780, 10 Feb.–28 June 1782.
Princeton University Library, Manuscript Collection, Princeton, New Jersey
Ensign Thomas Glyn Journal.
Royal Artillery Institute, London
Royal Artillery Brigade Orderly Book, 28 Sept. 1777–21 Feb. 1778.
William L. Clements Library, Ann Arbor, Michigan
Loftus Cliffe Papers.
British 10th Regt. Orderly Book, 8 Mar.–25 Apr. 1775.

## Published Primary Sources

Abbatt, W., ed. *Major André's Journal*. Tarrytown, New York: W. Abbatt, 1930. Reprint, New York: New York Times, 1968.

"The Actions at Brandywine and Paoli, Described by a British Officer." *Pennsylvania Magazine of History and Biography* 29 (1905): 368.

Adlum, J. *Memoirs of the Life of John Adlum in the Revolutionary War.* Edited by H. H. Peckham. Chicago: Caxton Club, 1968.

Allaire, A. *Diary of Lieut. Anthony Allaire*. Edited by L. C. Draper. New York: New York Times, 1968.

Anburey, T. *Travels through the Interior Parts of North America in a Series of Letters by an Officer.* 2 vols. London: William Lane, 1789. Reprint, New York: New York Times, 1969.

Anderson, T. "Journal of Lieutenant Thomas Anderson of the Delaware Regiment, 1780–1782." *Historical Magazine* 1 (1867): 207–11.

Atkinson, C. T., ed. "Some Evidence for Burgoyne's Expedition." *Journal of the Society for Army Historical Research* 26 (1948): 132–42.

Balderston, M., and D. Syrett, eds. *The Lost War: Letters from British Officers during the American Revolution*. New York: Horizon, 1975.

"Bamford's Diary: The Revolutionary Diary of a British Officer." *Maryland Historical Magazine* 27 (1932): 240–59, 296–314; 28 (1933): 9–26.

Bardeleben, J. H. von. *The Diary of Lieutenant von Bardeleben*. Translated and edited by B. E. Burgoyne. Bowie, Md.: Heritage Books, 1998.

Barker, J. *The British in Boston: Being the Diary of Lieutenant John Barker of the King's Own Regiment from November 15, 1774 to May 31, 1776.* Edited by E. E. Dana. Cambridge, Mass.: Harvard University Press, 1924. Reprint, New York: New York Times, 1969.

"Battle of Princeton, by Sergeant R——." *Pennsylvania Magazine of History and Biography* 20 (1896): 515–19.

Baurmeister, C. L. *Revolution in America: Confidential Letters and Journals, 1776–84, of Adjutant General Major Baurmeister of the Hessian Forces.* Translated and edited by B. A. Uhlendorf. New Brunswick, N.J.: Rutgers University Press, 1957.

Baxter, J. P., ed. *The British Invasion from the North: The Campaigns of Generals Carleton and Burgoyne, with the Journal of Lt. William Digby, of the 53d. or Shropshire Regiment of Foot.* Albany, N.Y.: J. Munsell's Sons, 1887. Reprint, New York: DaCapo, 1970.

Beatson, R. *Naval and Military Memoirs of Great Britain, from 1727 to 1783.* 6 vols. 2nd ed. London: Longman, 1804.

Bell, A. "Copy of a Journal by Andrew Bell, Esq., at One Time the Confidential Secretary of General Sir Henry Clinton. Kept during the March of the British Army through New-Jersey in 1778." *Proceedings of the New Jersey Historical Society* 6 (1851): 15–19.

Bense, J. *The Journal of Johann Bense in North America, 1776–83.* Translated and edited by C. Reuter. German-Canadian Museum of Applied History, Canada (undated pamphlet).

Biddulph, R. "Letters of Robert Biddulph." Edited by V. Biddulph. *American Historical Review* 29 (1923): 87–109.

Blanchard, C. *The Journal of Claude Blanchard, Commissary to the French Auxiliary Army sent to the United States during the American Revolution, 1780–1783.* Translated by W. Duane. Edited by T. Balch. Albany, N.Y.: J. Munsell, 1876. Reprint, New York: New York Times, 1969.

Bland, H. *A Treatise of Military Discipline: In which is Laid Down and Explained the Duty of the Officer and Soldier, through the Several Branches of the Service.* 9th rev. ed. London: R. Baldwin, 1762.

Bolton, C. K., ed. *Letters of Hugh, Earl Percy, from Boston and New York, 1774–1776.* Boston: Charles E. Godspeed, 1902. Reprint, Boston: Gregg, 1972.

Bostwick, E. "A Connecticut Soldier under Washington: Elisha Bostwick's Memoirs of the First Years of the Revolution." Edited by W. S. Powell. *William and Mary Quarterly*, 3rd ser., 6 (1949): 94–107.

Boudinot, E. *Journal of Events in the Revolution.* Philadelphia: F. Bourquin, 1894. Reprint, New York: New York Times, 1968.

Bradford, S. S., ed. "A British Officer's Revolutionary War Journal, 1776–1778." *Maryland Historical Magazine* 56 (1961): 150–75.

——, ed. "Lord Francis Napier's Journal of the Burgoyne Campaign." *Maryland Historical Magazine* 57 (1962): 285–333.

Burgoyne, B. E., trans. and ed. *Defeat, Disaster, and Dedication: The Diaries of the Hessian Officers Jakob Piel and Andreas Wiederhold.* Bowie, Md.: Heritage Books, 1997.

——, trans. and ed. *Diaries of Two Ansbach Jaegers.* Bowie, Md.: Heritage Books, 1997.

——, comp., trans., and ed. *Enemy Views: The American Revolutionary War as Recorded by Hessian Participants.* Bowie, Md.: Heritage Books, 1996.

——, trans. and ed. *A Hessian Officer's Diary of the American Revolution.* Bowie, Md.: Heritage Books, 1994.

Burgoyne, B. E., trans., and M. E. Burgoyne, eds. *Journal of the Hesse-Cassel Jaeger Corps: and, Hans Konze's List of Jaeger Officers.* Westminster, Md.: Heritage Books, 2005.

Burgoyne, B. E., trans., and M. E. Burgoyne, eds. *Order Book of the Hesse-Cassel von Mirbach Regiment.* Westminster, Md.: Heritage Books, 2004.

Burgoyne, J. *A State of the Expedition from Canada as Laid before the House of Commons.* 2nd ed. London: J. Almon, 1780. Reprint, New York: New York Times, 1969.

——. *A Supplement to the State of the Expedition from Canada, Containing General Burgoyne's Orders, Respecting the Principal Movements, and Operations of the Army to the Raising of the Siege of Ticonderoga.* London: J. Robson, 1780.

Campbell, Sir A. *Journal of an Expedition against the Rebels of Georgia in North America under the orders of Archibald Campbell, Esquire, Lieut. Colo. of His Majesty's 71st Regimt., 1778.* Edited by C. Campbell. Darien, Ga.: Ashantilly, 1981.

Carter, W. *A Genuine Detail of the Several Engagements, Positions, and Movements of the Royal and American Armies, during the Years 1775 and 1776.* London: N.p., 1784.

Cavan, R. Lambart, 6th Earl of. *A New System of Military Discipline, Founded upon Principal by — a General Officer.* Philadelphia: R. Aitken, 1776.

Chastellux, F. J. Marquis de. *Travels in North America in the Years 1780, 1781, and 1782.* 2 vols. London: G. G. J. & J. Robinson, 1787. Reprint, New York: New York Times, 1968.

Chesney, A.. *Journal of Alexander Chesney, a South Carolina Loyalist in the Revolution and After.* Edited by E. A. Jones. Columbus: Ohio State University, 1921.

Clarke, J. C. *An Impartial and Authentic Narrative of the Battle Fought on the 17th of June, 1775 between His Britannic Majesty's Troops and the American Provincial Army, on Bunker's Hill, Near Charles-town, in New England.* London: N.p., 1775.

Clinton, Sir H. *The American Rebellion: Sir Henry Clinton's Narrative of His Campaigns, 1775–1782.* Edited by W. B. Willcox. New Haven, Conn.: Yale University Press, 1954.

Closen, Baron L. von. *The Revolutionary Journal of Baron Ludwig von Closen, 1780–1783.* Translated and edited by E. M. Acomb. Chapel Hill: University of North Carolina Press, 1958.

Cohen, S. S., ed. "Captain William Leslie's Paths to Glory." *New Jersey History* 108 (1990): 54–81.

Coleman, C. W., ed. "The Southern Campaign, 1781, from Guilford Courthouse to the Siege of York, Narrated in the Letters from Judge St. George Tucker to his Wife." *Magazine of American History* 7 (1881): 36–46, 201–16.

Collins, V. L., ed. *A Brief Narrative of the Ravages of the British and Hessians at Princeton in 1776–1777: A Contemporary Account of the Battles of Trenton and Princeton.* Princeton: University Library, 1906. Reprint, New York: New York Times, 1968.

Commager, H. S., and R. B. Morris, eds. *The Spirit of 'Seventy-Six: The Story of the American Revolution as Told by Participants.* Rev. ed., New York: Harper, 1975. Reprint, New York: DaCapo, 1995.

[Congreve, W.]. "The Battle of Long Island: A New Account." Edited by J. Black. *Journal of the Society for Army Historical Research* 69 (1991): 201–205.

*Considerations upon the Different Modes of Finding Recruits for the Army.* London: T. Cadell, 1775.

Corsar, K. C., ed. "Letters from America, 1780 and 1781." *Journal of the Society for Army Historical Research* 20 (1941): 130–35.

Cresswell, N. *The Journal of Nicholas Cresswell, 1774–1777.* Edited by S. Thornely. London: J. Cape, 1925.

Cumming, W. P., and H. F. Rankin, eds. *The Fate of a Nation: The American Revolution through Contemporary Eyes.* London: Phaidon, 1975.

Cuthbertson, B. *A System for the Compleat Interior Management and Oeconomy of a Battalion of Infantry.* 2nd ed. Bristol: A. Gray, 1776.

Dalrymple, W. *Tacticks.* Dublin: W. & H. Whitestone, 1782.

Dann, J. C., ed. *The Revolution Remembered: Eyewitness Accounts of the War for Independence.* Chicago: University of Chicago Press, 1980.

Davies, K. G., ed. *Documents of the American Revolution.* 21 vols. Dublin: Irish University Press, 1972–81.

Dearborn, H. *Revolutionary War Journals of Henry Dearborn, 1775–83.* Edited by L. A. Brown and H. H. Peckham. New York: Caxton Club, 1939. Reprint, New York: DaCapo, 1971.

[De Berniere, J.]. "Narrative of Occurrences." *Massachusetts Historical Society Collections* 2nd ser., 4 (1816): 204–19.

De Krafft, J. C. P. "Journal of Lieutenant John Charles Philip von Krafft of the Regiment von Bose, 1776–1784." Edited by T. H. Edsall. In *Collections of the New-York Historical Society for the Year 1882,* 1–202. New York: The Historical Society, 1883.

Denny, E. "The Military Journal of Major Ebeneezer Denny, an Officer in the Revolutionary and Indian Wars." Edited by W. H. Denny. *Memoirs of the Historical Society of Pennsylvania* 7 (1860): 205–409.

*The Detail and Conduct of the American War under Generals Gage, Howe, Burgoyne, and Vice Admiral Lord Howe.* 3rd ed. London: N.p., 1780.

"Diary of a French Officer." *Magazine of American History* 6 (1880): 205–14, 293–308, 376–85, 441–52; 7 (1881): 283–95.

*Discord and Civil Wars: Being a Portion of the Journal Kept by Lieutenant Williams of His Majesty's Twenty-Third Regiment while Stationed in British North America during the Time of the Revolution.* Buffalo, N.Y.: Salisbury Club, 1954.

Döhla, J. C. *A Hessian Diary of the American Revolution by Johann Conrad Döhla.* Translated and edited by B. E. Burgoyne. Norman: University of Oklahoma Press, 1990.

Donkin, R. *Military Collections and Remarks.* New York: H. Gaine, 1777.

[Dowdeswell, T.]. "The Operations in New Jersey: An English Officer Describes the Events of December 1776." *Proceedings of the New Jersey Historical Society* 70 (1952): 133–36.

Downman, F. *The Services of Lieut.-Colonel Francis Downman in France, North America, and the West Indies, between the Years 1758 and 1784.* Edited by F. A. Whinyates. London: Royal Artillery Institution, Woolwich, 1898.

Drake, S. A., ed. *Bunker Hill: The Story Told in Letters from the Battle Field, by British officers Engaged.* Boston: Nichols & Hall, 1875.

——, ed. *Burgoyne's Invasion of 1777,* Boston: Lee & Shepard, 1889.

Drewe, E. *Military Sketches.* Exeter: N.p., 1784.

Dundas, D. *Principles of Military Movements, Chiefly Applied to Infantry. Illustrated by Manoeuvres of the Prussian Troops, and by an Outline of the British Campaigns in Germany, during the War of 1757.* London: T. Cadell, 1788.

Enys, J. *The American Journals of Lt. John Enys.* Edited by E. Cometti. Syracuse, N.Y.: Syracuse University Press, 1976.

Evelyn, W. G. *Memoir and Letters of Captain W. Glanville Evelyn, of the 4th Regiment ("King's Own"), from North America, 1774–1776.* Edited by G. D. Scull. Oxford: J. Parker, 1879. Reprint, New York: New York Times, 1971.

Ewald, J. von. *Diary of the American War: A Hessian Journal.* Translated and edited by J. P. Tustin. New Haven, Conn.: Yale University Press, 1979.

———. *Treatise on Partisan Warfare.* Translated and edited by R. A. Selig and D. C. Skaggs. New York: Greenwood, 1991.

"Extracts from the Letterbook of Captain Hinrichs." *Pennsylvania Magazine of History and Biography* 22 (1898): 137–70.

Fanning, D. *The Narrative of Colonel David Fanning, Giving Account of his Adventures in North Carolina, from 1775 to 1783, as Written by Himself.* Richmond, Va.: N.p., 1861.

Force, P., ed. *American Archives: Fourth Series, Containing a Documentary History of the English Colonies in North America from the King's Message to Parliament of March 7, 1774, to the Declaration of Independence by the United States.* 6 vols. Washington, D.C.: M. St. Clair Clarke & Peter Force, 1837–46.

———, ed. *American Archives: Fifth Series, Containing a Documentary History of the United States of America from the Declaration of Independence, July 4, 1776, to the Definitive Treaty of Peace with Great Britain, September 3, 1783.* 3 vols. Washington, D.C.: M. St. Clair Clarke & Peter Force, 1848–53.

Fortescue, J., ed. *The Correspondence of King George the Third: From 1760 to December 1783.* 6 vols. London: Macmillan, 1927–28.

"A Frenchman's Comments on the Discipline of the American and British Armies in 1777." *Pennsylvania Magazine of History and Biography* 35 (1911): 365–68.

Fyers, E. W. H., ed. "General Sir William Howe's Operations in Pennsylvania, 1777. The Battle of the Brandywine Creek—11 September—and the Action at Germantown—4 October." *Journal of the Society for Army Historical Research* 8 (1929): 228–41; 9 (1930): 27–42.

Gage, T. *The Correspondence of General Thomas Gage with the Secretaries of State, 1763–1775.* Edited C. E. Carter. 2 vols. New Haven, Conn.: Yale University Press, 1931–33. Reprint, Hamden, Conn.: Archon Books, 1969.

Galloway, J. *Letters to a Nobleman, on the Conduct of the War in the Middle Colonies.* London: J. Wilkie, 1779.

"George Inman's Narrative of the American Revolution." *Pennsylvania Magazine of History and Biography* 7 (1883): 237–48.

Gibbes, R. W., ed. *Documentary History of the American Revolution: Consisting of Letters and Papers Relating to the Contest for Liberty, Chiefly in South Carolina, from Originals in the Possession of the Editor, and Other Sources, 1776–1782.* 3 vols. Columbia, S.C.: Banner, 1853; and New York: D. Appleton, 1855, 1857. Reprint, New York: New York Times, 1971.

Graham, S. "An English Officer's Account of His Services in America, 1779–1781: Memoirs of Lt.-General Samuel Graham." *Historical Magazine* 9 (1865): 241–49, 267–74, 301–308, 329–35.

[———]. "A Recollection of the American Revolutionary War by a British Officer." *Virginia Historical Register* 6 (1853): 204–11.

[Graydon, A.]. *Memoirs of a Life, Chiefly Passed in Pennsylvania, Within the Last Sixty Years; with Occasional Remarks upon the General Occur-*

*rences, Character, and Spirit of that Eventful Period.* Harrisburg, Pa.: John Wyeth, 1811.

Greene, N. *The Papers of Nathanael Greene.* Edited by R. K. Showman and D. M. Conrad. 13 vols. Chapel Hill: University of North Carolina Press, 1976–2005.

[Grose, F.]. *Advice to the Officers of the British Army: With the Addition of Some Hints to the Drummer and Private Soldier.* 6th ed. London: G. Kearsley, 1783. Reprint, Schenectady, N.Y.: Unites States Historical Research Service, 1992.

Gruber, I. D., ed. *John Peebles' American War, 1776–1782.* Stroud, Gloucs.: Sutton, 1998.

Hadden, J. M. *Hadden's Journal and Orderly Books: A Journal Kept in Canada and upon Burgoyne's Campaign in 1776 and 1777. Also Orders Kept by Him and Issued by Sir Guy Carleton, Lieutenant-General John Burgoyne, and Major General William Phillips in 1776, 1777, and 1778.* Edited by H. Rogers. Albany, N.Y.: J. Munsell's Sons, 1884. Reprint, Boston: Gregg, 1972.

Hanger, G. *An Address to the Army, in Reply to Strictures, by R. M'Kenzie . . . on Tarleton's History of the Campaigns of 1780 and 1781.* London: James Ridgeway, 1789.

Harcourt, E. W., ed. *The Harcourt Papers.* 13 vols. Oxford: J. Parker, 1880–1905.

[Haslewood, W.]. "Journal of a British Officer during the American Revolution." Edited by L. P. Kellogg. *Mississippi Valley Historical Review* 7 (1920): 51–58.

Hawkins, J. "Journal of Sgt. Maj. John Hawkins." *Pennsylvania Magazine of History and Biography* 20 (1896): 420–21.

Hayes, J. T., ed. *Stephen Jarvis: The King's Loyal Horseman, His Narrative.* Fort Lauderdale, Fla.: Saddlebag, 1996.

Heath, W. *Memoirs of Major-General William Heath, by Himself, to which Is Added the Accounts of the Battle of Bunker Hill by Generals Dearborn, Lee, and Wilkinson.* Edited by W. Abbatt. New York: W. Abbatt, 1901. Reprint, New York: New York Times, 1968.

Historical Manuscripts Commission. *Report on the Manuscripts of the Late Reginald Rawdon Hastings, Esq., of the Manor House, Ashby de la Zouche.* 4 vols. London: H.M. Stationary Office, 1930–47.

———. *Report on the Manuscripts of Mrs. Stopford-Sackville, of Drayton House, Northamptonshire.* 2 vols. London: H.M. Stationary Office, 1904, 1910.

Honyman, R. *Colonial Panorama, 1775: Dr. Robert Honyman's Journal for March and April.* Edited by P. Padelford. San Marino, Calif.: Henry E. Huntington Library, 1939.

Houlding, J. A., and G. K. Yates, eds. "Corporal Fox's Memoir of Service, 1766–1783: Quebec, Saratoga, and the Convention Army." *Journal of the Society for Army Historical Research* 48 (1990): 146–68.

Howe, Sir W. *The Narrative of Lieutenant General William Howe, in a Committee of the House of Commons, on the 29th of April, 1779, Relative to His Conduct during His Late Command of the King's Troops in North*

*America: To which are Added Some Observations upon a Pamphlet.* London, H. Baldwin, 1780.

Hubbs, V. C., trans. and ed. *Hessian Journals: Unpublished Documents of the American Revolution.* Columbia: University of South Carolina Press, 1981.

Hughes, T. *A Journal by Thos. Hughes. For His Amusement, and Designed Only for His Perusal by the Time He Attains the Age of 50 if He Lives so Long, 1778–1789.* Introduction by E. A. Benians. Cambridge: Cambridge University Press, 1947.

Hunt, G., ed. *Fragments of Revolutionary History.* New York: Historical Printing Club, 1892. Reprint, New York: New York Times, 1971.

Hunter, M. *The Journal of Gen. Sir Martin Hunter, G.C.M.G., G.C.H., and Some Letters of His Wife, Lady Hunter.* Edited by A. Hunter and E. Bell. Edinburgh: Edinburgh Press, 1894.

Huth, H., ed. "Letters from a Hessian Mercenary." *Pennsylvania Magazine of History and Biography* 62 (1938): 488–501.

Inman, G. "Losses of the Military and Naval Forces Engaged in the War of the American Revolution." *Pennsylvania Magazine of History and Biography* 27 (1903): 176–205.

Innes, R. A., ed. "Jeremy Lister, 10th Regiment, 1770–83." *Journal of the Society for Army Historical Research* 41 (1963): 31–41, 59–73.

*John Robert Shaw: An Autobiography of Thirty Years, 1777–1807.* Edited by O. M. Teagarden and J. L. Crabtree. Athens: Ohio University Press, 1992.

Jones, C. C., ed. "Memorandum of the Road, and the March of a Corps of Troops from Savannah to Augusta, and Some Subsequent Occurrences." *Magazine of American History* 18 (1887): 256–58, 342–48.

Jordan, J. W., ed. "Extracts from the Order Book of Major Robert Clayton, of the Seventeenth Regiment British Foot, 1778." *Pennsylvania Magazine of History and Biography* 25 (1901): 100–103.

*Journal of Du Roi the Elder, Lieutenant and Adjutant, in the Service of the Duke of Brunswick, 1776–1778.* Translated by C. S. Epping. Philadelphia: Americana Germanica, 1911.

Kemble, S. "The Kemble Papers." 2 vols. *Collections of the New-York Historical Society for the Year 1883, . . . 1884.* New York: The Historical Society, 1884–85.

Kingsley, R. F., ed. "Letters to Lord Polwarth from Sir Francis-Carr Clarke, Aide-de-Camp to General John Burgoyne." *New York History* 79 (1998): 393–424.

Lafayette, Marquis de. *Memoirs, Correspondence, and Manuscripts of General Lafayette.* 3 vols. London: Saunders & Otley, 1837.

Lamb, R. *A British Soldier's Story: Roger Lamb's Narrative of the American Revolution.* Edited by D. N. Hagist. Baraboo, Wis.: Ballindalloch, 2004.

———. *Memoir of his own Life, by Roger Lamb.* Dublin: J. Jones, 1811.

———. *An Original and Authentic Journal of Occurrences during the Late American War, from Its Commencement to the Year 1783.* Dublin: Wilkinson & Courtney, 1809. Reprint, New York: New York Times, 1968.

Lee, H. *The Revolutionary War Memoirs of General Henry Lee.* 3rd ed. Edited by R. E. Lee. New York: University Publishing, 1869. Reprint, New York: DaCapo, 1998.

"Letters of British Officers in America in 1776." *Historical Magazine* 5 (1861): 68–70.

Linn, J. B., and W. H. Egle, eds. "Diary of the Pennsylvania Line, May 26, 1781–April 25, 1782." *Pennsylvania Archives* 2nd ser., 11 (1880): 707–62.

Luvaas, J., trans. and ed. *Frederick the Great on the Art of War*. New York: Free Press, 1966. Reprint, New York: DaCapo, 1999.

Lynderberg, H. M., ed. *Archibald Robertson, Lieutenant General, Royal Engineers: His Diaries and Sketches in America, 1762–1780*. New York: New York Public Library, 1930. Reprint, New York: New York Public Library, 1971.

[MacDowell, W.]. "Journal." *Pennsylvania Archives*, 2nd ser., 15 (1890): 296–340.

Mackenzie, F. *A British Fusilier in Revolutionary Boston: Being the Diary of Lieutenant Frederick Mackenzie, Adjutant of the Royal Welch Fusiliers, January 5–April 30, 1775; with a Letter Describing His Voyage to America*. Edited by A. French. Cambridge, Mass.: Harvard University Press, 1926.

——. *The Diary of Frederick Mackenzie*. Edited by A. French 2 vols. Cambridge, Mass.: Harvard University Press, 1930. Reprint, New York: New York Times, 1968.

Mackenzie, R. *Strictures on Lt.-Col. Tarleton's History "Of the Campaigns of 1780 and 1781, in the Southern Provinces of North America."* London: R. Jameson, 1787.

*The Manual Exercise, as Ordered by His Majesty, in 1764. Together with Plans and Explanations of the Method Generally Practis'd at Reviews and Field-Days, &c.* New York: H. Gaine, 1775.

Marshall, D.W., and H. H. Peckham, comps. and eds. *Campaigns of the American Revolution: An Atlas of Manuscript Maps*. Ann Arbor: University of Michigan Press, 1976.

Martin, J. P. *Private Yankee Doodle. Being a Narrative of the Adventures, Dangers, and Sufferings of a Revolutionary Soldier*. Edited by G. F. Scheer. Boston: Little, Brown, 1962. Reprint, Eastern Acorn Press, Eastern National Park and Monument Association, 1995.

"Mathew's Narrative." *Historical Magazine* 1 (1857): 102–106.

McCarty, T. "The Revolutionary War Journal of Sergeant Thomas McCarty." Edited by J. C. Lobdell. *Proceedings of the New Jersey Historical Society* 82 (1964): 29–46.

McDonald, A. "Letter-Book of Captain Alexander McDonald, of the Royal Highland Emigrants, 1775–1779." In *Collections of the New-York Historical Society for the Year 1882*, 203–498. New York, 1883.

McMichael, J. "Diary of Lieut. James McMichael." *Pennsylvania Archives*, 2nd ser., 15 (1890): 193–218.

"Memorial of Capt. Charles Cochrane." *Massachusetts Historical Society Proceedings*, 2nd ser., 6 (1891): 433–42.

[Montagu-Stuart-Wortley, V. H. G, ed.]. *A Prime Minister and His Son; from the Correspondence of the 3rd Earl of Bute and of Lt.-General The Hon. Sir Charles Stuart, K.B.* London: J. Murray, 1925.

Moore, F., ed. *Diary of the American Revolution: From Newspapers and Original Documents.* 2 vols. New York: C. Scribner, 1860. Reprint, New York: New York Times, 1969.

Morton, R. "The Diary of Robert Morton, kept in Philadelphia while that City Was Occupied by the British Army in 1777." *Pennsylvania Magazine of History and Biography* 1 (1877): 1–39.

Muenchhausen, F. von. *At General Howe's Side, 1776–1778: The Diary of General William Howe's Aide de Camp, Captain Friedrich von Muenchhausen.* Translated by E. Kipping. Edited by S. Smith. Monmouth Beach, N.J.: Philip Freneau, 1974.

Murdoch, D. H., ed. *Rebellion in America: A Contemporary British Viewpoint, 1765–1783.* Santa Barbara, Calif.: Clio Books, 1979.

Murray, J. *Letters from America, 1773 to 1780: Being the Letters of a Scots Officer, Sir James Murray, to His Home during the War of American Independence.* Edited by E. Robson. Manchester: Manchester University Press, 1951.

*A Narrative, of the Excursion and Ravages of the King's Troops under the Command of General Gage, on the Nineteenth of April 1775.* Edited by V. L. Collins. Princeton: University Library, 1906. Reprint, New York: New York Times, 1968.

Nebenzahl, K., and D. Higginbotham, comps. and eds. *Atlas of the American Revolution.* Chicago: R. McNally, 1974.

Newsome, A. R., ed. "A British Orderly Book, 1780–1781." *North Carolina Historical Review,* 9 (1932): 57–78, 163–86, 273–98, 366–92.

O'Hara, C. "Letters of Charles O'Hara to the Duke of Grafton." Edited by G. C. Rogers. *South Carolina Historical Magazine* 65 (1964): 158–80.

*Orderly Book of the Three Battalions of Loyalists Commanded by Brigadier-General Oliver De Lancey, 1776–1778.* Compiled by W. Kelby. New York: New York Historical Society, 1917. Reprint, Baltimore, Md.: Genealogical Publishing, 1972.

Papet, F. J. von. *Canada during the American Revolutionary War: Lieutenant Friedrich Julius von Papet's Journal of the Sea Voyage to North America and the Campaign Conducted There.* Translated and edited by B.E. Burgoyne. Bowie, Md.: Heritage Books, 1998.

Pattison, J. "Official Letters of Major General James Pattison." In *Collections of the New-York Historical Society for the Year 1875,* 1–430. New York: The Historical Society, 1876.

Pausch, G. *Georg Pausch's Journal and Reports of the Campaign in America.* Translated and edited by B. E. Burgoyne. Bowie, Md.: Heritage Books, 1996.

Peckham, H. H., ed. "Sir Henry Clinton's Review of Simcoe's Journal." *William and Mary Quarterly,* 2nd ser., 21 (1941): 361–70.

——, ed. *Sources of American Independence: Selected Manuscripts from the Collections of the William L. Clements Library.* 2 vols. Chicago: University of Chicago Press, 1978.

Pell, J. "Diary of Joshua Pell, Junior: An Officer of the British Army in America, 1776–1777." Edited by J. L. Onderdonk. *Magazine of American History* 2 (1878): 43–47, 107–12.

Pettengill, R. W., trans. and ed. *Letters from America, 1776–1779: Being Letters of Brunswick, Hessian, and Waldeck Officers with the British Armies during the Revolution.* Boston: Houghton, 1924. Reprint, Port Washington, N.Y.: Kennikat Press, 1964.

Pickering, T. *An Easy Plan of Discipline for a Militia.* Salem, Mass.: S. & E. Hall, 1775.

Piecuch, J., ed. *The Battle of Camden: A Documentary History.* Charleston, S.C.: History Press, 2006.

Potts, W. J., ed. "Battle of Germantown from a British Account." *Pennsylvania Magazine of History and Biography* 11 (1887): 112–14.

Raymond, W. O., ed. *Winslow Papers, A.D. 1776–1826.* St. John, N.B.: New Brunswick Historical Society, 1901.

*Remarks on General Burgoyne's State of the Expedition from Canada.* London: G. Wilkie, 1780.

Resseguie, T. "Journal of Timothy Resseguie, a British Soldier during the War of the Revolution." *Journal of American History* 4 (1910): 127–31.

Riedesel, F. A. *Memoirs, Letters, and Journals of Major General Riedesel during his Residence in America.* Translated by William L. Stone. 2 vols. Albany, N.Y.: J. Munsell, 1868. Reprint, New York: New York Times, 1969.

Riedesel, F. C. L. *Baroness von Riedesel and the American Revolution: Journal and Correspondence of a Tour of Duty, 1776–1783.* Translated and edited by M. L. Brown and M. Huth. Chapel Hill: University of North Carolina Press, 1965.

Robertson, J. *The Twilight of British Rule in Revolutionary America: The New York Letter Book of General James Robertson, 1780–1783.* Edited by M. M. Klein and R. W. Howard. Cooperstown, New York: New York State Historical Association, 1983.

Rosengarten, J. G., trans. "The Battle of Germantown Described by a Hessian Officer." *Pennsylvania Magazine of History and Biography* 16 (1892): 197–201.

——, trans. "Popp's Journal, 1777–1783." *Pennsylvania Magazine of History and Biography* 26 (1902): 25–41, 245–54.

Ross, C., ed. *Correspondence of Charles, First Marquis Cornwallis.* 3 vols. London: J. Murray, 1859.

Russell, P. "The Siege of Charleston: Journal of Captain Peter Russell, December 25, 1779, to May 2, 1780." Edited by J. Bain. *American Historical Review* 4 (1899): 478–501.

Scheer, G. F., and H. F. Rankin, eds. *Rebels and Redcoats: The American Revolution through the Eyes of Those Who Fought and Lived It.* New York: World, 1957. Reprint, New York: DaCapo, 1987.

Schmidt, A. *The Hesse-Cassel Mirbach Regiment in the American Revolution.* Translated by B. E. Burgoyne. Bowie, Md.: Heritage Books, 1998.

Scull, G. D., ed. "The Montresor Journals." *Collections of the New-York Historical Society for the Year 1881.* New York: The Historical Society, 1882.

Serle, A. *The American Journal of Ambrose Serle, Secretary to Lord Howe, 1776–1778.* Edited by E. H. Tatum. San Marino, Calif.: Huntington Library, 1940. Reprint, New York: New York Times, 1969.

Seybolt, R. F. ed. "A Contemporary British Account of General Sir William Howe's Military Operations in 1777." *Proceedings of the American Antiquarian Society*, n.s., 40 (1931): 69–92.

Simcoe, J. G. *Simcoe's Military Journal. A History of the Operations of a Partisan Corps, Called the Queen's Rangers, Commanded by Lieut. Col. J. G. Simcoe, during the War of the American Revolution.* New York: Bartlett & Welford, 1844. Reprint, New York: New York Times, 1968.

Simes, T. *A Military Course for the Government and Conduct of a Battalion, Designed for Their Regulations in Quarter, Camp, or Garrison; with . . . Observations and Instructions for Their Manner of Attack and Defence.* London: N.p., 1777.

Skelly, F. "Journal of Brigade Major F. Skelly." Edited by C. C. Jones, *Magazine of American History* 26 (1891): 152–54, 392–93.

Smith, G. *An Universal Military Dictionary.* London: J. Millan, 1779. Reprint, Ottawa, Ontario: Museum Restoration Service, 1969.

Smith, J. "Diary of Jacob Smith—American Born." Edited by C. W. Heathcote. *Pennsylvania Magazine of History and Biography* 56 (1932): 260–64.

Smith, S. S., and J. R. Elting, eds. "British Light Infantry, 1775–1800." *Military Collector and Historian* 27 (1975): 87–89.

Specht, J. F. *The Specht Journal: A Military Journal of the Burgoyne Campaign.* Translated by H. Doblin. Edited by M. C. Lynn. Westport, Conn.: Greenwood, 1995.

Stang, G. *The Diary of Georg Stang, a Military Musician Serving in the Anspach-Bayreuth Corps, 1777–1783.* Translated and edited by C. Reuter. German-Canadian Museum of Applied History, Canada (undated pamphlet).

Stanley, G. F. G., ed. *For Want of a Horse: Being a Journal of the Campaigns against the Americans in 1776 and 1777 Conducted from Canada, by an Officer Who Served with Lt. Gen. Burgoyne.* Sackville, N.B.: Tribune, 1961.

Stedman, C. *The History of the Origin, Progress, and Termination of the American War.* 2 vols. London: J. Murray, 1794. Reprint, New York: New York Times, 1969.

Steuben, F. W. *Baron von Steuben's Revolutionary War Drill Manual. A Facsimile Reprint of the 1794 Edition.* New York: Courier Dover Publications, 1985.

Stevens, B. F., ed. *General Sir William Howe's Orderly Book at Charlestown, Boston, and Halifax, June 17, 1775, to 26 May 1776.* London: N.p., 1890.

Stewart, D. *Sketches of the Character, Manners, and Present State of the Highlanders of Scotland, with Details of Highland Regiments.* 2 vols. Edinburgh: Longman, 1822.

Stone, W. L., ed. *Orderly Book of Sir John Johnson during the Oriskany Campaign, 1776–1777.* Albany, N.Y.: J. Munsell's Sons, 1882.

Sullivan, T. *From Redcoat to Rebel: The Thomas Sullivan Journal.* Edited by J. L. Boyle. Bowie, Md.: Heritage Books, 1997.

Tarleton, B. *A History of the Campaigns of 1780 and 1781 in the Southern Provinces of North America.* London: T. Cadell, 1787. Reprint, New York: New York Times, 1968.

———. "New War Letters of Banastre Tarleton." Edited by R. M. Ketchum. *New-York Historical Society Quarterly* 51 (1967): 61–81.

Thacher, J. *A Military Journal during the American Revolutionary War, from 1775–1783*. 2nd rev. ed. Boston: Cottons & Barnard, 1827.

"Three Letters written by British Officers from Boston in 1774 and 1775." *Bostonian Society Proceedings*, 12–15. Boston, 1919.

Townshend, J. "Some Account of the British Army under General Howe, and of the Battle of Brandywine." *Bulletin of the Historical Society of Pennsylvania* 1 (1846): 17–29.

Tucker, L. L., ed. " 'To My Inexpressible Astonishment': Admiral Sir George Collier's Observations on the Battle of Long Island." *New-York Historical Society Quarterly* 48 (1964): 292–305.

Tyler, J. E., ed. "An Account of Lexington in the Rockingham Mss. at Sheffield." *William and Mary Quarterly*, 3rd ser., 10 (1953): 99–107.

Uhlendorf, B. A., trans. and ed. *The Siege of Charleston, with an Account of the Province of South Carolina: Diaries and Letters of Hessian Officers from the Von Jungkenn Papers in the William L. Clements Library*. Ann Arbor, Mich.: University of Michigan Publications, 1938.

Washington, G. *The Papers of George Washington. Revolutionary War Series*. Edited by Philander D. Chase et al. 16 vols. to date. Charlottesville: University Press of Virginia, 1985–.

———. *The Writings of George Washington*. Edited by J. C. Fitzpatrick. 39 vols. Washington, D.C.: Government Printing Office, 1931–44.

Wasmus, J. F. *An Eyewitness Account of the American Revolution and New England Life: The Journal of Julius Friedrich Wasmus, German Company Surgeon, 1776–1783*. Translated by H. Doblin. Edited by M. C. Lynn. New York: Greenwood, 1990.

Wilkinson, J. *Memoirs of My Own Times*. 3 vols. Philadelphia: N.p, 1816.

Williams, J. *Considerations on the American War*. London: T. Hookham, 1782.

Williamson, J. *The Elements of Military Arrangement; comprehending the tactick, exercise, manoevres, and discipline of the British infantry, with an appendix, containing the substance of the principal standing orders and regulations for the army*. London: N.p., 1781.

Wolfe, J. *General Wolfe's Instructions to Young Officers: Also His Orders for a Battalion and an Army. Together with the Orders and Signals Used in Embarking and Debarking an Army by Flat-Bottom'd Boats, &c....* 2nd ed. London: J. Millan, 1780.

Young, W. "Journal of Sergeant William Young." *Pennsylvania Magazine of History and Biography* 8 (1884): 255–78.

Young, Maj. W. *Manoeuvres, or Practical Observations on the Art of War*. 2 vols. London: J. Millan, 1771.

## SECONDARY SOURCES

### Books

Anderson, M. S. *The War of the Austrian Succession, 1740–1748*. London: Longman, 1995.

Anderson, T. S. *The Command of the Howe Brothers during the American Revolution.* New York: Oxford University Press, 1936.

Atwood, R. *The Hessians: Mercenaries from Hessen-Kassel in the American Revolution.* Cambridge: Cambridge University Press, 1980.

Babits, L. E. *A Devil of a Whipping: The Battle of Cowpens.* Chapel Hill: University of North Carolina Press, 1998.

Baker, N. *Government and Contractors: The British Treasury and war supplies, 1775–1783.* London: Athlone, 1971.

Barrington, S. *The Political Life of William Wildman, Viscount Barrington.* 2nd ed. London: Payne & Foss, 1815.

Bilias, G. A., ed. *George Washington's Generals and Opponents.* New York: DaCapo, 1994.

Black, J. *European Warfare, 1660–1815.* London: UCL, 1994.

——. *War for America: The Fight for Independence, 1775–83.* Stroud, Gloucs.: Sutton, 1991.

Blanning, T. C. W. *The French Revolutionary Wars.* London: E. Arnold, 1996.

Boatner, M. M. *Encyclopedia of the American Revolution.* 3rd ed. Mechanicsburg, Pa.: Stackpole Books, 1994.

Boaz, T. *"For the Glory of the Marines!" The Organization, Training, Uniforms, and Combat Role of the British Marines during the American Revolution.* Devon, Pa.: Dockyard, 1993.

Bowler, R. A. *Logistics and the Failure of the British Army in America, 1775–83.* Princeton: Princeton University Press, 1975.

Bowman, A. *The Morale of the American Revolutionary Army.* Washington, D.C.: American Council on Public Affairs, 1943.

Browning, R. *The War of the Austrian Succession.* New York: St. Martin's, 1993. Reprint, Stroud, Gloucs.: Sutton, 1995.

Brumwell, S. *Redcoats: The British Soldier and War in the Americas, 1755–1763.* Cambridge: Cambridge University Press, 2002.

Camus, R. F. *Military Music of the American Revolution.* 2nd ed. Chapel Hill: University of North Carolina Press, 1977.

Chandler, D. *The Art of Warfare in the Age of Marlborough.* London: Batsford, 1976. 2nd ed. Staplehurst, Kent: Spellmount, 1990.

Conway, S. *The British Isles and the American War of Independence.* Oxford: Oxford University Press, 2000.

——. *The War of American Independence, 1775–1783.* London: E. Arnold, 1995.

Crow, J. J., and L. E. Tise, eds. *The Southern Experience in the American Revolution.* Chapel Hill: University of North Carolina Press, 1978.

Curtis, E. E. *The Organization of the British Army in the American Revolution.* New Haven, Conn.: Yale University Press, 1926.

Darling, A. D. *Red Coat and Brown Bess.* Bloomfield, Ontario: Museum Restoration Service, 1971.

Davis, R. P. *Where a Man Can Go: Major General William Phillips, British Royal Artillery, 1731–1781.* Westport, Conn.: Greenwood, 1999.

De Fonblanque, E. B. *Political and Military Episodes in the Latter Half of the Eighteenth Century Derived from the Life and Correspondence of the*

*Right Hon. John Burgoyne, General, Statesman, Dramatist.* London: Macmillan, 1876. Rev. ed. Boston: Gregg, 1972.

Duffy, C. *The Army of Frederick the Great.* 2nd ed. Chicago: Emperor's, 1996.

———. *Frederick the Great: A Military Life.* London: Routledge and Kegan Paul, 1985.

———. *The Military Experience in the Age of Reason.* London: Routledge and Kegan Paul, 1987.

Dwyer, W. *The Day Is Ours! An Inside View of the Battles of Trenton and Princeton, November 1776–January 1777.* New York: Viking, 1983. Reprint, New Brunswick, N.J.: Rutgers University Press, 1998.

Eelking, M. von. *The German Allied Troops in the North American War of Independence, 1776–1783.* Translated by J. G. Rosengarten. Albany, N.Y.: J. Munsell's Sons, 1893. Reprint Baltimore, Md.: Genealogical Publishing, 1972.

Elting, J. R. *The Battle of Bunker's Hill.* Monmouth Beach, N.J.: Philip Freneau, 1975.

———. *The Battles of Saratoga.* Monmouth Beach, N.J.: Philip Freneau, 1977.

Ferling, J., ed. *The World Turned Upside Down: The American Victory in the War of Independence.* Westport, Conn.: Greenwood, 1988.

Field, T. W. *The Battle of Long Island, with Connected Proceeding Events, and the Subsequent American Retreat.* Brooklyn, N.Y.: Long Island Historical Society, 1869.

Fortescue, J. *The War of Independence: The British Army in North America, 1775–1783.* London: Greenhill Books, 2001.

Fowler, W. M., and W. Coyle, eds. *The American Revolution: Changing Perspectives.* Boston: Northeastern University Press, 1979.

French, A. *The First Year of the American Revolution.* Boston: Houghton Mifflin, 1934.

Frey, S. *The British Soldier in America: A Social History of Military Life in the Revolutionary Period.* Austin: University of Texas Press, 1981.

Fuller, J. F. C. *British Light Infantry in the Eighteenth Century.* London: Hutchinson, 1925.

Furneaux, R. *Saratoga: The Decisive Battle.* London: Allen & Unwin, 1971.

Gallagher, J. J. *The Battle of Brooklyn, 1776.* New York, 1995.

Galvin, J. R. *The Minute Men: The First Fight: Myths and Realities of the American Revolution.* Rev. ed. Washington, D.C.: Pergamon-Brassey's International Defense Publisher, 1996.

Gates, D. *The British Light Infantry Arm, c.1790–1815: Its Creation, Training, and Operational Role.* London: Batsford, 1987.

Gilchrist, M. M. *Patrick Ferguson: "A Man of Some Genius."* Edinburgh: NMS Enterprises, 2003.

Glover, M. *General Burgoyne in Canada and America: A Scapegoat for a System.* London: Gordon & Cremonesi, 1976.

———. *Peninsular Preparation: The Reform of the British Army, 1795–1809.* Cambridge: Cambridge University Press, 1963.

Gross, R. A. *The Minutemen and their World.* New York: Hill & Wang, 1976.

Graham, J. *The Life of General Daniel Morgan, with Portions of his Correspondence.* New York: Derby & Jackson, 1856.

Gruber, I. D. *The Howe Brothers and the American Revolution.* Chapel Hill: University of North Carolina Press, 1972.

Harding, D. F. *Smallarms of the East India Company, 1600–1856.* Vol. 3, *Ammunition and Performance.* London: Foresight, 1999.

Hatch, C. E. *The Battle of Guilford Courthouse.* Washington, D.C.: National Park Service, 1971.

Higginbotham, D. *The War of American Independence: Military Attitudes, Policies, and Practices, 1763–1789.* New York: Macmillan, 1971.

Hoffman, R., and P. J. Albert, eds. *Arms and Independence: The Military Character of the American Revolution.* Charlottesville: University Press of Virginia, 1984.

Houlding, J. A. *Fit for Service: The Training of the British Army, 1715–95.* Oxford: Oxford University Press, 1981.

Hughes, B. P. *Firepower: Weapons Effectiveness on the Battlefield, 1630–1850.* London: Arms & Armour, 1974. Reprint, Staplehurst, Kent: Spellmount, 1997.

Jackson, J. W. *With the British Army in Philadelphia, 1777–1778.* San Rafael, Calif.: Presidio, 1979.

Jervis, J. *Three Centuries of Robinsons: The Story of a Family.* Rev. ed., Toronto: T.H. Best, 1967.

Johnson, W. *Sketches of the Life and Correspondence of Nathanael Greene, Major General of the Armies of the United States, in the War of the Revolution.* 2 vols. Charleston, S.C.: N.p., 1822.

Johnston, H. P. *The Campaign of 1776 around New York and Brooklyn; including a New and Circumstantial Account of the Loss of Long Island, and the Loss of New York, with a Review of Events to the Close of the Year.* Brooklyn, N.Y.: Long Island Historical Society, 1878.

Katcher, P. R. N. *King George's Army, 1775–1783: A Handbook of British, American, and German Regiments.* Reading, Berks.: Osprey, 1973.

Kennett, L. *The French Armies in the Seven Years' War.* Durham, N.C.: Duke University Press, 1967.

Ketchum, R. *Decisive Day: The Battle for Bunker Hill.* Garden City, N.Y.: Doubleday, 1962.

———. *The Winter Soldiers.* London: Macdonald, 1973.

Kipping, E. *The Hessian View of America.* Monmouth Beach, N.J.: Philip Freneau, 1971.

Kwasny, M. *Washington's Partisan War, 1775–1783.* Kent, Ohio: Kent State University Press, 1996.

Lawrence, A. A. *Storm over Savannah: The Story of Count d'Estaing and the Siege of the Town in 1779.* Athens: University of Georgia Press, 1951.

Lefkowitz, A. S. *The Long Retreat: The Calamitous American Defense of New Jersey.* Metuchen. N.J.: Upland, 1998. Reprint, New Brunswick, N.J.: Rutgers University Press, 1999.

Lenman, B. *Britain's Colonial Wars, 1688–1783.* Harlow, Essex: Longman, 2001.

Lindsay, A. W. C. *Lives of the Lindsays; or, a Memoiur of the Houses of Crawford and Balcarres, by Lord Lindsay.* 3 vols. London: J. Murray, 1849.

Lowell, E. J. *The Hessians and the Other German Auxiliaries of Great Britain in the Revolutionary War*. New York: Harper & Bros., 1884. Reprint, Williamstown, Mass.: Corner House, 1970.

Lunt, J. *The Duke of Wellington's Regiment (West Riding)*. London: Leo Cooper, 1971.

Lushington, S. R. *The Life and Services of General Lord Harris, G.C.B. during His Campaigns in America, the West Indies, and India*. London: J. W. Parker, 1840.

Lynn, J. A. *The Bayonets of the Republic: Motivation and Tactics in the Army of Revolutionary France, 1791–1794*. Urbana: University of Illinois Press, 1984.

Mackesy, P. *The War for America*. London: Longmans, 1964. Reprint, Lincoln: University of Nebraska Press, 1993.

Martin, J. K., and M. E. Lender, *A Respectable Army: The Military Origins of the Republic, 1763–1789*. Arlington, Ill.: Harlan Davidson, 1982.

May, R., and G. Embleton. *The British Army in North America, 1775–83*. Reading: Osprey, 1974.

McGuire, T. J. *The Battle of Paoli*. Mechanicsburg, Pa.: Stackpole Books, 2000.

——. *The Philadelphia Campaign. Volume One: Brandywine and the Fall of Philadelphia*. Mechanicsburg, Pa.: Stackpole Books, 2006.

——. *The Philadelphia Campaign. Volume Two: Germantown and the Road to Valley Forge*. Mechanicsburg, Pa.: Stackpole Books, 2007.

——. *The Surprise of Germantown, October 4th 1777*. Gettysburg, Pa.: Thomas Publications, 1994.

Milborne, A. J. B. "British Military Lodges in the American War of Independence." *Transactions of the American Lodge of Research* 10 (1966): 22–85.

Mintz, M. M. *The Generals of Saratoga*. New Haven, Conn.: Yale University Press, 1990.

Mollo, J., and M. McGregor. *Uniforms of the American Revolution*. Poole: Blandford, 1975. Reprint, New York: Sterling Publishing, 1991.

Murdock, H. *Bunker Hill: Notes and Queries on a Famous Battle*. Boston: Houghton Mifflin Co., 1927. Reprint, n.p.: Wee Bee Publishing, 1995.

Nafziger, G. *Imperial Bayonets: Tactics of the Napoleonic Battery, Battalion, and Brigade as Found in Contemporary Regulations*. London: Greenhill Books, 1996.

Neimeyer, C. P. *America Goes to War: A Social History of the Continental Army*. New York: New York University Press, 1996.

Nelson, P. D. *General James Grant: Scottish Soldier and Royal Governor of East Florida*. Gainesville: University Press of Florida, 1993.

——. *Sir Charles Grey, First Earl Grey: Royal Soldier, Family Patriarch*. Madison, N.J.: Fairleigh Dickenson University Press, 1996.

——. *William Tryon and the Course of Empire: A Life in British Imperial Service*. Chapel Hill: University of North Carolina Press, 1990.

Newlin, A. I. *The Battle of New Garden*. Greensboro: North Carolina Friends Historical Society, 1977. Reprint, Greensboro: North Carolina Yearly Meeting Publications Board, 1995.

Nosworthy, B. *The Anatomy of Victory: Battle Tactics, 1689–1763.* New York: Hippocrene Books, 1992.

——. *Battle Tactics of Napoleon and His Enemies.* London: Constable, 1995.

Novak, G. *"Rise and Fight Again': the War of Independence in the South.* Champaign, Ill.: Rue Sans Joie, 1988.

——. *"We Have Always Governed Ourselves": The War of Independence in the North.* 2nd ed. Champaign, Ill.: N.p., 1990.

Pancake, J. S. *1777: The Year of the Hangman.* Tuscaloosa: University of Alabama Press, 1977.

——. *This Destructive War: The British Campaign in the Carolinas, 1780–1782.* Tuscaloosa: University of Alabama Press, 1985.

Paret, P., ed. *Makers of Modern Strategy from Machiavelli to the Nuclear Age.* Princeton: Princeton University Press, 1971.

Peckham, H. H. *The Toll of Independence: Engagements and Battle Casualties of the American Revolution.* Chicago: University of Chicago Press, 1974.

Peterkin, E. *The Exercise of Arms in the Continental Infantry.* Alexandria Bay, N.Y.: Museum Restoration Service, 1989.

Reid, S. *Wolfe: The Career of General James Wolfe from Culloden to Quebec.* Staplehurst, Kent: Spellmount, 2000.

Reid, S., and R. Hook. *British Redcoat, 1740–93.* London: Osprey Military, 1996.

Richardson, E. W. *Standards and Colors of the American Revolution.* Philadelphia: University of Pennsylvania Press, 1982.

Robson, E. *The American Revolution in its Political and Military Aspects, 1763–1783.* London: Batchworth, 1955.

Rogers, H. C. B. *The British Army of the Eighteenth Century.* London: Allen & Unwin, 1977.

Ross, S. *From Flintlock to Rifle: Infantry Tactics, 1740–1866.* Cranbury, N.J.: Associated University Presses, 1979. 2nd ed. London: Frank Cass, 1996.

Royster, C. *A Revolutionary People at War: The Continental Army and American Character, 1775–1783.* Chapel Hill: University of North Carolina Press, 1979.

Sampson, R. *Escape in America: The British Convention Prisoners, 1777–1783.* Chippenham, Wilts.: Picton, 1995.

Shy, J. *A People Numerous and Armed: Reflections on the Military Struggle for American Independence.* New York: Oxford University Press, 1976. Rev. ed. Ann Arbor: University of Michigan Press, 1990.

——. *Toward Lexington: The Role of the British Army in the Coming of the American Revolution.* Princeton: Princeton University Press, 1965.

Smith, P. H. *Loyalists and Redcoats: A Study in British Revolutionary Policy.* Chapel Hill: University of North Carolina Press, 1964.

Smith, S. S. *The Battle of Brandywine.* Monmouth Beach, N.J.: Philip Freneau, 1976.

——. *The Battle of Monmouth.* Monmouth Beach, N.J.: Philip Freneau, 1964.

——. *The Battle of Princeton.* Monmouth Beach, N.J.: Philip Freneau, 1967.

Smythies, R. H. R. *Historical Records of the 40th (2nd Somersetshire) Regi-*

ment, now *1st Battalion the Prince of Wales's Volunteers (South Lanca-shire Regiment), from its formation in 1717 to 1893*. Devonport, Devon: printed for the subscribers, 1894.

Starkey, A. *European and Native American Warfare 1675–1815*. London: UCL, 1998.

Strachan, H. *European Armies and the Conduct of War*. London: Allen & Unwin, 1983.

Syrett, D. *Shipping and the American War, 1775–83: A Study of British Transport Organisation*. London: Athlone, 1970.

Symonds, C. L. *A Battlefield Atlas of the American Revolution*. Annapolis, Md.: Nautical & Aviation Publishing, 1986.

Van Creveld, M. *Supplying War: Logistics from Wallenstein to Patton*. 2nd ed. Cambridge: Cambridge University Press, 2004.

Ward, C. *The War of the Revolution*. Edited by J. R. Alden. 2 vols. New York: Macmillan, 1952.

Ward, H. M. *The War for Independence and the Transformation of American Society*. London: UCL Press, 1999.

Wickwire, F., and M. Wickwire. *Cornwallis and the War of Independence*. London: Faber & Faber, 1971.

Wilkin, W. H. *Some British Soldiers in America*. London: Hugh Rees, 1914.

Willcox, W. B. *Portrait of a General: Sir Henry Clinton in the War of Independence*. New York: Alfred A. Knopf, 1964.

Winstock, L. *Songs and Music of the Redcoats, 1642–1902*. London: Leo Cooper, 1970.

Wood, W. J. *Battles of the Revolutionary War, 1775–81*. Chapel Hill: University of North Carolina Press, N.C., 1990.

## Articles and Theses

Ashmore, O., and C. H. Olmstead. "The Battles of Kettle Creek and Briar Creek." *Georgia Historical Quarterly* 10 (1926): 85–125.

Beattie, D. J. "The Adaptation of the British Army to Wilderness Warfare, 1755–1763." In *Adapting to Conditions: War and Society in the Eighteenth Century*, edited by M. Ultee, 56–83. Tuscaloosa: University of Alabama Press, 1986.

Black, J. "Could the British Have Won the American War of Independence?" *Journal of the Society for Army Historical Research* 74 (1996): 145–54.

Bowler, R. A. "Logistics and Operations in the American Revolution." In *Reconsiderations on the Revolutionary War*, edited by D. Higginbotham, 54–71. Westport, Conn.: Greenwood, 1978.

Brumwell, S. "Rank and File: A Profile of One of Wolfe's Regiments." *Journal of the Society for Army Historical Research* 79 (2001): 3–24.

——. "The British Army and Warfare with the North American Indians." *War in History* 5 (1998): 147–75.

Burke, W. W., and L. M. Bass. "Preparing a British Unit for Service in America: The Brigade of Foot Guards, 1776." *Military Collector and Historian* 47 (1995): 2–11.

Burns, R. E. "Ireland and British Military Preparations for War in America." *Cithara* 2 (1963): 42–61.

Calderhead, W. L. "British Naval Failure at Long Island: A Lost Opportunity." *New York History* 57 (1976): 321–38.

Caruana, A. B. "The Dress of the Royal Artillery in North America." *Military Collector and Historian* 35 (1983): 124–29.

Conway, S. "British Army Officers and the American War for Independence." *William and Mary Quarterly*, 3rd ser., 41 (1984): 265–76.

——. "British Mobilization in the American War of Independence." *Historical Research* 72 (1999): 58–76.

——. " 'The Great Mischief Complain'd Of': Reflections on the Misconduct of British Soldiers in the Revolutionary War." *William and Mary Quarterly*, 3rd ser., 47 (1990): 370–90.

——. "The Politics of British Military and Naval Mobilization, 1775–83." *English Historical Review* 112 (1997): 1179–1201.

——. "The Recruitment of Criminals into the British Army, 1775–81." *Bulletin of the Institute of Historical Research* 58 (1985): 46–58.

——. "To Subdue America: British Army Officers and the Conduct of the Revolutionary War." *William and Mary Quarterly*, 3rd ser., 43 (1986): 381–407.

Demarest, T. "The Baylor Massacre—Some Assorted Notes and Information." In *Bergen County Historical Society 1971 Annual*, 28–93. River Edge, N.J.: Bergen County Historical Society, 1971.

Dornfest, W. T. "John Watson Tadwell Watson and the Provincial Light Infantry, 1780–1781." *Journal of the Society for Army Historical Research* 75 (1997): 220–29.

Embleton, G., and P.J. Haythornwaite. "British Troops on Campaign, 1775–81." *Military Illustrated* 55 (1992): 24–28.

——. "Reversed Colours: British Infantry Musicians in the Eighteenth-Century." *Military Illustrated* 57 (1993): 30–35.

Frey, S. "Courts and Cats: British Military Justice in the Eighteenth Century." *Military Affairs* 43 (1979): 5–11.

Gilbert, A. N. "Charles Jenkinson and the Last Army Press, 1779." *Military Affairs* 42 (1978): 7–11.

——. "Law and Honour among Eighteenth Century British Army Officers." *Historical Journal* 19 (1976): 75–87.

——. "Why Men Deserted from the Eighteenth-Century British Army." *Armed Forces and Society* 6 (1980): 553–67.

Gilbert, S. "An Analysis of the Xavier della Gatta Paintings of the Battles of Paoli and Germantown, 1777." *Military Collector and Historian* 46 (1994): 98–108; 47 (1995): 146–62.

Gruber, I. D. "The American Revolution as a Conspiracy: The British View." *William and Mary Quarterly*, 3rd ser., 26 (1969): 360–72.

——. "For King and Country: The Limits of Loyalty of British Officers in the War for American Independence." In *Limits of Loyalty*, edited by E. Denton, 21–40. Waterloo, Ont.: Wilfrid Laurier University Press, 1980.

——. "Britain's Southern Strategy." In *The Revolutionary War in the South:*

*Power, Conflict, and Leadership: Essays in Honor of John Richard Alden,* edited by W. R. Higgins, 205–38. Durham, N.C.: Duke University Press, 1979.

Haarmann, A. W. "The Royal Artillery and 62nd Regiment of Foot: Campaign Dress in North America, 1777." *Journal of the Society for Army Historical Research* 54 (1976): 134–35.

Hatch, C. E. "The 'Affair near James Island' (or, 'The Battle of Green Spring') July 6, 1781." *Virginia Magazine of History and Biography* 53 (1945): 172–96.

Higginbotham, D. "The Early American Way of War: Reconnaissance and Reappraisal." *William and Mary Quarterly,* 3rd ser., 44 (1987): 230–73.

Howard, J. B. "'Things Here Wear a Melancholy Appearance': The American Defeat at Briar Creek." *Georgia Historical Quarterly* 88 (2004): 477–98.

Hubner, B. E. "The Formation of the British Light Infantry Companies and their Employment in the Saratoga Campaign of 1777." M.A. thesis, University of Saskatchewan, 1986.

Kopperman, P. E. "'The Cheapest Pay': Alcohol Abuse in the Eighteenth-Century British Army." *Military History* 60 (1996): 445–70.

——. "The British High Command and Soldiers' Wives in America, 1755–83." *Journal of the Society for Army Historical Research* 60 (1982): 14–34.

Lawrence, A. A. "General Robert Howe and the British Capture of Savannah in 1778." *Georgia Historical Quarterly* 36 (1952): 303–27.

Lynn, J. "Food, Funds, and Fortresses: Resource Mobilization and Positional Warfare in the Campaigns of Louis XIV." In *Feeding Mars: Logistics in Western Warfare from the Middle Ages to the Present,* edited by J. Lynn, 137–59. Boulder, Colo.: Westview, 1993.

Mackesy, P. "The Redcoat Revived." In *The American Revolution: Changing Perspectives,* edited by W. M. Fowler and W. Coyle, 173–88. Boston: Northeastern University Press, 1979.

Massey, G. "The British Expedition to Wilmington." *North Carolina Historical Review* 66 (1989): 387–411.

Moomaw, W. H. "The Denouement of General Howe's Campaign of 1777." *English Historical Review* 79 (1964): 498–512.

Nelson, P. D. "Citizen Soldiers or Regulars: The Views of the American General Officers on the Military Establishment, 1775–1781." *Journal of Military Affairs* 43 (1979): 126–32.

Odintz, M. "The British Officer Corps, 1754–83." Ph.D. diss., University of Michigan, 1988.

Papenfuse, E. C., and G. A. Stiverson. "Smallwood's Recruits." *William and Mary Quarterly,* 3rd ser., 30 (1973): 117–32.

Paret, P. "Colonial Experience and European Military Reform at the End of the Eighteenth Century." *Bulletin of the Institute for Historical Research* 37 (1964): 47–59.

Perjés, G. "Army Provisioning, Logistics, and Strategy in the Second Half of the 17th Century." *Acta Historica* 16 (1970): 1–51.

Pugh, R. C. "The Revolutionary Militia in the Southern Campaigns, 1780–81." *William and Mary Quarterly,* 3rd ser., 14 (1957): 154–75.

Robson, E. "British Light Infantry in the Mid-Eighteenth Century: The Effect of American Conditions." *The Army Quarterly* 63 (1952): 209–22.

———. "Purchase and Promotion in the British Army in the Eighteenth Century." *History* 36 (1951): 57–72.

———. "Raising a Regiment in the War of American Independence: The 80th Foot, the Edinburgh Regiment." *Journal of the Society for Army Historical Research* 27 (1949), 107–15.

Russell, P. E. "Redcoats in the Wilderness: British Officers and Irregular Warfare in Europe and North America, 1740–1760." *William and Mary Quarterly*, 3rd ser., 35 (1978): 629–52.

Stacy, K. R. "Crime and Punishment in the 84th Regiment of Foot, 1775–84." *Journal of the Society for Army Historical Research* 79 (2001): 108–18.

Starkey, A. "Paoli to Stony Point: Military Ethics and Weaponry during the American Revolution." *Journal of Military History* 58 (1994): 7–27.

———. "War and Culture, a Case Study: The Enlightenment and the Conduct of the British Army in America, 1755–1781." *War and Society* 8 (1990): 1–28.

Strach, S. G. "A Memoir of the Exploits of Captain Alexander Fraser and his Company of British Marksmen, 1776–77." *Journal of the Society for Army Historical Research* 63 (1985): 91–98, 164–79.

Surtees, G. "British Colours at Saratoga." *Journal of the Society for Army Historical Research* 45 (1967): 102–104. See also 53 (1975): 123–24; 54 (1976): 55, 177.

Syrett, D. "The Methodology of British Amphibious Operations during the Seven Years' and American Wars." *Mariner's Mirror* 59 (1972): 269–80.

Tiedemann, J. S. "Patriots by Default: Queens County, New York, and the British Army, 1776–1783." *William and Mary Quarterly*, 3rd ser., 43 (1986): 35–63.

Urwin, G. J. W. "Cornwallis in Virginia: A Reappraisal." *Military Collector and Historian* 37 (1985): 111–26.

Vivian, F. "A Defence of Sir William Howe with a New Interpretation of His Action in New Jersey, June 1777." *Journal of the Society for Army Historical Research* 44 (1966): 63–83.

Ward, M. C. " 'The European Method of Warring Is Not Practiced Here': The Failure of British Military Policy in the Ohio Valley, 1755–1759." *War in History* 4 (1997): 249–63.

Weller, J. "Irregular but Effective: Partizan Weapons Tactics in the American Revolution, Southern Theatre." *Military Affairs* 21 (1957): 118–31.

Wright, J. W. "The Rifle in the American Revolution." *American Historical Review* 29 (1924): 293–99.

Yates, G. K. "His Majesty's 47th Regiment of Foot in Canada: 1777–82." *Journal of the Society for Army Historical Research* 74 (1996): 212–17.

# Index

6423446

LIBRARY
THE UNIVERSITY OF TEXAS
AT BROWNSVILLE
Brownsville, TX 78520-4991